PELICAN BOOKS
A 484

THE NUDE
KENNETH CLARK

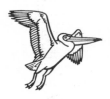

D1438024

KENNETH CLARK

THE NUDE

A STUDY OF IDEAL ART

*

PENGUIN BOOKS

Penguin Books Ltd, Harmondsworth, Middlesex
AUSTRALIA: Penguin Books Pty Ltd, 762 Whitehorse Road,
Mitcham, Victoria

—

First published 1956
Published in Pelican Books 1960

—

Made and printed in Great Britain
by Hazell Watson & Viney Ltd
Aylesbury and Slough

Dedicated to
BERNARD BERENSON

Contents

	Preface	xxi
I	THE NAKED AND THE NUDE	1
II	APOLLO	26
III	VENUS I	64
IV	VENUS II	113
V	ENERGY	162
VI	PATHOS	214
VII	ECSTASY	264
VIII	THE ALTERNATIVE CONVENTION	300
IX	THE NUDE AS AN END IN ITSELF	335
	List of Books referred to in Abbreviated Form	359
	Notes	361
	Index	399

Illustrations

1. VELASQUEZ. Rokeby Venus. *London, National Gallery* — 1

2. GREEK. 2nd century B.C. Mirror. *Louvre* — 2

3. PICASSO. Bathers. *Cambridge, Mass., Fogg Museum* — 3

4. COURBET. 'La Source.' *Louvre* — 5

5. REJLANDER. Photograph. *Gernsheim Collection* — 6

6. KYONAGA. Colour print. *Boston* — 7

7. ETRUSCAN TOMB. 'L'Obeso.' *Tarquinia* — 8

8. VILLARD DE HONNECOURT. Antique figures. *Paris, Bibliothèque Nationale* — 9

9. LEONARDO DA VINCI. Vitruvian Man. *Venice, Accademia* — 12

10. CESARINO. Vitruvian Man, from the Como *Vitruvius.* 1521 — 13

11. DÜRER. Nemesis. Engraving — 14

12. DÜRER. Measured nude. *Vienna, Albertina* — 15

13. FRENCH. 16th century. Bronze cast of Venus of the Belvedere. *Louvre* — 16

14. MEMLINC WORKSHOP. Eve. *Vienna* — 17

15. SANSOVINO. Apollo. *Venice, Loggetta* — 18

16. GRAECO-ROMAN. Apollo. *Naples* — 18

17. ATTIC. Early 5th century B.C. Palestra scene. *British Museum* — 20

18. 12TH-CENTURY AUSTRIAN (?) MS. Three Graces. *British Museum* — 21

19. MICHELANGELO. Crucifixion. *British Museum* — 24

20. ATTIC. *c.* 600 B.C. Kouros. *New York, Metropolitan Museum* — 26

21. ATTIC. 6th century B.C. Apollo of Tenea. *Munich* — 27

22. 'KRITIOS.' *c.* 480 B.C. Youth. *Athens, Acropolis Museum* — 28

23. MAGNA GRAECIA. *c.* 490 B.C. The Apollo of Piombino. *Louvre* — 29

24. AFTER POLYCLITUS. *c.* 450 B.C. Doryphoros. *Naples* — 32

25. AFTER POLYCLITUS. *c.* 430 B.C. Diadumenos. *Athens* — 33

26. AFTER POLYCLITUS. *c.* 450 B.C. Torso of the Doryphoros. *Uffizi* — 34

27. GREEK. ? 4th century B.C. The Idolino. *Florence, Museo Archeologico*   36

28. GREEK. ? *c.* 400 B.C. After the Discophoros of Polyclitus. *Louvre*   37

29. GREEK. *c.* 450 B.C. Apollo. *Olympia*   38

30. STYLE OF PHIDIAS. Apollo of the Tiber. *Rome*   40

31. PRAXITELES. *c.* 350 B.C. Hermes. *Olympia*   42

32. AFTER PRAXITELES. *c.* 350 B.C. Apollo Sauroctonos. *Louvre*   43

33. STYLE OF PRAXITELES. Bronze Boy from Marathon. *Athens*   44

34. CELLINI. Perseus. *Florence*   45

35. GREEK. ? 2nd century B.C. The Apollo Belvedere. *Vatican*   46

36. EARLY CHRISTIAN. 5th century A.D. *Florence, Bargello*   47

37. NICOLA PISANO. Fortitudo. *Pisa, Cathedral*   48

38. DONATELLO. David. *Florence, Bargello*   49

39. PERUGINO. Apollo and Marsyas. *Louvre*   51

40. DÜRER. Apollo. *British Museum*   52

41. MICHELANGELO. Nude Youth. *Louvre*   54

42. MICHELANGELO. An antique god. *Louvre*   55

43. MICHELANGELO. Detail of David. *Florence, Accademia*   56

44. MICHELANGELO. Creation of Adam. *Vatican, Sistine Chapel*   57

45. PHIDIAS. *c.* 435 B.C. Dionysus from the Parthenon. *British Museum*   58

46. MICHELANGELO. Apollo—David. *Florence, Bargello*   59

47. MICHELANGELO. Detail from Last Judgment. *Vatican, Sistine Chapel*   60

48. POUSSIN. Apollo crowning Virgil, frontispiece to the royal Virgil of 1641   61

49. MENGS. Parnassus. *Rome, Villa Albani*   62

50. CANOVA. Perseus. *Vatican*   63

51. PREHISTORIC. Figure of a woman. *Vienna*   64

52. CYCLADIC DOLL. *British Museum*   65

53. GREEK. Early 6th century B.C. Venus mirror handle. *Munich*   66

54. ATTIC. 6th century B.C. Black figure vase. *Berlin*   68

55. PANPHAIOS. *c.* 500 B.C. Vase (detail). *Louvre*   69

56. ATTIC. 5th century B.C. Terra-cotta doll. *Louvre*   70

57. GREEK. 5th century B.C. Torso (replica). *Louvre*   72

58. GREEK. 5th century B.C. Esquiline Venus (replica). *Rome, Conservatori*   73

59. IONIAN. Early 5th century B.C. Flute player on Ludovisi throne. *Rome, Terme*   74

60. IONIAN. Early 5th century B.C. Venus on Ludovisi throne. *Rome, Terme*   75

61. HELLENISTIC. 'Venus Genetrix.' *Rome, Terme*   76

62, 63. GREEK. *c.* 400 B.C. Bronze figure of a girl. *Munich*   77

64. AFTER PRAXITELES. *c.* 350 B.C. Cnidian Venus. *Vatican*   78

65. AFTER PRAXITELES. *c.* 350 B.C. Cnidian Venus. *Vatican*   80

66. HELLENISTIC. Capitoline Venus. *Rome*   81

67. HELLENISTIC. Medici Venus. *British Museum*   81

68. GREEK. *c.* 100 B.C. Venus of Milo. *Louvre*   82

69. HELLENISTIC. Bronze Venus. *British Museum*   84

70. GRAECO-ROMAN. Venus of Cyrenaica. *Rome, Terme*   86

71. GRAECO-ROMAN. Three Graces. *Siena*   87

72. GRAECO-ROMAN. Three Graces. *Louvre*   88

73. GRAECO-ROMAN. 1st century A.D. Three Graces. *Naples*   89

74. GIOVANNI PISANO. Temperance. *Pisa, Cathedral*   90

75. FLORENTINE. *c.* 1420. Marriage Tray. *Louvre*   91

76. BOTTICELLI. Three Graces (detail from *Primavera*). *Uffizi*   93

77. BOTTICELLI. Birth of Venus (detail). *Uffizi*   95

78. BOTTICELLI. Truth (detail from Calumny of Apelles). *Uffizi*   96

79. LORENZO DI CREDI. Venus. *Uffizi*   97

80. SIGNORELLI. Nude (detail from School of Pan). *Formerly Berlin*   98

81. RAPHAEL. Three Graces. *Chantilly*   99

82. RAPHAEL. Leda. *Windsor, Royal Library*   100

83. RAPHAEL. Adam and Eve. *Vatican*   101

84. MARCANTONIO. Adam and Eve. Engraving   102

85. FEDERIGHI. Adam and Eve. *Siena, Cathedral*   102

86. RAPHAEL. Venus (drawing). *Uffizi*   104

87. RAPHAEL. Kneeling Girl (drawing). *Chatsworth Collection*   105

88. BELLINI. Woman at her toilet. *Vienna*   107

89. GIORGIONE. Venus. *Dresden*   108

90. TITIAN. Venus of Urbino. *Uffizi*   111

91. CESARE DA SESTO. After Leonardo da Vinci. Leda. *Wilton House*   141

92. GIORGIONE. 'Concert Champêtre.' *Louvre*   116

93. SEBASTIANO DEL PIOMBO. Life drawing of a woman. *Louvre*   117

94. TITIAN. Sacred and Profane Love. *Rome, Borghese Gallery*   118

95. TITIAN. Venus. *Ellesmere Collection*   120

96. TITIAN. Venus and the Organ Player. *Madrid, Prado*   122

97. TITIAN. Danaë. *Madrid, Prado*   123

98. TITIAN. Diana and Actaeon. *Ellesmere Collection*   124

99. CORREGGIO. Jupiter and Antiope. *Louvre*   126

100. CORREGGIO. Danaë. *Rome, Borghese Gallery*   128

101. BRONZINO. Allegory of Passion. *London, National Gallery*   129

102. AMMANATI. Venus. *Florence, Bargello*   130

103. GIOVANNI DA BOLOGNA. Astronomy. *Vienna*   131

104. RUBENS. Three Graces. *Madrid, Prado*   132

105. RUBENS. Venus and Cupid with Bacchus and Area. *Kassel*   134

106. RUBENS. Rape of the Daughters of Leucippus. *Munich*   135

107. RUBENS. Perseus and Andromeda. *Berlin*   136

108. WATTEAU. Judgment of Paris. *Louvre*   138

109. BOUCHER. Miss O'Murphy. *Munich*   140

110. BOUCHER. Diana. *Louvre*   141

111. RUBENS. Life drawing of a woman. *Louvre*   142

112. CLODION. Nymph and Satyr. *New York, Metropolitan Museum*   144

113. INGRES. 'Baigneuse.' *Louvre*   146

114. INGRES. Venus Anadyomene. *Chantilly*   148

115. INGRES. 'La Grande Odalisque.' *Louvre*   150

116. INGRES. Study for 'L'Âge d'or'. *Cambridge, Mass., Fogg Museum*   151

117. INGRES. 'Le Bain Turc.' *Louvre*   152

118. COURBET. 'L'Atelier du peintre' (detail). *Louvre*   153

119. MANET. Olympia. *Musée du Jeu de Paume*   154

120. RENOIR. 'Baigneuse au griffon.' *Brazil, São Paulo*   155

121. RENOIR. 'La Baigneuse blonde.' *Kenneth Clark Collection*   157

122. RENOIR. Three Bathers. *Louvre*   158

123. RENOIR. Bather seated. *Chicago, Art Institute*   160

124. PAN-ATHENAIC AMPHORA. 6th century B.C. *New York, Metropolitan Museum* 162

125. ATTIC. *c.* 480 B.C. Wrestlers. *Athens* 164

126. POLLAJUOLO. Nude men fighting. Engraving 165

127. ATTIC. *c.* 470 B.C. Bearded God of Histiaea. *Athens* 166

128. ATTIC. *c.* 440 B.C. Lapith and Centaur, from metope of Parthenon. *British Museum* 168

129. AFTER MYRON. *c.* 450 B.C. Discobolos (reconstruction). *Rome, Terme* 169

130. AFTER MYRON. *c.* 450 B.C. Discobolos of Castel Porziano. *Rome, Terme* 170

131. MICHELANGELO. Athlete. *Vatican, Sistine Chapel* 171

132. GREEK. 3rd century B.C. Wrestlers. *Uffizi* 172

133. ATTIC. *c.* 440 B.C. Iris from west gable of Parthenon. *British Museum* 173

134. WORKSHOP OF SCOPAS. *c.* 350 B.C. An Amazon. From frieze of Mausoleum. *British Museum* 174

135. WORKSHOP OF SCOPAS. *c.* 350 B.C. Battle of Greeks and Amazons. From frieze of Mausoleum. *British Museum* 175

136. WORKSHOP OF SCOPAS. *c.* 350 B.C. Greeks and Amazons. From frieze of Mausoleum. *British Museum* 176

137. WORKSHOP OF SCOPAS. *c.* 350 B.C. Greeks and Amazons. From frieze of Mausoleum. *British Museum* 177

138. GREEK. (?) 3rd century B.C. Borghese Warrior. *Louvre* 178

139. LATE ANTIQUE. 4th century. Hercules and Stag. *Ravenna* 179

140. TUSCAN. 12th century. Samson and Lion. *Lucca* 180

141. ANTICO. Hercules and Lion. *Florence, Bargello* 181

142. POLLAJUOLO. Hercules slaying Hydra. *Formerly Uffizi* 182

143. POLLAJUOLO. Hercules and Antaeus. *Formerly Uffizi* 183

144. POLLAJUOLO. Hercules and Antaeus. *Florence, Bargello* 184

145. GRAECO-ROMAN. Dancing Faun. *Naples* 185

146. SIGNORELLI. Drawing. *Louvre* 186

147. SIGNORELLI. The Blessed. *Orvieto, Cathedral* 187

148. SIGNORELLI. The Damned. *Orvieto, Cathedral* 188

149. BERTOLDO. Battle piece. *Florence, Bargello* 189

150. MICHELANGELO. Battle of the Centaurs. *Florence, Casa Buonarroti* 190

151. AFTER MICHELANGELO. Copy of cartoon for Battle of Cascina. *Holkham Hall* 191

152. MICHELANGELO. Bathing soldier for Cascina cartoon. *British Museum*   192

153. MICHELANGELO. Study for Cascina cartoon. *Vienna, Albertina*   193

154. LEONARDO DA VINCI. Muscular legs. *Windsor, Royal Library*   194

155. RAPHAEL. Men fighting. *Oxford, Ashmolean Museum*   195

156. MICHELANGELO. Athlete. *Vatican, Sistine Chapel*   196

157. MICHELANGELO. Three Labours of Hercules. *Windsor, Royal Library*   197

158. MICHELANGELO. Victory. *Florence, Palazzo Vecchio*   198

159. AFTER MICHELANGELO. Samson defeating Philistines. *Florence, Casa Buonarroti*   199

160. VINCENZO DANTI. Honour. *Florence, Bargello*   200

161. GIOVANNI DA BOLOGNA. Mercury. *Florence, Bargello*   201

162. RUBENS. Abduction of Hippodamia. *Brussels*   202

163. GREEK. 2nd century B.C. Torso of Satyr. *Uffizi*   203

164. BLAKE. From 'Europe'   205

165. BLAKE. Glad Day. Colour print. *British Museum*   206

166. VITRUVIAN MAN from Scamozzi's 'Architettura universale'. *Venice, 1615*   207

167. GÉRICAULT. Leda. *Louvre*   208

168. DELACROIX. Girls wrestling. *Louvre*   209

169. DEGAS. Woman sponging her back. *Kenneth Clark Collection*   210

170. DEGAS. Spartan Girls. *London, National Gallery*   212

171. GREEK. (?) 5th century B.C. Son of Niobe. *Copenhagen, Ny-Carlsberg Glyptotek*   214

172. GREEK. (?) 5th century B.C. Daughter of Niobe. *Rome, Terme*   215

173. GRAECO-ROMAN. Soldier's Gravestone. *Rome, Capitoline*   216

174. PERGAMENE. 3rd century B.C. Marsyas. *Rome, Conservatori*   217

175. ? PERGAMENE. 2nd century B.C. Laocoön. *Vatican*   218

176. ROME. (?) 4th century. Crucifixion. Ivory plaque. *British Museum*   220

177. CONSTANTINOPLE. 10th century. Crucifixion. *New York, Metropolitan Museum*   221

178. GERMAN. 10th century. Gero Cross. *Cologne*   222

179. CIMABUE. Cross. *Arezzo*   224

180. MASACCIO. The Expulsion. *Florence, Brancacci Chapel*   226

181. GHIBERTI. Sacrifice of Isaac. *Florence, Bargello*   227

182. PROVENÇALE. 15th century. 'Pietà' from Villeneuve-lès-Avignon. *Louvre*   228

183. DONATELLO. Dead Christ with Angels. *London, Victoria and Albert Museum*   229

184. GIOVANNI BELLINI. Dead Christ with Angels. *Rimini*   230

185. MICHELANGELO. 'Pietà.' *Rome, St. Peter's*   231

186. RAPHAEL. Entombment. *Rome, Borghese Gallery*   232

187. MICHELANGELO. Dying Captive. *Louvre*   233

188. MICHELANGELO. Struggling Captive. *Louvre*   234

189. MICHELANGELO. Athlete. *Vatican, Sistine Chapel*   236

190. MICHELANGELO. Captive. *Florence, Accademia*   237

191. MICHELANGELO. Day. *Florence, Medici Chapel*   238

192. GRAECO-ROMAN. The Torso Belvedere. *Vatican*   239

193. MICHELANGELO. Night. *Florence, Medici Chapel*   240

194. MICHELANGELO. Dawn. *Florence, Medici Chapel*   241

195. GREEK. (?) 2nd century. Ariadne. *Vatican*   242

196. MICHELANGELO. Crucifixion. *British Museum*   244

197. MICHELANGELO. Crucifixion. *Louvre*   245

198. MICHELANGELO. Crucifixion. *Windsor, Royal Library*   246

199. MICHELANGELO. Palestrina 'Pietà' (detail). *Florence, Accademia*   247

200. MICHELANGELO. 'Pietà.' *Florence, Cathedral*   248

201. MICHELANGELO. 'Pietà.' *Milan, Castello*   249

202. ROSSO FIORENTINO. Moses and the Children of Jethro. *Uffizi*   251

203. TITIAN. St. Sebastian (detail). *Brescia*   252

204. CARAVAGGIO. Entombment. *Vatican*   253

205. RUBENS. Deposition (detail). *Antwerp, Cathedral*   255

206. RUBENS. Three Crosses. *Holland, Van Beunigen Collection*   256

207. RUBENS. Mourning over the Dead Christ. *Berlin*   258

208. POUSSIN. Death of Narcissus. *Louvre*   259

209. POUSSIN. Mourning over the Dead Christ. *Munich*   260

210. DELACROIX. Barque of Dante. *Louvre*   261

211. RODIN. Three Shades. *Paris, Musée Rodin*   262

212. HELLENISTIC. 1st century B.C. The Borghese Vase. *Louvre*   265

213. AFTER CALLIMACHUS. (?) 4th century B.C. Spartan Girl dancing. *Berlin*   266

214. AFTER CALLIMACHUS. (?) 4th century B.C. Spartan Girl dancing. *Berlin*   267

215. GRAECO-ROMAN. Three Maenads. *Uffizi*   268

216. AFTER SCOPAS. 4th century B.C. Maenad. *Dresden*   269

217. GRAECO-ROMAN. Dionysiac procession. *Naples*   270

218. GRAECO-ROMAN. Dionysiac sarcophagus (detail). *Rome, Terme*   271

219. AFTER SCOPAS (?). A Tritoness. *Ostia*   272

220. GRAECO-ROMAN. Nereid sarcophagus. *Louvre*   273

221. GRAECO-ROMAN. Nereid sarcophagus. *Vatican*   273

222. LATE ANTIQUE. *c.* A.D. 350. Silver dish from the Mildenhall Treasure. *British Museum*   274

223. GRAECO-ROMAN. 1st century A.D. Nereid. Wall painting from Stabia. *Naples*   275

224. LATE ANTIQUE. *c.* A.D. 380. The Casket of Projecta. *British Museum.*   276

225. INDIAN. 6th century A.D. Flying Gandharvas. *Gwalior*   276

226. HANS FRIES. Last Judgment (detail of a triptych). *Munich*   277

227. LORENZO MAITANI. The Creation of Eve. *Orvieto, Cathedral*   278

228. GHIBERTI. The Creation of Eve. *East doors of Baptistery, Florence*   279

229. PISANELLO. Luxury. *Vienna, Albertina*   280

230. DONATELLO. Detail from Cantoria. *Florence, Opera del Duomo*   281

231. POLLAJUOLO. Dancing Nudes. *Florence, Torre del Gallo*   282

232. BOTTICELLI. The Winds (detail from Birth of Venus). *Uffizi*   283

233. TITIAN. Bacchus (detail from Bacchus and Ariadne). *London, National Gallery*   285

234. TITIAN. Reclining Maenad (detail from Bacchanal). *Madrid, Prado*   286

235. TITIAN. Europa. *Boston, Gardner Collection*   287

236. CORREGGIO. Io. *Vienna*   288

237. LOTTO. Triumph of Chastity. *Rome, Galleria Rospigliosi*   289

238. BERNINI. Apollo and Daphne. *Rome, Borghese Gallery*   290

239. RAPHAEL. Triumph of Galatea. *Rome, Farnesina*   291

240. CARRACCI. Triumph of Galatea. *Rome, Farnese Palace*   292

241. POUSSIN. Triumph of Galatea. *Philadelphia*   293

242. CARPEAUX. Dance. Model for Paris Opera. *Louvre*   294

243. MATISSE. Dance. *Moscow, Museum of Modern Western Art*   295

244. MICHELANGELO. Resurrection. *Windsor, Royal Library*   296

245. MICHELANGELO. Risen Christ. *Windsor, Royal Library*   297

246. MICHELANGELO. Resurrection. *British Museum*   298

247. ROGIER VAN DER WEYDEN. Last Judgment (detail). *Beaune*   300

248. GERMAN. *c.* 1235. Adam and Eve. *Bamberg, Cathedral*   302

249. WILIGELMO. *c.* 1105. Adam and Eve. *Modena, Cathedral*   303

250. GERMAN. *c.* 1010. The Fall. Bronze doors. *Hildesheim*   304

251. GERMAN. *c.* 1010. The Expulsion. Bronze doors. *Hildesheim*   305

252. FRENCH. 12th century. Eve. *Autun, Cathedral Museum*   306

253. FRENCH. 13th century. Last Judgment. *Bourges, Cathedral*   307

254. MAITANI. Last Judgment. *Orvieto, Cathedral*   308

255. DE LIMBOURG. The Fall. 'Très Riches Heures.' *Chantilly*   309

256. VAN EYCK. Eve (detail of altar-piece). *Ghent*   310

257. VAN DER GOES. Adam and Eve. *Vienna*   311

258. SCHOOL OF MEMLINC. Vanitas. *Strasbourg*   312

259. BELLINI. Vanitas. *Venice, Accademia*   312

260. KONRAD MEIT. Judith. *Munich*   313

261. DÜRER. Naked Hausfrau. *Bayonne*   314

262. DÜRER. Women's Bath. *Bremen*   315

263. DÜRER. Four Witches. Engraving   316

264. NIKLAUS MANUEL DEUTSCH. Masked flute player. *Basle*   318

265. URS GRAF. Woman stabbing herself. *Basle*   319

266. CRANACH. Venus and Cupid. *Hermitage*   320

267. LORENZO COSTA. Venus. *Budapest*   321

268. CRANACH. Venus. *Frankfurt*   322

269. CRANACH. Judgment of Paris. *Karlsruhe*   324

270. INDIAN. 8th century. *From the painted caves at Ajanta*   325

271. GERMAIN PILLON (?). Diana of Anet. *Louvre*   326

272. REMBRANDT. Diana. Etching   328

273. REMBRANDT. Cleopatra. *London, Villiers David Collection*   329

274. REMBRANDT. Old woman bathing her feet. Etching. *British Museum*   330

275. REMBRANDT. Bathsheba. *Louvre*   331

276. RODIN. 'La Belle Heaulmière.' *Paris, Musée Rodin*   332

277. CÉZANNE. Nude. *Louvre*   333

278. ROUAULT. A Prostitute. *New York, Bakwin Collection*   334

279. GREEK. *c.* 438 B.C. Ilissus. From west front of Parthenon. *British Museum*   336

280. MICHELANGELO. River god. *Florence, Accademia*   337

281. DOIDALSUS (?). Early 4th century. Crouching Venus. *Louvre*   338

282. POLLAJUOLO. Bowmen (detail from Martyrdom of St. Sebastian). *London, National Gallery*   339

283. RAPHAEL. Drawing for 'Disputa'. *Frankfurt*   341

284. MARCANTONIO. Engraving after Raphael. Massacre of the Innocents   342

285 MARCANTONIO. Engraving after Raphael. Judgment of Paris   343

286. MATISSE. Blue Nude. *Baltimore Museum of Art*   345

287. MATISSE. Nude. From 'Poésies de Mallarmé'   347

288. BRANCUSI. Torso. *Cleveland Museum of Art*   348

289. PICASSO. 'Les Demoiselles d'Avignon.' *New York, Museum of Modern Art*   349

290. PICASSO. Woman in an armchair. *New York, Museum of Modern Art*   350

291. PICASSO. Four of the 18 stages of 'Les Deux Femmes nues'   352

292. HENRY MOORE. Recumbent Figure. *London, Tate Gallery*   355

293. HENRY MOORE. Reclining Figure. *New York, Curt Valentine*   356

294. ROMAN. The Emperor Trebonius Gallus. *New York, Metropolitan Museum*   368

295. GRAECO-ROMAN. Hermaphrodite. *Louvre*   377

296. GREEK. 5th century. The River Alpheus. *Olympia*   385

297. METZ. *c.* 850. The Crucifixion. *Paris, Bibliothèque Nationale*   388

298. BOLDRINI. After Titian. The Monkey Laocoön (woodcut)   390

Acknowledgments

I acknowledge my indebtedness to Her Majesty The Queen for gracious permission to reproduce six pictures in the Royal Library, Windsor.

My thanks are due to the following who have kindly helped me in securing the photographs used for reproduction in this book :

Professor Bernard Ashmole.
Lord Ellesmere.
Lord Herbert.
The Earl of Leicester.
G. Zarnecki, Esq.

Acknowledgments are due to the Curators of the following Galleries and Museums ; and Photographers :

A.C.L., Brussels ; The Acropolis Museum, Athens ; The Albertina, Vienna ; The Alte Pinakothek, Munich ; Alinari, Florence ; Anderson, Rome ; The Archaeological Museum, Gwalior ; Archives Photographiques, Paris ; The Art Institute, Chicago ; The Arts Council, London ; The Ashmolean Museum, Oxford ; The Bakwin Collection, New York ; The Baltimore Museum of Art ; Bildarchiv-Foto-Marburg, Lahn ; The Boston Museum of Fine Art ; Braun et Cie, France (courtesy Soho Gallery, London) ; The British Museum ; Brogi, France ; Bruckmann, Munich ; Bulloz, France ; Paul Bytebier, Brussels ; The Capitoline Museum, Rome ; Virginie Chauffourier, Rome ; The Cleveland Museum of Art ; The Courtauld Institute, London ; The Devonshire Collection, Chatsworth (courtesy of the Trustees of the Chatsworth Settlement) ; The Fogg Art Museum, Harvard University ; Foto Grassi, Siena ; A. Frequin, The Hague ; The Gemäldegalerie, Kassel ; Giraudon, Paris ; · The Glyptotek, Copenhagen ; The Glyptothek, Munich ; The Isabella Stewart Gardner Museum, Boston ; The Kunsthistorisches Museum, Vienna ; The Kunstinstitut, Frankfurt ; The Kupferstichcabinett, Basel ; The Lahore Museum, Pakistan ; The Louvre, Paris ; The Mansell Collection, London ; The Metropolitan Museum, New York ; The Museum of Art, São Paulo, Brazil ; The Museum of Modern Art, New York ; The National Gallery, London ; The National Museum, Athens ; The Phaidon Press, London ; The Philadelphia Museum of Art ; Photo Estel, Paris ; The Rheinisches Museum, Cologne ;

ACKNOWLEDGMENTS

The Rijksmuseum, Amsterdam ; The Royal Academy of Arts, London ; The Staatliches Museum, Berlin ; The Staatliche Kunsthalle, Karlsruhe ; The Staatliche Kunstsammlungen, Dresden ; The Tate Gallery, London ; The Uffizi, Florence ; The Vatican Museum ; The Victoria and Albert Museum ; Roger Viollet, Paris ; The Warburg Institute, London.

Preface

IN the spring of 1953 I had the honour to give the A. W. Mellon Lectures in the Fine Arts at the National Gallery of Art in Washington. I have never spoken to a more responsive and intelligent audience, and I should like to have given every member of it a copy of this book as a token of gratitude as soon as the course was over. But the lectures had to be considerably lengthened, three new chapters had to be written, and at the last minute my American publishers persuaded me to add a section of notes. This has meant a delay of almost three years, and I would like to thank the Mellon Lectureship and the Bollingen Foundation for the patience they have shown in waiting for the book to be finished.

Considering how the Nude dominated sculpture and painting at two of the chief epochs in their history, one might have expected a small library on the subject. But in fact there are only two general studies of any value, Julius Lange's *Die menschliche Gestalt in der Geschichte der Kunst*, Strasburg (1903) and Wilhelm Hausenstein's *Der nackte Mensch* (1913) in which much useful material is cooked into a Marxist stew. The fact is, as I soon discovered, that the subject is extremely difficult to handle. There is a difficulty of form ; a chronological survey would be long and repetitive, but almost every other pattern is unworkable. And there is a difficulty of scope ; since Jacob Burckhardt no responsible art historian would have attempted to cover both antique and post-mediaeval art. I recognise that it is imprudent for a student of renaissance painting to have written so many pages about classical sculpture ; but I am unrepentant—indeed I believe that these constitute the most useful part of the book. The dwindling appreciation of antique art during the last fifty years has greatly impoverished our understanding of art in general ; and professional writers on classical archaeology, microscopically re-examining their scanty evidence, have not helped us to understand why it was that for four hundred years artists and amateurs shed tears of admiration before works which arouse no tremor of emotion in us.

But although I believe that this attempt to revalue the once familiar monuments of antiquity was worth making, I cannot claim that I was fully qualified to make it. The reader should be warned that my pages on classical art are peppered with heresies, some intentional, some, no doubt, due to ignorance. From the Renaissance onwards I am more orthodox, but even then I have had to enter certain fields of scholarship, Michelangelo for example, or Rubens, which bear the sign 'Trespassers will be prosecuted'.

In trying to find my way through these dense and intricate subjects I have received generous help from eminent scholars and would like to express my gratitude to them. Professor Ashmole and M. Jean Charbonneau have answered my questions about antique art ; Professor Johannes Wilde has given me the benefit of his unequalled knowledge of Michelangelo, and on all matters concerning the survival of antique imagery I have received much help from Dr. Ettlinger of the Warburg Institute. On this last subject I must acknowledge a debt to a recent book by A. von Salis, *Antike und Renaissance*, which came to my notice when I was already at work on the Nude and amplified many of my own conclusions. In the troublesome business of collecting photographs, of which only about a quarter have found a place in this book, I was greatly helped by Mrs. Anthony P. Millman. Finally I must record my especial gratitude to Miss Caryl Whineray, who compiled the index and without whom the notes could never have been completed.

Les belles filles, que vous aurez vues à Nîmes, ne vous auront, je m'assure, pas moins délecté l'esprit par la vue que les belles colonnes de la Maison Carrée, vu que celles-ci ne sont que de vieilles copies de celles-là.

NICOLAS POUSSIN to CHANTELOU
20th March 1642

J'ai passé hier une grande heure à regarder se baigner les dames. Quel tableau ! Quel hideux tableau.

FLAUBERT to LOUISE COLET
14th August 1853

For soule is forme, and doth the bodie make.

SPENSER, *Hymne in Honour of Beautie*
1596

CHAPTER I

The Naked and the Nude

THE English language, with its elaborate generosity, distinguishes between the naked and the nude. To be naked is to be deprived of our clothes and the word implies some of the embarrassment which most of us feel in that condition. The word nude, on the other hand, carries, in educated usage, no uncomfortable overtone. The vague image it projects into the mind is not of a huddled and defenceless body, but of a balanced, prosperous and confident body: the body re-formed. In fact the word was forced into our vocabulary by critics of the early 18th century in order to persuade the artless islanders that in countries where painting and sculpture were practised and valued as they should be, the naked human body was the central subject of art.

For this belief there is a quantity of evidence. In the greatest age of painting the nude inspired the greatest works; and even in periods when it ceased to

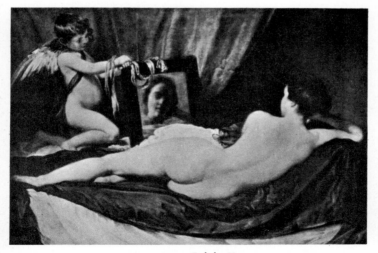

1. VELASQUEZ. Rokeby Venus

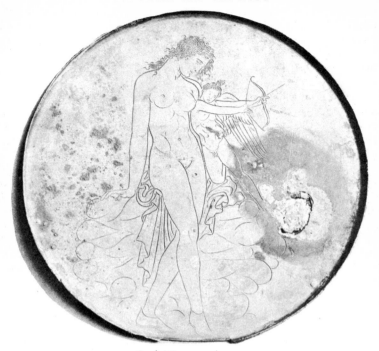

2. Greek Mirror. 2nd cent. B.C.

be a compulsive subject it has held its position as an academic exercise and a demonstration of mastery. Velasquez, living in the prudish and corseted court of Philip IV and admirably incapable of idealisation, yet felt bound to paint the Rokeby Venus [1]. Sir Joshua Reynolds, wholly without the gift of formal draughtsmanship, set great store by his Cymon and Iphigenia. And in our own century, when we have shaken off one by one those inheritances of Greece which were revived at the Renaissance, discarded the antique armour, forgotten the subjects of mythology and disputed the doctrine of imitation, the nude alone has survived. It may have suffered some curious transformations, but it remains our chief link with the classic disciplines. When we wish to prove to the philistine that our great revolutionaries are really respectable artists in the tradition of European painting, we point to their drawings of the nude. Picasso has often exempted it from that savage metamorphosis which he has inflicted on the visible world and has produced a series [3] of nudes which might have walked unaltered off the back of a Greek mirror [2] ; and Henry Moore, searching in stone for the ancient laws of its material and seeming to find there some of those elementary creatures of whose fossilised bones it is composed, yet gives to his constructions the same fundamental character which was invented by the sculptors of the Parthenon in the 5th century before Christ.

These comparisons suggest a short answer to the question 'What is the nude?' It is an art form invented by the Greeks in the 5th century B.C., just as opera is an art form invented in 17th-century Italy. The conclusion is certainly too abrupt, but it has the merit of emphasising that the nude is not the subject of art, but a form of art.

It is widely supposed that the naked human body is in itself an object upon which the eye dwells with pleasure and which we are glad to see depicted. But anyone who has frequented art schools and seen the shapeless, pitiful model which the students are industriously drawing will know that this is an illusion. The body is not one of those subjects which can be made into art by direct transcription—like a tiger or a snowy landscape. Often in looking at the natural and animal world we joyfully identify ourselves with what we see and from this happy union create a work of art. This is the process which

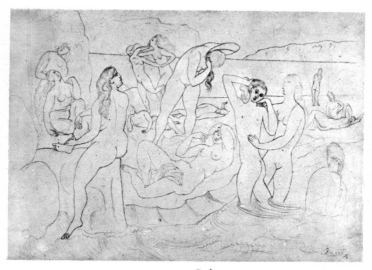

3. PICASSO. Bathers

students of aesthetics call empathy, and it is at the opposite pole of creative activity to the state of mind which has produced the nude. A mass of naked figures does not move us to empathy, but to disillusion and dismay. We do not wish to imitate ; we wish to perfect. We become, in the physical sphere, like Diogenes with his lantern looking for an honest man ; and, like him, we may never be rewarded. Photographers of the nude are presumably engaged in this search, with every advantage ; and having found a model who pleases them, they are free to pose and light her in conformity with their notions of beauty ; finally they can tone down and accentuate by retouching. But in spite of all their taste and skill, the result is hardly ever satisfactory to those whose eyes have grown accustomed to the harmonious simplifications of antiquity. We are immediately disturbed by wrinkles, pouches and other small imperfections which, in the classical scheme, are eliminated. By long habit we do not judge it as a living organism, but as a design ; and we discover that the transitions are inconclusive, the outline faltering. We are bothered because the various parts of the body cannot be perceived as simple units and have no clear relationship to one another. In almost every detail the body is not the shape which art had led us to believe that it would be. Yet we can look with pleasure at photographs of trees and animals, where the canon of perfection is less strict. Consciously, or unconsciously, photographers have usually recognised that in a photograph of the nude their real object is not to reproduce the naked body, but to imitate some artist's view of what the naked body should be like. Rejlander was the most philistine of the early photographers, but, perhaps without knowing it, he was a contemporary of Courbet [4], and with this splendid archetype somewhere in the background he produced one of the finest (as well as one of the first) photographs of the nude [5]. He has succeeded partly because his unconscious archetype was a realist. The more ideal the model, the more unfortunate the photographs which try to imitate it—as those in the style of Ingres or Whistler prove.

Although the naked body is no more than the point of departure for a work of art, it is a pretext of great importance. In the history of art, the subjects which men have chosen as nuclei, so to say, of their sense of order, have often been in themselves unimportant. For hundreds of years, and over an area stretching from Ireland to China, the most vital expression of order was an imaginary animal biting its own tail. In the middle ages drapery took on a life of its own, the same life which had inhabited the twisting animal, and became the vital pattern of Romanesque art. In neither case had the subject any independent existence. But the human body, as a nucleus, is rich in associations, and when it is turned into art these associations are not

4

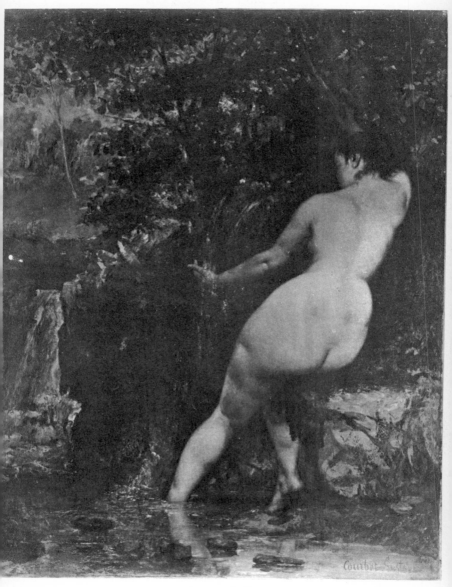

4. COURBET. *La Source*

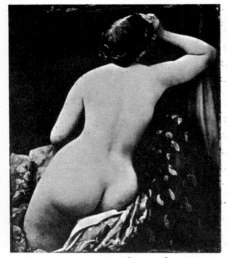

5. REJLANDER. Photograph

entirely lost. For this reason it seldom achieves the concentrated aesthetic shock of animal ornament, but it can be made expressive of a far wider and more civilising experience. It is ourselves, and arouses memories of all the things we wish to do with ourselves; and first of all we wish to perpetuate ourselves.

This is an aspect of the subject so obvious that I need hardly dwell on it; and yet some wise men have tried to close their eyes to it. 'If the nude', says Professor Alexander, 'is so treated that it raises in the spectator ideas or desires appropriate to the material subject, it is false art, and bad morals.' This high-minded theory is contrary to experience. In the mixture of memories and sensations aroused by the nudes of Rubens or Renoir are many which are 'appropriate to the material subject'. And since these words of a famous philosopher are often quoted, it is necessary to labour the obvious and say that no nude, however abstract, should fail to arouse in the spectator some vestige of erotic feeling, even although it be only the faintest shadow—and if it does not do so, it is bad art and false morals. The desire to grasp and be united with another human body is so fundamental a part of our nature, that our judgment of what is known as 'pure form' is inevitably influenced by it; and one of the difficulties of the nude as a subject for art is that these instincts cannot lie hidden, as they do for example in our enjoyment of a piece of pottery, thereby gaining the force of sublimation, but are dragged into the foreground, where they risk upsetting the unity of responses from which a work of art derives its independent life. Even so, the amount of erotic content which a work of art can hold in solution is very high. The temple sculptures of 10th-century India are an undisguised exaltation of physical desire; yet they are great works of art because their eroticism is part of their whole philosophy.

Apart from biological needs, there are other branches of human experience

6

of which the naked body provides a vivid reminder—harmony, energy, ecstasy, humility, pathos ; and when we see the beautiful results of such embodiments, it must seem as if the nude as a means of expression is of universal and eternal value. But this we know historically to be untrue. It has been limited both in place and in time. There are naked figures in the paintings of the Far East ; but only by an extension of the term can they be called nudes. In Japanese prints they are part of *ukioye*, the passing show of life, which includes without comment certain intimate scenes usually allowed to pass unrecorded [6]. The idea of offering the naked body for its own sake as a serious subject of contemplation simply did not occur to the Chinese or Japanese mind, and to this day raises a slight barrier of misunderstanding. In the Gothic north the position was fundamentally very similar. It is true that German painters in the Renaissance, finding that the naked body was a respected subject in Italy, adapted it to their needs, and evolved a remarkable convention of their own. But Dürer's struggles show how artificial this creation was. His instinctive responses were curiosity and horror, and he had to draw a great many circles and other diagrams before he could brace himself to turn the unfortunate body into the nude.

Only in countries touching on the Mediterranean has the nude been at

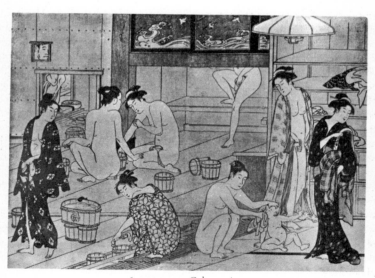

6. KYONAGA. Colour print

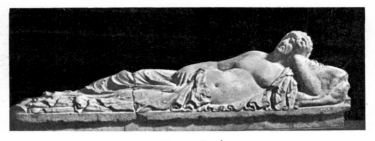

7. Etruscan Tomb

home ; and even there its meaning was often forgotten. The Etruscans, owing three-quarters of their art to Greece, never abandoned a type of tomb figure in which the defunct displays his stomach with a complacency which would have shocked a Greek profoundly [7]. Hellenistic and Roman art produced statues and mosaics of professional athletes who seem satisfied with their monstrous proportions. More remarkable still, of course, is the way in which the nude, even in Italy and Greece, is limited by time. It is the fashion to speak of Byzantine art as if it were a continuation of Greek ; the nude reminds us that this is one of the refined excesses of specialisation. Between the nereids of late Roman silver and the golden doors of Ghiberti the nudes in Mediterranean art are few and insignificant—a piece of modest craftsmanship like the Ravenna ivory of Apollo and Daphne, a few *objets de luxe*, like the Veroli Casket, with its strip-cartoon Olympus, and a number of Adams and Eves whose nakedness seldom shows any memory of antique form. Yet during a great part of that millennium the masterpieces of Greek art had not yet been destroyed, and men were surrounded by representations of the nude more numerous and, alas, infinitely more splendid than any which have come down to us. As late as the 10th century the Cnidian Venus of Praxiteles, which had been carried to Constantinople, it is said, by Theodosius, was praised by the Emperor Constantine Porphyrogenitus ; and either the original or a copy is mentioned by Robert de Clari in his account of the taking of Constantinople by the Crusaders. Moreover the body itself did not cease to be an object of interest in Byzantium : this we may deduce from the continuation of the race. And athletes performed in the circus, workmen, stripped to the waist, toiled at the building of St. Sophia. There was no want of opportunity for artists. That their patrons did not demand representations of the nude during this period may be explained by a number of reasonable-looking causes—fear of idolatry, the fashion for asceticism, or the influence of eastern art. But in fact such answers are incomplete. The nude had ceased to be the subject of art almost a century before the official establishment of Christianity. And during the middle ages there would have been ample opportunity to introduce it both into profane decoration and into such sacred subjects as show the beginning and end of our existence.

Why, then, does it never appear? An illuminating answer is to be found in the notebook of the 13th-century architect Villard de Honnecourt [8]. This contains many beautiful drawings of draped figures, some of them showing a high degree of skill. But when Villard draws two nude figures in what he believes to be the antique style the result is painfully ugly. It was impossible for him to adapt the stylistic conventions of Gothic art to a subject which depended on an entirely different system of forms. There can be few more hopeless misunderstandings in art than his attempt to render that refined abstraction, the antique torso, in terms of Gothic loops and pot-hooks. Moreover, Villard has constructed his men according to the pointed geometrical scheme of which he himself gives us the key on another page. He still felt that the human body was sufficiently divine to require the blessing of geometry. Cennino Cennini, the last chronicler of mediaeval practice, says, 'I will not tell you about irrational animals, because I have never learned any of their measurements. Draw them from nature, and in this respect you will achieve a good style.' The Gothic artists could draw animals because this involved no intervening abstraction. But they could not draw the nude because it was an idea: an idea which their philosophy of form could not assimilate.

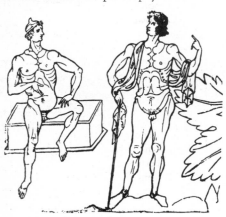

8. VILLARD DE HONNECOURT. Notebook

I said just now that, in our Diogenes search for physical beauty, our instinctive desire is not to imitate but to perfect. This is part of our Greek inheritance, and it was formulated by Aristotle with his usual deceptive simplicity. 'Art', he says, 'completes what nature cannot bring to a finish. The artist gives us knowledge of nature's unrealised ends.' A great many assumptions underlie this statement, the chief of which is that everything has an ideal form of which the phenomena of experience are more or less corrupted replicas. This beautiful fancy has teased the minds of philosophers and writers on aesthetics for over two thousand years, and although we need not plunge into a sea of speculation, we cannot discuss the nude without considering its practical application, because every time we criticise a figure, saying that a neck is too long, hips too wide or breasts too small, we are admitting, in concrete terms, the existence of ideal beauty. Critical opinion has varied between two interpretations of the ideal, one unsatisfactory because it is too prosaic, the other because it is too mystical. The former begins with the belief that although no individual body is satisfactory as a whole, the artist can choose the perfect parts from a number of figures and then combine them into a perfect whole. Such, we are told by Pliny, was the procedure of Zeuxis when he constructed his Venus out of the five beautiful maidens of Croton, and the advice reappears in the earliest treatise on painting of the post-antique world, Alberti's *Della pittura*. Dürer went so far as to say that he had 'searched through two or three hundred'. The argument is repeated again and again for four centuries, never more charmingly than by the French 17th-century theorist Du Fresnoy, whom I will quote in Mason's translation :

> For tho' our casual glance may sometimes meet
> With charms that strike the soul and seem complete,
> Yet if those charms too closely we define,
> Content to copy nature line for line,
> Our end is lost. Not such the master's care,
> Curious he culls the perfect from the fair ;
> Judge of his art, thro' beauty's realm he flies,
> Selects, combines, improves, diversifies ;
> With nimble step pursues the fleeting throng,
> And clasps each Venus as she glides along.

Naturally the theory was a popular one with artists : but it satisfies neither logic nor experience. Logically it simply transfers the problem from the whole to the parts and we are left asking by what ideal pattern Zeuxis accepted or rejected the arms, necks, bosoms and so forth of his five maidens. And even admitting that we do find certain individual limbs or features which, for some mysterious reason, seem to us perfectly beautiful, experience shows us that we cannot often recombine them. They are right in their setting, organically, and to abstract them is to deprive them of that rhythmic vitality on which their beauty depends.

To meet this difficulty the classic theorists of art invented what they called 'the middle form'. They based this notion on Aristotle's definition of nature, and in the stately language of Sir Joshua Reynolds' *Discourses* it seems to carry some conviction. But what does it amount to, translated into plain speech ? Simply that the ideal is composed of the average and the habitual. It is an uninspiring proposition, and we are not surprised that Blake was provoked into replying, 'All Forms are Perfect in the Poet's Mind but these are not Abstracted or compounded from Nature, but are from the Imagination'. Of course he is right. Beauty is precious and rare, and if it were like a mechanical toy, made up of parts of average size which could be put together at will, we should not value it as we do. But we must admit that Blake's interjection is more a believer's cry of triumph than an argument, and we must ask what meaning can be attached to it. Perhaps the question is best answered in Crocean terms. The ideal is like a myth, in which the finished form can be understood only as the end of a long process of accretion. In the beginning no doubt there is the coincidence of widely diffused desires and the personal tastes of a few individuals endowed with the gift of simplifying their visual experiences into easily comprehensible shapes. Once this fusion has taken place, the resulting image, while still in a plastic state, may be enriched or refined upon by succeeding generations. Or, to change the metaphor, it is like a receptacle into which more and more experience can be poured. Then, at a certain point, it is full. It sets. And, partly because it seems to be completely satisfying, partly because the mythopoeic faculty has declined, it is accepted as true. What both Reynolds and Blake meant by ideal beauty was really the diffused memory of that peculiar physical type which was developed in Greece between the years 480 and 440 B.C., and which, in varying degrees of intensity and consciousness, furnished the mind of western man with a pattern of perfection from the Renaissance until the present century.

Once more we have returned to Greece, and it is now time to consider some peculiarities of the Greek mind which may have contributed to the formation of this indestructible image.

The most distinctive is the Greek passion for mathematics. In every branch of Hellenic thought we encounter a belief in measurable proportion which, in the last analysis, amounts to a mystical religion ; and as early as Pythagoras it had been given the visible form of geometry. All art is founded on faith, and inevitably the Greek faith in harmonious numbers found expression in their painting and sculpture ; but precisely how we do not know. The so-called canon of Polyclitus is not recorded, and the rules of proportion which have come down to us in Pliny and a few writers of antiquity are of the most elementary kind. Probably the Greek sculptors were familiar with a system as subtle and elaborate as that of their architects, but we have scarcely

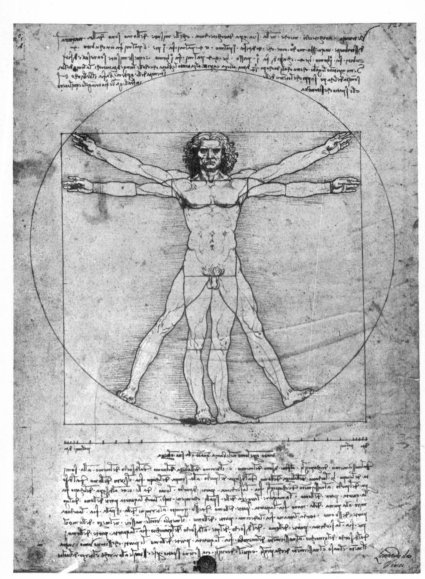

9. LEONARDO DA VINCI. Vitruvian Man

any indication as to what it was. There is, however, one short and obscure statement in Vitruvius which, whatever it meant in antiquity, had a decisive influence on the Renaissance. At the beginning of the third book, in which he sets out to give the rules for sacred edifices, he suddenly announces that these buildings should have the proportions of a man. He gives some indication of correct human proportions and then throws in a statement that man's body is a model of proportion because with arms or legs extended it fits into those

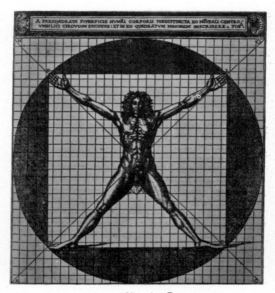

10. CESARINO. *Vitruvius*, Como, 1521

'perfect' geometrical forms, the square and the circle. It is impossible to exaggerate what this simple-looking proposition meant to the men of the Renaissance. To them it was far more than a convenient rule: it was the foundation of a whole philosophy. Taken together with the musical scale of Pythagoras, it seemed to offer exactly that link between sensation and order, between an organic and a geometric basis of beauty which was (and perhaps remains) the philosopher's stone of aesthetics. Hence the many diagrams of figures standing in squares or circles which illustrate the treatises on architecture or aesthetics from the 15th to the 17th centuries.

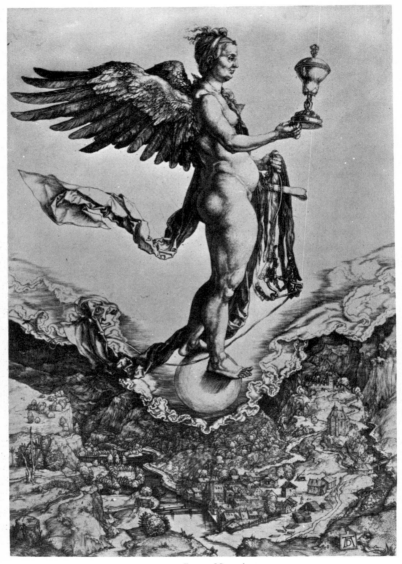

11. DÜRER. Nemesis

Vitruvian Man, as this figure has come to be called, appears earlier than Leonardo da Vinci, but it is in Leonardo's famous drawing in Venice that he receives his most masterly exposition [9] ; also, on the whole, the most correct, for Leonardo makes only two slight deviations from Vitruvius, whereas most of the other illustrations follow him very sketchily. This is not one of Leonardo's most attractive drawings, and it must be admitted that the Vitruvian formula does not provide any guarantee of a pleasant-looking body. The most carefully worked-out illustration of all, in the Como *Vitruvius* of 1521, shows an ungraceful figure with head too small and legs and feet too big [10]. Particularly troublesome was the question how the square and the circle, which were to establish the perfect form, should be related to one another. Leonardo, on no authority that I can discover, said that in order to fit into a circle the figure should stretch apart his legs so that he was a fourteenth shorter than if they were together. But this arbitrary solution did not please Cesarino, the editor of the Como *Vitruvius*, who inscribed the square in the circle, with unfortunate results. We see that from the point of view of strict geometry a gorilla might prove to be more satisfactory than a man.

How little systematic proportion alone can be relied on to produce physical beauty is shown by Dürer's engraving known as the Nemesis or Large Fortune [11]. It was executed in 1501, and we know that in the preceding year Dürer had been reading Vitruvius. In this figure he had applied Vitruvian principles of measurement down to the last detail : according to Professor Panofsky even the big toe is operative. He has also taken his subject from a work by the same humanist poet who inspired Botticelli's Birth of Venus and Raphael's Galatea, Poliziano. But in spite of these precautions he has not achieved the classical ideal. That he did so later was due to the practice of relating his system to antique figures [12]. It was not his

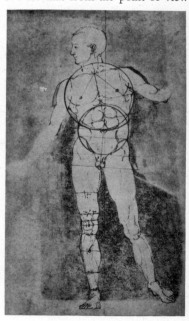

12. DÜRER. Measured nude

squares and circles which enabled him to master classical proportions, but the fact that he applied them to memories of the Apollo Belvedere and the Medici Venus—forms 'perfected in the poet's mind'. And it was from these, in the end, that he derived the beautiful nude figure of Adam in his famous engraving of the Fall.

Francis Bacon, as we all know, said, 'There is no excellent beauty that hath not some strangeness in the proportion. A man cannot tell whether Apelles or Albrecht Dürer were the more trifler ; whereof the one would make a personage by geometrical proportions : the other by taking the best part out of divers faces to make one excellent.' This very intelligent observation is unfair on Dürer, and suggests that Bacon, like the rest of us, had not read his book on human proportions, only looked at the plates. For, after 1507, Dürer abandoned the idea of imposing a geometrical scheme on the body, and set about deducing ideal measurements from nature, with a result, as may be imagined, somewhat different from his analyses of the Antique ; and in his introduction he forcefully denies the claim that he is providing a standard of absolute perfection. 'There lives no man upon earth', he says, 'who

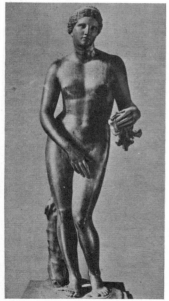

can give a final judgment upon what the most beautiful shape of a man may be ; God only knows that. . . . "Good" and "better" in respect of beauty are not easy to discern, for it would be quite possible to make two different figures, neither conforming with the other, one stouter, the other thinner, and yet we might scarce be able to judge which of the two excelled in beauty.'

So the most indefatigable and masterly constructor of ideal proportions abandoned them half-way through his career, and his work, from the Nemesis onwards, is a proof that the idea of the nude does not depend on analysable proportions alone. And yet when we look at the splendidly schematised bodies of Greek sculpture, we cannot resist the conviction that some system did exist. Almost every artist or writer on art who has thought seriously about the nude has concluded that it must

have some basis of construction which can
be stated in terms of measurement ; and I
myself, when trying to explain why a
photograph did not satisfy me, said that I
missed the sense of simple units, clearly
related to one another. Although the artist
cannot construct a beautiful nude by mathematical rules, any more than the musician
can compose a beautiful fugue, he cannot
ignore them. They must be lodged somewhere at the back of his mind or in the
movements of his fingers. Ultimately he is
as dependent on them as an architect.

Dipendenza : that is the word used by
Michelangelo, supreme as a draughtsman of
the nude and as an architect, to express his
sense of the relationship between these two
forms of order. In the pages which follow
I often make use of architectural analogies.
Like a building, the nude represents a balance
between an ideal scheme and functional
necessities. The figure artist cannot forget
the components of the human body any
more than the architect can fail to support
his roof or forget his doors and windows.
But the variations of shape and disposition
are surprisingly wide. The most striking
instance is, of course, the change in proportion between the Greek and the Gothic
idea of the female body. One of the few
classical canons of proportion of which we
can be certain is that which, in a female
nude, took the same unit of measurement
for the distance between the breasts, the
distance from the lower breast to the navel,
and again from the navel to the division of
the legs. This scheme we shall find carefully maintained in all figures of the classical

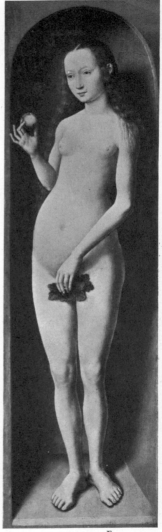

14. MEMLINC. Eve

epoch [13] and in most of those which imitated them down to the 1st century.

17

Contrast a typical Gothic nude of the 15th century, Memlinc's Eve from Vienna [14]. The components are—naturally—the same. The basic pattern of the female body is still an oval, surmounted by two spheres; but the oval has grown incredibly long, the spheres distressingly small. If we apply our unit of measurement, the distance between the breasts, we find that the navel is exactly twice as far down the body as it is in the classic scheme. This increased length of body

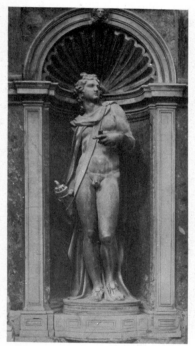

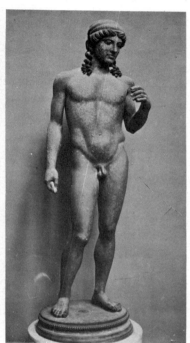

15. SANSOVINO. Apollo

16. Graeco-Roman Apollo

is made more noticeable because it is unbroken by any suggestion of ribs or muscles. The forms are not conceived as individual blocks, but seem to have been drawn out of one another as if they were made of some viscous material. It is usual to speak of this kind of Gothic nude as 'naturalistic', but is Memlinc's Eve really closer to the average (for this is what the word means) than the antique nude? Such, at all events, was certainly not the painter's intention. He aimed at producing a figure which should conform to the ideal of his time, which should be the kind of shape which men liked to see ; and by some strange interaction of flesh and spirit this long curve of the stomach has become the means by which the body has achieved the ogival rhythm of late Gothic architecture.

A rather less obvious example is provided by Sansovino's Apollo on the Loggetta in Venice [15]. It is inspired by the Apollo Belvedere, but although Sansovino, like all his contemporaries, thought that the antique figure was of unsurpassable beauty, he has allowed himself a fundamental difference in his construction of the body. We may describe this by saying that the antique male nude is like a Greek temple, the flat frame of the chest being carried on the columns of the legs [16] ; whereas the renaissance nude is related to the architectural system which produced the central-domed church ; so that instead of the sculptural interest depending on a simple, frontal plane, a number of axes radiate from one centre. Not only the elevations but, so to say, the ground plans of these figures would have an obvious relationship to their respective architectures. What we may call the multiple-axis nude continued until the classicistic revival of the 18th century. Then, when architects were reviving the Greek temple form, sculptors once more gave to the male body the flatness and frontality of a frame building. Ultimately the *dipendenza* of architecture and the nude expresses the relationship which we all so earnestly desire between that which is perfected by the mind and that which we love. Poussin, writing to his friend Chantelou in 1642, said, 'The beautiful girls whom you will have seen in Nîmes will not, I am sure, have delighted your spirit any less than the beautiful columns of Maison Carrée ; for the one is no more than an old copy of the other'. And the hero of Claudel's *Partage de midi*, when at last he puts his arms round his beloved, utters, as the first pure expression of his bliss, the words '*Ô Colonne!* '

So our surmise that the discovery of the nude as a form of art is connected with idealism and faith in measurable proportions seems to be true, but it is only half the truth. What other peculiarities of the Greek mind are involved ? One obvious answer is their belief that the body was something to be proud of, and should be kept in perfect trim.

We need not suppose that many Greeks looked like the Hermes of Praxiteles, but we can be sure that in the 5th-century Attica a majority of the young men had the nimble, well-balanced bodies depicted on the early red figure vases. On a vase in the British Museum is a scene which will arouse sympathy in most of us, but to the Athenians was ridiculous and shameful— a fat youth in the gymnasium embarrassed by his ungraceful figure, and apparently protesting to a thin one, while two young men of more fortunate

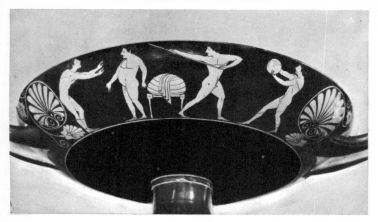

17. Attic vase. Early 5th cent. B.C. Palestra scene

development throw the javelin and the discus [17]. Greek literature from Homer and Pindar downwards contains many expressions of this physical pride, some of which strike unpleasantly on the Anglo-Saxon ear and trouble the minds of schoolmasters when they are recommending the Greek ideal of fitness. 'What do I care for any man,' says the young man, Critobalus, in the *Symposium* of Xenophon, 'I am beautiful.' And no doubt this arrogance was increased by the tradition that in the gymnasium and the sports-ground such young men displayed themselves totally naked.

The Greeks attached great importance to their nakedness. Thucydides, in recording the stages by which they distinguished themselves from the Barbarians, gives prominence to the date at which it became the rule in the Olympic games, and we know from vase paintings that the competitors at the pan-Athenaic festival had been naked since the early 6th century. Although the presence, or absence, of a loin-cloth does not greatly affect questions of form, and in this study I shall include figures which are lightly draped, psychologically the Greek cult of absolute nakedness is of great importance. It implies the conquest of an inhibition which oppresses all but the most backward people ; it is like a denial of original sin. This is not, as is sometimes supposed, simply a part of paganism: for the Romans were shocked by the nakedness of Greek athletes, and Ennius attacked it as a sign of decadence. Needless to say he was wide of the mark, for the most determined nudists of all were the Spartans, who scandalised even the Athenians by allowing women to compete, lightly clad, in their games. He and subsequent moralists considered the matter in purely physical terms : but in fact Greek confidence in the body can be understood only in relation to their philosophy. It expresses above all their sense of human wholeness. Nothing which related to the whole man could be isolated or evaded ; and this serious awareness of how much was implied in physical beauty saved them from the two evils of sensuality and aestheticism.

At the same party where Critobalus brags about his beauty Xenophon describes the youth Autolycus, victor of the Pancration, in whose honour the feast was being given. 'Noting the scene,' he says, 'the first idea to strike the mind is that beauty has about it something regal ; and the more so if it chance to be combined (as now in the person of Autolycus) with modesty and self-respect. Even as when a splendid object blazes forth at night, the eyes of men are riveted, so now the beauty of Autolycus drew on him the gaze of all ; nor was there one of those onlookers but was stirred to his soul's depth by him who sat there. Some fell into unwonted silence, while the gestures of the rest were equally significant.'

This feeling, that the spirit and body are one, which is the most familiar of all Greek characteristics, manifests itself in their gift of giving to abstract ideas a sensuous, tangible and, for the most part, human form. Their logic is conducted in the form of dialogues between real men ; their gods take visible shape, and on their appearance are usually mistaken for half-familiar human beings—a maidservant, a shepherd or a distant cousin ; and woods, rivers, even echoes are shown in painting as bodily presences, solid as the living protagonists, and often more prominent. Here we reach what I take to be the central point of our subject. Greek statues, said Blake in his *Descriptive Catalogue*, 'are all of

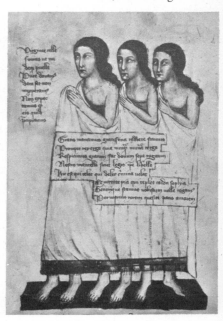

18. The Three Graces. 12th-cent. MS.

them representations of spiritual existences, of gods immortal, to the mortal, perishing organ of sight ; and yet they are embodied and organised in solid marble'. The bodies were there, the belief in the gods was there, the love of rational proportion was there. It was the unifying grasp of the Greek imagination which brought them together. And the nude gains its enduring value from the fact that it reconciles several contrary states. It takes the most sensual and immediately interesting object, the human body, and puts it out of reach of time and desire ; it takes the most purely rational concept of which mankind is capable, mathematical order, and makes it a delight to the senses ; and it takes the vague fears of the unknown and sweetens them by showing that the gods are like men, and may be worshipped for their life-giving beauty rather than their death-dealing powers.

To recognise how completely the value of these spiritual existences depends on their nudity, we have only to think of them as they appear, fully clothed, in the middle ages or early Renaissance. They have lost all their meaning. When the Graces are represented by three nervous ladies hiding behind a blanket, they no longer convey to us the civilising influence of beauty [18]. When Hercules is a lumbering *landsknecht* weighed down by fashionable armour he does not increase our sense of well-being by his own superabundant strength. Conversely, when nude figures which had been evolved to express an idea ceased to do so, and were represented for their physical perfection alone, they lost their value. This was the fatal legacy of neo-classicism, and Coleridge, who lived through the period, summed up the situation in some lines which he added to the translation of Schiller's *Piccolomini* :

> The intelligible powers of ancient poets,
> The fair humanities of old religion,
> The Power, the Beauty and the Majesty,
> That had their haunts in dale or piny mountain,
>   . . . all these have vanished.
> They live no longer in the faith of reason.

The academic nudes of the 19th century are lifeless because they no longer embodied real human needs and experiences. They were among the hundreds of devalued symbols which encumbered the art and architecture of the utilitarian century.

The nude had flourished most exuberantly during the first hundred years of the classical Renaissance, when the new appetite for antique imagery over-lapped with the mediaeval habits of symbolism and personification. It seemed then that there was no concept, however sublime, which could not be expressed by the naked body, and no object of use, however trivial, which would not be the better for having been given human shape. At one end of the scale was Michelangelo's Last Judgment ; at the other the door-knockers, candelabra or even handles of knives and forks. To the first it might be objected—and frequently was—that nakedness was unbecoming in a representation of Christ and His saints. This was the point put forward by Paul Veronese when he was tried by the Inquisition for including drunkards and Germans in his picture of the marriage of Cana : to which the chief inquisitor gave his immortal reply, 'Do you not know that in these figures by Michelangelo there is nothing which is not spiritual—*non vi è cosa se non de spirito*'. And to the second it might be objected—and frequently is—that the similitude of the naked Venus is not what we need in our hand when we are cutting up our food or knocking at a door, to which Benvenuto Cellini would have replied that since the human body is the most perfect of all forms we cannot see it too often. In between these two extremes was that forest of nude figures, painted or carved, in stucco, bronze or stone, which filled every vacant space in the architecture of the 16th century.

Such an insatiable appetite for the nude is unlikely to recur. It arose from a fusion of beliefs, traditions and impulses very remote from our age of essence and specialisation. Yet even in the new self-governing kingdom of the aesthetic sensation the nude is enthroned. The intensive application of great artists has made it into a sort of pattern for all formal constructions, and it is still a means of affirming the belief in ultimate perfection. 'For soule is forme, and doth the bodie make', wrote Spenser in his *Hymne in Honour of Beautie*, echoing the words of the Florentine neo-Platonists, and although in life the evidence for this doctrine is inconclusive, it is perfectly applicable to art. The nude remains the most complete example of the transmutation of matter into form.

Nor are we likely once more to reject the body, as in the ascetic experiment of mediaeval Christianity. We may no longer worship it, but we have come to terms with it. We are reconciled to the fact that it is our lifelong companion, and since art is concerned with sensory images the scale and rhythm of the body is not easily ignored. Our continuous effort, made in defiance of the pull of gravity, to keep ourselves balanced upright on our legs affects every judgment on design, even our conception of which angle shall be called 'right'. The rhythm of our breathing and the beat of our hearts are part of the experience by which we measure a work of art. The relation of head to body determines the standard by which we assess all other proportions in nature. The disposition of areas in the torso is related

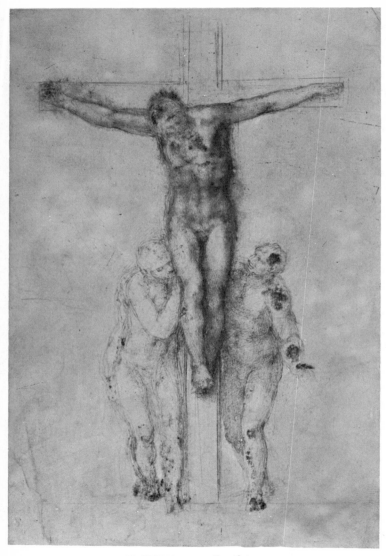

19. MICHELANGELO. Crucifixion

to our most vivid experiences, so that abstract shapes, the square and the circle, seem to us male and female ; and the old endeavour of magical mathematics to square the circle is like the symbol of physical union. The starfish diagrams of renaissance theorists may be ridiculous, but the Vitruvian principle rules our spirits and it is no accident that the formalised body of the 'perfect man' became the supreme symbol of European belief. Before the Crucifixion of Michelangelo [19] we remember that the nude is, after all, the most serious of all subjects in art ; and that it was not an advocate of paganism who wrote, 'The Word was made flesh and dwelt among us . . . full of grace and truth'.

CHAPTER II

Apollo

THE Greeks had no doubt that the god Apollo was like a perfectly beautiful man. He was beautiful because his body conformed to certain laws of proportion and so partook of the divine beauty of mathematics. The first great philosopher of mathematical harmony had called himself Pythagoras, son of the Pythian Apollo. So in the embodiment of Apollo everything must be calm and clear : clear as daylight, for Apollo is the god of light. Since justice can exist only when facts are measured in the light of reason, Apollo is the god of justice ; *sol justitiae*. But the Sun is also fierce ; neither graceful athlete nor geometrician's dummy, nor an artful combination of the two, will embody Apollo, the python slayer, the vanquisher of darkness. The god of reason and light superintended the flaying of Marsyas.

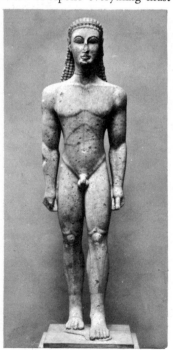

20. Attic. *c.* 600 B.C. Kouros

But the earliest nudes in Greek art, traditionally known as Apollos, are not beautiful. They are alert and confident, members of a conquering race, 'the young, light-hearted masters of the waves'. But they are stiff, with a kind of ritual stiffness ; the transitions between their members are abrupt and awkward, and they have a curious flatness, as if the sculptor could think only of one plane at a time [20]. They are less natural and less easy than the Egyptian figures upon which, to a large extent, they are modelled, and which over a thousand years earlier had achieved a limited perfection. Stage by stage, in less

26

than a century they grew into models which were to satisfy our western notion of beauty till the present day. They have two characteristics, and only two, which foreshadow this momentous evolution. They are clear and they are ideal. The shapes they present—their members and the areas of their bodies—are neither pleasant in themselves nor comfortably related to one another, but each one is firmly delineated and aspires to a shape which the measuring eye can easily grasp. Historians who have written in the belief that all art consists in a striving for realism have sometimes expressed surprise that the Greeks, with their vivid curiosity, should have approached nature so reluctantly ; that in the fifty years between the Moscophoros and the funeral stele of Aristeion, there should have been so little 'progress'. This is to misconceive the basis of Greek art. It is fundamentally ideal. It starts from the concept of a perfect shape and only gradually feels able to modify that shape in the interests of imitation. And the character of the shapes chosen is expressed in the word used to describe the earliest form of Greek art, geometric ; a dreary, monotonous style and at first ill-adapted to realisation in the round. But the head yields easily to geometric treatment and already in the most archaic heads of Apollo we see how geometry can be combined with plastic vitality. In a century the same unifying power will subordinate the dispersed and intractable forms of the body.

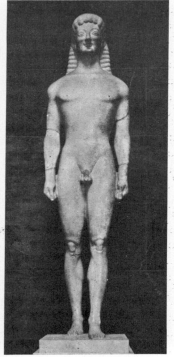

21. Attic. 6th cent. B.C.
Apollo of Tenea

So Apollo is clear and ideal before he is beautiful. How and when did the transformation take place ? If we examine in a hypothetical order of time the nude male figures of the 6th century B.C. [21], we see the transitions from shape to shape becoming smoother, and absorbing, in the process, details which had been left as decorative notations. Then, quite suddenly, in about the year 480, there appears before us the perfect human body, the marble figure from the Acropolis known

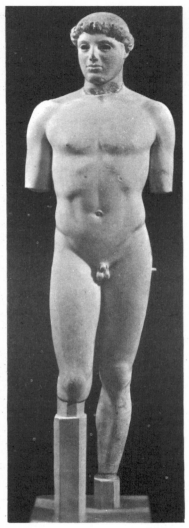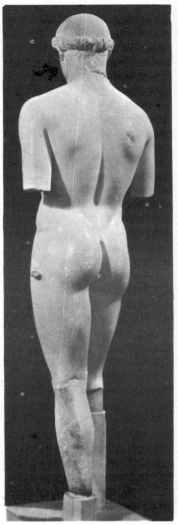

22. 'KRITIOS.' *c.* 480 B.C. Youth

as the Ephebe of Kritios [22]. Of course he was not really a sudden isolated creation. We have only a slender reason to attribute him to the sculptor Kritios, and we have even less reason to suppose that Kritios, though eminent in his day, was the initiator of so momentous a change. Literary sources give the name of Pythagoras of Rhegium as the sculptor who 'first gave rhythm and proportion to his statues'. All the evidence suggests that the new concept of form would have been first expressed in bronze and not in marble; and a bronze in the Louvre, known as the Apollo of Piombino [23], although slightly earlier and stiffer, may give some notion of what had been going on in the first twenty years of the 5th century. But since almost every bronze statue made in Greece in classic times has been melted down, the Ephebe of Kritios remains the first beautiful nude in art. Here for the first time we feel the passionate pleasure in the human body which is familiar to all readers of Greek literature; for the eagerness with which the sculptor's eye has followed every muscle, or watched the skin stretch and relax as it passes over a bone, could not have been achieved without a heightened sensuality. We all have a mental picture of that strange institution, Greek athletics, so like and yet so unlike its 19th-century Anglo-Saxon

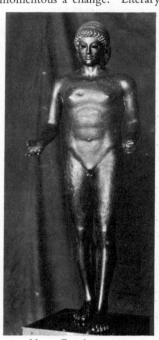

23. Magna Graecia. *c.* 490 B.C.
The Apollo of Piombino

counterpart. In our study of the nude it is the unlikeliness which is significant: not simply because Greek athletes wore no clothes, although that is of real importance, but because of two powerful emotions which dominated the Greek games and are largely absent from our own : religious dedication and love. These gave to the cult of physical perfection a solemnity and a rapture which have not been experienced since. Greek athletes competed in almost the same poetical and chivalrous spirit as knights, before the eyes of their loves, jousted in the lists: but all that pride and devotion which mediaeval contestants expressed through the flashing symbolism of heraldry was, in the games of antiquity, concentrated in one object, the naked body. No wonder that it has never again been looked at with such a keen sense of its qualities, its proportion, symmetry, elasticity and aplomb ; and when we consider that this passionate scrutiny of the individual was united to the intellectual need for geometric form, we can estimate what a rare coincidence brought the male nude to perfection.

Perfection hangs by a thread and is weighed in the jeweller's balance. We must therefore submit the classic nude, at its first appearance, to an examination which may seem fastidious, until we remember how the rhythmic organisation of this form was still dominating sculpture two thousand three hundred years after its invention. Looking at the Apollo of Piombino as an example of bronze casting, how strikingly it brought out the classic character of the Kritios youth. In twenty years a basic alteration of style has taken place. It can be illustrated by examining the lower part of the torso, to be precise, the junction of the hips, abdomen and thorax. One of the most peculiar features of the early Kouroi, for example the Apollo of Tenea [21], is their thin, flat stomachs. They are inscribed within elongated ovals such as we associate with Gothic decoration. The nudes of late mediaeval art, dominated by the pointed arch form, do in fact display very much the same characteristics, and one of the earliest figure studies which have come down to us, a drawing in the Uffizi from the circle of Uccello, combines Gothic and naturalistic forms with a remarkable likeness to a 6th-century Kouros. In the Apollo of Piombino these ogival forms are less marked. The thorax is of classic rectangularity ; but it bears an uneasy relationship to the flat triangle of the stomach. Like Perrault's façade of the Louvre, we feel that a richly classical upper storey is resting on a base too stiff and thin to support it. In the Kritios youth this uneasiness has vanished altogether. The legs and divisions of the torso flow together with the same full and fruitful rhythm. How is this achieved ? To begin with the hips are not parallel, but since he rests his weight on his left leg, that hip is slightly higher. The full implications of this pose are more easily seen from behind, for, as usual in early Greek sculpture, the back is more naturalistic and more plastically developed than the front. But even from the front we can perceive that subtle equilibrium of outline and axis which is to be the basis of classical art. This delicate balance of movement gives the torso its unity of rhythm. It also allows the sculptor to solve the problem of the abdomen by realising it as a dominant, as opposed to a recessive, form : and this has involved an anatomical emphasis which was to be exaggerated to the point of distortion in the next fifty years : I refer to the muscles which lie above the pelvis and mark the junction of the thighs and the torso. They are largely absent from archaic sculpture, and since it seems unlikely that between

500 and 450 B.C. Greek athletes really did develop these muscles to such an un-equalled extent, we must reckon them chiefly a device by which the rhythmic structure of the torso might be set in motion, and its lower half supported by two buttresses, before descending to the arc of the abdomen. They were elements in the classic architecture of the human body and as such they lasted as long as metopes and triglyphs.

All this we discover in the youth of Kritios when we compare him to the nude figures which precede him. But it is not obtruded. He is so straight-forwardly beautiful that we do not willingly use him to demonstrate the mechanics of form or the rules of an aesthetic theory. To the sculptors of the next generation this grace and naturalness was a defect, or at least a danger. It is as if they foresaw the frivolous beauty of Hellenistic art, and wished to defend themselves against it as long as possible. Of such austere taste there is ample evidence in the earlier specimens of Attic sculpture, but it was given concentrated and individual expression through the peculiar genius of Polyclitus.

The great puritans of art are a curious study. They seem to be divided into two groups, those who renounce a rich, early sensuality, like Poussin and Milton, and those who hope, like Malherbe and Seurat, to purify art by giving it the logic and finality of an intellectual theorem. Our knowledge of Poly-clitus, fragmentary and unreliable as it is, leaves little doubt that he belonged to the second group ; yet he often reminds us of Poussin by a heavy physical momentum, a Dorian obstinacy, on account of which, no doubt, his intel-lectualism has survived. Few great artists have concentrated their forces with such single-minded economy. His general aim was clarity, balance and completeness ; his sole medium of communication the naked body of an athlete, standing poised between movement and repose. He believed that this could be achieved only by the strictest application of measurement and rule. He would make no concessions. He was a fighting highbrow. Aelian tells us that he executed two statues of the same model, one according to popular taste, which we may assume, then as always, to have been naturalistic; and one according to the rules of art. He invited his visitors to suggest im-provements and modifications to the former, all of which were duly carried out. He then exhibited the two statues. The former was received with ridicule, the latter with admiration ; and Polyclitus did not fail to point the moral. How many artists since that time would have liked to try a similar experiment ; but, except in the Italian Renaissance, they could not have expected it to turn out in their favour. That Polyclitus, pursuing his narrow specialised aim, should have been accepted as the equal of Myron and Phidias, proves how closely the Greeks associated their art with their mathematics, as being a demonstration of order, capable of accurate conclusions.

No sculptures by Polyclitus have come down to us in the original, and to judge of their effect from the existing copies is almost impossible. As usual

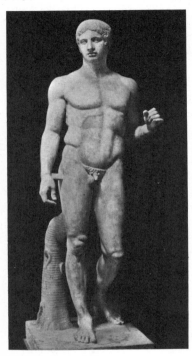

24. After Polyclitus. *c.* 450 B.C.
Doryphoros

they were in bronze and the surviving full-size copies are all in marble. Polyclitus said that 'a well-made work is the result of numerous calculations, carried to within a hair's breadth'. What chance have we, then, of appreciating his art in those blockish parodies, the oldest and grubbiest inhabitants of any cast-room, with which, alas, his name is usually associated? The general effect of his art is better appreciated in small replicas, in bronze and terra-cotta, which although far removed from the strict precision of the originals, seem to have preserved some of their general rhythm. But the problems which Polyclitus envisaged, and the finality with which he solved them, are so cardinal to subsequent representations of the nude that we must force ourselves to endure the distasteful quality of a marble copy in order to know more precisely what he achieved. His first problem was to find some means by which the figure should combine repose with the suggestion of potential movement. To stand firmly is inert; to record a given point in a violent movement is, as we shall see in a later chapter, limiting and finite. Polyclitus invented a pose in which the figure is neither walking nor standing, but simply establishing a point of balance. Of his two famous figures, it is arguable that the Doryphoros [24] is walking : at least his pose was thus interpreted in antiquity. On the other hand the Diadumenos [25] must be reckoned as standing—a victor would not walk when crowning himself—and the movement of his legs is almost identical with that of the Doryphoros. In both the body has been used as the basis of a carefully adjusted composition, carried through with such consistency that we do not realise how artificial a pose has been evolved until we see it in a different context, for example in the procession of horsemen on the Parthenon frieze. Since the movement of the leg destroys the old stiff symmetry of exact correspondence, a new symmetry has to be created by a balance of axes. Up and down, in and out : one could easily reduce the figures of Polyclitus to the rods and sheet-metal of modern sculpture, and they would still work; although of course they would be miserably impoverished. For, as Polyclitus told his contemporaries, from the toes to the last hair on the head every line was calculated, and every surface depended on the scratch of a finger-nail.

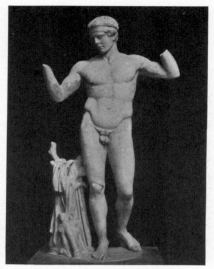

25. After Polyclitus. *c.* 430 B.C.
Diadumenos

This perfection of symmetry by balance and compensation is the essence of classical art. A figure may have within itself the rhythms of movement, but yet always comes to rest at its true centre. It is complete and self-sufficient. But balance is only half the problem. The parts balanced must have some measurable relation to one another : there must be a canon of proportion, and we know that Polyclitus composed such a canon, of which nothing has come down to us but a few elementary rules—seven and a half heads to a figure, and so forth ; and attempts to rediscover the canon by measuring his figures have been unsuccessful probably because it was geometrical, not arithmetical, and so is extremely difficult to reconstruct. I have said that a system of mathematical proportion appears in the nude long before the element of beauty ; Polyclitus codified it, and made it, no doubt, more elaborate. In doing so he sacrificed the enchanting youth and grace which had flowered so suddenly in the Ephebe of Kritios : for, even in the originals, the athletes of Polyclitus must have been square-set and rigidly muscular. To some extent he was following an earlier tradition, as seen in a large torso from Miletus, now in the Louvre, which must date from fifty years before his time. And this heavy physique, long accepted as appropriate

33

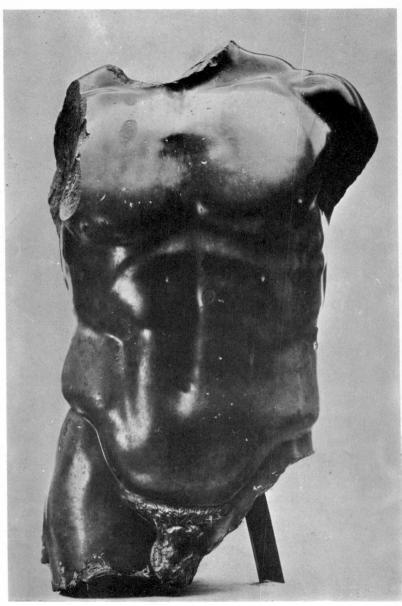

26. **After Polyclitus.** *c.* 450 B.C. Torso of the Doryphoros

to a hero, both gratified his taste for the deliberate and was more easily adapted to his calculations.

Beside these problems of balance and proportion, Polyclitus set himself to perfect the internal structure of the torso. He recognised that it allowed for the creation of a sculptural unit in which the position of humps and hollows evokes some memory and yet can be made harmonious by variation and emphasis. There is the beginning of such a system in the torso from Miletus and that of the Kritios youth ; but Polyclitus' control of muscle-architecture was evidently far more rigorous, and from him derives that standard schematisation of the torso known in French as the *cuirasse esthétique*, a disposition of muscles so formalised that it was in fact used in the design of armour, and became for the heroic body like the masks of the antique stage. The *cuirasse esthétique*, which so greatly delighted the artists of the Renaissance, is one of the features of antique art which has done most to alienate modern taste. It seems to us ungraceful in itself, and lacking in vitality. But although a row of formalised torsos in the Galleries of the Vatican or the Naples Museum may not cause the pulse to vary its beat, we can see from certain replicas that this was originally a construction of great power. Such is the copy of the Doryphoros in the Uffizi [26], which being in a hard smooth basalt, conveys the effect of bronze, and is executed with unusual care. It preserves some of the urgency and concentration of the original, and proves that Polyclitus' scheme of the body, like all abstractions which have survived, not only contained life, but was bursting with a vitality all the more potent because forced into so narrow a channel.

With all great artists who have thus sharpened their aims to a single point of perfection, we are sometimes tempted to ask whether the sacrifices involved are worth while. Such concentration has its negative aspect, its element of refusal, and also its element of self-hallucination. In the end our feelings are our only guide, and to test our feelings about Polyclitus is, alas, almost impossible. But something may be achieved by comparing a direct copy of one of his works with a freer version, in which the rigour of perfection has been relaxed. Our scales are weighted heavily in favour of the latter, for we can take as example an elegant figure in Florence known as the Idolino [27], which although of much later date, retains the freshness of an original Greek bronze. And yet when we look at it critically, how unstable and incomplete this figure seems, compared even to the lifeless copies of Polyclitus' athletes. The legs are not within the rhythm of the whole, and seem to lose themselves half-way down. A similar break appears in the body, and the shoulders are axially unrelated to the hips. Even the small bronze copy of the Discophoros [28] in

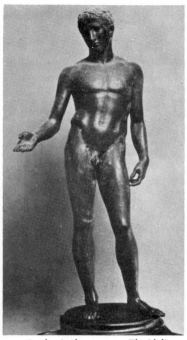

27. Greek. ? 4th cent. B.C. The Idolino

the Louvre, only a high-class commercial product and of uncertain date,
shows more of Polyclitan compactness.
Now let us try to imagine such a figure
as the Diadumenos with all the freshness of the Idolino, and a feeling for
bronze even more sensuous and fastidious. Does it not seem that the
dangerous doctrine of salvation through
exclusion was for once justifiable ?

Nor is it correct to discuss Polyclitus solely in aesthetic terms, for his
work was based on an ethical ideal, to
which formal questions were subservient. Though his purity of aim may
recall the Chinese potter, continually
refining upon a single shape, the human
body is, in fact, inexhaustibly complex
and suggestive, and to a Greek of the
5th century it stood for a set of values
of which restraint, balance, modesty,
proportion and many others would be
applied equally in the ethical and the
aesthetic sphere. Polyclitus himself
would probably have recognised no
real distinction between them, and we need not hesitate to pronounce before
his work the word 'moral', that vague but not altogether meaningless word
which rumbles in the neighbourhood of the nude till the academies of the
19th century.

The writers of antiquity recognised that Polyclitus had created a perfectly
balanced man, but added that he could not create the likeness of a god. This,
they said, was the achievement of Phidias. From 480 to 440 B.C., parallel with
the series of athletes was a series of votive statues which culminated in the
great Apollos of Phidias. Of these Apollos we can derive some notion from
an insensitive copy at Cassel. They represent a perfecting of the image complementary to Polyclitus' perfecting of form ; and in the survival of Apollo
this power to satisfy our imaginations, though it came later, had the more
lasting influence. One great image of Apollo from the beginning of the Classic
period has survived in the original : he who rises above the struggle in the west

pediment of the Temple of Olympia [29], and, with a gesture of sovereign authority, reproves the bestial fury of the centaurs. Nowhere else, perhaps, is the early Greek ideal so perfectly embodied : calm, pitiless, and supremely confident in the power of physical beauty. Not a shade of doubt or compunction could soften the arc of cheek or brow ; the *Phaedo* is still far away and the Beatitudes would be totally incomprehensible. But all this we deduce from his head ; his body, though not without a certain passive magnificence, is flat and inexpressive. Like all the sculptures at Olympia, it lacks the rigorous precision of Attic work. It is twenty years later than the youth of Kritios, but is plastically less evolved. No doubt it was given an archaic character in order to enhance its godlike authority, for the other figures on the pediments are almost too experimental. They attempt more than was within the compass of pure classic art : greater naturalism, freer poses, more various expressions. There are nudes at Olympia of a character which never occurs again in Greek sculpture ; and those who regret the limited perfection of antique art may feel that Olympia was like a last burst of freedom. From that starting-point Greek art might have gone anywhere. But just as pre-Socratic philosophy is made up largely of inspired guesses, so the nudes at Olympia seem haphazard and fundamentally formless. This was decorative sculpture, where certain rough and picturesque experiments were permissible. The real work of refining on the classic ideal took place in bronze.

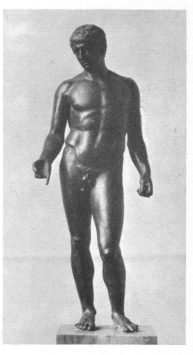

Our surviving copies of these bronze Apollos happen to be of finer quality than those of the Polyclitan athletes and may be looked at with pleasure, not merely with critical curiosity. How far they go back to early works of Phidias himself is an insoluble problem, but one at least seems to reflect his style as we know it in the frieze

28. Greek. ? *c.* 400 B.C. After the Discophoros of Polyclitus

37

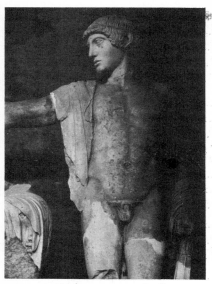

29. Greek. *c.* 450 B.C. Apollo

of the Parthenon, the Apollo of the Tiber [30], in Rome. Although a copy of bronze, it is in a beautiful piece of marble, and must be by a fine Greek craftsman. It shows most clearly the difference between Polyclitan athlete and Phidian god. This Apollo is taller and more graceful, and still bears a trace of hieratic frontality, consciously preserved to enhance his god-like remoteness. The flat, square shoulders seem lifted up into a different plane, from which the head looks down with a calm and dreamy interest ; the torso, less in-sistently schematic than those of Polyclitus, renders vividly the taut-ness of skin stretched over muscle. If only this figure had been known to Winckelmann instead of the Apollo Belvedere, his insight and gift of literary recreation would have been better supported by the sculptural qualities of his subject. The Apollo of the Tiber is worthy of the 'maker of Gods', the title by which Phidias is described in ancient literature, and seems to me to give a truer reflection of his style, as we know it, from the Parthenon, than does the Apollo at Cassel ; but this may be due to the relative transparency of the medium through which the original is seen. The copy of the Cassel Apollo is unusually opaque, but straining our eyes to penetrate it, we can just catch sight of a firm, full image of the god at his most prosperous. It is the moment of balance—a physical balance be-tween strength and grace, a stylistic balance between naturalism and the ideal, a spiritual balance between the old worship of the god and the new philo-sophy, in which that worship was recognised as being no more than a poetic exercise. And of these three the last was never achieved again. During the next century the frontiers of physical beauty were extended materially. Apollo became more human and more elegant. But never again in antiquity was he transfigured by the aspect of divine authority which, as we can guess from our fragments of evidence, he derived from the imagination of Phidias.

Of the humanised beauty of the 4th century we can speak from a more direct experience, for at least one example survives which seems to be an original work by a great sculptor, the Hermes of Praxiteles [31]. True, the documentary evidence which associates the figure at Olympia with Praxiteles is not such as would carry any weight in a field of study where documents were less scanty, being no more than a reference in Pausanias' travel diaries, made over four hundred years after the figure was carved. We should not place much confidence in Horace Walpole's opinion of a work by Giotto ; but in the history of art, as in all history, we accept or reject documentary evidence exactly as it suits us, that is to say, according to our feelings about the object referred to ; and our feelings about the Hermes of Olympia are rather different from those aroused by any other work of antiquity. Almost alone of antique marbles it retains that translucent, sensuous quality which we know to have been a characteristic of 4th-century art in general, and of Praxiteles in particular. Majesty is not lost, and the body is firm and muscular ; but the overwhelming impression is one of grace and of a gentle sweetness, achieved partly by the flowing design and partly by an almost morbid delicacy of execution. The Hermes is the climax of that passion for physical beauty first apparent in the Kritios youth, which had been arrested by the schematic austerity of Polyclitus and by Phidias' belief in the rectangular majesty of Apollo. We know how easily beauty of this kind may be exploited, till it dwindles into prettiness. With Praxiteles, however, it was not an instrument, but a mode of being. Like Correggio, he was incapable of setting up an abrupt or uneasy relationship. Every form glides into the next with that smoothness which, at all periods, has been part of the popular concept of beauty. How much the value of this *legato* depends on the precision of a sensitive execution we can tell from the copies of Praxiteles' works, the Faun, the Sauroctonos, the Apollino, where the smoothness of transition has degenerated into slipperiness, and the forms themselves have been reduced, in section, to a few commonplace radial curves. So the Hermes, although itself one of the most obscure of Praxiteles' works, of which no replica exists, persuades us to look again at the copies of his more famous pieces, and try to imagine their ravishing beauty when surface design and material all obeyed the orders of a single sensibility.

The Hermes of Praxiteles represents the last triumph of the Greek idea of wholeness. Physical beauty is one with strength, grace, gentleness and benevolence. For the rest of its course we witness, in antique art, the fragmentation of the perfect man and the human body becomes either very graceful, or very muscular, or merely animal. Praxiteles himself contributed to this creation of specialised types. In his Apollo Sauroctonos [32] the python slayer has been diminished into a boy of feminine delicacy who is about to transfix with his

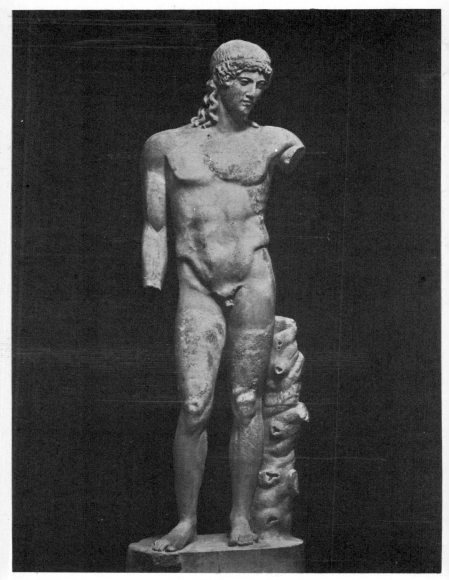

30. Style of Phidias.   Apollo of the Tiber

dart a harmless lizard. His head, as so often in 4th-century sculpture, is indistinguishable from that of a girl, and instead of the majestic breadth and squareness of the Phidian torso, the lines of his body flow in an elegant curve. Conversely Hercules, who, in the 5th-century metopes of Selinunte, is active and compact, becomes in the 4th century a professional strong man whose bulging muscles seem to weigh him down like a load of sausages. To these exaggerations must be added certain figures of athletes which aim at physical perfection, but yet have lost the radiance and the *ethos* in which true beauty is to be found. Amongst these are three or four original bronzes, the so-called Hermes from Antikythera, the Athlete with the Strigil from Ephesus and the Praxitelean boy from Marathon [33]. They are representative of Greek art at a high routine level, and may fairly be made the basis of generalisation ; and the first thing which strikes us about them is their lack of accent. We do not feel behind them, as we do behind quite mediocre work of the Renaissance, the personal sensibility of an individual artist. Moreover, the 16th-century Italians, emphatic in their admiration of a *bel corpo ignudo*, valued it ultimately as a means of expressing energy, heroism or spiritual victory. If we compare the boy from Marathon with the two Davids of Michelangelo, how clearly they belong to the world of the spirit. They are the visible form of Michelangelo's aspirations, whereas the Marathon boy is simply a young body, and his physical complacency blocks up precisely those means of communication, those chinks and cracks through which some ray of light may enter our shuttered world. In the average nude of later Greek sculpture this lack of inner life is perceptible in every articulation. Cellini was not one of the great sculptors of the Renaissance, but how living and sensitive his modelling appears to be, if we compare his bronze model of the Perseus [34] with the Hermes of Antikythera. And yet the Antique has retained, from the first passionate researches of the 5th century, a kind of stability, a sense of absolute norm, which has been the envy of artists ever since. That, in the end, is the remarkable thing about these bronze athletes. They were the ordinary routine productions of antique art, equivalent to a painting of the Virgin and Child in the 15th century. They represent the high plateau of achievement from which alone the summits of art can spring.

The last great name in Greek sculpture is Lysippus. Ancient writers tell us that he invented a new proportion, with smaller head, longer legs and a slenderer body. We also know that he did the figure of an athlete scraping himself, which was popular in ancient Rome, and a marble of such a subject in the Vatican fits so well with literary descriptions of his style that it may reasonably be taken as a basis for further attributions. It is in a position of

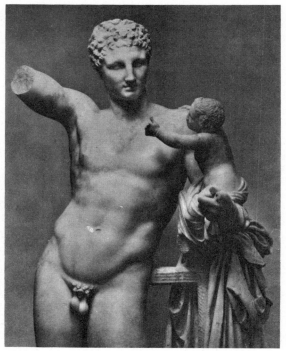

31. PRAXITELES. *c.* 350 B.C. Hermes

arrested action more complex and more suggestive of impending movement than the earlier figures of athletes ; and in fact all the works credibly claimed as copies of Lysippus show a consciousness of existence in space and a multiplicity of view very different from the austere frontality of Polyclitus. With this technical freedom went a new attitude towards nature, and in contrast with Polyclitus' defiance of popular opinion is a story in Pliny that Lysippus, when asked who were his masters, pointed to a crowd of men in the street. Such developments used to be called advances by evolutionary art historians, and perhaps under certain circumstances all additional mastery is a gain. But in the calculated programme of the Greek nude freedom and promiscuity were by no means an advantage. Among the works claimed as Lysippic are some graceful figures of young men, the resting Hermes in Naples or the praying boy in Berlin, which have a strong appeal to those who do not normally care for sculpture. In originals by Lysippus this pleasant obviousness was evidently accompanied by a powerful control of means; but for those who followed, the absence of limitations imposed by rules and traditional treatment meant also the absence of order and lawful harmony.

The result was the anarchy of Hellenistic art, with on one side its drunken fauns and boxers, on the other its eternal repetitions of accepted motives. No wonder that our spirits sink as we look at the multitude of marble nudes which confront us in the Galleries of the Vatican or in the Museum at Naples. No civilisation has been so artistically bankrupt as that which, for four hundred years, on the shores of the Mediterranean, enjoyed a fabulous material prosperity. During those centuries of blood-stained energy, the figure arts were torpid—a kind of token currency, still accepted because based on those treasures of the spirit accumulated in the 5th and 4th centuries before Christ. By artfully adapting and recombining the inventions of that distant epoch, it was sometimes possible to produce the illusion of novelty, though hardly ever of vitality; but in general the means taken to make a dead style acceptable

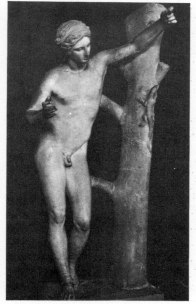

32. After Praxiteles. c. 350 B.C.
Apollo Sauroctonos

were of the kind made familiar by many subsequent attempts at vulgarisation—smoother finish, more elaborate detail, more explicit narrative: to which, in sculpture, restorers have added the last deadly touches.

There is, however, one peculiar practice which has a certain bearing on our subject: the placing of a portrait head on the ideal nude body. This error of taste—for such I think we must allow it to be—has been attributed, like all errors of taste, to the Romans; but it appears in works executed before the rise of the Roman empire, such as the so-called Hellenistic Prince in the Museo delle Terme. Evidently it was thought that the divinity of a ruler could be enhanced by giving him the authorised body of a god. In consequence the practice was approved by the early Roman emperors and became an accepted convention. To us,

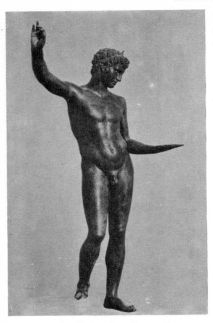

33. Style of Praxiteles. Bronze Boy
from Marathon

who look first at the head, there is something comic about these academic Phidian nudes, from which every trace of individuality has been erased centuries ago, being surmounted by the likenesses of the unhappy Claudius or the maniac Caligula. But at a later date there did appear, in the Imperial household, one individual who by his strange perfection created a new ideal of beauty, Antinous. It was the wish of the Emperor Hadrian that the beautiful features of his favourite should appear on the statues of the gods ; and so we find this dark Arabian head on the bodies of Apollo, Hermes and Dionysus, the traditional proportions being modified to suit the heavier torso of Antinous. For almost the first time since the 4th century a type of beauty is taken from a real head and not from a copy-book. That is why, in drifting round a gallery of antique sculpture, our attention is so often caught by these sultry features : we feel once more, though remotely enough, the warmth of an individual attachment. No doubt the men of the Renaissance, those supreme individualists, felt the same ; and for that reason the physical character of Antinous is still perceptible when, after its long banishment, the Apollonian nude returns in the person of Donatello's David.

Before leaving the antique world one more figure of Apollo remains to be described ; for, whatever its status as a work of art, it has been an image of almost magical efficacy : the Apollo Belvedere [35]. A hundred and fifty years ago it was, without question, one of the two most famous works of art in the world. In the volume printed by Didot to celebrate Napoleon's triumphs one page contains nothing but the words *'L'Apollon et le Laocoön emportés à Paris'*. From Raphael to Winckelmann artists and critics, whose understanding of art was at least equal to our own, vied with each other in its praise. 'It is', says Winckelmann, 'the highest ideal of art among all the works of antiquity. Enter, O reader, with your spirit into this kingdom of beauty incarnate, and there seek to create for yourself the images of the divine nature.' Unfortunately for the modern reader this kingdom is closed. He can only imagine that for three hundred years the Apollo satisfied the same sort of uncritical hunger which was later to crave for the plumes and pinnacles of romanticism; and as long as it did so, the eye could overlook weak structure and slack surfaces which, to the aesthetic of pure sensibility, annul its other qualities. In no other famous work of art, perhaps, are idea and execution more distressingly divorced, and in so far as we believe that they must be inseparable if art is to take on the

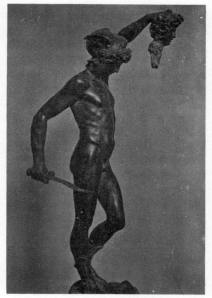

34. CELLINI. Perseus

quality of new life, the figure of the Vatican is dead. But in the bronze cast made for Francis I, and now in the Louvre, some of the mechanical smoothness of the marble is disguised, and with no great effort of the imagination we can picture the shining original, delicately modelled, scrupulously chiselled, with cloak and hair of gold. What an exquisite messenger of the gods he must have been! This is the antique epiphany, the god come to earth, alighting with the radiance of his celestial journey still about him.

A messenger, a visitor from another world, an intermediary: that is the impression the Apollo makes on us, and that, in fact, is what he became. A touch of self-consciousness in his ideal beauty and something un-Greek in the turn of his head made him all the more acceptable to the men of the Renaissance. He seems to look beyond the enclosed Greek world, as if awaiting an answering glance of recognition from the great romantics of the early 16th century.

Long before the façade of classical culture finally collapsed Apollo had ceased to satisfy any imaginative need. Hermes, accompanier of the dead,

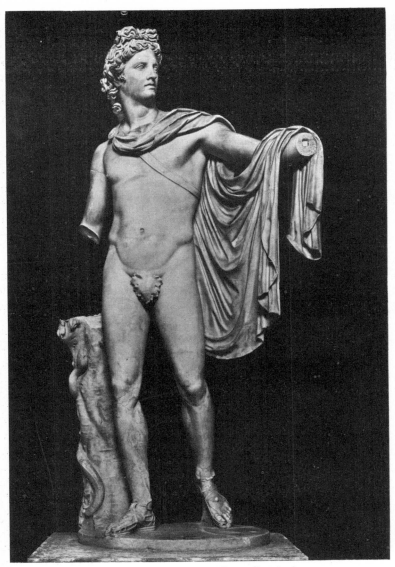

35. Greek. ? 2nd cent. B.C. The Apollo Belvedere

could be associated with religions of mystery; Dionysus with religions of enthusiasm. But Apollo, the embodiment of calm and reason, had no place in the uneasy, superstitious world of the 3rd century A.D., and the idea of naked perfection appears relatively seldom in the art of late antiquity. When at last Christianity began to evolve its own symbols there were few contemporary models from which Apollo might be transpersonalised into Adam. From the 5th century there has survived an ivory panel carved with the scene

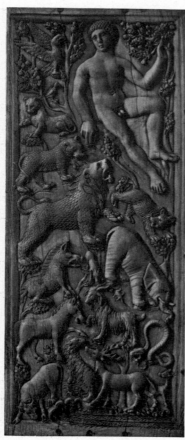

36. Early Christian. 5th cent. A.D.

of Adam sitting in his newly created kingdom [36], and although, by classical standards, his head and members are disproportionately big, his body is still intended to demonstrate the belief that man is distinguished from the animals by superior physical beauty. But the Bargello ivory has no surviving equal. Only in the Far East does the Apollonian ideal take on a new life and significance; for we can hardly doubt that the measured harmony of early Buddhist art represents a Greek conquest more lasting than the victories of Alexander. From the 5th to the 12th centuries the various cultures of Eastern Asia produced male nude figures which have the dignity and frontal authority of some pre-Phidian Apollo. The likeness of the finest Boddhisatvas in Khmer sculpture to 6th-century Ionian Kouroi is unmistakable, and proves how, given certain conditions and ingredients, a style may follow its own logic in which space and time are relative terms.

In the Christian west, during the same centuries, nude figures are occasionally to be found, but they are echoes or meaningless doxologies, repeated on account of some magic which has long since evaporated from them. The ideal form of Apollo scarcely appears again

47

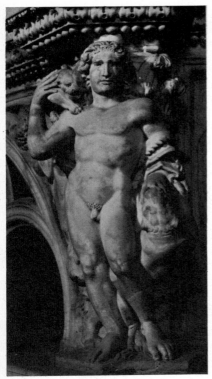

37. NICOLA PISANO. Fortitudo

before that false dawn of the Renaissance, Nicola Pisano's pulpit in the Baptistery of Pisa [37]. Characteristically, it is transferred to a personification of strength; for, as we shall see, Hercules alone of the Olympian gods was moralised into survival. But formally Nicola's figure remains an Apollo, heavier than his Hellenistic model, but conforming with a kind of obstinacy to the canonical image of 5th-century Attica. What is lacking is the belief in physical beauty, which underlies even the squarest athletes of Polyclitus, a belief which had been so long accepted as sinful that another century and a half had to pass before it could re-enter the mind. How pleasure in the human body once more became a permissible subject of art is the unexplained miracle of the Italian Renaissance. We may catch sight of it in the Gothic painting of the early 15th century, revealed in the turn of a wrist and forearm or the inclination of a neck; but nothing prepares us for the beautiful nakedness of Donatello's David [38].

Donatello's first innovation, which was to be followed many times in the Renaissance, is the transformation of the King of Israel into a young Greek god. In his youth David had been comely and, like Apollo, had conquered, by his purity of purpose, an embattled monster. He was also the canonised patron of music and poetry. But the image of David most familiar in mediaeval art was an old man, bearded and crowned, playing on the harp or on a chime of bells; and although the young David was not unknown in the middle ages, it was by a prodigious leap of the imagination that Donatello saw him as a god of antiquity. Strictly speaking he is not an Apollo but a young Dionysus, with dreamy smile and flexible pose; and the Goliath head

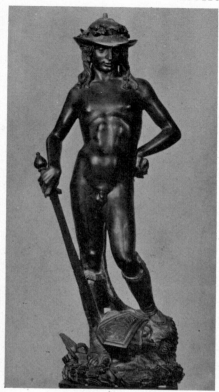

38. DONATELLO. David

at his feet is simply the old satyr head often found at the base of Dionysiac statues. One of these Donatello must have known, and combined it with the memory of an Antinous ; and he must also have been familiar with certain antique bronzes, for the sense of form in relation to material is identical with such work as the Spinario. But these obvious sources of inspiration do not prevent the David from being a work of almost incredible originality, which nothing else in the art of the time leads us to anticipate. One would gladly know the comments made upon it when it was first exhibited, for during the rest of the century it continues to be far beyond the current of contemporary taste. It is curiously different, even, from the rest of Donatello's work, in which he appears as the sculptor of drama, and of man's moral and emotional predicament, and not of physical perfection. Yet we feel that in the David he has looked as eagerly as a Greek of the 4th century at those tensions and transitions which make the youthful body sensuously appealing. Donatello's deviations from the canon of classical proportion are obvious. He has represented a real boy whose chest was narrower and flank less rounded than the Greek ideal. No doubt his model was younger and less developed than the boy athletes to whom instinctively we compare him. But allowing for these accidental differences, there remains a fundamental difference of construction. In the antique nude the flat rectangular chest is supported by a formalised stomach—the *cuirasse esthétique* already described ; in the David, and in practically all subsequent nudes of the Renaissance, the waist is the centre of plastic interest, from which radiate all the other planes

49

of the body. Donatello's contemporaries, however, would scarcely have recognised these differences of proportion and construction, and would have been conscious only of some pagan god returned to earth. Of both him and Brunellesco it was said, giving to their genius a kind of alchemical interpretation, that they had rediscovered the secrets of the ancient world ; amongst which was the secret of physical beauty.

There are several reasons why for fifty years or more Donatello's David had no successors. One is the Gothic reaction which took place in Florentine art at the middle of the 15th century, when a fashion for the decorative tapestries and minutely finished panels of the Low Countries superseded the heroic humanism of Donatello and Masaccio. Another is the inherent restlessness of the Florentine temperament. Apollo is static. His gestures are dignified and calm. But the Florentines loved movement, the more violent the better. The two great masters of the nude in the late *quattrocento*, Pollajuolo and Botticelli, are concerned with embodiments of energy or ecstatic motion, with a wrestling Hercules or a flying angel, and only once, in Botticelli's St. Sebastian, achieve a satisfactory nude in repose. Thus, although the Florentines were the first to be influenced by the remains of antiquity, the tranquil, static painting of Central Italy, scarcely awakened from its Gothic dream, was more fundamentally classical. The nude figures in Piero della Francesca's Death of Adam have the large gravity of pre-Phidian sculpture. A man seen from behind, leaning on a spade, seems to be mid-way between Myron and Polyclitus, and the brother and sister, Adam's grandchildren, are like the Orestes and Electra at Naples. How far this classicism was innate, how far the result of study it is hard to say, but I have come to believe that Piero was more closely acquainted with antique art, including antique painting, than recent students have allowed.

His pupil, Perugino, belonged to the generation which made free use of antiquarian pattern books, and in his drawings of the nude the Umbrian sense of harmony is applied to Hellenistic models. In spite of slender proportions and willowy Gothic legs there is a classical ease of transition between one form and another which leads directly to Raphael ; and to Raphael himself was attributed for many years Perugino's masterpiece of pagan imagery, the Apollo and Marsyas in the Louvre [39]. It is the perfection of *quattrocento* classicism. For the lower part of the figure Perugino has followed his lifedrawing in the Uffizi, but by squaring the shoulders he has given it a Hellenistic character. This Apollo is as graceful as a bronze from Herculaneum and, in contrast to the gentle Marsyas, pot-bellied and spindle-shanked like a faun, as confidently ideal : and yet the total effect is entirely of its time, and no more

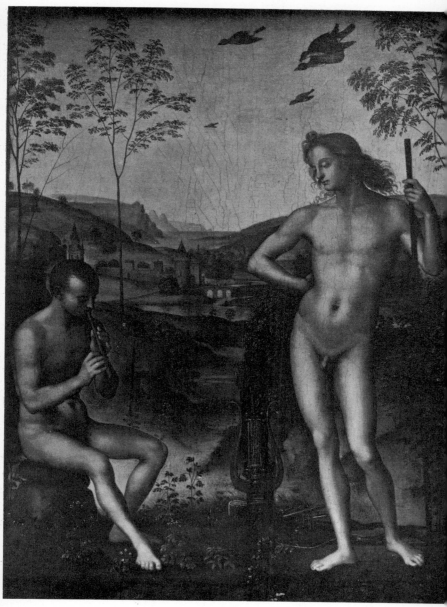

39. PERUGINO. Apollo and Marsyas

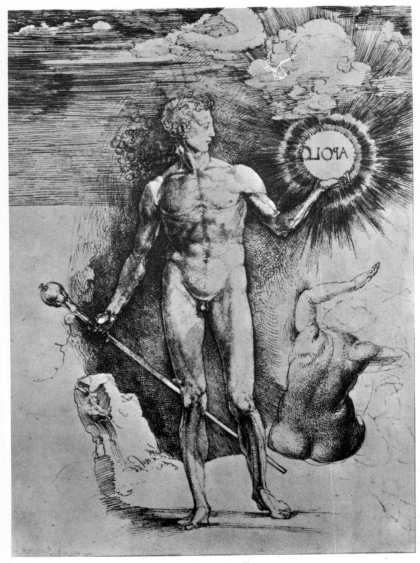

40. DÜRER. Apollo

resembles a painting of antiquity than the poems of Poliziano resemble those of Ovid. Walter Pater was fond of describing works of the Renaissance by the word 'dainty', a word which, before its recent degradation, carried a train of chivalric associations. It is not a word which should be applied to the Apollos of ancient Greece, but it comes unbidden to the mind before Perugino's picture, expressing both the jewel-setter's delicacy of the execution, and also some element of make-believe, as of an exquisitely learned pageant. Even at this moment which precedes his triumph over a lower order of enthusiasm, this Apollo lacks the impartial ferocity of the sun. He is, rather, the elegant leader of the muses ; and as such he appears again in that most beautiful representation of his realm, Raphael's Parnassus.

At this point the Apollo Belvedere reappears. The exact circumstances of its excavation are not known, but is seems to have taken place about the year 1479 ; it appears twice in the Ghirlandajesque pattern-book known as the Escurialensis, and shortly afterwards is transformed into a David in an early engraving by Marcantonio, thus continuing the precedent of Donatello. It was engraved again by Marcantonio in its unrestored state, and inspired imitations, ranging from the bronze statuette of the Mantuan court sculptor, Antico, a copy so exact that we can scarcely credit its date, to the free adaptation of Bernini's Apollo and Daphne. One of the first to feel its influence was an artist who cannot have seen it. Albrecht Dürer never reached Rome, but on his first visit to Italy he must have been shown drawings of the famous antique ; and, as we have seen, he made them the basis of his exercises in proportion. Almost immediately after his return, in 1501, he executed the drawing in the British Museum of a nude man bearing in his hand a disc on which is written (in reverse) the word *Apolo* [40]. The figure is made up of *souvenirs d'Italie*. The legs are copied from a Mantegna engraving, the style, both in penmanship and degree of emphasis, shows knowledge of early drawings by Michelangelo : but above all it is the image he had formed of the figure in the Belvedere which has given this Apollo its godlike bearing. The flat rectangularity of the torso, the absence of articulation in the outline of the thighs and the way in which they are joined to the waist—in these, and many other points, Dürer's drawing is far more antique than the restless figures of the Florentines. Not for the last time a German artist has constructed a work of irreproachable classicism ; yet a construction it remains, concealing only temporarily Dürer's real conviction that the body was a curious and rather alarming organism.

Raphael's response to the Apollo was exactly the reverse. Of the drawings he did direct from the figure only one has survived, a slight sketch, significantly on the back of a drawing of the Adam in the Disputa. But from the time of his arrival in Rome the rhythm and, we may say, the *ethos* of the Apollo are perceptible in some of his noblest creations. Not only the grace of move-

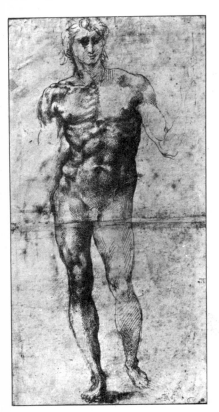

41. MICHELANGELO. Nude Youth

ment, but the sense of epiphany and the glance towards a more radiant world, which are peculiar to the Apollo Belvedere, reappear in the saints, poets and philosophers of the *Stanze*. Raphael, with his unequalled power of assimilation, practically never borrowed a form directly, and the three Apollos in the *Stanza della Segnatura* are his own creations. Even the figure in the School of Athens which is intended to represent an ancient statue in a niche displays the same structural difference from antique art which has just been observed in Donatello's David; and the figure in the centre of the Parnassus is a mild and harmonious god, *Apollo Musagetes*, in whom the pride of the original Olympian has been subdued to fit him for the Christian company which surrounds him.

Since the Greeks of the 4th century no man felt so certain of the godlike character of the male body as Michelangelo. 'And held it for something divine':

this phrase which occurs so often in Vasari's life when describing his hero's work is not rhetoric, but the statement of a conviction; and Michelangelo expresses the same belief in his sonnets to Cavalieri. It was a belief born of emotion. Michelangelo, like the Greeks, was passionately stirred by male beauty, and with his serious, Platonic cast of mind he was bound to identify his emotions with ideas. This passage of violent sensuous attachment into the realm of non-attachment, where nothing of the first compulsion is lost but much gained of purposeful harmony, makes his nudes unique. They are both poignant and commanding. The Apollo of Olympia is commanding but not at all poignant, for he has grown naturally out of an assumption which no man of the post-Christian world can make, least of all the hungry soul of Michelangelo. There can never be, in his work, the Olympian calm or the Apollonian clarity of reason. But what Michelangelo could give, as no man since, was the fierce Apollonian authority, the character of *sol justitiae*.

In his youth, as we know, he strove for the perfection of antique beauty, producing imitations of classic art which were even used to deceive the collectors of the day. The Bacchus shows that he would go so far as to imitate the lifeless surface of a marble copy. But his drawings of the nude have from the start a Tuscan strength and that nervous articulation which I have already contrasted with the bland forms of antiquity. In the Louvre is a drawing of a nude youth [41], whose godlike body has a Phidian splendour; but on analysis how un-Greek it becomes.

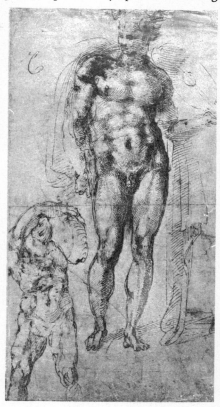

42. MICHELANGELO. An antique god

The outlines of the torso flow with a restless, vital movement, and within them the modelling is so rich and continuous that the old, geometric divisions on which the classic architecture of the body is founded, have almost disappeared. The eye never seems content to move peacefully over a plane, but either extorts from it the last fraction of incident, or omits the passage altogether, as the arms and left breast are omitted here. There are, moreover,

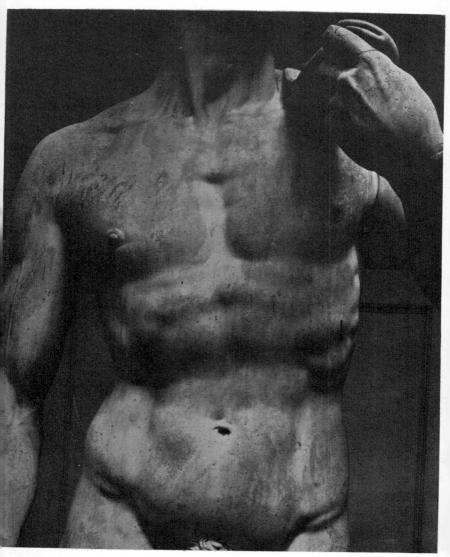

43. MICHELANGELO. Detail of David

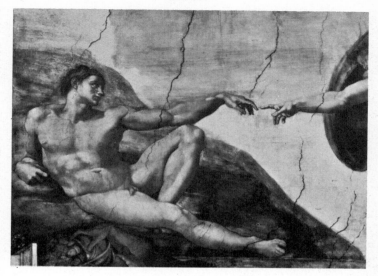

44. MICHELANGELO. Creation of Adam

several anatomical details, such as the right clavicle and surrounding muscles, which would have offended the Greeks, but satisfied Michelangelo's love of knotted, hard-gripping form. The drawing which comes nearest to antiquity is one of an Olympian god, half Mercury, half Apollo, also in the Louvre, which is evidently done from memory [42]. The forms are more generalised than in the life drawings and flow with an easier movement ; but already there is that peculiar thickening of the torso (increased, even, in a correction) which in his later work was to become almost a deformation. It would be a mistake, however, to suppose that he disregarded the classical system of proportion. On the contrary, he studied it, and himself used one which was probably derived from Pliny's account of Polyclitus. Of this we have evidence in a study at Windsor which has been marked and measured in great detail, as if for the instruction of some other painter. Michelangelo has exaggerated the Polyclitan stance, so that the axis of the shoulders contrasts violently with that of the hips, and has indicated the muscles with anatomical exactness. Since the aim of the drawing was scientific he has made no attempt at classical idealisation, and the result is more like Andrea del Castagno than Polyclitus. It shows us what a confluence of mental activities,

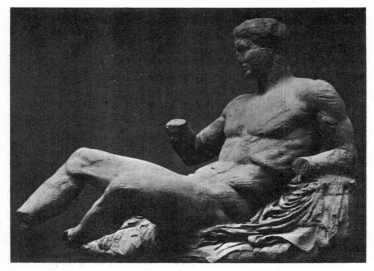

45. PHIDIAS. *c.* 435 B.C. Dionysus from the Parthenon

calculation, idealisation, scientific knowledge and sheer ocular precision contributed to the final effect of his masterpieces.

Michelangelo's greatest embodiment of the Apollonian idea is the first marble David. The torso alone [43] might be claimed as the climax of that long search for harmony which started with the fragment from Miletus, or the Kritios youth. True there is a ripple of ribs and muscles, and beneath it, scarcely perceptible, the ground swell of some distant storm, which distinguishes the David's torso from those of the most vigorous antiques ; but if it had remained a fragment we should have been astonished at the strictness with which Michelangelo had accepted the classical scheme. However, we have the entire figure ; and long before our eye can take in the torso it has been caught by the head on its strained, defiant neck, the enormous hands and the potential movement of the pose which force him far outside the sphere of Apollo. This overgrown boy is both more vehement and less secure. He is a hero rather than a god. He sums up, and with a turn of the head destroys, the whole of that trusting, reverent and romantic attitude towards antiquity which Michelangelo had learnt from Bertoldo in the garden of Lorenzo the Magnificent. Michelangelo himself was scarcely conscious of this. The drawings already mentioned were certainly done after the David ;

and at a far later date he returned to the idea of Apollonian perfection. The most symbolic of these perfect men is the awakening Adam of the Sistine [44]. Nowhere else does Michelangelo concede so much to the accepted notion of physical beauty ; but in this very image he shows the balanced body receiving that charge which was to disturb for ever its equilibrium. The Adam is in a pose not very different from that of the figure from the pediment of the Parthenon known as the Dionysus [45]. The distribution of balance, the sense of noble relaxation and the general architecture of their bodies are the same ; and yet how strikingly the Adam differs from the Dionysus in total effect. It is the difference between being and becoming. The Dionysus, in its timeless world, obeys an inner law of harmony; the Adam gazes out to some superior power which will give him no rest.

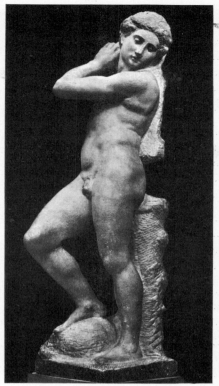

46. MICHELANGELO. Apollo—David

In two other nude figures Michelangelo has given form to aspects of Apollo, strangely different from one another, and perhaps complementary. The first is the marble figure in the Bargello, which he seems to have intended as an Apollo (for the shadowy suggestion of a quiver is still visible), and then changed into a David with his sling [46]. Apollo it remains, for the sleepy, sensuous movement of the body cannot be interpreted as the action of the young hero ; indeed, this round-limbed youth entirely lacks the heroic indignation of the earlier figure. He is like a romantic dream, a poem of vanishing love, in which already the details are slightly blurred. In structure, in proportion, in movement, in sentiment, nothing of the antique nude remains ; nothing except the worship of physical beauty.

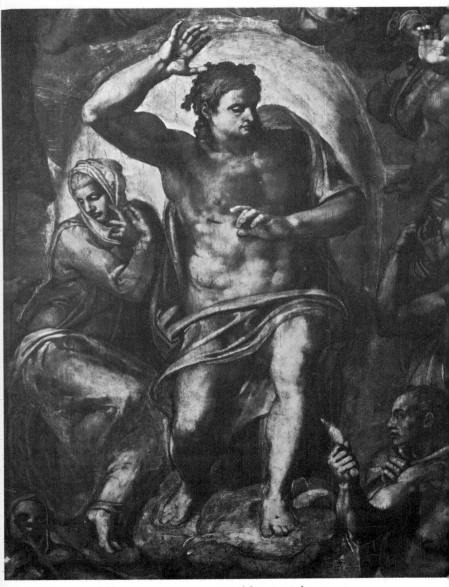

47. MICHELANGELO. Detail from Last Judgment

The other figure is the exact reverse. It is the Judge who, in the enormous Doom of the Sistine Chapel, confounds the powers of darkness [47]. We have returned to the most primitive aspect of Apollo, the solar energy which creates and destroys, the embodiment of *sol justitiae*. His gesture is more imperious even than that of the Apollo of Olympia, for the heights to which he summons the blessed are more radiant, the depths to which he condemns the unruly more atrocious. In spite of his un-Greek proportions, and Michelangelo has not tried to resist that strange compulsion which made him thicken a torso till it is almost square, this Pantocrator remains Apollonian. Michelangelo has discarded the bearded Syrian figure in its stiff robes, which even the most pagan spirits of the Renaissance had preserved from the Judges of Byzantine tradition, and has found his inspiration in the conquering image of Alexander the Great. His arrogant head, slightly modified in spiritual conquest, is set on the naked body of an athlete, and it is partly through the crushing strength of this body that his divine authority is expressed. Looking back

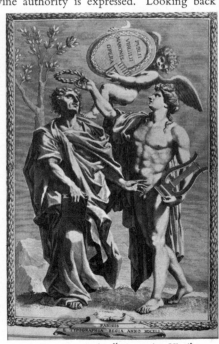

48. POUSSIN. Apollo crowning Virgil

to the Apollos of 5th-century Greece, we recognise how much the impressiveness of the Phidian nude depended on a latent fear of Olympus and we remember, with Mexican art in mind, that, next to love, there is no more powerfully form-creating emotion than fear of the wrath of God.

It is precisely this feeling of dread that is absent from all subsequent representations of Apollo, and turns him into the complacent bore of classicism. One example will do for all, Poussin's title-page to the royal Virgil of 1641 [48]. The poet is crowned by a nude figure with short legs, broad chest and heavy shoulders which, since the 16th century, had been thought of as iconographically appropriate to Apollo; and not even Poussin's mastery

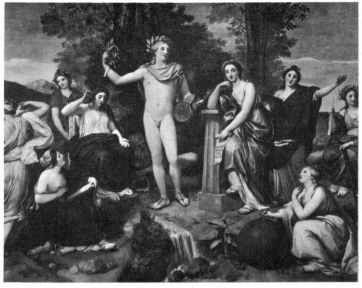

49. MENGS. Parnassus

of design can make this type of body anything but dull. In fact Poussin usually had the tact to avoid such figures, and represented Apollo seated and two-thirds draped. But the neo-classicists of the next century, lacking his creative insight, were aware only of the convenience of this respectable-looking form. Winckelmann had asserted that the highest beauty should be free from all flavour, like perfectly pure water, and when his disciple, Raphael Mengs, painted for the Gallery of the Villa Albani a decoration which should be in keeping with its contents, he aimed at an ideal insipidity. In his Apollo he achieved it [49]. The muses of his Parnassus, although uninspiring, are average specimens of 18th-century decoration ; the flat, formless body of their leader is on a different plane of unreality, and so looks as absurd to us as it looked admirable to Winckelmann's contemporaries. In the next generation Canova, a brilliant portraitist and master of contemporary chic, could produce ideal figures as ridiculous as the Perseus of the Vatican [50], in which a fashion-plate version of the Apollo Belvedere holds at arm's length a caricature of the Rondanini Medusa. Apollo, with all those beliefs which clustered round his name, had lost his place in the human imagination ; and the husk of Apollo alone remained to provide a meaningless discipline in academies of art.

Myths do not die suddenly. They pass through a long period of respectable retirement, decorating the background of the imagination, until some new hot-gospeller decides that their destruction is necessary to his salvation. Apollo, who, in the early 19th century, was lost sight of in the smoke of materialism, has become in this century the object of positive hostility. From Mexico, from the Congo, even from the cemeteries of Tarquinia, those dark gods, of which D. H. Lawrence made himself the prophet, have been brought out to extinguish the light of reason. The individual embodi-

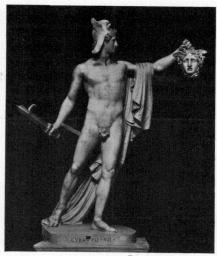

50. CANOVA. Perseus

ment of calm and order is to be supplanted by communal frenzy and the collective unconscious. Such impulses were well known to the Greeks. They are embedded in Greek religion ; they are at the root of antique tragedy ; and they are made beautifully visible to us on reliefs and drinking cups depicting Dionysus and his companions. Dionysiac enthusiasm, as we shall see in a later chapter, produced a series of nude figures which had a longer and more continuous life than the embodiments of Olympian calm. Yet when we look at the earliest representations of enthusiasm, the satyrs and rumba dancers on 6th-century Greek vases, we realise why the Greeks felt that their art could not rest on this basis alone. Without some element of lawful harmony it would have been no different from the arts of the surrounding cultures, Hittite, Assyrian, or as we may speculate, Minoan ; and like them have dwindled into decoration, anecdote or propaganda. This is the justification of Apollo in his cruel triumph over Marsyas. The union of art and reason, in whose name so many lifeless works have been executed and so many ludicrous sentiments pronounced, is after all a high and necessary aim ; but it cannot be achieved by negative means, by coolness or non-participation. It demands a belief at least as violent as the impulses it controls ; and if today, in the wailing of the saxophone, Marsyas seems to be avenged, that is because we lack the spiritual energy to accept the body and to superintend it.

CHAPTER III

Venus I

PLATO, in his *Symposium*, makes one of the guests assert that there are two Venuses, whom he calls Celestial and Vulgar, or, to give them their later titles, *Venus Coelestis* and *Venus Naturalis*; and because it symbolised a deep-seated human feeling, this passing allusion was never forgotten. It became an axiom of mediaeval and renaissance philosophy. It is the justification of the female nude. Since the earliest times the obsessive, unreasonable nature of physical desire has sought relief in images, and to give these images a form by which Venus may cease to be vulgar and become

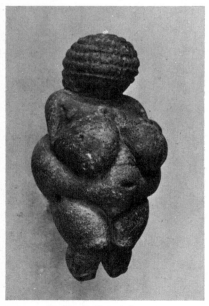

51. Prehistoric figure of a woman

celestial has been one of the recurring aims of European art. The means employed have been symmetry, measurement and the principle of subordination, all refining upon the personal affections of individual artists. But perhaps the purification of Venus could not have taken place had not some abstract notion of the female body been present in the Mediterranean mind from the first. Prehistoric images of women are of two kinds, the bulging statuettes from palaeolithic caves, which emphasise the female attributes till they are little more than symbols of fertility [51], and the marble dolls of the Cyclades in which already the unruly human body has undergone a geometrical discipline [52]. Following Plato's example, we might call them Vege-

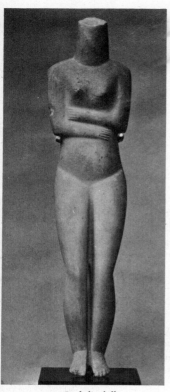

52. Cycladic doll

table and Crystalline Venus. These two basic conceptions never quite disappear, but since art involves the application of laws, the distinction between the two Venuses grows very slight; and even when most unlike one another they partake of each other's characters. Botticelli's Venus 'born of the crystalline sea of thought and its eternity' has a piercing strain of sensuality; Rubens' Venus, a cornucopia of vegetable abundance, still aspires to the idea. Plato made his two goddesses mother and daughter; the renaissance philosophers, more perceptively, recognised that they were twins.

Since the 17th century we have come to think of the female nude as a more normal and appealing subject than the male. But this was not so originally. In Greece no sculpture of nude women dates from the 6th century, and it is still extremely rare in the 5th. There were both religious and social reasons for the scarcity. Whereas the nakedness of Apollo was a part of his divinity, there were evidently ancient traditions of ritual and taboo that Aphrodite must be swathed in draperies. The fables by which she arose from the sea or came from Cyprus represent a truth, for naked Venus was an eastern concept, and when she first appears in Greek art she has a shape which clearly denotes her origin. This is the figure in Munich forming the handle of a bronze mirror, which is as straight and slim as if it were Egyptian, and without a hint of that system of curves from which the classic Venus was to be constructed [53]. Even as late as the 4th century, the naked Venus was embarrassingly associated with oriental cults, and it was because the beauty of her body might seem an inducement to heresy and not for moral reasons that Phryne, the model of Praxiteles, became an object of clerical disapproval. Socially the restrictions were equally strong. Whereas the young men stripped naked for exercise and habitually wore no more than a short cloak, Greek women went about heavily

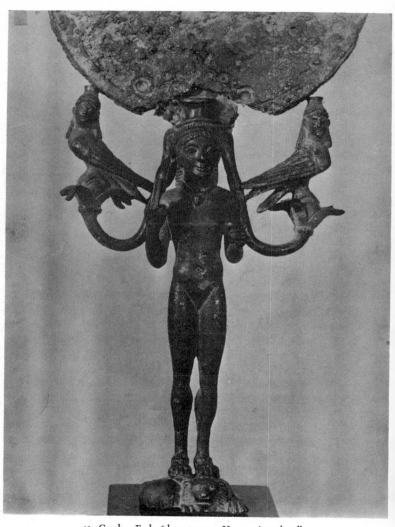

53. Greek.   Early 6th cent. B.C.   Venus mirror handle

draped from head to foot, and were confined by tradition to their domestic duties. The Spartans alone were an exception. Their women scandalised the rest of Greece by showing their thighs and competing in athletic sports. The Girl Runner in the Vatican must certainly have been a Spartan. Nor must we discount the influence of that peculiar institution of Greek life, so earnestly celebrated in the odes of Pindar and the dialogues of Plato, by which the love of two young men for one another was considered nobler and more natural than that between opposite sexes. It is from the rapturous scrutiny of passion that ideal beauty is born ; and there is no feminine equivalent to the youth of Kritios. The rare drawings of naked women on early vases are almost comically unideal, for example the ladies on a black figure vase in Berlin enjoying a shower-bath [54], who are closer to the eternal feminine of Thurber than to that of Praxiteles. By the middle of the 5th century the female figures on drinking cups have become more attractive [55]. These were ladies whose physical charm was their fortune and no doubt the artist has tried to make them look as neat and sprightly as possible. But they are no more idealised than their Japanese equivalents in the print of Kyonaga. The most revealing of all these chance survivors from the minor arts is a terra-cotta doll in the Louvre, from which, since it was intended to be clothed, the sculptor has not removed any of the imperfections and irregularities of nature [56]. It shows us what observation, what grasps of truth and substance, even a humble artisan could command in 5th-century Greece.

Such is the short and scrappy prelude to Venus. And although it contains evidence of vitality and a sense of physical charm, it is entirely without that search for finality of form which, on our definition, is the basis of the nude. But at about the same date as the terra-cotta doll there was produced a bronze figure of a nude girl, perhaps a priestess of Isis, binding her hair, which must have been a masterpiece. It is known to us in two marble replicas, of which the more complete is the statue in Rome, known as the Esquiline Venus, the more vivid a torso in the Louvre [57, 58]. No doubt the original has been changed and elaborated by translation into marble, yet the copies have not lost the unity of the first idea. Somewhere not very far behind them is the work of an individual artist who, on the surviving evidence, must be reckoned the creator of the female nude. Not that the Esquiline girl represents an evolved notion of feminine beauty. She is short and square, with high pelvis and small breasts far apart, a stocky little peasant such as might be found still in any Mediterranean village. Maillol maintained that he could find 300 in the town of Banyuls alone. Her elegant sisters from the metropolis would smile at her thick ankles and thicker waist. But she is solidly desirable, compact, proportionate ; and in fact her proportions have been calculated on a simple mathematical scale. The unit of measurement is her head. She is seven heads tall ; there is the length of one head between her breasts, one from breast to navel, and one from the navel to the division of the legs. More important than these calculations which, as we have seen from Dürer, can be misleading, the sculptor has discovered what we may call the plastic essentials of the feminine body. Breasts will become fuller, waists narrower and hips will describe a

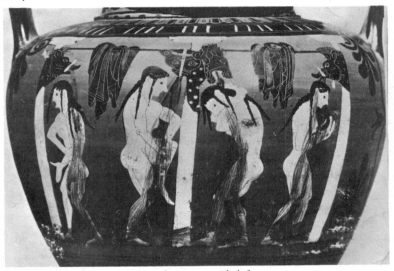

54. Attic. 6th cent. B.C. Black figure vase

more generous arc ; but fundamentally this is the architecture of the body which will control the observations of classically minded artists till the end of the 19th century and has been given fresh life in our own day by Renoir.

So rare are nude figures of women in the great period of Greek art that to follow the evolution of Venus before Praxiteles we must not look for absolute nudity, but must include those carvings in which the body is covered by a light, clinging garment, what the French call a *draperie mouillée*. This device was used from archaic times onward, the earliest sculptors seeming to recognise how drapery may render a form both more mysterious and more comprehensible. The section of a limb, as it swells and subsides, may be delineated precisely, or left to the imagination ; parts of the body which are plastically satisfying can be emphasised, those which are less interesting can be concealed ;

and awkward transitions can be made smooth by the flow of line. Drapery makes the bodies of the 6th-century maidens as beautiful as those of the young men, and consoles us for the absence of female nudes by the presence of the Korai ; and in that isolated masterpiece, the Ludovisi throne, the body of the naked flute player moves us less than that of the lightly draped Venus [59, 60]. The flute player's pose has not allowed the sculptor to develop the leading motives of the nude, whereas in the Venus, who rises with such benign

confidence between the arms of her attendants, he has discovered that landscape of the breasts and thorax which for some mysterious reason, connected, perhaps, with our earliest physical needs, is one of the most satisfying the eye can rest upon. In the execution of this passage, how skilfully he has used the pleats of her shift, which outline her shoulders, vanish under the pressure of her breasts and occupy with delicate curves that plane of her chest which, without them, would have seemed too flat for continuous beauty. The modelling of her attendants' legs, half seen through their flimsy skirts, is done with equal subtlety and

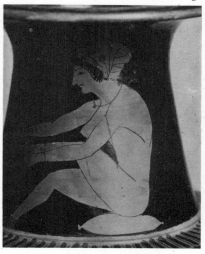

55. Greek. *c.* 500 B.C. Panphaios Vase (detail)

sensuous understanding. Clearly the schools of Ionia and Magna Graecia brought to the problem of clinging drapery a long tradition of technical skill. It was an artist trained in this tradition, but with an imperfect grasp of construction, who designed the draped nudes of the Nereid monument, and another, whose name, Paionios, has come down to us, who carved the figure of Victory in the Museum of Olympia.

In the Nike of Paionios almost every trace of archaic accent has disappeared. Her limbs have the youthful fullness which we find in the early nudes of Titian or Poussin. In fact, her body must first have been modelled in the nude and the drapery added to bring out, rather than to conceal, its rotundities. A lack of rhythmic unity suggests that Paionios did not himself invent the style which he employs, and it may well be that his contemporaries had already executed draped nudes with a more confident structure, which have been lost to us.

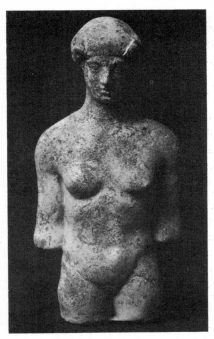

56. Attic. 5th cent. B.C. Terra-cotta doll

The Fates of the Parthenon leave us in no doubt that the sculptors under the supervision of Phidias could dispose the female body with the noblest and most natural effect ; and towards the end of the 5th century this tradition of the draped nude produced a famous Aphrodite. She has come down to us, under the misleading name of Venus Genetrix, in replicas, of which those which are fragmentary are beautiful, those which are complete are dull. Of the latter, a figure in the Louvre may give a more or less correct idea of the whole, but we come nearer to sharing the sculptor's emotions when we look at a torso in Rome [61] which reproduces the same design in reverse. The original was certainly by a pupil of Phidias, and one of the same circle as the sculptor who executed the famous relief of Nike tying her sandal. In both her chlamys has slipped from her shoulder and is tied in a knot on her arm, and in both the folds of drapery flow round the body, but are drawn tight over breasts and belly, so that the modelling, traversed by one vagrant line, makes its full effect. But in the Nike the revelation of her physical beauty is incidental, in the Venus it is essential, and the drapery is used to accentuate it. Perhaps this was the first Venus, in the sense that the beauty which arouses physical passion was celebrated and given a religious status. No longer need we complain that the response to femininity is half-hearted or incomplete. The plays of Aristophanes and Euripides are often quoted to prove that, in the last quarter of the 5th century, Athenian women acquired a new importance ; and to such literary examples may be added this figure, in which the subtlest rhythms of the female body are noted with an eager delicacy unsurpassed by Correggio or Clodion.

It has been suggested that the original of this lovely motive was the garden

Aphrodite of Alcamenes, fervently praised by Pliny and Lucian ; but as we do not even know if this figure was draped or nude, marble or bronze, this is only an archaeologist's day-dream. That nude bronze figures of women were made in this period is shown by a statuette in Munich of a girl who, in pose and proportions, is almost the undraped sister of the marble in the Terme [62, 63]. Her turbaned head suggests a date not more than twenty years after the Esquiline Venus, but in these years the classical type has almost completed its evolution. Polyclitus has perfected his ideal of equilibrium, the weight resting on the right leg, the left bent as if to move ; and the girl in Munich is in this attitude. The pose was invented for the male figure, but by one of those happy accidents which often accompany the discoveries of genius, the female figure has drawn from it a more lasting profit ; for this disposition of balance has automatically created a contrast between the arc of one hip, sweeping up till it approaches the sphere of the breast, and the long, gentle undulation of the side which is relaxed ; and it is to this beautiful balance of form that the female nude owes its plastic authority to the present day. The swing of the hip, what the French call the *déhanchement*, is a motive of peculiar importance to the human mind, for by a single line, in an instant of perception, it unites and reveals the two sources of our understanding. It is almost a geometric curve ; and yet, as subsequent history shows, it is a vivid symbol of desire. This pose seems obvious enough to us now ; yet such are the strange limitations of plastic intelligence that sculptors might have continued for thousands of years, as they did in Egypt and Mesopotamia, without ever discovering it. Yet as soon as it emerged, it became one of the dominant rhythms of humanist art, and carried some evidence of the Greek mental pattern far beyond the confines of Greek philosophy. Every art in which the motive appears has been touched by Hellenistic influence ; and although the austere Polyclitus might shudder at the luxurious *déhanchements* of Amaravati he is ultimately responsible for them.

Incredible as it seems, the Munich statuette and the Esquiline Venus are the only sculptural records of the female nude in the 5th century. The old ritualistic feeling that the beauty of Venus should not be uncovered lasted till well into the 4th century, and no doubt influenced the people of Cos when they rejected Praxiteles' nude Venus in favour of one which was draped. The people of Cnidos, profiting by their piety, thus became possessed of the most famous statue of antiquity.

The Cnidian Venus of Praxiteles [64] seems to have been executed in about 350 B.C., soon after his collaboration on the Mausoleum. Whether or not Pliny's story of her rejection by the people of Cos is true, there is no doubt

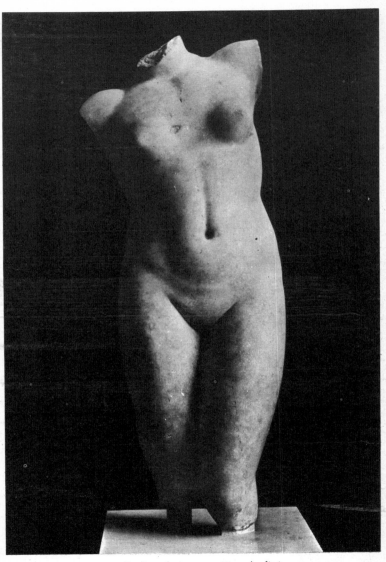

57. Greek. 5th cent. B.C. Torso (replica)

that she was ideally suited to Cnidos, an island off the south coast of Asia Minor where Venus had long been an object of devotion. A Greek author of late antiquity whose writings were formerly confused with those of Lucian, has left a vivid account of a visit to her sanctuary. Instead of the usual paved courtyard, it was surrounded by fruit trees of the finest growth between which hung festoons of generous grapes. In the midst of this refreshing verdure was a small shrine, open at the front so that pilgrims might see the figure of the goddess, white and radiant in contrast to the surrounding greenery. She was about to step into a ritual bath, and one hand still held the shift which she had drawn from her shoulders. Her lips were parted in a gentle smile; yet she had not altogether laid aside the majesty of an Olympian. The false Lucian and his companions, however, were not overawed, and made no pretence of aesthetic detachment. They spoke of her exactly as if she had been a living woman of overwhelming beauty. One of them, carried away by his excitement, leapt on her pedestal and threw his arms round her neck. The sacristan was mildly shocked, but later, for a gratuity, unlocked the door at the back of the shrine, so that they could admire this aspect of the goddess also; and their enthusiasm was redoubled. Not all pilgrims, perhaps, were quite so direct in their appreciation. The diligent Pliny

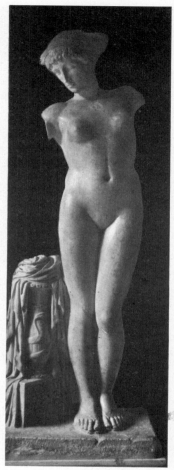

58. Greek. 5th cent. B.C. Esquiline Venus (replica)

writes of her as befits a professor. But no one questioned the fact that she was an embodiment of physical desire, and that this mysterious, compulsive force was an element in her sanctity.

Such sentiments may seem to us incompatible with an object of religious veneration ; but that is because the Hebrew basis of our religion has accustomed us to a literary rather than to a visual evocation of physical desire. Compared to the imagery of the Song of Songs, the appeal of the Cnidian is mild and restrained. Both derive from the same state of mind, and perhaps even from the same cult, because the Venus of desire was, as we have seen, a Syrian divinity ; but the luxuriant sensuality of the form is modified by the Greek sense of decorum, so that the gesture of Venus' hand, which in eastern religions indicates the source of her powers, in the Cnidian modestly conceals it. Perhaps

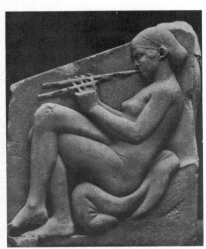

59. Ionian. Early 5th cent. B.C. Flute player on Ludovisi throne

no religion ever again incorporated physical passion as calmly, as sweetly and as naturally so that all who saw her felt that the instincts they shared with beasts they also shared with the gods. It was a triumph for beauty ; and to the Greek mind this beauty was not simply created by Praxiteles, but was already present in the person of his model Phryne. She shared with him the credit for the beautiful figures with which he enriched the Greek world ; and a nude statue of her in gilt bronze, openly a portrait, was erected in the sacred precincts of Delphi by a grateful community.

So much we know from literary records. Alas, when we turn for ocular confirmation of this epiphany, it is visible no longer. Of our forty-nine full-size replicas of the Cnidian, not one can give us even the faintest notion of the original. They are unusually bad because the delicately painted surface did not allow of a cast being taken and copying was probably discouraged. To add to our misfortunes, the three best replicas are in the Vatican where they have long been more or less inaccessible to students. Of these the so-called Venus of the Belvedere is obviously the copy of a bronze, and therefore at two removes from Praxiteles' original ; while the Venus from the Palazzo Colonna, although the main lines of the pose are convincing, has a head which does not belong to her, set on a stupid neck, and is as insensitive in modelling as the most commonplace garden statue. This is particularly fatal

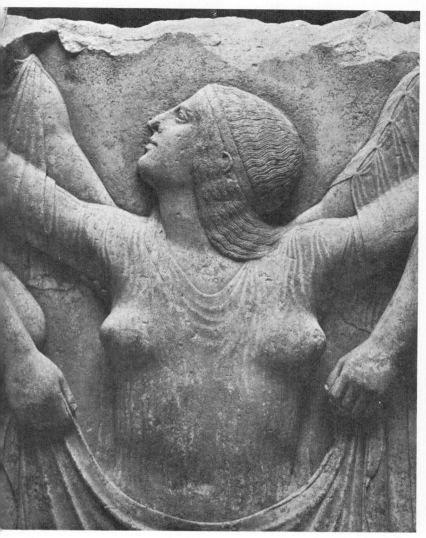

60. Ionian. Early 5th cent. B.C. Venus on Ludovisi throne

to work of Praxiteles who, as we have seen, took an almost morbid pleasure in delicacy of texture. The translucent surface still apparent in the Hermes, and more appropriate to a Venus, must have added that sensual tremor which, for five hundred years, led poets, emperors and boat-loads of tourists to linger in the sanctuary of Cnidos.

But in spite of this direct appeal to the senses the Venus of Praxiteles remains an ideal creation, complying with the abstract harmonies of art. At this distance of time we see that she belongs to the crystalline side of the family. Although she is so much taller, the proportions of her torso still conform to the first simple scheme established in the Esquiline girl. And, beyond this geometrical harmony, there is, in her whole bearing, a harmonious calm, a gentleness even, much at variance with the amatory epigrams which she inspired. To us she may even seem less desirable than the nudes which preceded her ; but in this one must make allowance not only for the dismal nature of our replicas, but for the interference of her innumerable successors. The classic nude, which Praxiteles invented, became, in less sensitive hands, the conventional nude, and as we try to look at his Cnidian Aphrodite we seem to see a forest of marble females, filling a vast conservatory with their chaste, monotonous forms.

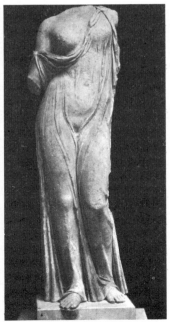

61. Hellenistic 'Venus Genetrix'

There is no more curious example of conspicuous waste than the smooth white marble nudes which in the 19th century were considered symbolic of art. In fact these figures do not usually derive from the Cnidian [65], but from two Hellenistic statues of great celebrity, the Venus of the Capitol [66] and the Venus of the Medici [67]. Fundamentally these are versions of the Praxitelean idea, but they involve an important difference. The Cnidian is thinking only of the ritual bath which she is about to enter. The Capitoline is posing. Herself self-conscious, she is the product of self-conscious art. Her pose, whenever it was evolved, is the most complete solution in antique art of certain formal

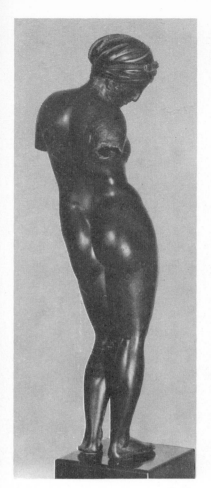
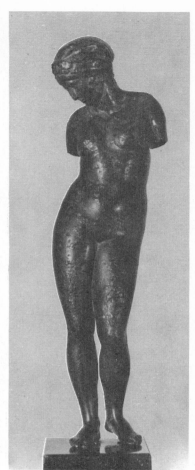

62, 63. Greek.　*c.* 400 B.C.　A girl

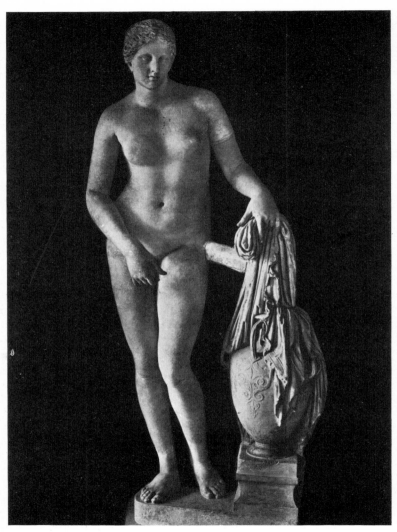

64. After Praxiteles. *c.* 350 B.C.   Cnidian Venus

problems presented by the naked female body ; and it is worth trying to see how this has been achieved. The variations on the Cnidian are subtle, but decisive. The weight has been transferred from one leg to the other, but is more evenly distributed, so that the axes of the body are nearly parallel. The action of the Cnidian's right arm has been given to the Capitoline's left, but both heads look in the same direction. Finally, the most obvious change, the arm of her 'free' side, instead of holding her drapery, is bent over her body, just below her breasts. All these changes are designed to produce compactness and stability. At no point is there a plane or an outline where the eye may wander undirected. The arms surround the body like a sheath, and by their movement help to emphasise its basic rhythm. The head, left arm and weight-bearing leg form a line as firm as the shaft of a temple. Approach the Cnidian from the direction to which her gaze is directed, and her body is open and defenceless ; approach the Capitoline, and it is formidably enclosed. This is the pose which is known to history as the Venus Pudica, the Venus of Modesty, and although the Capitoline is more carnally realistic than the Cnidian and the action of her right hand does nothing to conceal her magnificent breasts, a formal analysis shows that the title has some justification. We can see why in later replicas this attitude was adopted when the more candid nudity of Praxiteles would have given offence. We can also understand why, through all the misfortunes and mutations which Venus was to suffer during two thousand years, this impregnable design was the chief survivor.

Curiously enough it owes a great part of its authority in post-renaissance art to a version in which the rhythmic completeness of the whole is almost lost : the famous Medici Venus, which so long reigned unchallenged in the Tribuna of the Uffizi. The breakdown of rhythm is partly due to a faulty restoration of the right arm which, in an effort genuinely to cover the breasts and deserve her reputation for modesty, is bent at too sharp an angle, and does not sustain the flow of movement round the body. But at every point the Medici Venus is stilted and artificial. The physical opulence of the Capitoline has been reduced to refined complacency. The line of the body tapers up to the tiny, Praxitelean head, with the vapid elegance of a Victorian fashion-plate. It was perhaps inevitable that for two centuries this modish elegance should have been confused with ideal beauty. In the literature of praise the Medici Venus fills almost as many pages as the Apollo Belvedere, and with less reason. Byron, who considered the ideal 'all nonsense', devoted to the Venus a stanza of *Childe Harold* :

> We gaze and turn away, and know not where,
> Dazzled and drunk with Beauty, till the heart

Reels with its fulness ; there—forever there—
Chained to the chariot of triumphal Art,
We stand as captives, and would not depart,
Away !—There need no words, nor terms precise
The paltry jargon of the marble mart,
Where Pedantry gulls Folly—we have eyes.

In fact Byron was not using his eyes at all and, like most people of his class and temperament, had himself been gulled by fashion. Wordsworth,

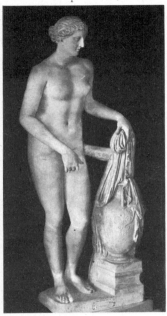

65. After Praxiteles. *c. 350 B.C.*
Cnidian Venus

with a firmer grasp of fact and, as we know from Hazlitt, a stronger feeling for art, confessed that in the Tribuna of the Uffizi he had turned his back on the Venus and fallen asleep. Nevertheless, we must admit that a number of good judges, from Winckelmann downwards, have considered the Medici Venus a model of feminine beauty, and it is clear that the narrow boundary which separates the affected from the graceful, the insipid from the pure, has slightly changed its position. No doubt it will continue to fluctuate, but, like the waist-line, within limits : and if we think that we can place it more accurately than a great critic like Winckelmann, that is because we have the advantage of knowing at least a few of those original works of 5th-century Greece which to him were only dreams. Fortified by knowledge of the Hermes of Olympia and the sculpture from the Acropolis, we can return to our lifeless copies of the Cnidian Venus, and find in them traces of a purity and serene humanity compared to which the Medici Venus is no more than a large drawing-room ornament.

The Cnidian was not the only famous Venus by Praxiteles. He also executed for the Thespians a statue in which the legs were draped and the breasts nude ; and this, too, has come down to us in several replicas. Once more the most complete is in the Louvre, the so-called Venus of Arles, and once more our heart sinks as we contemplate it. Not the faintest tremor of the artist's original feeling has been permitted to reach us, and if she were placed on the staircase of an old-fashioned hotel we should not give her a second glance. This is largely due to the restorations of the sculptor Girardon, who, on the instructions of Louis XIV, not only added the arms and changed the angle of the head, but smoothed down the whole body, since the King was offended by the sight of ribs and muscles. We can see from a cast at Arles,

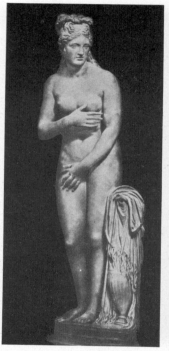 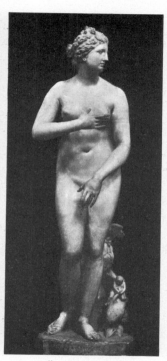

66. Hellenistic. Capitoline Venus   67. Hellenistic. Medici Venus

made before the statue was taken to Versailles, that the Thespian Venus embodied a noble idea, and one which was to prove more fruitful than the extreme perfection of the Cnidian. She solves one of the chief problems of sculpture with the simplicity of Columbus' egg. It has always been the despair of sculptors that the torso, that perfect, plastic unity, should rest on tapering, spindly supports. Praxiteles has simply draped the legs and left the

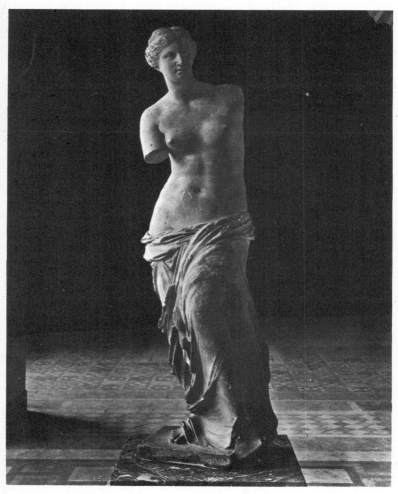

68. Greek. *c.* 100 B.C. Venus of Milo

torso bare. He has thus achieved so firm a foundation for his figure that he can dispense with any support—vase, pillar or dolphin—and allow the arms free play. Perhaps, as sometimes happens with a new discovery, he has failed to take full advantage of his freedom. The conventional appearance of the Venus of Arles is not due solely to her inarticulate surface, but to a rather quiet design, which is all that a replica can transmit. In particular, the axes of the body are so nearly parallel as to deprive it of vitality ; and it is in this respect that later sculptors were able to develop Praxiteles' idea. Already in the 4th century it was adapted to the motive of Venus admiring herself in the mirror of Mars' shield, supported on her knee, and the figure was recomposed on the basis of emphatic, ascending diagonals. The Venus of Capua in Naples is the chief replica of this statue ; and for about two hundred years may seem to have exhausted the possibilities of the motive. It was, however, to undergo a further development. The Venus of Capua had been conceived in profile, like a relief : about the year 100 B.C. it occurred to some sculptor of genius to re-design the figure in terms of depth. The result was the last great work of antique Greece, the Venus of Milo [68].

Within a few years of her discovery in 1820, the Venus of Milo had taken the central, impregnable position formerly occupied by the Venus de' Medici, and even now that she has lost favour with connoisseurs and archaeologists she has held her place in popular imagery as a symbol, or trade mark, of Beauty. There must be hundreds of products, from lead pencils to face tissues, from beauty parlours to motor-cars which use an image of the Venus of Milo in their advertisements implying thereby a standard of ideal perfection. Vast popular renown of song, novel and poem is always hard to explain and in a piece of sculpture is more mysterious still. Coincidence, merit and momentum are imponderably combined. The Venus of Milo gained some of her celebrity from an accident : that until 1893, when Furtwängler subjected her to a stricter analysis, she was believed to be an original of the 5th century, and the only free-standing figure of a woman which had come down from the great period with the advantage of a head. She thus profited by the years of devoted partisanship which had established the supremacy of the 'Elgin Marbles'. They had been praised for their heroic naturalness, their lack of affectation and self-conscious art, and the same terms could be used in contrasting the Venus of Milo with the frigid favourites of classicism. It remains true that she is fruitful and robust beyond the other nude Venuses of antiquity. If the Medici Venus reminds us of a conservatory, the Venus of Milo makes us think of an elm tree in a field of corn. Yet there is a certain irony in this justification through naturalness, for in fact she is of all works of antiquity one of the most complex and the most artful. Her author has not only used the inventions of his own time, but has consciously attempted to give the effect of a 5th-century work. Her proportions alone demonstrate this. Whereas in the Venuses of Arles and Capua the distance between the breasts is considerably less than from breast to navel, in the Venus of Milo the old equality is restored. The planes of her body are so large and calm that at first we do not realise the number of angles through which they pass. In architectural terms, she is a baroque composition with classic effect, which is perhaps exactly why the 19th century placed her in the same category of excellence as Handel's *Messiah* and Leonardo da Vinci's Last Supper. Even now when we realise that she is not a work of the heroic age of Phidias, and is perhaps somewhat lacking in the modern merit of 'sensibility', she remains

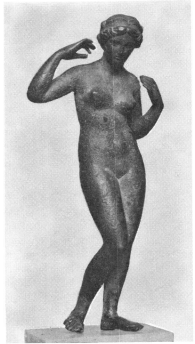

69. Hellenistic.   Bronze Venus

one of the most splendid physical ideals of humanity, and the noblest refutation of contemporary critical cant that a work of art must express its own epoch.

The genesis of the Venus of Milo exemplifies how the later Hellenistic artists approached the problems of creation. Not being blessed with great powers of invention, they used all their skill in combination and development. In the history of art this is neither unusual nor discreditable. In China and Egypt, for example, it was the rule, and the extreme restlessness of European art since the Renaissance has not been an unmixed advantage. But it is remarkable that in the female nude there is hardly a single formal idea of lasting value which was not originally discovered in the 4th century. An example is the beautiful motive of the crouching Venus, from which Rubens and French artists of the 18th century were to derive so much profit. On the evidence of epigraphy this is usually attributed to a late Hellenistic sculptor from Bithynia, named Doidalsus, and no doubt he did execute a statue in this pose. But the motive occurs on a 4th-century amphora decorated by the painter Camiros, whose figures seem to have been inspired by the sculpture of Scopas ; so that the splendid wholeness of the crouching Venus must also go back to the great age of plastic energy.

The variations on the theme of Venus which have come down to us from Hellenistic and early Roman times, especially those in the form of small bronzes, are often of great charm and ingenuity. Venus putting on her necklace [69], Venus with the girdle of Mars' sword, above all Venus newly risen from the waves and wringing the sea water from her hair—in all of these a slight change of motive refreshes, but does not disturb, the basic inventions of Scopas and Praxiteles. There are also several marbles, such as a splendid sensual torso in the Bibliothèque Nationale, which suggests that in Alexandria there were distinguished sculptors capable of altering the classical canon of proportion. But nearly all the surviving marble figures are memories and mixtures, and lack both the vitality and the unity of a fresh impulse. Even the Venus of Cyrenaica, whose combination of elegance and naturalism takes our eyes at the first glance, proves on analysis to be a pasticcio of Roman date [70]. Yet she is more delicately carved than almost any other Venus which has survived from antiquity, and still imparts some thrill of refined sensuality such as was the glory of the Cnidian.

The Venus of Cyrenaica, by her rhythm and proportions, reminds us of one of the last beautiful inventions of antique art : the Three Graces. Renaissance artists have made us feel that this interlacing of the three nude figures was usual and inevitable, but in fact it was not known in the great ages of classicism and its origins are obscure. The complicated pose may be derived from a row of dancers with arms on each other's shoulders, front to back, a motive still common in Greek choreography. From this row some artist had the happy idea of cutting off three figures, to form a closed, symmetrical group, and offering them as the sweet and charitable companions of Venus. It is impossible to say precisely when this occurred, but in all surviving versions of the Graces their proportions are those of the 1st century. Nor are any of our survivors of high quality. On the contrary, they are either mediocre commercial pieces or such rough imitations as local masons might make of a subject which was popular, but not yet sanctified by time. The marble group in Siena which was to assume such importance in the Renaissance was not, even then, considered a masterpiece of sculpture, but only the repository of a beautiful idea [71]. A relief in the Louvre [72], headless, alas, and of unpretentious workmanship, may still speak to us, as it spoke to the artists of the 16th century, of an art more complete and consistent than any which has succeeded it. For some reason the nakedness of the Graces was free from moral opprobrium, and in consequence they furnished the subject through which pagan beauty was first allowed to reappear in the 15th century ; they also offer an early example of the abandonment of that canon of proportion which had been followed without question since the 5th century B.C. In two

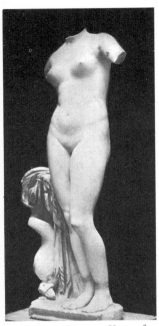

70. Graeco-Roman. Venus of
Cyrenaica

wall paintings from Pompeii their torsos have grown so long that the distance from the breasts to the division of the legs is three units instead of two [73] ; the pelvis is wide, the thighs absurdly short, and the whole body seems to have lost its structural system. It is interesting to find that this deformation of the classic nude, which we think of as characteristic of late antique art, had already reached such lengths before Pompeii was destroyed in the 1st century A.D. Probably the painter was one of those artisans from Alexandria who occupied, in the Roman world, rather the same position as Italian decorators in 18th-century England ; and the Graces of Pompeii are one of the first symptoms of that oriental influence which was to play so large a part in the disintegration of the classic style. Even the Hellenising art of Alexandria, as we can see from terra-cotta figurines, never quite abandoned the wide hips and narrow chest of the Egyptian body ; the influence of this ideal is apparent in all those nudes of late antiquity, in silver ware, needle-work or decorative carving which originated in the Eastern Mediterranean.

But it would be a mistake to suppose that the change in the female nude was due solely to the pressure of an outside influence. Styles, like civilisations, collapse from within, and to a large extent the shape of these Graces represents one of those standard, popular deformations which take place whenever the discipline of an ideal scheme is relaxed. All through antiquity the nudes engraved on the backs of mirrors or painted on inexpensive pottery tended to assume this curious proportion when the craftsmen were careless, incompetent or provincial. Perhaps there is in this, besides incompetence, a kind of naïve realism. The drift of all popular art is towards the lowest common denominator, and there are more women whose bodies look like a potato than like the Cnidian Venus. The shape to which the female body tends to return is one which emphasises its biological functions ; Venus is always ready to relapse into her first vegetable condition.

The representations of the female nude in late antiquity from which I have drawn these conclusions are scanty and, for the most part, crude. Long before it had become the object of moral or religious reprobation it had practically ceased to be the subject for art. As far as I know there is not a single nude statue of a woman which can be dated with any probability after the 2nd century A.D. Venus had suffered the fate of any motive in art which loses its meaning. She had passed from religion to entertainment, from entertainment to decoration : and then she had disappeared. When she emerged again everything made by man had changed its shape : clothes, buildings, written characters, systems of thought and morals ; and the female body had

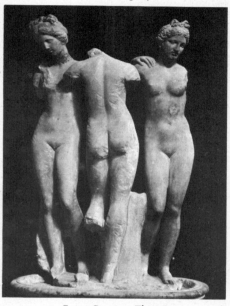

71. Graeco-Roman. Three Graces

changed also. A new convention, which I try to define in a later chapter, had been invented to combine in the body of Eve the humble character appropriate to our first unfortunate mother and the ogival rhythms of Gothic ornament ; and some consciousness of this convention is perceptible in the work of those artists who first attempted, in the early phase of the Italian Renaissance, to revive the canon of antique nudity.

The Renaissance, as we know, was preceded by several false alarms ; and so it was with the re-emergence of Venus. In Italy she lay buried very near the surface, and even in the middle ages might be dug up by chance. The sculptor Ghiberti, in his book of historical anecdotes, describes one such exhumation, which took place in the middle of the 14th century in Siena. A statue came to light signed by Lysippus, and at first the citizens were

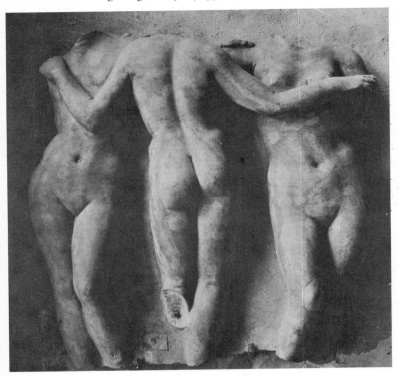

72. Graeco-Roman. Three Graces

delighted. They set it up in triumph on the Fonte Gaja, the centre of the town, and it was drawn by the chief official painter, Ambrogio Lorenzetti. But the tradition of iconoclasm was still strong. In 1357 a citizen made a patriotic speech pointing out the disasters which had befallen the city ever since the figure had been discovered ; 'and since idolatry is prohibited by our faith there can be no doubt whence these disasters arise'. And on November 7th, by public decree, the statue was taken down and buried in Florentine territory in order to bring bad luck to the enemy. It is important to notice that this decision was not taken because the figure was nude, but because it was a heathen idol. Ghiberti, who had seen Lorenzetti's drawing, does not mention its nudity, nor even its sex ; only that it was supported by a dolphin, and so was, presumably, a Venus. In the Latin countries nudity adds only a very little fuel to the fire of iconoclasm, and in a number of contexts was accepted by the Catholic Church. Fifty years earlier than the expulsion of Venus from Siena, the architect of Siena Cathedral, Giovanni Pisano, had included an almost exact replica of the Venus Pudica as one of the Cardinal

Virtues on the pulpit of the cathedral of Pisa [74]. This figure, now thought to represent Temperance or Chastity, was executed between 1300 and 1310, and is one of the most surprising false alarms in art-history. Giovanni's father, Nicola, working in a style formed before the conquering influence of the north, could easily incorporate pieces of sarcophagi and reliefs into his Christian subjects. But for Giovanni, the prophet of Italian Gothic, to assimilate such a completely classical pattern was an extraordinary feat of imagination.

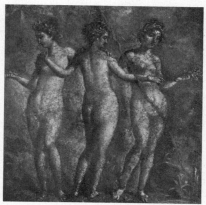

73. Graeco-Roman. 1st cent. A.D. Three Graces

The means by which he has, so to say, christianised Venus, is in the turn and expression of her head. Instead of looking in the same direction as her body, and thus confirming her existence in the present, she turns and looks upwards over her shoulder towards the promised world of the future. Her right arm, bent so that the hand comes higher on her breast and really covers it, leads the eye back to her head. Giovanni Pisano has discovered a gesture which was to become the recognised expression of other-worldly longing, and be used again and again, till its meaning was exhausted by the ecstatic saints of the counter-Reformation.

Pisano's figure is a complete anachronism. We must wait for over a hundred years before naked beauty is no longer the accidental endowment of our first parents, but can claim, once more, to be represented among the worshipful symbols of human impulse. Venus, as was to be expected, was not at first admired for her celestial attributes. There remained a large section of conservative opinion which regarded her simply as the embodiment of lust. The sculptor Filarete, in his treatise on art, describes as a possible subject a Garden of Vice in which Venus is the central object of attraction, and it is thus that she appears in those pieces of decorative art which preserve the popular imagery of the time. She is *Venus Naturalis* with a vengeance, and her body, in consequence, is unidealised [75]. She is simply a lady of easy manners who has taken off her clothes, and if her outlines follow, to some

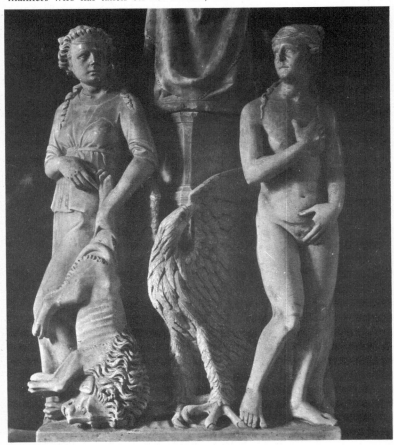

74. GIOVANNI PISANO. Temperance

extent, the Gothic convention, that is because the craftsmen did not know how to draw in any other way. But above this popular prejudice there existed a group of scholar-philosophers who, loving antiquity and delighting in the pleasures of the eyes, were determined that, by hook or by crook, Venus should be given back some of her divine attributes. By hook or by crook : the homely expression comes to mind as we read the complicated and disingenuous arguments by which she is transformed from the object of physical desire into the pattern of spiritual excellence ; but of course it is an error to think of them as arguments at all, in the rational modern sense. They are a series of allegories in which the relationships are suggested by the merest accidents of association, astrology or even euphony.

So Venus was rescued from her mediaeval disgrace by mediaeval means ;

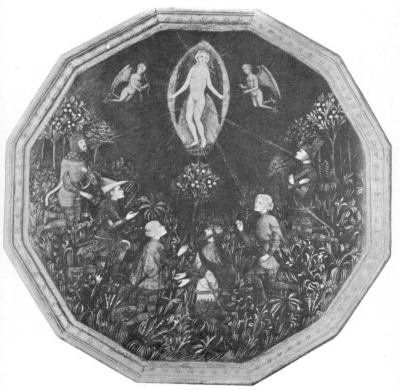

75. Florentine. *c. 1420.* Marriage Tray

but the vision which floated before her rescuers, leading them on to fresh feats of exegesis, was a vision of antiquity. It was because he could not resist this vision nor believe that such perfection of form could be harmful, that Marsilio Ficino wove his impenetrable web of commentary round the *Symposium* of Plato. The arguments were cloudy, the image was clear. And from this background of metaphor, shifting, dissolving, contradicting, there emerged, with sharp outlines, one of the greatest poets of Venus, Botticelli. His appeal is so irresistible that we may ask what is gained by associating him with the fantasies of neo-Platonic philosophers. The answer is that without them it is impossible to understand how the painter of pensive Madonnas invented the *Primavera*. His connection with the neo-Platonist circle can be demonstrated. Both the *Primavera* and the Birth of Venus come from the Villa of Lorenzo di Pierfrancesco de' Medici, a second cousin of Lorenzo the Magnificent. Marsilio Ficino had elected himself the mentor of this rich and promising youth, and in one of his numerous letters to his pupil there is a passage which illustrates the kind of allegorical thought I have just described, and anticipates the position which Venus was to hold during the next fifty years. Lorenzo, he says, 'should fix his eyes on Venus, that is on Humanitas. For Humanitas is a nymph of excellent comeliness, born of Heaven and more than others beloved by God on high. Her soul and mind are Love and Charity, her eyes Dignity and Magnanimity, her hands Liberality and Magnificence, her feet Comeliness and Modesty. The whole, then, is Temperance and Honesty, Charm and Splendour. Oh, what exquisite beauty!' Pico della Mirandola writes in the same strain. 'She has as her companions and her maidens the Graces, whose names in the vulgar tongue, are Verdure, Gladness and Splendour ; and these three Graces are nothing but the three properties appertaining to ideal Beauty.' Such, we may suppose, were the incantations which the shy young painter heard on the lips of the learned men who surrounded his patron ; and although himself unable to follow their meaning, they seemed to justify a vision of physical grace which had formed itself in his mind. But where, in the visual rather than the literary sense, did the vision come from ? That is the mystery of genius. From antique sarcophagi, from a few gems and reliefs, and perhaps some fragments of Aretine ware ; from those drawings of classical remains by contemporary artists which were circulated in the Florentine workshops, like the architects' pattern-books of the 18th century ; from such scanty and mediocre material, Botticelli has created one of the most personal evocations of physical beauty in the whole of art, the Three Graces of the *Primavera* [76]. The *Primavera* is, of course, ten years earlier than the Birth of Venus, and it is significant that Botticelli should

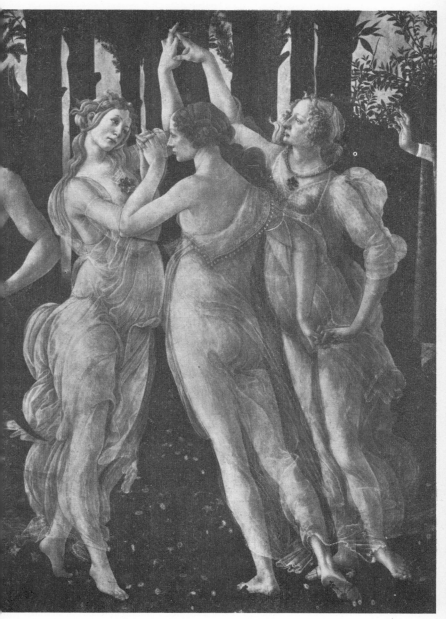

76. BOTTICELLI. Three Graces (detail from *Primavera*)

have felt his way back to antiquity through the image of the Graces, for their nudity had been sanctioned, as emblematic of sincerity, by Christian writers who condemned the nakedness of Venus. What antique representations of the subject he had seen remains uncertain ; perhaps it was a relief now lost, perhaps a drawing of the Siena statue, similar to that in Vienna attributed to Francesco di Giorgio. In either case he has penetrated beyond the Hellenistic replica to the impulse from which it derives, and has achieved an extraordinary affinity with Greek figures which he cannot possibly have seen. He has recognised that the Graces were part of a frieze of dancers, and has given them back their movement, animated by the rhythm of drapery. So naked beauty reappears in the Renaissance as it first emerged in Greece, protected and enhanced by *draperie mouillée*. In the management of flowing lines he was no doubt influenced by the figures of maenads which were such a frequent motive in Hellenistic decoration. In a later chapter, where I discuss the maenads as embodiments of ecstatic energy, I suggest that they may have been first invented by a painter ; and it is remarkable that the works of art which most closely resemble Botticelli's Graces are the antique paintings of the Seasons from Herculaneum. Obviously his figures are more slender and fragile than the ample nudes of antiquity, though not more so than those in the stucco reliefs from Prima Porta or Hadrian's Villa, some of which he may have known. The real difference lies in the more nervous articulation of each form and the more intricate pattern of line. Botticelli has ignored the volumetric character of the classical nude which, in such a figure as the Torso in the Terme, persists under the linear drapery. And yet, how incredibly close to the Greek rhythm, in one inspired leap of the imagination, Botticelli has come.

To see how far it has taken him, we should look again at the Three Graces as the middle ages pictured them [18], three timid ladies huddling behind the straight lines of their single blanket, yet not without a suggestion of impropriety ; and then turn back to Botticelli's Graces, where the body is not hidden, but transposed into a melody of celestial beauty : celestial but humanly touching, like a melody of Gluck. In the end it is by their human quality that Botticelli's Graces dissociate themselves from antiquity. The most famous lines in Virgil remind us how the sense of human pathos permeates antique literature, but in the visual arts how limited it is ! No doubt it is the strength of Venus that her face reveals no thought beyond the present. It is a fruit among fruits, and by excluding the further dimension of thought, it gives to the whole body an equal degree of permanence. That is a condition which we, of the Christian world, cannot reproduce ; we cannot dehumanise the face, and it was with a correct instinct that de Chirico, when he produced

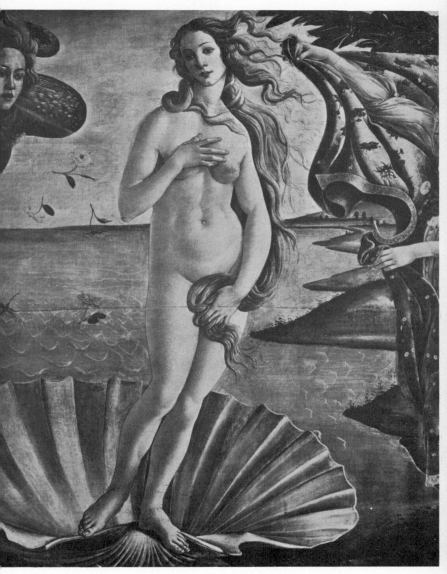

77. BOTTICELLI. Birth of Venus (detail)

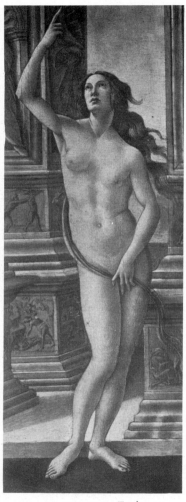

78. BOTTICELLI. Truth
(detail from Calumny of Apelles)

his travesties of classicism, replaced the heads by footballs. The heads of Botticelli's Graces, seen in isolation, are extraordinarily real. They are individual souls ; and so their beautiful bodies take on an added poignancy. They are immortal on account of their harmonious perfection, yet they are fragile because, as we can tell from their faces, they have no firm belief in the physical world. In this, as in much else, the *Primavera* rests on a point of balance between classic and mediaeval thought ; and the inspired certainty of Botticelli's imagination is shown by the way in which he has combined two apparently irreconcilable concepts. Just as the humanists incorporated their classical learning in a framework of scholastic thought, so the Ionian grace of Botticelli's figures is set in the framework of a Gothic tapestry; and as the neo-Platonists sacrificed reason to a fluid interpretation of symbols, so Botticelli has made no attempt to represent space or solidity, but has offered each beautiful shape on its own, like jewels on a velvet cushion, uniting them, as symbols are united, by their decorative affinities. Most of the other figures, moreover, are quite unclassical. The Venus herself, decorously clothed, raises her hand with a gesture of a Virgin Annunciate ; and the figure of Spring, fleeing from the icy embraces of the East Wind, is a Gothic nude. Her attitude, and the sweeping line of her stomach, are close to the little Eve who tempts Adam in the *Très Riches Heures* ; yet by a more ample rhythm she is made to harmonise with the classic figure opposite. Perhaps Botticelli himself was aware that this laying side by side of different types could not be repeated, for in his other great poem of neo-paganism, painted over ten years later, he has aimed at a more classical synthesis.

Between the *Primavera* and the Birth of Venus, Botticelli spent some time in Rome, at work on his frescoes in the Sistine Chapel. Antiques which in Florence were confined to a few collections, lay all around him. No foundations could be laid, no field freshly dug without there coming to light some fragments of an ideal world. It was as if every day the dreams of the preceding night were to find solid, but casual, confirmation. From the thickets and vineyards of the Palatine, nude figures emerged without shame or comment, and Botticelli, who had already penetrated so far into the Greek spirit, could recognise a Venus different from the gentle priestess of the *Primavera*, and

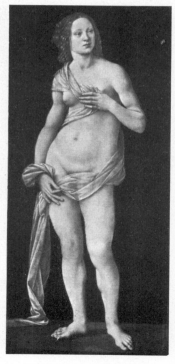

no less ideal. So when, on his return to Florence, his patron Lorenzo di Pierfrancesco asked him to paint a subject illustrating the lines of Poliziano's poem of the *Giostra*, in which he describes the goddess rising from the sea, Botticelli had perfected in his mind a clear image of her naked body [77]. Poliziano's lines were taken almost direct from one of the Homeric Hymns, and the same passage seems to have inspired a picture of Venus Anadyomene by Apelles mentioned in Pliny. Botticelli's commission was therefore intended as a tribute to antiquity; and the whole conception is far more classical than the *Primavera*. Instead of the tapestry composition, with its figures spread out decoratively against a background of Gothic verdure, the Birth of Venus is so concentrated and sculptural that it could almost be carried out as a relief. Yet, from the time of Ruskin onwards, it has been observed that the Venus herself is not classical, but Gothic. This is not due, as is usually said, to her slender proportions, for the cardinal measurements of her torso

79. LORENZO DI CREDI. Venus

follow exactly the classical scheme. She is, in fact, considerably less elongated than many pieces of Hellenistic sculptures, for example the Three Graces on Plate 73. Her differences from antique form are not physiological, but rhythmic and structural. Her whole body follows the curve of a Gothic ivory. It is entirely without that quality so much prized in classical art, known as aplomb ; that is to say, the weight of the body is not distributed evenly either side of a central plumb line. Indeed the Venus' foot makes no pretence of supporting

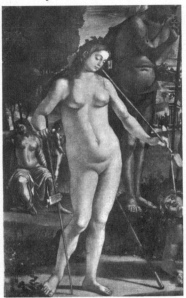

80. SIGNORELLI. Nude
(detail from School of Pan)

her body, and almost the whole of her weight is to the right of it. She is not standing, but floating. This is the rhythm of the whole picture, and without appearing anywhere to compromise the classical scheme, it has spread to each part of her body and subtly modified its shape. Her shoulders, for example, instead of forming a sort of architrave to her torso, as in the antique nude, run down into her arms in the same unbroken stream of movement as her floating hair. Every movement is related to every other by a line of unbroken grace, and Botticelli, like a great dancer, cannot make a gesture without revealing the harmonious perfection of his whole being. By this innate rhythmic sense he has transformed the solid ovoid of the antique Venus Pudica into the endless melody of Gothic line, the melody of 12th-century drapery, of Celtic interlacings, even, but made more poignant by a delicate perception of the human predicament. Flow of line is the most musical element in the visual arts, continually urging us on in time, and this gives a unity to the form and content of Botticelli's Venus. For her head is even further than those of the Graces from the expressionless, time-free pumpkins of antique sculpture. The word wistful which comes to the lips of every tourist who tries to describe her expression, is correct, and cannot be translated into Greek or Latin. It is the same head which Botticelli uses for his Madonnas, and this fact, at first rather shocking, is seen, on reflection, to reveal a summit of the human mind shining in the pure air of the imagination. That the head of our Christian goddess, with all her tender apprehension and scrupulous inner life, can be set on a naked body without a shadow of discord, is the supreme triumph of Celestial Venus.

Although she is raised above the first impulses of nature by the melody of line, Botticelli's Venus does not deny the empire of the senses. On the contrary,

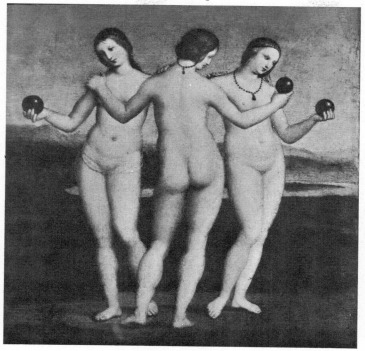

81. RAPHAEL. Three Graces

the flow of her body is like some hieroglyphic of delight, and behind the severe economy of Botticelli's drawing we can feel how his hand quickens or hesitates as he follows with his eye those inflections of the body which awaken desire.

This sensuous character is made clear when we compare the Venus with the only other female nude by Botticelli which has come down to us, the figure of Truth [78] in his Calumny of Apelles. Again he has reproduced an antique work of art on the basis of literary descriptions ; but by this time the aesthetic impact of antiquity on Botticelli was over. The preaching and martyrdom of Savonarola had persuaded him that the pleasures of the senses, even when purified of all grossness, were vain and contemptible. He had returned to the waning enchantments of the middle ages from which, by some wonderful accident, the humanist philosophers had temporarily removed him. In consequence, the Truth in the Calumny is, of all nudes which are not positively ugly, the least desirable. Superficially she resembles the Venus

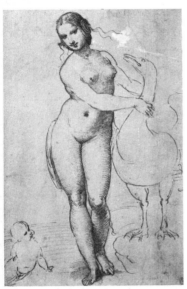

82. RAPHAEL. Leda

(although she must, I think, have involved a separate study), but at almost every point the flow has been broken. Instead of the classic oval of Venus, her arms and the angle of her head create the zigzag diamond-shaped pattern of mediaeval dialectics. The long strand of hair which winds round her right hip deliberately refuses to describe it. Botticelli could not draw without firmness and grace, but in every inflection he is at pains to deny himself the smallest tremor of delight and this puritanism has forced him to give her form a distressing meagreness. Only when the body emerges from draperies, as do the arms of Calumny, does he permit himself some physical response; and we almost regret the iconographic tradition by which even the most austere moralists permitted Truth to be naked.

With that strange indifference which visionary artists have shown towards their creations, Botticelli allowed his Venus to be copied in his workshop a number of times, and two of these copies have survived the general destruction which was visited on such pagan vanities under the influence of Savonarola. One of these, formerly in Berlin, was evidently done from the cartoon of the Venus, for it shows a difference which is perceptible in the under painting of the Uffizi picture. Venus is represented alone, standing before a dark background ; and as she is no longer floating forward, her figure is tilted more to the left in order to preserve her balance. The other, although slightly gothicised, is in a similar taste. Evidently they were popular and they seem to have been exported to France

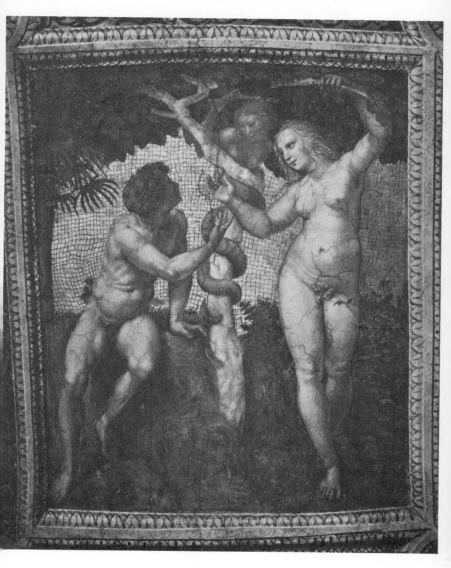

83. RAPHAEL. Adam and Eve

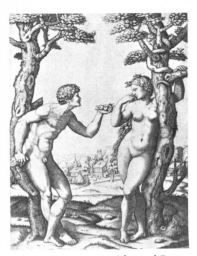

84. MARCANTONIO. Adam and Eve

and Germany : at least, I cannot believe that the naked Venus standing before a black background which Cranach painted in 1509 is an altogether independent invention. A curious survivor of this fashion is by Lorenzo di Credi, who, of all the Florentine painters of his time, was least equipped with the idealising faculties which the subject demands. His Venus is a model posed in the attitude of the Pudica, and the memory of Botticelli, perceptible in her left hand and legs, has hardly been enough to save him from a literal materialism [79].

There is, perhaps, only one other female nude of the *quattrocento* which need be mentioned separately, the noble figure to the left of Signorelli's School of Pan [80]. Whatever the allegorical meaning of the whole group, there can be little doubt that she is a personification of natural instincts, simple and uncorrupted. Iconographically she is *Venus Naturalis*. But this has in no way affected the form of her body, which is as geometrically ideal as the Celestial Venus of Botticelli. It is, of course, designed on a very different scheme. Signorelli (with one exception) had no sympathy with the suavities of antique art, and spent no time in examining them. He makes no attempt to conform to classic proportions, and in his nymph the distance between breasts and navel is of Gothic length. And yet in some respects she is more classical than the Botticelli. Her body is felt as mass and not as line ; it is constructed like architecture, the

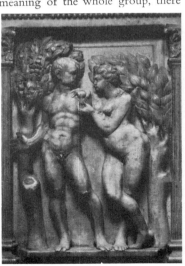

85. FEDERIGHI. Adam and Eve

102

weight resting on a point of balance. We approach it, as we do classic sculpture, grateful for the way in which every shape has been given its simplest and most satisfying character. Signorelli's transformation of the nude, as we shall see in a later chapter, is so personal and complete in itself that it could not be developed. The great enduring forms of art, from sonnet to symphony, must evolve step by step, so that each fresh departure is a development, with behind it an accumulated weight of ideas, to carry the next adventurer still further. We are grateful for the individual vision of Signorelli, but we can recognise that in the evolution of ideal form it is less important than the synoptic vision of Raphael.

Of all Raphael's marvellous gifts, that which was most completely his own, and seems to come from the radiant centre of his personality, was his power of grasping the ideal through the senses. The harmony by which he gives a lovable perfection to the human race was never the product of calculation or conscious refinement. It was a part of his physical apprehension. He was thus endowed to be the supreme master of Venus, the Praxiteles of the post-classical world. His employers willed otherwise ; and no artist ever served his employers more faithfully. He never painted the perfect picture of Venus which, as we know from his drawings, was always at the front of his mind. His contemporaries, less concerned than we are with sensitive execution, sought his ideal in engravings and the works of pupils ; and we must force ourselves to follow their example. Fortunately the nude is the subject of one original painting, the earliest perhaps, in which he was entirely himself, the Three Graces at Chantilly [81]. On the other side was the Dream of a Knight, now in London, and it has been convincingly suggested that the two were originally painted as a visible exhortation to the young Scipio Borghese to follow the path of duty, with Celestial Venus as his goal. Released from the conventional subjects and formalised style of Perugino, Raphael discovers that innate classicism through which he could come so close to antique art without pedantry. Which antique Graces he had seen we do not know. Probably the group in Siena first stirred his imagination, but the poses and proportions are more like those of a relief in Rome, of which a drawing may already have been in circulation. Raphael's little group has the flowing rhythm of a formal 15th-century lyric, a *villanella* or *terzetto*, both naïve and elaborate. It is far from the ethereal music of Botticelli. These sweet, round bodies are as sensuous as strawberries, and although their attitude must be derived from art, their power to please us is due to a grasp of nature. At that date the young Raphael could not have studied the nude from a living model, but some friend or relation has evidently allowed him to draw her bare arms and shoulders, for these are observed with a delicate naturalism beyond memory. That is what makes Raphael's vision of antiquity from the first so much more classical than the learned reconstructions of Mantegna. We see also that the qualities of classic art so admirably defined by Wölfflin, the sparing ornament, the uninterrupted outline, the concentration on essentials, all came to Raphael by nature and were by preference applied to the female nude. Yet from the formative years he spent in Florence, when he drew the male nude with matchless vigour and resilience, only one study of a naked woman survives. The strenuous Florentines, who delighted in the movement of a muscular back or an extended arm, took no interest in the bland and static form of Venus ; and Raphael submitted himself to their authority, always retaining from those years some taste for knotty

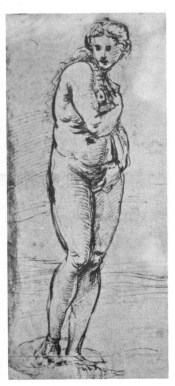

86. RAPHAEL. Venus

modelling. The single exception is revealing. It is not drawn from life nor from the Antique, but is a copy of one of Leonardo da Vinci's studies for the Leda [82] ; and when a year or so later, Raphael began to decorate the Papal apartments almost his first work was a scene of the Temptation [83] in which the lower part of Eve's body is directly derived from this design. In the places where he has had to vary Leonardo's pose, the action of the left arm and the set of the head on the shoulders, the rhythm of his figure breaks down, proving how little Raphael had yet been able to study the female body. We may be permitted to guess that he was himself dissatisfied with this Eve, for at a later stage he produced a more memorable image of the Temptation, known to us in an engraving by Marcantonio [84], in which, by the shapes of their bodies, he has expressed the primal relationship between man and woman. Adam, hollow and recessive, looks questioningly at his partner, whose assurance is symbolised by the dominating curve of her hip, sweeping up to her breasts, just as the curve of her arm leads up to her wilful head. Seldom

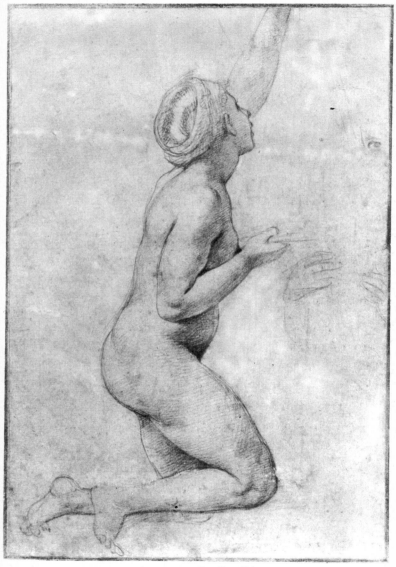

87. RAPHAEL. Kneeling Girl

in antiquity was this *déhanchement* quite so emphatic, so purposefully expressive of sexual difference; and I believe that Raphael may have been influenced by the memory of a piece of *quattrocento* sculpture which he had seen in Siena, a few yards away from the Three Graces in the Cathedral, the relief of Adam and Eve on Antonio Federighi's font [85].

Of this same period, roughly drawn on the back of a sheet of studies for the Orleans Madonna, is Raphael's first Venus [86]. Probably it was done with no purpose in mind, and has survived by chance, yet how warmly it illuminates our knowledge of his feeling for antiquity. Since classic times no other painter has absorbed so completely the principles of the nude. The forms are as firmly inscribed within the ovoid as in the Capitoline Venus; more firmly even, for Raphael has screwed them in with the twist of the body and final, frontal turn of the head. And how classically substantial she is ! This Venus may just have risen from the foam, but she is weighty and dense and demonstrates, by her frank acceptance of the flesh, the essential difference between Raphael and his classicising imitators. Maratta and Mengs, we feel, were less close to him than Rubens.

That such a project as this Venus Anadyomene should remain unrealised was inevitable. Raphael was working for the head of the Church in the centre of Christendom; and it is characteristic of his resourceful pliability that in these years he should have made a careful study of the draped nude—*draperie mouillée*—using as his models the two most famous examples of antiquity, the Venus Genetrix and the Ariadne; and incorporated their rhythms into that vision of spiritual harmony expressed through sensuous means, the Parnassus. Naked Venus did in fact enter one apartment of the Vatican, Cardinal Bibiena's bathroom where she has remained in strict retirement until the present day. Actually some of the nudes with which Raphael and his pupils decorated this enchanting room were engraved by Marcantonio, and through him enriched the iconography of Venus down to the time of Poussin.

In 1516 when Agostino Chigi invited Raphael to decorate his new villa on the banks of the Tiber, it seemed that his opportunity had come. The architect, Baldassare Peruzzi, had already employed a young painter newly arrived in Rome, Sebastiano del Piombo, who had been the companion and executor of Giorgione. Only a few years earlier the Venetians had discovered how to give the nude a sensuous warmth which made it one with the landscape, and Raphael, as we know from the Mass of Bolsena, had set himself to imitate Venetian colour. When, therefore, Chigi chose as subject the story of Cupid and Psyche he must have looked forward to a triumph of physical beauty richer and more circumstantial than anything which the revival of

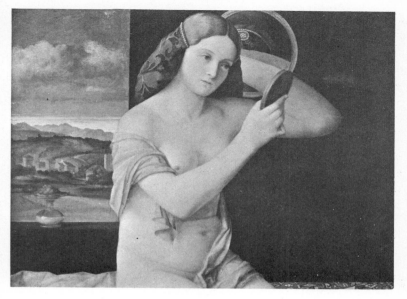

88. BELLINI. Woman at her toilet

paganism had yet achieved. Alas, he was too late. Raphael was already over-worked, and forced to let his designs be carried out by pupils. As a result the decorations in the loggia of the Farnesina lack just that sensuous delight, that palpitation which we can feel in Raphael's drawings. They are masterly inventions, but pushed through with a determination which makes them almost dogmatic. Some of the surviving studies for them show what has been lost by insensitive execution. A drawing of the Three Graces is as fully modelled as the fresco, but still vigorous ; a study from life of a kneeling girl has a feeling of round, firm flesh, conveyed by the outline and a few touches of shadow—the economy of conviction [87]. We recognise the real Raphael to whom a tangible presence was essential, and who could only be induced to work continuously when Agostino Chigi sent for his mistress and imprisoned her in the Farnesina.

By far Raphael's finest work in the Farnesina, and the only one entirely from his hand, is the Galatea [239]. Evidently this fresco was executed a few years before the Cupid and Psyche series, and has a radiance which they lack. Nothing in painting gives us a more convincing idea of the lost masterpieces of

89. GIORGIONE. Venus

antiquity, for Raphael had studied such surviving fragments of painted decoration as were then to be seen in the Golden House of Nero, and has adopted their light shadows and blonde tonality. The Galatea herself is a most conscious and elaborate construction. Raphael told Castiglione that, like the painters of classical legend, he had been unable to find any one model of sufficient beauty, but had used the best parts of several. In fact the Galatea does not seem to have been inspired by nature, but by other works of art. Her upper half may be found, appropriately enough, in a Nereid sarcophagus in Siena. Ultimately she derives from a Venus of the Capua type, to which Raphael has added the head of one of his saints. Instead of looking down, like Venus, at her reflection in Mars' shield, she is looking upwards to the skies. It is the same turn of the head which Giovanni Pisano gave to the Venus Pudica in his figure of Temperance, and proves by its application to a pagan subject how deeply the yearning for another world had entered the post-Christian spirit.

Beautiful as she is, the Galatea is not a dominating image of Venus. She is the central part of magnificent decoration, subordinate to its space-filling symmetry ; and as such will reappear in a later chapter. She did not contribute to the ideal. Yet it was during these years, the first two decades of the 16th century, that the mature image of Venus was formed, and one of the chief elements in its formation was, no doubt, the wide diffusion of engravings by Marcantonio and his imitators. These made accessible reproductions of recently discovered antiques and the most memorable inventions of Raphael and the Venetians. The antique fragments were, of course, shown as complete figures, sometimes in a very misleading fashion ; for example a print by Giovanni Antonio da Brescia, inscribed *noviter repertus*, represents the Cnidian Venus in the Belvedere version, but the engraver has forfeited the honour of being the first to record her resurrection, for his guess at the position of her right arm is so far from correct that the Praxitelean idea is lost. On the other hand, Marcantonio's engraving of the Crouching Venus was evidently taken from a well-preserved original and imparts a correct notion of its character. The renaissance appetite for articulation had led him to exaggerate the modelling ; yet how classical this Venus looks compared to another, done directly from Raphael's design, who sits with leg crossed over knee in the attitude of the Spinario. We recognise once more the enclosed finality, the cameo quality, of antique art which even the most Greek of renaissance artists could not, or did not wish to, achieve.

The study of Marcantonio's engravings confirms an impression that the Venus of the high-Renaissance was not invented in Rome, but in Venice. True, a long-established intercourse with Germany and the Tyrol gave to the early figures of early Venetian art a proportion more pronouncedly Gothic than can be found elsewhere in Italy. Rizzo's Eve is almost as ogival as a Konrad Meit ; and Bellini himself, in his little panel of the naked Vanitas, has cheerfully followed the model of Van Eyck, or perhaps of Memlinc. But soon after 1500 he painted a more graceful figure, the lady at her toilet, now in Vienna, where for the first time we see the ample forms which were to be characteristic of Venetian art in its next phase [88]. Although apparently untouched by classic influence she is the sister of the woman seated on the ground in Giorgione's *Concert Champêtre*. Did Bellini see her for himself, or did the old master, with his undiminished powers of absorption, see through the eyes of his dazzling pupil ? We shall never know. But as the evidence has come down to us we can say that the classic Venetian nude was invented by Giorgione. He may have known a few antiques in Venice and Padua ; there were paintings and engravings of the nude by Mantegna, and perhaps drawings by Perugino, who, as we can see from the Castelfranco altar-piece, played a leading part in giving his style its classic simplicity. But far beyond such quasi-accidents was an appetite for physical beauty more eager and more delicate than had been bestowed on any artist since 4th-century Greece. It is because he suddenly found the shape and colour of those desires which had been floating half-formed in the minds of his contemporaries, that Giorgione's work has reached us inextricably confused with that of other artists. He had no sooner found the password than all could enter at the same door, and one, or two, may have pushed past him. In the nude we can be sure that he was the real inventor. Engravings of his vanished masterpiece, the frescoes of the Fondaco de' Tedeschi, show nude figures of women used for the first time in isolation, as units in a decorative scheme ; and a nude woman is the subject of the picture in which his peculiar graces are most clearly apparent, the Dresden Venus.

In European painting the Dresden Venus holds almost the same place as is held in antique sculpture by the Cnidian [89]. Her pose is so satisfying that for four hundred years the greatest painters of the nude, Titian, Rubens, Courbet, Renoir, even Cranach, continued to compose variations on the same theme. Unlike the Cnidian she was herself relatively unknown, hidden in the Cà Marcello ; but Titian's variants, the Venuses of Urbino and of the Pardo, were royally famous from the first. Her pose seems so calm and inevitable that we do not at once recognise its originality. Giorgione's Venus is not antique. The reclining figure of a nude woman does not seem to have been the subject of any famous work of art in antiquity, although it is sometimes to be found in the corners of Bacchic sarcophagi. And apart from the absence

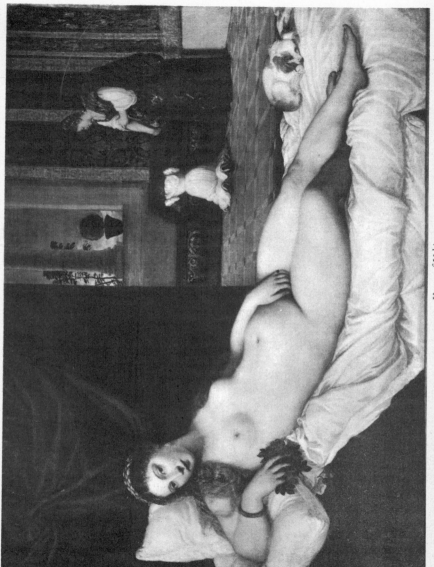

90. TITIAN. Venus of Urbino

of models, she is not a Hellenistic shape. She lacks the weighty sagging rhythm, as of a laden branch, in which the antique world paid equal tribute to growth and to gravity. There remains something Gothic in her movement, confirmed by the gentle swell of her stomach, and perhaps after all her real predecessors were those figures of naked brides which were traditionally painted on the inside of the 15th-century marriage chests. When this is said, how un-Gothic she is in the cylindrical smoothness of every form. If, as Winckelmann maintained, classic beauty depends on a perfect ease of transition from one comprehensible shape to another, the Dresden Venus is as classically beautiful as any nude of antiquity.

The Venus of Praxiteles had just laid aside her chlamys, and was modestly poised on the steps of a ritual bath. The Venus of Giorgione is sleeping, without a thought of her nakedness, in a honey-coloured landscape : but her outline forbids us to identify her as *Venus Naturalis*. Compared with Titian's Venus of Urbino, who seems, at first, so closely to resemble her, she is like a bud, wrapped in its sheath, each petal folded so firmly as to give us the feeling of inflexible purpose. With Titian [90] the bud has opened, the continent outline is broken, and, to change from metaphor to measurement, the sharp-pointed triangle formed by the breasts of the Giorgione Venus and the base of the neck, has become in the Titian almost equilateral. The swift Gothic movement, by which the Dresden Venus seems to be lifted above the material world, is replaced by renaissance satisfaction in here and now ; and we scarcely need the closed eyes of the Giorgione or the inviting gaze of the Titian to point the difference between them. If the distinction between the twin sisters can ever be sustained, Giorgione's Venus is celestial. Yet this isolation of the nude from the vegetable life which surrounded it could not be maintained for long : it resulted from a moment of balance as delicate as that which produced Botticelli's *Primavera*. And in the culmination of the Giorgionesque, the *Concert Champêtre*, the bodies have lost all sense of Gothic virginity. Far from being buds, they have the opulent maturity of an Italian summer. We have entered the realm of *Venus Naturalis*.

CHAPTER IV

Venus II

I N Florence Celestial Venus had risen from the sea of neo-Platonic speculation. In Venice her sister was born in the more tangible environment of
thick grasses, rustic wells and abundant foliage ; and for four hundred
years painters have recognised that Natural Venus is originally and
essentially a Venetian. Yet by a strange quirk of genius the first renaissance
artist to represent a naked woman as a symbol of creative and generative life
was a Florentine, Leonardo da Vinci. Between 1504 and 1506 he executed at
least three designs of Leda and the Swan, one of which was carried out as a
painting and was taken to Fontainebleau, where it survived till the end of
the 17th century. The reasons which led him to depict this subject are characteristically oblique. On the surface it would seem to be wholly unsuited
to him. He was not moved by classical mythology ; he had no patience with
the fancies of neo-Platonism, and little feeling for that kind of geometrical
harmonisation of the body from which the classic nude was derived. Above
all, he was not emotionally or sensually attracted by women. But this last
was, no doubt, the determining factor. Since women did not arouse in him
any feelings of desire, he was all the more curious about the mysterious character of generation. He could consider the sexual act as part of that endless
flux of growth, decay and rebirth which formed for him the most fascinating
and fundamental of all intellectual problems. In about the year 1504 he began
to study the process of generation scientifically, accompanying his questions,
as always, with exquisitely precise illustrations ; and beside one of the
anatomical drawings of this series is the first sketch of a Leda.

Even without this scrap of evidence the surviving copies of Leonardo's
Leda leave us in no doubt that he intended her as an allegory of generation
[91]. He has invented a pose which ingeniously emphasises those parts of
the body which the Cnidian Venus and her descendants had concealed. True,
a similar pose was known to antiquity. A Bacchic sarcophagus in the Terme
[218] contained a maenad with her arm bent across her chest, leaving the
lower part of the body open, and it is conceivable that some such figure was

known to Leonardo. But the word 'invented' may stand, for in antique examples the arm covers the breasts, whereas Leonardo has so contrived that the same action reveals them and gives them an oriental prominence. Oriental is, indeed, one of the first epithets we think of applying to the Leda, a word suggested by the swing of the hip, by the continuous flow of the modelling and, above all, by a sort of tropical redundancy of rhythm. Leonardo was aware of this and in the first cartoon his figure was surrounded by a jungle growth of heavy leaves, twisting grasses and upstanding bulrushes, for which the preliminary drawings, marvellously uniting love and science, are at Windsor. As so often in his work, 'nature' has been given a more urgent life than the human body.

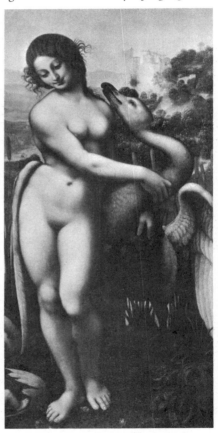

Making every allowance for the repulsive quality of all Leonardesque replicas, it is hard to believe that Leonardo's Leda can ever have been an attractive work. The exploitation by the intellect of a theme usually governed by the emotions must always be disturbing to a normal sensibility. Almost the only analogous effect in European painting is to be found in the *Bain Turc* of Ingres, but even at eighty-two Ingres felt the tug of physical desire, which makes his Hindu contortions both more and less disquieting. Yet what an undeniable work of genius Leonardo's Leda remains. The writhing, intricate rhythms of growth are carried through from the pose of her figure to the plaits of her headdress and the grasses at her feet. Incapable of the feeling and

91. CESARE DA SESTO. After Leonardo da Vinci. Leda

contemptuous of the philosophy from which, in harmonious union, Venus was born, Leonardo still holds us fascinated by the purposeful consistency of every form and every symbol.

Leonardo's Leda achieves intellectually, we may even say scientifically, the conception of *Venus Naturalis* which, in the very same year, was taking shape in the sensuous imaginations of the Venetians. Whether the design was also known in Venice is an unanswerable question. Other works by Leonardo had a considerable influence on Venetian art, and there is no reason why some drawing for, or copy of, the Leda should not have reached Venice during the first years in which Giorgione and Titian were putting nude figures in a setting of leaves and grasses. But there is no direct reminiscence of the figure, and the way in which the forms slide and twist round each other is contrary to the open, frontal presentation of Venetian art. The first great celebration of Natural Venus in Venice is the so-called *Concert Champêtre* in the Louvre [92].

As Pater pointed out, in some of the finest pages of English criticism, the aim of the *Concert Champêtre* is to create a mood through the medium of colour, form and association. Our participation is sensuous and direct. Although it tells no story, and the most determined iconologists have been unable to saddle it with a subject, its theme is not altogether new, for artists had enjoyed painting picnics since the 14th century. But the *Concert Champêtre* has this peculiarity, that the ladies have undressed ; and we may speculate how Giorgione has persuaded us to accept as natural this unusual freedom. Several memories, no doubt, pictorial and literary, had helped to strengthen and clarify his imagination. There was the memory of Bacchic sarcophagi, with their naked Bacchantes seated in the corner, of whom Titian later was to make so superb a use ; and there was the antique habit of personification by which the essence of every pleasant thing in nature—springs, flowers, rivers, trees, even the elusive echo—could be thought of as having the shape of a beautiful girl. This, the imaginative legacy of Ovid, became fused with the imaginative legacy of Virgil, the myth of the Golden Age. So naked figures could be introduced into a landscape partly because they could be thought of as embodying some of its elements, and partly because, in the youth of the world, human beings did not need to cut themselves off from nature by the artificial integuments of dress. These are the ingredients of Arcadian poetry ; and Giorgione could be represented as part of the same movement which produced Sannazaro and Tebaldeo. But the poets were encumbered with learned allusions. Their equivalent is Raphael's Judgment of Paris, known through Marcantonio's engraving [285], which was to inspire a long line of academic compositions, ending, most surprisingly, with Manet's *Déjeuner sur l'herbe*. In spite of the classical completeness of each group the engraving has an air of frigid and fanciful pedantry, as of some old-fashioned cabinet of antiquities. Paris is a stock figure, the Olympians jostle one another in the sky, and the personifications on either side add to the sense of overcrowding. Only the naiads on the left seem to be imaginatively related to the spring they personify.

In contrast to this intellectual Mount Ida, Giorgione's *Concert Champêtre* is as simple, sensuous and passionate as the poetry of Keats ; and the nude figures, which sound artificial in a description, seem, when apprehended through the eye, to embody, or bring to a point of physical apprehension, all the fruitful elements of nature which surround them. The two women, although they might have been painted from the same model, differ greatly from one another in conception. She who is seated on the ground is painted with an unprejudiced sensuality as if she were a peach or a pear. In this she is the forerunner of Courbet, Etty, Renoir and of those life studies which were the chief product of art schools throughout the 19th century. She gives an impression of directness unprecedented in the nude, but in fact the aspect of the female body which Giorgione has selected is quite arbitrary, and the forms

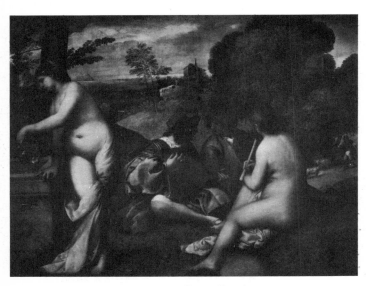

92. GIORGIONE. *Concert Champêtre*

have been drastically simplified. The standing woman is not so datelessly naturalistic. Her draperies indicate that she is a figure of art, and her complex pose seems to have been derived from an antique relief similar to that in Plate 218, although by turning the Bacchante's head into profile Giorgione has changed her heated urgency into a gentle calm. He has also given her more generous proportions than were usual in antiquity. Even figures of Alexandrian origin seldom show such width of pelvis or such ample expanse of stomach. This is the type of female nude which was to dominate Venetian art for a century, and, through Dürer, greatly to influence the physical ideal of Germany ; and it seems reasonable to attribute its invention to Gior-

gione, for it appears in such works as the Marcantonio engraving of a woman watering a plant which antedate stylistically the *Concert Champêtre*. The most famous and influential of Giorgione's nudes, those which decorated the Fondaco de' Tedeschi, have perished, and we are left with the reminiscences and developments of his two companions who, as we know, completed his unfinished works and carried out his ideals, Sebastiano del Piombo and Titian. Sebastiano, with that taste for the heroic which was later to draw him into the inner circle of Michelangelo, carried to their furthest point the sweeping proportions — long-armed, widehipped and tall—of the woman to the left of the *Concert Champêtre*. He was so imbued with this ideal that he could find it in nature, as we can tell from a splendid drawing of a nude model, one of the first 'life drawings' of a woman which have

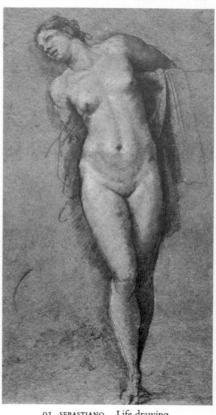

93. SEBASTIANO. Life drawing

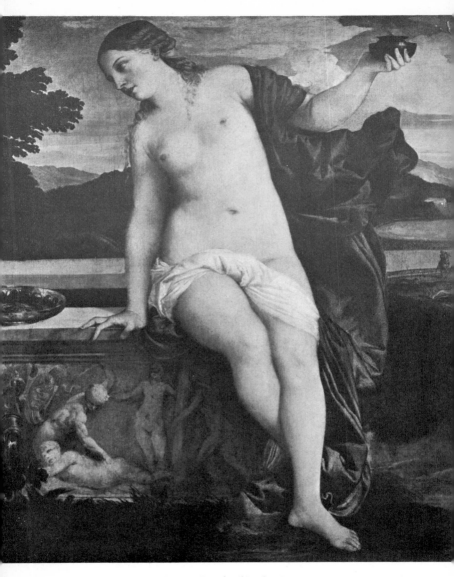

94. TITIAN. Sacred and Profane Love

come down to us [93]. Titian, on the other hand, developed the sensuous aspect of the Giorgionesque nude till he became one of the two supreme masters of Natural Venus.

The most beautiful of Titian's Giorgionesque nudes is in the picture known as Sacred and Profane Love [94]. It has been claimed that she represents Celestial Venus while her clothed sister is Natural. But to anyone who looks at Titian's painting as a poem and not as a puzzle, her significance is clear enough. Beyond almost any figure in art she has what Blake called 'the lineaments of gratified desire'. The evening light of the Veneto, with which Bellini had affirmed the unity of vegetable creation, is now made to include that tender fruit, the human body. She is generous, natural and calm. Her outline is more classical than the women in the *Concert Champêtre*, more idealised than the pipe player, more compact than the dipper in the well. No doubt it has been inspired by an antique, and Titian has even broken the line of the arm by a cast of crimson drapery exactly where it would have been broken by time. But marble, even the sunny, time-softened marble of some statue recently brought to light in vineyard or garden, is the last thing we remember before this glowing panoply of flesh ; and this, for antique art, as we now realise, was an art of colour, is what brings the Venetians so much closer to antiquity than the industrious archaeologists of Rome.

Nor would the idea that he was re-creating antique painting have seemed to Titian, in the 1520's, altogether surprising. The subjects of his Bacchanals are taken from the classical repertoire of pictorial themes, Philostratus, and, quite as much as the classic architecture of Vignola or Sansovino, they were intended to support the illusion that paganism had been reborn. We may question whether any painter of antiquity achieved their palpable full-ness and warmth. Yet as in all midsummer celebrations, the promise of an earlier season has been lost, so in the Bacchanals we lose the shadowy invitations, the poetical mystery of the first Giorgionesque pastorals. A few years later Titian the friend of Giorgione and native of Cadore has been pushed out of the way by Titian the friend of Princes ; and the inspired idea that naked beauty could be a natural feature of the landscape has ceased to be a reality. Titian's employers were not averse from naked women, but they wanted them in their proper place ; and there follows a series of nude figures reclining on beds and couches, of which the first is the Venus of Urbino.

To this there is one exception : the Venus Anadyomene of the Ellesmere Collection [95]. She has suffered from time and restoration. Her carmines have faded, some insensitive restorer has altered the outline of her left arm and shoulder ; and Titian himself has repainted her head, which is now out of

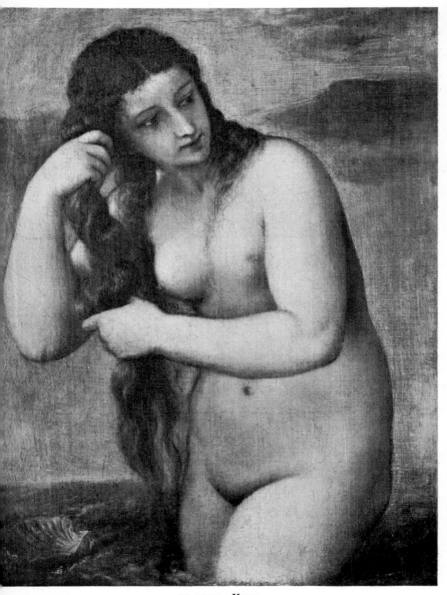

95. TITIAN. Venus

keeping with her body. In spite of this she remains one of the most complete and concentrated embodiments of Venus in post-antique art. If the pipe-player in the *Concert Champêtre* anticipates the shape of the female nude in the 19th century, the Ellesmere Venus anticipates the whole conception of the subject which ended, for our generation, in the nudes of Renoir : that is to say, the female body, with all its sensuous weight, is offered in isolation, as an end in itself. This presentation of the nude, with no pretext of fable or setting, was in fact extremely rare before the 19th century, and it would be interesting to know under what circumstances Titian conceived it. Perhaps he was asked to preserve in the medium of oil paint a specimen of the single nude figures with which he and Giorgione had frescoed the Fondaco de' Tedeschi. His point of departure is of course an antique, presumably the same one which inspired an engraving by Marcantonio of Venus wringing the water from her hair ; but Titian has changed the flowing rhythm of the Hellenistic original into the firm rectangular design of the two arms, to which even the thigh, in some measure, conforms.

That an austere tradition of design is an essential of the nude has been one of the chief themes of this book, but I will re-state it here, for the nudes of Titian provide its most impressive illustrations. An epic poet of sensuality, an absolute master of flesh painting, one might have supposed that an infinite variety of poses and situations was available to him. And yet the number of attitudes which seemed to him to achieve finality was extremely small. It is, to begin with, astonishing that in 1538, thirty years after he had put the finishing touches on Giorgione's Venus, he should have used identically the same pose for almost the whole body of the Venus of Urbino, varying only, as we have seen, the position of the right arm and breast ; and the same form, much coarsened, serves in that laboured attempt to recapture his early style, the Venus del Pardo.

In the 1540's he discovered two fresh patterns for a recumbent Venus which were to satisfy him for a decade. One of them is the figure reclining on her left arm, her body turned round towards the spectator, who appears first alone with Cupid, in the Uffizi picture, and thereafter, in numerous replicas, with an admirer seated at her feet making music on an organ or a lute [96]. In this series only the position of her head is varied : her body remains the same, and there can be no doubt that Titian found it unusually satisfying. This is the nude which is most nearly Titian's own creation. In his other figures Giorgione, Michelangelo and the Antique provide at least the outlines ; but the Venus of the Organ Player series has a quality which is entirely Titianesque. It is, as has often been observed, the quality of the full-blown rose, rich, heavy

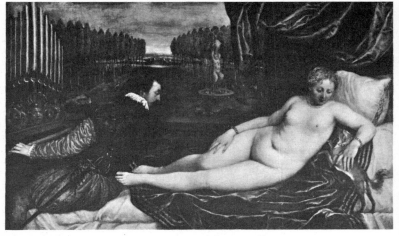

96. TITIAN. Venus and the Organ Player

and a trifle coarse. The rose is held frontally, so that we look towards its heart, still covered by curving petals, and although the outline is clear enough, the inscape has lost its tenseness and precision. This frontality, reflecting the magnificent obviousness of Titian's nature, is no doubt what chiefly pleased him in the Venus with the Organ Player and led him to repeat her form so often. It also gave him the opportunity of rendering in paint his admiration for an expanse of soft skin, fully and evenly illuminated. But in spite of this pleasure in the flesh, the Venuses of this series are not provocative. The almost brutal directness with which their bodies are presented to us makes them, now that their delicate texture has been removed by restoration, singularly un-aphrodisiac. Moreover, they are far more conventionalised than is evident at first sight. Comparison with Rembrandt's Danaë shows how much of the natural appearances Titian has suppressed or subordinated to his ideal scheme. Even such a highly stylised figure as Goujon's Nymph retains a sag of the stomach and a movement of the torso which is more naturalistic than the Titian, and thus arouses more natural feelings.

The Venus with the Organ Player is entirely Venetian, younger sister of all those expansive ladies whom Palma Vecchio, Paris Bordone and Bonifazio painted for local consumption ; in the rest of Italy bodies of an entirely different shape had long been fashionable, and in 1546–7 Titian himself, who was in Rome, receiving the freedom of the city, came to terms with the new

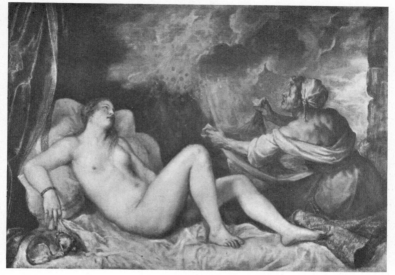

97. TITIAN. Danaë

convention. The result was the Danaë, of which during the next years he was to paint an almost equally large number of versions [97]. Her pose is clearly based on drawings of Michelangelo, and is in fact similar to that of the Night, reversed and opened out. Her head, instead of drooping forward in melancholy slumber, is stretched back on her pillow, voluptuously contemplating the shower of gold ; her arm is no longer twisted behind her, but rests comfortably on a cushion as do the arms of Titian's Venuses. Needless to say the harsh furrows of the stomach have been smoothed away into a gentle undulation and the extruding animal breast has been brought into conformity with human expectations. At every point Michelangelo's grandiose invention has been transformed from an embodiment of spiritual malaise into an embodiment of physical satisfaction.

Suddenly, in the 1550's, all Titian's self-imposed restraints and limitations are broken through. The frontal poses and decisive contours are abandoned, and in the two great 'poesies' in the Ellesmere Collection, the *Actaeon* and the *Callisto*, the female body is seen with a freedom from stylistic preconception never achieved before [98]. True, some of the principal figures, in particular the Diana rebuking Callisto, have an elegance which must owe something to Parmigiano ; but in both pictures the attendant maidens are of an amazing

123

naturalness. Rubens never surrendered himself more whole-heartedly to pleasure in the sight of the naked body, nor greeted with better appetite generous developments of the flesh. The figure on the left of the *Callisto* is, indeed, so far outside the canon of desirable beauty that Courbet might have hesitated to accept her. The crouching figure in the centre of the *Actaeon*, on the other hand, is one of the most seductive nudes in all painting, and was

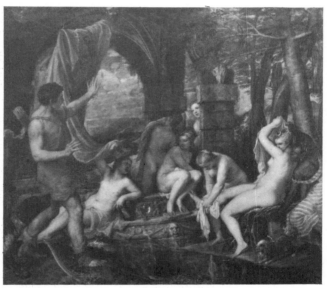

98. TITIAN. Diana and Actaeon

recognised as such by both Rubens and Watteau. This freedom of imagery is supported by an equal freedom of composition and handling. The forms are no longer evenly illuminated, but pass through cast shadows and reflected lights, and the paint is put on with large, broken touches of bright colour. This is the final mastery of execution which appears in the latest works of Rembrandt, Velasquez and Cézanne, and perhaps it was this feeling that at last his brush could do anything which led Titian to give free rein to his un-diminished sensuality. The controlling factor, even in such an eager approach, is still the technical medium. Thus Titian could maintain that balance between intense participation and absolute detachment which distinguishes art from other forms of human activity.

Contemporary with Titian and complementary to him was another great poet of the body, Correggio. The difference between them is like a difference of sex or the difference between day and night. Where Titian saw form like a full, frontal relief, Correggio saw it gliding into depth. Where Titian seems to place his figures before an open window with daylight falling directly on them, Correggio seems to place them in the penumbra of a curtained gallery where the light comes from several sources. We seize upon the mass of Titian's Venus immediately and abruptly ; Correggio's Antiope we caress [99]. This feeling of tenderness he achieves by the fellowship of line and shadow, which ultimately derives from Leonardo da Vinci. It was Leonardo who had advised the painter to penetrate the secrets of expression by looking at the faces of women in the mysterious illumination of twilight ; and it was he who had studied scientifically the passage of light round a sphere. The delicately perceived continuum of shadow and reflection in his diagrams had its own sensuous beauty even before it was transferred from geometric spheres to the soft irregular sphere of the breast. Moreover, light which passes gently along a form, be it an old wall, a landscape or a human body, produces an effect of physical enrichment not solely because of the fullness of texture which it reveals but because it seems to pass over the surface like a stroking hand. In Correggio's Antiope this effect is used with the greatest delicacy. As our eye follows every undulation it passes refreshed from shadow to light. The arm on which she rests her ecstatically sleeping head is clouded with shadows and reflections. Every form has the melting quality of a dream. This, of course, is achieved as much by linear movement as by chiaroscuro. Correggio was a natural lyricist who gave a flowing metre to everything he made, from the whole design down to the curve of a little finger. Here, too, he was influenced by Leonardo, and was perhaps the only artist who gained something from the oriental flexibility of the Leda. But those curves which in Leonardo have an alienating detachment—curves of marsh grass or of swirling water—become in Correggio warm and delicately human. They are, and have remained, the signature of feminine grace ; and although in the last century they have been vulgarised and shamefully exploited, when we meet them first they have the freshness of morning. No painter, as Mr. Berenson said long ago, was ever more penetrated by femininity, so that his most warlike saints are tender, his most venerable anchorites have the graceful gestures of a girl. Like Botticelli, he passed easily from Christian to pagan subjects, but whereas the earlier painter thought first of woman as the Madonna, with all her sorrows and apprehensions, and was persuaded by learned poets to transform her into Celestial Venus, Correggio thought of her as a tangible

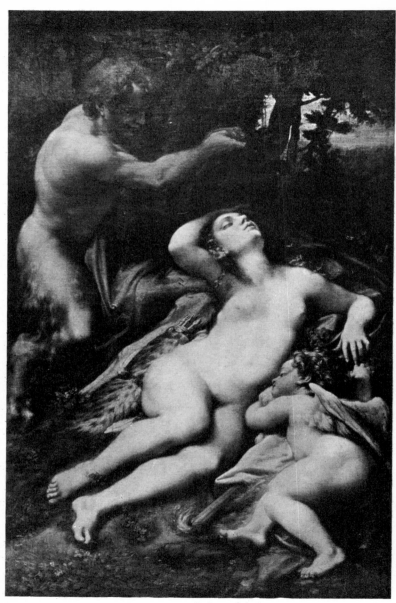

99. CORREGGIO. Jupiter and Antiope

human body and was happiest when the subject allowed him to show it un-draped and enjoying the amorous enterprises of Jupiter. We can be thankful that he did not live twenty years later when such subjects were generally prohibited.

Correggio's gentle character was devoid of pruriency. His nudes are the reverse of obscene. Nevertheless he has tried to make them as seductive as possible, and this has involved a relaxation of the classic norm and a removal, so to say, of the armour of geometry. The body of his Antiope is entirely feminine, small, warm and relaxed. The Danaë, prettier and less passionate, is incredibly *dix-huitième*, and late *dix-huitième* at that, for she is closer to Clodion than to Boucher [100]. The silvery light which passes with a kind of sub-aqueous tremor over her little body, models her breasts to a form which inspired both Prud'hon and Chasseriau, though neither ventured so far from the mould of antiquity. It is hard to believe that this charming creature, with her rococo complexity of movement and subtlety of expression, was painted earlier than Titian's Venus of Urbino ; even harder to think of Cor-reggio's Leda as almost contemporary with Michelangelo's heroic version of the same subject. It is composed with a freedom scarcely regained in the later Renoir and has a heedless gaiety which is not only contrary to the grandiose spirit of the high-Renaissance, but far away from that kind of animal earnestness with which antique art treated everything to do with sexual intercourse.

Between Correggio's invention of sheer prettiness and its reappearance in the 18th century, Venus underwent two further incarnations. The first may be for convenience labelled mannerism, a word which, however often it is mis-applied, cannot lose its association with a definite ideal of feminine beauty, with an unnatural length of limb, an impossible slenderness of body and a self-conscious elegance of bearing. In this scheme of proportions the classic norm is sometimes consciously rejected, and I therefore return to it in the chapter called the Alternative Convention, where I examine the Gothic nude. This is historically justifiable, for during the years of collapsing humanism Italian art borrowed shapes, subjects and actual figures from Germany and the Low Countries. But what we call mannerism has its origin in the ex-pressive distortions of Michelangelo to which, in the female nude, must be added the elegance of Parmigiano ; and both these physical schemes start from inside classic art. Michelangelo hardly became more contorted than the Laocoön, nor Parmigiano more elongated than the stucco reliefs of Hadrian's Villa and other late antique decorations from which his style must be derived. It is paradoxical that Michelangelo, who took so little pleasure in the female body, should have had an influence on the image of Venus. But his powers of formal invention so dominated his contemporaries that his poses reappear in unexpected contexts. An example is the Venus in Bronzino's Allegory of Passion, who seems to be the epitome of Medicean elegance, polished, slender and coolly lascivious [101]; yet her zigzag pose derives from that of Christ's dead body in the *Pietà* of the Duomo. Michelangelo himself gave a lead to such transformations when, to please the Duke of Ferrara, he used the pose of the Night as the basis of his cartoon for Leda. And the two female figures of the Medici Chapel continued, for half a century, to provide basic material for the decorative nudes of mannerism. The tapering limbs of the Dawn become longer and more streamlined, until the accidents of the flesh are almost forgotten, as in the nymph elegantly balanced on the edge of Ammanati's fountain in the Piazza della Signoria.

Nevertheless the embodiments of Venus in the sculpture of mid-16th-century Florence and Venice have hardly been surpassed in variety and grace. An equal mastery of human anatomy and of the antique convention gave to Italian sculptors of that date perfect freedom to approach and withdraw from

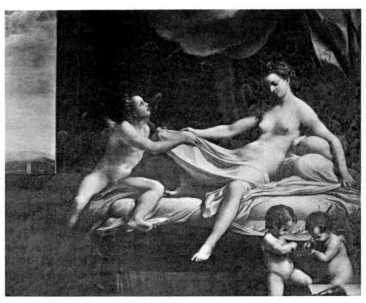

100. CORREGGIO. Danaë

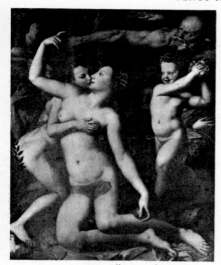

101. BRONZINO. Allegory of Passion
(*after cleaning*)

the facts of the body. In Venice the figures of Tiziano Aspetti or Gerolamo Campagna retain, on the whole, the large oval forms of Giorgione ; but in Florence the sculptors who worked for the Grand Dukes were more adventurous. Three bronzes from the Studiolo of Francesco I show their range. One, by Stoldo di Lorenzo, is almost Hellenistic in its proportions and easy-going sensuality ; another, by Ammanati, is more elongated, and shows a closer observation of the real body [102]. It is one of the most seductive nudes of the 16th century. In the third, by Calamecca, direct sensibility is almost excluded and in its place is a useful formula of elegance for the mass-produced nudes of mannerism.

More than once in this study I have emphasised how much formalisation the female body can undergo and still preserve some tremor of its first impact. The nudes of Giambologna are the most polished example of this survival. They are probably further from actuality than anything in antique art ; yet we accept them as the material of sculpture which, although it does not warm the heart, achieves its ends with remarkable assurance. The finality of such a figure as his Astronomy [103] led to hundreds of imitations, yet compared with the original they are all slightly awkward or amateurish. It is the last triumph of *disegno* in Italian art, and, perhaps inevitably, the work of a non-Italian. For Giambologna is not solely a stylist. He had a northern vigour, manifested also in his enormous output, which no formula could freeze, and a certain largeness of spirit which gives nobility even to his smallest bronze figurines. Perhaps no other living artist (for he lived till 1604) had so decisive an effect on Rubens' conception of the nude when, as a young man, he first visited Italy.

Mannerism spread to France in the first years of its evolution. Rosso, Primaticcio, Nicolo del Abate and Cellini found employment in Fontainebleau denied to them in their disrupted country, and, removed from the chastening influence of the classic tradition, they produced nudes of fantastic slenderness and elongation. Cellini's Nymph of Fontainebleau is so far from the antique canon of proportion that her legs alone are six heads long ; and yet Cellini, in his native Florence, had made for the base of the Perseus a figure of Danaë as neat and trim as any nude of the Renaissance. The fact that mannerism flourished so luxuriantly when transplanted is due partly to the latent Gothicism of French art, but also to the fact that, even in the middle ages, France had been the centre of *chic*. The goddess of mannerism is the eternal feminine of the fashion-plate. A sociologist could no doubt give ready answers why embodiments of elegance should take this somewhat ridiculous shape—feet and hands too fine for honest work, bodies too thin for child-bearing, and heads too small to contain a single thought. But elegant proportions may be found in many objects which are exempt from these materialist explanations—in archi-

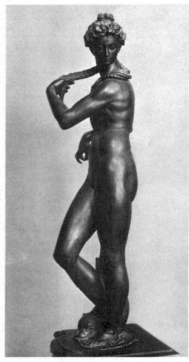

tecture, pottery or even handwriting. The human body is not the basis of these rhythms but their victim. Where the sense of *chic* originates, how it is controlled, by what inner pattern we unfailingly recognise it—all these are questions too large and too subtle for a parenthesis. One thing is certain : *chic* is not natural. Congreve's Millamant or Baudelaire's dandy warn us how hateful, to serious votaries of *chic*, is everything that is implied by the word 'nature'. So strictly speaking the exquisite ladies of Fontainebleau should not be classified with *Venus Naturalis*. Nor are they narrowly celestial, for in spite of their remoteness from ordinary experience they are calculated to arouse desire ; indeed their very strangeness of proportion seems to invite erotic fantasies for which the substantial bodies of Titian offer less opportunity.

But it is this lack of substance which, in the end, makes northern mannerism no more than a bewitching

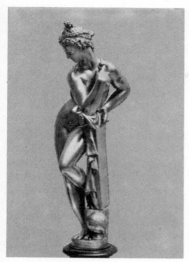

103. GIOVANNI DA BOLOGNA. Astronomy

by-way in the history of European art. However much we enjoy the seasoning of style, by the year 1600 we are in need of some more solid nourishment. In that year the Duke of Mantua engaged as court painter a young man from the north, Peter Paul Rubens.

We have reached the unchallenged master of *Venus Naturalis*, and all the familiar words stand ready to flow from the pen — gusto, exuberance, mastery of execution. But they are not enough. Why do we burn with indignation when we hear people who believe themselves to have good taste dismissing Rubens as a painter of fat naked women, and even applying the epithet 'vulgar'? What is it, in addition to sheer pictorial skill, that makes his nudes noble and life-giving creations?

The answer is partly in his character and partly in the discipline through which he mastered his profession. Both are evident if we compare him with the contemporary who seems at first sight to resemble him, Jacob Jordaens. There is indeed something amiable about Jordaens' hearty, farmyard approach to the body. It is at least easier and more natural than that of the post-Reformation Germans. But how stupid and grossly material his naked women appear if we put them beside the nudes of Rubens. Rubens, after all, was the greatest religious painter of his time, and in his splendidly unified character, sensuality could not be dissociated from praise.

> We thank Thee then, O Father,
>   For all things bright and good,
> The seed-time and the harvest,
>   Our life, our health, our food ;
> Accept the gifts we offer . . .

As we sing these words on a bright Sunday in September we may approach for a minute the spirit in which Rubens painted his pictures. The golden hair and swelling bosoms of his Graces are hymns of thanksgiving for abundance, and they are placed before us with the same unselfconscious piety as the sheaves

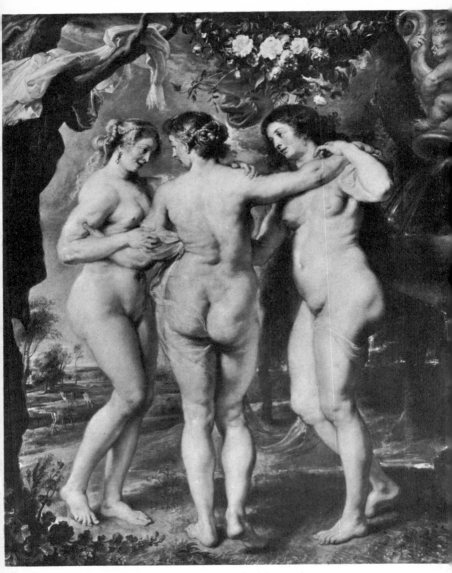

104. RUBENS. Three Graces

of corn and piled-up pumpkins which decorate a village church at Harvest Festival. Rubens never doubted that 'The spring of pure delight can never be defiled'. This is what gives an air of innocence to all his nudes, even when they are most conscious of their charms. They are a part of nature ; and they embody a view of nature more optimistic than that of the Greeks, for thunder and the treacherous sea, the capricious cruelty of Olympus, are absent. The worst that can happen is a surprise attack by satyrs and 'The lust of the goat is the Bounty of God'. In the 17th century the Triumph of the Sacrament, that subject to which Rubens gave so much of his time, was felt to coincide with a faith in natural order, and this gave an extraordinary wholeness to all phenomena. The human mind had begun to conceive a universe governed by beneficent cause and effect but had not yet subjected it to analysis. It was still expressible through personifications, that is to say, still within the grasp of popular understanding. This philosophy of participation was the background for the harmonious personality of Rubens. Few men can have been so free from pettiness or perversity, jealousy or frustration. His figures never pause to calculate material advantage or nurse an unacted desire. They have the sweetness of flowing water.

Not unconnected with his gratitude for God's bounty is Rubens' humble devotion to the art of design. No great painter has ever made such a prolonged, laborious and fruitful study of his predecessors' work. From antique cameos to Flemish primitives, from the tiny panels of Elsheimer to the vast canvases of the Venetians, Rubens copied everything which could conceivably add to his already overflowing resources. For the nude his models were, of course, the Antique, Michelangelo and Marcantonio. Titian he copied for his colour, but altered his form. From them he learnt what a severe formal discipline the naked body must undergo if it is to survive as art. Rubens' nudes seem at first sight to have been tumbled out of a cornucopia of abundance ; the more we study them the more we discover them to be under control. His procedure was that which has become the dogma of academies : he drew from the Antique and copied from his predecessors till certain ideals of formal completeness were absolutely fixed in his mind ; then when he drew from nature he instinctively subordinated the observed facts to the patterns established in his imagination. The average student cannot make a success of this procedure because accident is more attractive than substance. He seizes upon tricks of style, and overlooks essential structure. Rubens did the reverse. He gave to his learned reminiscences so much of his own peculiar style and his own responsiveness to nature that we are seldom conscious of his sources. An exception is a picture at Cassel, where the figure of Area is obviously taken from

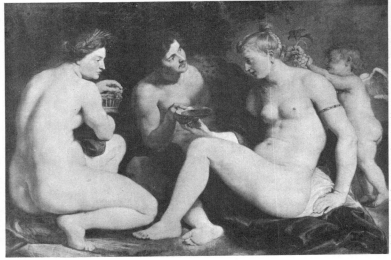

105. RUBENS. Venus and Area

the crouching Venus of Doidalsus and Venus from a memory of Michelangelo's Leda [105] ; but this, with its full, relief-like treatment, is the most classical of all Rubens' compositions. A few years later, when the same Michelangelesque motive is used in the Rape of the Daughters of Leucippus [106], it is assimilated into a baroque design. In fact the actual borrowings in Rubens' work are rare ; what is important is the evidence of formal discipline, demonstrable in his drawings and implicit in his paintings. But he knew that at a certain point the constraints of classic form could be abandoned. He made copies from those great liberations of the female nude, Titian's Diana pictures, and his own Diana and Callisto contains figures as freely drawn from nature, Diana herself squatting on the ground or the girl who leans forward with her elbows on the rim of a fountain. To the left of the same composition is a woman in a pose of exceptional beauty which reappears in several of his other works, in the Outbreak of War and in the Crowning of a Victorious Hero. With her hips still frontal she turns the upper part of her body violently to the left and her right arm is stretched across her breasts. She is the Bacchante whom we have already noticed on a sarcophagus in the Terme, and who must have existed in other reliefs in the 16th century. Naturally Rubens was attracted by her twist and sweep, by the large arc of her hip and shining expanse of her stomach ; and he has made her one of the most characteristic of all his figures. Since this is an unusually good example of his transformation of the classical body I may pause to ask what this change involves.

Rubens wished his figures to have weight. So did the men of the Renaissance, and they sought to achieve it by enclosed forms, which had the ideal solidity of the sphere or the cylinder. Rubens sought to achieve it by overlapping contours and rich internal modelling. In this way he hoped to gain a greater fullness and a more pervasive movement. Even if he had not felt a natural fondness for fat girls, he would have looked for accidents of the flesh

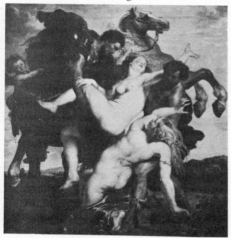

as necessary to his system of modelling. That suggestion of movement flowing across a torso, which, in the female body, antiquity had rendered by the device of clinging drapery, Rubens could reveal by the wrinkles and puckers of delicate skin, stretched or relaxed. Wölfflin in his masterly analysis of baroque form spoke of a change from a tactile to a painter-like, or visual, approach. But if the word tactile be allowed its normal meaning this definition cannot be applied to Rubens. He does not abandon the ideated sensation of

106. RUBENS. Rape of the Daughters of Leucippus

solidity confirmed by touch ; on the contrary he refines upon it by transferring it from the whole hand to the finger-tips. How intensely aware he was of the tactile sense is shown by his famous picture of Helena Fourment wrapping her naked body in a fur coat. The motive had been used already in a picture by Titian in the Hermitage. But the classical restraints which Titian exercised in painting the nude led him to suppress as accidental precisely that ideated sensation of texture which makes the contact of Helena Fourment's skin and her fur so stimulating.

The fact that Rubens was more concerned than his predecessors with the flesh and with the texture of the skin has sometimes been considered a symptom of superficiality. In European art there has always been a belief that the more a figure reveals its inner structure the more respectable it becomes. Perhaps

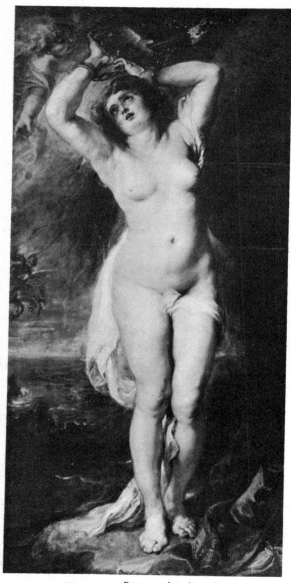

107. RUBENS. Perseus and Andromeda

there has been some confusion between physical and metaphysical terminology, and the word superficial has extended its meaning from thought to perception, reversing the mental process which leads up to Swift's famous defence of Delusion, 'Last week I saw a woman flayed, and you will hardly believe how much it altered her person for the worse'. But such speculations would have seemed meaningless to Rubens. He gave the solid form, the weight and movement of the body ; and in addition, inseparably, he gave that invigorating lustre, that brightness which even so grave a philosopher as St. Thomas Aquinas considered essential to his definition of beauty. It was an achievement demanding not only sensibility, but the highest technical skill. 'Mille peintres sont morts,' said Diderot, 'sans avoir senti la chair', and thousands more, we may add, have felt it, and not been able to render it. That strange substance, of a colour neither white nor pink, of a texture smooth yet variable, absorbing the light yet reflecting it, delicate yet resilient, flashing and fading, beautiful and pitiful by turns, presents surely the most difficult problem which the painter with sticky pigments and smearing brush has ever been called upon to solve ; and perhaps only three men, Titian, Rubens and Renoir, were sure how it should be done [107].

But in the end the greatness of Rubens does not lie in the realm of technique, but in that of imagination. He takes the female body, the plump, comfortable, clothed female body of the north, and transforms it imaginatively with less sacrifice of its carnal reality than had ever been necessary before. He creates a new, complete race of women. In this creation the face plays an important part. I have said already how determinant in any conception of the nude body is the character of the head which surmounts it. We look first at the face. It is through facial expression that every intimacy begins. This is true even of the classic nude, where the head often seems to be no more than an element in the geometry of the figure, and the expression is reduced to a minimum. In fact, try as we will to expunge all individuality in the interest of the whole, our responses to facial expression are so sensitive that the slightest accent gives a suggestion of mood or inner life. And so with the nude there is a double problem : the face must be subordinate, but it must not go by default, for inevitably it will colour our response to the body. The solution of this problem involves what is called 'creating a type'— of all forms of creation the most revealing of an artist's whole being. Rubens' women are both responsive and detached. To be so well favoured makes them happy, but not at all self-conscious, even when rejecting the advances of a satyr or accepting the apple of Paris. They are grateful for life, and their gratitude spreads all through their bodies.

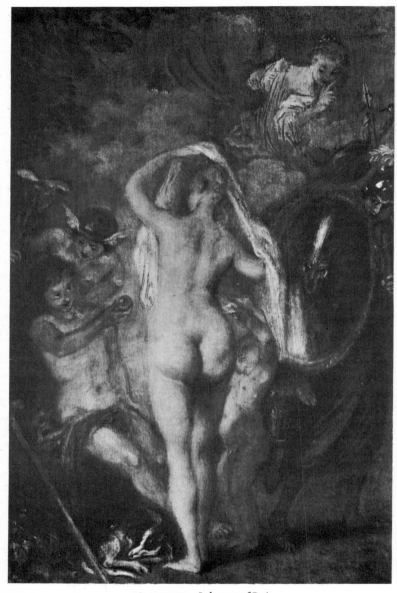

108. WATTEAU. Judgment of Paris

Rubens did for the female nude what Michelangelo had done for the male. He realised so fully its expressive possibilities that for the next century all those who were not the slaves of academism inherited his vision of the body as pearly and plump. It was the century of France, and French artists, from the illuminators of the 15th-century manuscripts onwards, had depicted the female body with a sharper sense of provocation than anything which we find in Italy. Round the Venuses or Dianas of the Fontainebleau School hangs a smell of stylish eroticism, impossible, like all smells, to describe, but strong as ambergris or musk. One reason is that a trace of Gothicism, with all that it implies of seductive guess-work, persists in their proportions. Up to the time of Lemoyne or even Houdon, the bodies of French goddesses retain the small breasts, long tapering limbs and slightly accented stomachs of the 16th century. To this tradition of quasi-Gothic elegance certain painters of the *dix-huitième*—Watteau above all—added Rubens' feeling for the colour and texture of skin. No painter has had a more sensitive eye for texture than Watteau, and the rarity of his nudes may even reflect a kind of shyness, born of too tremulous desire, which the spectacle of the living surface aroused in him. Perhaps the very unfrigid statues in his parks are telling us that he could only contain his excitement when the body was supposed to be of stone. The most beautiful of all his nudes, the Judgment of Paris in the Louvre [108], combines in one glowing vision the two traditions of French art, with its Venus as tall and tapering as a figure by Pillon, but displaying an area of flesh modelled with the fullness and delicacy of Rubens.

By the middle of the century slenderness has yielded to compactness and a new ideal of naked beauty has been established : the *petite*. The small, full, manageable body, which has always appealed to the average sensualist, is to be found in the less idealised minor arts of antiquity, and in certain *cassone* panels of the Italian Renaissance, notably in the David and Bathsheba of Franciabigio. Correggio's Leda made this kind of body more consciously seductive ; but the particular formalisation of this physical type which we associate with the *dix-huitième* seems to go back to the *Bassin des nymphes* of Girardon (himself a devoted student of Hellenistic art) and to have been perfected by François Boucher.

Both by nature and by the wish of his employers Boucher was a decorator, and decorators must be content with formulae. So Boucher was forced to reduce the female body to one serviceable type which appears in his compositions so frequently and with so even an accomplishment that we end by almost forgetting that she is a nude at all, and her body means little more to us than the clouds on which she floats. But in those works to which he could give individual attention, Boucher shows himself an eager and perceptive admirer of the body. Freshness of desire has seldom been more delicately expressed than by Miss O'Murphy's round young limbs, as they sprawl with undisguised satisfaction on the cushions of her sofa [109]. By art Boucher has enabled us to enjoy her with as little shame as she is enjoying herself. One false note and we should be embarrassingly back in the world of sin. The most artful of Boucher's nudes is the Diana in the Louvre [110], where not only the young body, with its fine wrists and ankles, but the graceful pose and the subtle reflected lighting combine to give an air of exaggerated refinement. We are reminded that Boucher's chief patron was Madame de Pompadour and that he was the willing servant of a civilisation in which women were in the ascendant. To this day a style derived from Boucher is considered appropriate for predominantly feminine establishments, coiffeurs and beauty parlours. He created the image which *Venus Naturalis* would like to see in the mirror, a magic reflection in which she ceases to be natural without ceasing to be desirable.

The Venus of the *dix-huitième* extends the range of the nude in one memorable way : far more frequently than any of her sisters, she shows us her back.

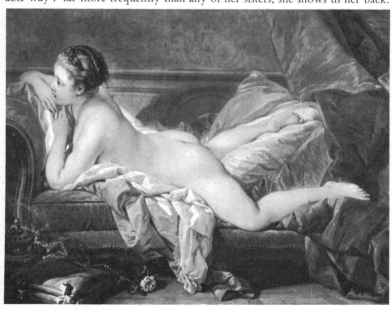

109. BOUCHER. Miss O'Murphy

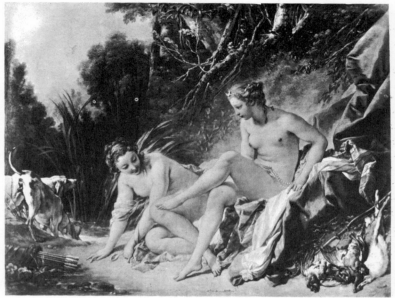

110. BOUCHER. Diana

Looked at simply as form, as relationship of plane and protuberance, it might be argued that the back view of the female body is more satisfactory than the front. That the beauty of this aspect was appreciated in antiquity we know from such a figure as the Venus of Syracuse. But the Hermaphrodite and the Venus Callipygas suggest that it was also considered symbolic of lust, and before the 18th century the number of female nudes depicted from behind solely on account of their plastic possibilities was remarkably small. A famous exception is the Rokeby Venus of Velasquez [1]; but that dispassionate work is outside all our preconceived notions of chronology, and seems closer to the *academies* of the 19th century than to the warmer images of Venus which precede and follow her. It might have been supposed that in this matter at least Velasquez had yielded to the influence of his great contemporary, but in fact the most beautiful of Rubens' goddesses are all frontal; only in the Three Graces in the Prado, and in some splendid drawings, does he show his appreciation of the other aspect [111]. Nevertheless it was Rubens who inspired both Watteau and Boucher. He was a master of the Baroque, and the bottom is a baroque form, harmonising with the clouds and garlands of late baroque decoration.

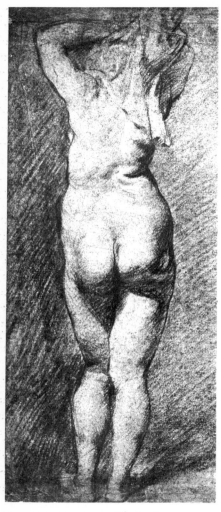

III. RUBENS. Life drawing

These decorative considerations certainly influenced Boucher and Fragonard when they so frequently depicted the nymphs of antiquity or the heroines of La Fontaine lying on their fronts, and leaning their elbows on a cushion or convenient cloud ; and we must also allow that the antique motive for this pose was not excluded, although conveyed with a lightness and finesse very different from the bestial frescoes of Pompeii.

The evolved formula of delicate nudity is not to be found in the painting of the *dix-huitième*, but in its sculpture, particularly in the small figures of terra-cotta or *biscuit de Sèvres* which we associate with the names of Clodion and Falconet. By Clodion Venus was observed with a more appreciative eye than by any other artist of the 18th century [112] ; Boucher himself had not so fine a sense of evocative accent. But both he and Falconet could suppress observation in favour of an ideal refinement, in which we surrender to politeness almost as much of our natural appetites as, in an earlier age, was surrendered to the spirituality of *Venus Coelestis*. As with the small bronzes of the Renaissance, we see how a theme can be civilised till its original impulse is lost in convention. At the close of the century the curious mixture of mannerism and

142

classicism, which was evolved by the painters of the Consulate—Boilly, Girodet and Prud'hon—added an inflection to our image of Venus. Prud'hon, by nature her sensitive votary, could combine, in his beautiful drawings of the model, classic wholeness of form with Correggiesque rapture.

The attempt to rescue Venus from her boudoir and restore to her some of the splendour of the Cnidian, an attempt for which Girodet had lacked the conviction and Prud'hon the stamina, was achieved by Ingres. 'Son libertinage est sérieux,' said Baudelaire, 'et plein de conviction. . . . Si l'île de Cythère commandait un tableau à M. Ingres, a coup sûr il ne serait pas folâtre comme celui de Watteau, mais robuste et nourrissant, comme l'amour antique.'

It is true that Ingres' response to the female body has a meridional earnestness, but this impulse was combined with a passion for form, or, to be more precise, with a need to externalise certain expressive shapes ; and his paintings are often no more than a sort of show-case in which to display those points where obsessive form and sensuality are brought into focus. In the Jupiter and Thetis, for example, the whole design is taken from two impoverished outlines by Flaxman, and the Jupiter is a piece of classical furniture ; but the figure of Thetis achieves a crescendo of sensual—we may even say sexual —excitement, starting with the outline of her body, which echoes so mysteriously that of the neophyte in the as yet undiscovered wall paintings of the Villa Item, following her swanlike neck and rising up her arm, boneless but disturbingly physical, till it culminates in her extraordinary hand, half octopus, half tropical flower. Ingres spent his whole life in an attempt to prize out of himself these nuggets of obsessive form ; and the intensity of this effort made him so narrow and obstinate as to seem unintelligent. But he recognised that he must reconcile his insatiable appetite for particularity with an ideal of classical beauty, and his greatness as a delineator of the nude could be described, in modern jargon, as a tension between the two. A contemporary critic made the same point more picturesquely when he referred to Ingres as 'un Chinois égaré dans les ruines d'Athènes'. The accusation of Gothicism, provoked by the work of his pre-Raphaelite phase, could still be applied to drawings of his Raphael-worshipping maturity, many of which show the accented details of northern form and even the morphological characteristics, small breasts and prominent stomachs, which in a later chapter I point out as characteristic of the Gothic nude. These observations made, as Baudelaire said, with the sharp, unprejudiced eye of a surgeon, were subservient to four or five formal ideas which came to him during his first years in Rome. They were his moments of inspiration, and he depended on them for the rest of his life. Like Titian, this great amateur of the female body knew that his excitement must be concentrated if it were to achieve finality ; and the number of his formal ideas which I have just given is meant to be taken literally.

Leaving out of account the beautiful but still experimental picture in the Bonnat Collection, the series opens with the so-called *Baigneuse de Valpinçon* (1808), a picture which fortunately he felt able to execute at the time of its conception [113]. Of all his works it is the most calmly satisfying and best exemplifies his notion of beauty as something large, simple and continuous, enclosed and amplified by an un-

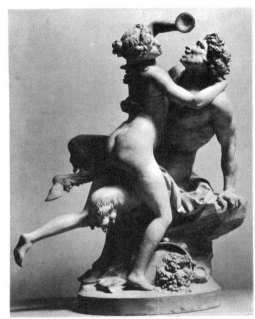

112. CLODION. Nymph and Satyr

broken outline. But in this instance the modelling suggested by the contour is supported by a passage of reflected light worthy of Correggio. Ingres never again attempted this naturalistic means, just as he never again felt satisfied by such a natural-looking pose. In fact the design of the *Baigneuse de Valpinçon* is of an inspired simplicity worthy of antique Greece. She speaks to us in the accents of fulfilment, and we are not surprised to find her reappearing in his work fifty-five years later. His other ideal presentations of the female body are more artificial, and, perhaps for this reason, were not carried out till long after the date of their conception. One of these is the standing figure who first appears in two pen drawings as a Venus Anadyomene. They suggest that in addition to the engraved backs of mirrors and other documents of antiquity, Ingres had been contemplating the Venus of Botticelli, and had there found confirmation for the sinuous embraces of his outline. How soon these drawings were used in the preparation of a painting we do not know. According to Charles Blanc, an unfinished painting of the subject existed as early as 1817, when Géricault saw it in Ingres' studio in Rome ; but for some reason it was carried no further, and the picture at Chantilly is dated 1848 [114]. The Botticellian line has been substantiated by a full Raphaelesque modelling, but in a few places, for example the outline of her left side, general-isation has become too dominant over particularity, and perhaps this is why eight years later the sight of his concierge's daughter, recalling his days in the via Gregoriana, set him to work on the *motif* again. It is said that already in 1820 he had thought of changing his Venus into a maiden with a pitcher of water. This was the version of his idea which in 1856 he decided to complete ; and the result was one of the most famous nudes in the history of art, *La Source*. Like the Medici Venus her fame has declined since Charles Blanc could call her, without fear of contradiction, the most beautiful figure in French painting ; and although we may still admire certain passages of drawing, the left hip, for example, or the relationship of the legs, we are put off by the softness of the actual execution ; and a generation which favours a sharper attack will prefer the clear accents of his earlier work. Of these the most uncompromisingly personal, and for this reason the least classical, is the *Grande Odalisque* of 1814 [115]. She could be claimed as the culminating work of the School of Fontainebleau, in which all that is approximate and provincial in the pupils of Primaticcio is at last given a metropolitan finality. Whereas *La Source* was the most immediately popular of his works, the *Grande Odalisque* was the most savagely criticised. It was discovered that she had two vertebrae too many, and in later years, when Ingres had made himself the high priest of academic orthodoxy, rebels and philistines united in repeating that she was out of drawing. In fact the drawings of which she is the culmination could be claimed as the most beautiful studies of the female nude ever executed, and show with what deliberation and sustained conviction Ingres had sought her peculiar pose.

The *Grande Odalisque* was painted as pendant to another reclining nude which had been purchased by Murat, King of Naples, in 1809. It was destroyed in the riots of 1815 and we have no certain record of its appearance, but, given Ingres' tenacity, we are probably right in assuming that the figure was in the pose repeated many years later in a series of pictures representing an Odalisque and her attendant. This idea certainly goes back to the first Roman period. It occurs in a drawing at Montauban inscribed *Maruccia, blonde, belle, via Margutta 116*. It is a pose of sinuous relaxation, which he felt he could justify by a setting in the Seraglio, although in fact the hand of Thetis shows us that the un-dulating contours of the east were a necessity to him, whatever their context. Purveyors of seduction were to repeat this pose throughout the 19th century, but without the archaic severity which Ingres was to impose on it. In the

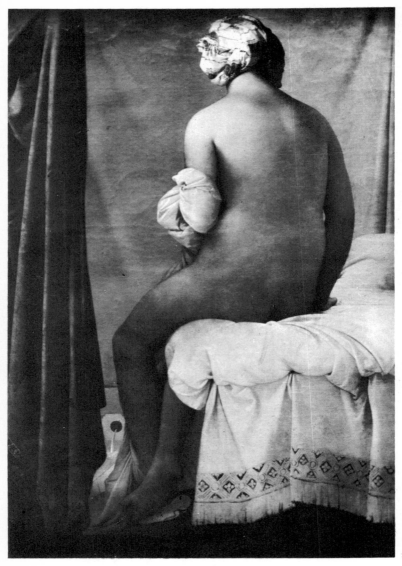

113. INGRES. *Baigneuse*

drawing of Maruccia we see him following, with breathless delight, every inflection of her beautiful body ; but when he used this study in the paintings (he executed two with his own hand, one dated 1839, the other 1842) the forms become weightier and more memorable. The hips and stomach approximate to comprehensible arcs, yet nothing is sacrificed of their physical splendour. It is a demonstration of his aesthetic beliefs which only the female nude could justify. Fifty years earlier Winckelmann had asserted that whereas the male nude might achieve character, the female nude alone could aspire to beauty : an assertion uninfluenced by personal preferences but by his theory that beauty consists in smoothness and continuity. It was largely because Ingres for so long dominated the centre of the academic system that this theory became reality, and naked women took the place of men as the models in art schools. Ingres could draw the male figure admirably, as he could everything else, but as a rule it bored him, and his studies of men lack that excited particularisation which sharpens the edge of his studies of women. A drawing in the Fogg Museum [116], done with even more than his usual diligence, shows a man and woman conceived in terms of their bodily contrast, very much as in Raphael's Adam and Eve ; but whereas in the Raphael the male figure is more naturalistic and more clearly seen, in the Ingres he is vapidly ideal, a composite memory of Praxitelean originals. The woman's body on the other hand, in spite of her conventional pose, is observed with almost embarrassing attention.

The drawing is one of the many hundreds of studies made for L' Âge d'or, the great mural painting at the Château de Dampierre, on which he was at work from 1840 to 1848. It consists entirely of nudes—what Ingres called 'un tas de beaux paresseux'—dancing, embracing, reclining and being joined in pagan matrimony. Many reasons, material and technical, have been given why the work is incomplete and, on the whole, unsuccessful ; and no doubt one of them is that Ingres' concentrated programme had not taught him to organise so large a space. But another reason is that these nude figures, beautifully observed though they are, do not come from the centre. They are the result of experiences, but they are not ideas.

On one of the notes for L'Âge d'or Ingres has written : 'One must not dwell too much on the details of the human body ; the members must be, so to speak, like shafts of columns : such they are in the greatest masters'. It is touching to find Ingres, at the height of his fame, warning himself against his own gifts ; and of course the advice was not—could not be—accepted. He continued to dwell on details and his figures, far from being like the columns of antique Greece, come more and more to resemble the temple sculpture of Southern India.

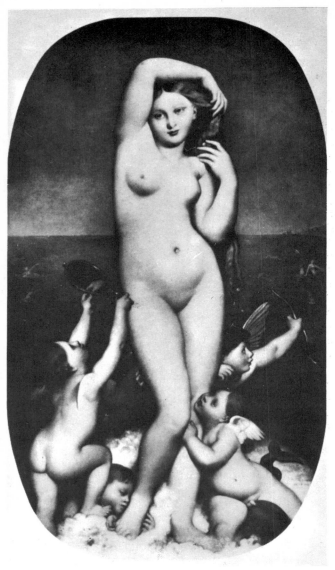

114. INGRES. Venus Anadyomene

The final expression of this Orientalism is the *Bain Turc* [117]. It is dated 1862, and Ingres, with justifiable pride, has added to his signature his age : Aetatis LXXXII. Like his fellow octogenarian in the Diana and Actaeon he has at last felt free to release his feelings, and all that was implied in the hand of Thetis or the sole of the Odalisque's foot is now openly attributed to thighs, breasts and luxurious *déhanchements*. The result is almost suffocating ; but in the middle of this whirlpool of carnality is his old symbol of peaceful fulfilment, the back of the *Baigneuse de Valpinçon*. Without her tranquil form the whole composition might have made us feel slightly sea-sick. The two reclining figures on the right are in attitudes of relaxed sensuality unparalleled in western art, and at the first glance we participate in their languor and satiety ; but after a minute we become aware of a design so densely organised that we derive from it the same intellectual satisfaction as is provided by Poussin and Picasso. Even in this moment of abandonment he still keeps his feet—*je suis solide sur mes ergots*—on the basis of ideal form.

The decade in which the *Bain Turc* was painted may be reckoned the high-water mark of 19th-century prudery, and perhaps only Monsieur Ingres, the 'petit éléphant bourgeois', with his seat in the Academy, his frock-coat and his absurdly orthodox opinions, could have persuaded public opinion to accept so open an evocation of eroticism. One can imagine what howls of outraged modesty it would have produced if it had been a work of the opposite school. Only one year later public and critics were screaming with horror at the nude in Manet's *Déjeuner sur l'herbe*, unaware that her outlines were taken direct from Raphael. That fear of the body which is usually called Victorian is a subject worthy of more disinterested examination than it has yet received. Unlike the scruples of the early Christians it had no religious motive and was not connected with a cult of chastity. Rather it seems to have been a necessary part of that enormous façade behind which the social revolution of the 19th century could adjust itself. The unwritten code of physical respectability which was then produced seems at first to be full of inconsistencies, but analysis proves it to have had one overriding aim, the calculated avoidance of reality : thus it was possible to fill a conservatory with nude figures in Carrara marble, although the mention of an ankle was held to be a gross indecency. The Crystal Palace contained a forest of marble nudes, but only one of them, Hiram Power's Captive Slave, caused a scandal, not because of her body, which was a blameless pastiche on the Cnidian Venus, but because her wrists were handcuffed. Stylistically the basis of these figures was the mannered classicism of Canova, from which a mechanical execution had removed the last tremors of excitement. Easier to get with child a mandrake root than consider the

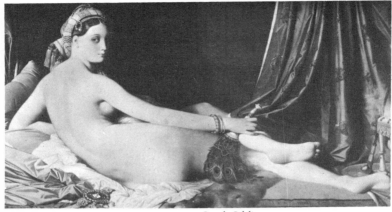

115. INGRES. *La Grande Odalisque*

marble Venuses of the Victorians as objects of desire. And yet so magical had been the first creation of the Cnidian that her insignificant progeny was considered a respectful form of furniture while the impulse which had brought her into existence was condemned.

The nude survived the great frost of Victorian prudery, partly owing to the prestige of classical art, never higher than in the first quarter of the 19th century, and partly to the system of academic instruction known as 'drawing from the life'. Even in England this was permitted and produced at least one modest but resolute devotee of Venus, William Etty. His daily visits to the life class did not escape censure—'I have been accused', said the poor fellow, 'of being a shocking and immoral man'—but a long series of nude studies, painted with obvious enjoyment, prove that he was undeterred. Etty was one of those who, in Diderot's words, *ont senti la chair*, and he might have been a considerable artist if he had known how to make his studies into finished pictures. But he lacked the imagination to use them in his compositions without surrendering their truthfulness, and he was too humbly the servant of his times to offer direct transcriptions of the body for their own sakes. To do so required the gargantuan self-confidence of Courbet.

Like all revolutionary realists, from Caravaggio onwards, Courbet was far more tied to tradition than he admitted, or than his critics, confused by the cataract of his talk, could recognise. His nudes are often little more than life studies and when he tries to give them the additional lustre of art, as in the *Femme au perroquet*, the result is as artificial in conception as the vulgarest salon favourite. The obvious way in which he asserted his realism was by indulging his preference for heavily built models. One of these, the *Baigneuse* of 1853, was intended to provoke and succeeded imperially, for Napoleon III struck at her with his riding crop. She is, in fact, the only one of his nudes whose proportions are far outside the contemporary canons of comeliness, as we know them from the life studies of other artists and from early photographs ; and even she is in a pose which reeks of the art school. How natural, compared to her, is the *Baigneuse* of Ingres ! When all this is conceded, however, Courbet remains an heroic figure in the history of the nude. His doctrine of realism, poor stuff when put into words but magnificent when expressed in paint, was the overflow of a colossal appetite for the substantial. In so far as the popular test of reality is that which you can touch, Courbet is the archrealist whose own impulse to grasp, to thump, to squeeze or to eat was so strong that it communicates itself in every stroke of his palette-knife. His eye embraced the female body with the same enthusiasm that it stroked a deer, grasped an apple or slapped the side of an enormous trout. Such thoroughgoing sensuality has about it a kind of animal grandeur, and there are paintings in which Courbet achieves comfortably and with hardly a trace of defiance that conquest of shame which D. H. Lawrence attempted in prose. A solid weight of flesh does in fact seem more real and enduring than elegance, and the woman who stands beside him at the centre of his realised dream, that vast canvas known as *L'Atelier du peintre* [118], although she has the patient carnality of the life class, is, after all, more representative of humanity than the Diana of Boucher.

Nor is this effect due solely to the body. It is, above all, in his faces that we realise how far Etty falls short of Courbet, for on bodies of ageless health he places heads of fashionable coyness ; whereas the bovine unselfconsciousness of Courbet's women gives them a kind of antique nobility.

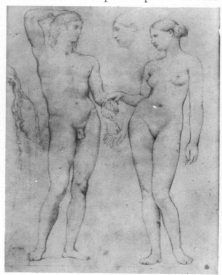

116. INGRES. Study for *L'Âge d'or*

To justify the epithet heroic, which I have just applied to him, one must look for those representations of the subject which during Courbet's lifetime and for another forty years won official favour in the Salon. They are not easily found, for the paintings of Ary Scheffer, Cabanel, Bouguereau and Henner are no longer exhibited in public galleries, and must be sought in provincial *mairies* or the saloons of mid-western hotels. Each of these artists had his

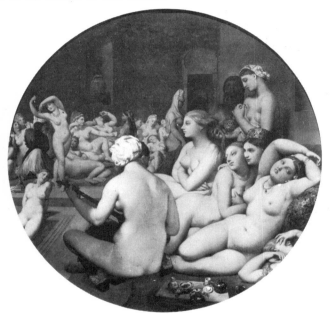

117. INGRES. *Le Bain Turc*

own recipe for success, ranging from the lubricity of Bouguereau to the high-minded sexlessness of Lord Leighton ; but all had one characteristic in common ; they glossed over the facts. They employed the same convention of smoothed-out form and waxen surface ; and they represented the body as existing solely in twilit groves or marble swimming baths. It was this grateful acceptance of unreality in both texture and circumstance which was to receive so painful a shock from the Olympia of Manet [119].

The Olympia is painted in the style of the young Caravaggio, with a more sensitive feeling for paint; but this alone would not have annoyed the amateurs,

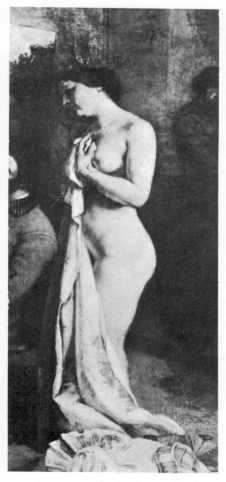

118. COURBET. *L'Atelier du peintre* (detail)

and no doubt the true reason for their indignation was that for almost the first time since the Renaissance a painting of the nude represented a real woman in probable surroundings. Courbet's women were professional models, and although their bodies were painted from nature, they were usually placed by woodland springs in the accepted convention. The Olympia is a portrait of an individual, whose interesting but sharply characteristic body is placed exactly where one would expect to find it. Amateurs were thus suddenly reminded of the circumstances under which actual nudity was familiar to them, and their embarrassment is understandable. Although no longer shocking, the Olympia remains exceptional. To place on a naked body a head with so much individual character is to jeopardise the whole premise of the nude, and Manet succeeds only because of his perfect tact and skill as a painter. He himself may have felt that so delicate a feat of balance could not be repeated, for he never again chose the female nude as the subject of his principal works. But he had shown that in spite of its long degradation the subject could be saved for the living art of the time, and two painters followed him in protesting against the falsity of salon nudes. The first was Degas who as a young man had done drawings of the female model as beautiful as those of Ingres, and yet realised that this

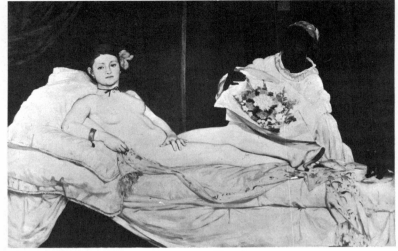

119. MANET. Olympia

kind of beauty was, for the time being, fatally compromised. The second was Toulouse-Lautrec whose revulsion from the hypocritical rotundities of Henner was even sharper, and whose quick eye noted with satisfaction precisely those accents and excrescences of the female body which the salon favourites had been at pains to suppress. His vivid notations of the naked gain in force precisely because at the back of his mind and ours is the concept of the nude, and our faculties are heightened by a reminder of how otiose this concept had become.

By 1881 it might have seemed that Venus had suffered the fate of Apollo ; that she had been cheapened, falsified and fragmented, so that between the frigid constructions of academicians and the vulgar provocations of the *Vie parisienne* she would never again dominate the imagination in her radiant entirety. In that year Renoir, who was forty years old, took his wife on a honeymoon to Rome and Naples.

Everyone who writes about Renoir refers to his adoration of the female body, and quotes one of his sayings to the effect that without it he would scarcely have become a painter. The reader must therefore be reminded that until his fortieth year his pictures of the nude are few and far between. The first to achieve celebrity was the *Baigneuse au griffon*, now in the Museum of S. Paulo [120]. It was exhibited in the Salon of 1870 and won for Renoir the only

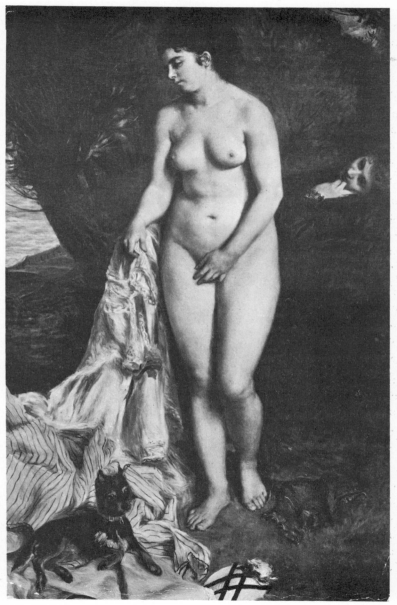

120. RENOIR. *Baigneuse au griffon*

popular success he was to enjoy for twenty years. With his usual simplicity he took no pains to conceal the origins of his composition. The pose is taken from an engraving of the Cnidian Venus, the lighting and way of seeing are derived from Courbet. These contrary sources indicate the problems which were to occupy him for half his life ; how to give the female body that character of wholeness and order which was the discovery of the Greeks and combine such order with a feeling for its warm reality. In the *Baigneuse au griffon*, admirable as it is, the two components are not yet united. The antique pose is too obvious and the earthiness of Courbet's style does not express Renoir's own sunny temperament.

We may suppose that Renoir would have corrected these inconsistencies immediately had it not been that during the next ten years he became absorbed in the theories of Impressionism. Now Impressionism in its first, doctrinaire condition could not easily accept a subject which was both artificial and formal. The nude being a kind of ideal art is closely connected with that first projection of an idea, the outline ; and during the '70's the Impressionists, Renoir amongst them, were at pains to demonstrate that the outline does not exist. When he painted the figure he broke up its contours by dappling them with patches of light and shadow. But even in these years his instinctive understanding of the European tradition showed him how the great Venetians had rendered form through colour and he painted two nudes, the Anna in Moscow and the Torso in the Barnes Collection, which might almost be details from Titian's Diana and Actaeon. In these the outline is minimised by overlapping forms and by the broken tones of the background, but the modelling is solid, and there seems to be no reason why Renoir should not have continued to paint a series of masterpieces in this manner. However, it did not satisfy his conviction that the nude must be simple and sculptural, like a column or an egg, and by 1881, when he had exhausted the possibilities of Impressionism, he began to look for an example on which such a conception of the nude would be based. He found it in Raphael's frescoes in the Farnesina and in the antique decorations from Pompeii and Herculaneum. The immediate result was a picture of his wife known as the *Baigneuse blonde* [121], painted at Sorrento towards the end of the year, in which her body, pale and simple as a pearl, stands out against her apricot hair and the dark Mediterranean sea as firmly as in a painting of antiquity. Like Raphael's Galatea and Titian's Venus Anadyomene, the *Baigneuse blonde* gives us the illusion that we are looking through some magic glass at one of the lost masterpieces extolled by Pliny, and we realise once more that classicism is not achieved by following rules—for young Madame Renoir's measurements are far removed from those of the

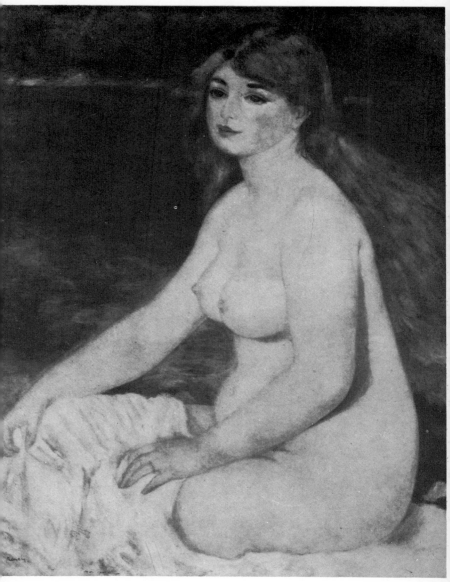

121. RENOIR. *La Baigneuse blonde*

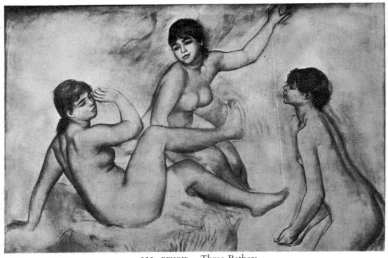

122. RENOIR. Three Bathers

Cnidian—but by acceptance of the physical life as capable of its own tranquil nobility.

The moment of revelation which inspired the *Baigneuse blonde* did not survive Renoir's return to France, and for the next three years he continued to struggle with the problems which he had solved by instinct beside the bay of Naples. To concentrate his forces he undertook a masterpiece, a composition of girls bathing, which should have all the qualities of classic French art from Goujon to Ingres. The general movement and some of the poses were inspired by a relief on Girardon's Fountain of the Nymphs at Versailles and throughout the many studies for the finished picture this sculptural conception persists. It is most marked in a large drawing, a cartoon worthy of the Renaissance [122], where the sense of relief and the flow of line are so perfectly satisfying that I cannot conceive why Renoir should have altered them ; yet in the finished picture every interval is worked out afresh. The execution is equally deliberate and although the tonality recalls Boucher, the use of paint has none of his decorative ease. In certain lights it almost seems as if the painstaking enamel of the surface has killed the first sensation of delight ; but a passing cloud or an unexpected reflection will soften those dry transitions so that the whole picture flatters the eye like a Gobelins tapestry.

The *Grandes Baigneuses* occupied Renoir from 1885 to 1887, and whether we consider it a masterpiece or a prodigious exercise of will, it liberated him from his anxieties. In the next twenty years his nudes still show to the perceptive eye evidence of labour and calculation, but it is artfully concealed. These charming creatures sit by the banks of streams, dry themselves or splash each other with an appearance of perfect naturalness and spontaneity. They are somewhat plumper than the classical norm and have an air of Arcadian health. Unlike the models of Rubens, their skin never has the creases and puckers of a body which is normally clothed, but fits them closely, like an animal's coat. In the unselfconscious acceptance of their nudity they are perhaps more Greek than any nudes painted since the Renaissance, and come closest to attaining the antique balance between truth and the ideal.

We know that Renoir, like Praxiteles, was dependent on his models. Madame Renoir complained that the maids had to be chosen because 'their skin took the light well', and at the end of his life, crippled and bereaved, it was the sight of a new model that gave him the impetus to start painting again. But to write of Renoir's nudes as if they were ripe peaches which he had only to stretch out a hand and pluck from the wall is to forget his long struggle with the classic style, a struggle which continued after the victory of 1887. Not only Boucher and Clodion, but Raphael and even Michelangelo are drawn upon ; and above all he studied antique Greece. Memories of Pompeii and the occasional sight of bronzes and terra-cottas in the Louvre lead him away from the official classicism of the cast room to the long, pear-shaped body of Alexandrian Hellenism. In these minor arts the nude, although still achieving the oneness of antiquity, had not been deadened by centuries of imitation, and no doubt their flavour of popular naturalism—their touch of Vegetable Venus —also appealed to him. The earliest example of this proportion known to me is the etching of a Venus Anadyomene which serves as frontispiece to the 1891 edition of Mallarmé's *Pages* ; but in general these Alexandrian figures belong to the period after 1900 when they are often combined in scenes of antique mythology, in particular the Judgment of Paris, wonderfully revived. In these years we watch Renoir gradually abandoning the fair, round girls who had won him popularity and creating a new race of women, massive, ruddy, unseductive but with the weight and unity of great sculpture [123]. Indeed it is as a piece of sculpture that Renoir's Venus achieves her most complete form, and by a strange paradox this master of oil paint has had little influence on subsequent painting, but a decisive influence on modern sculpture.

The series of nudes produced by Renoir between 1885 and his death in 1919, one of the most satisfying tributes ever paid to Venus by a great artist, knits together all the threads in this long chapter. Praxiteles and Giorgione, Rubens

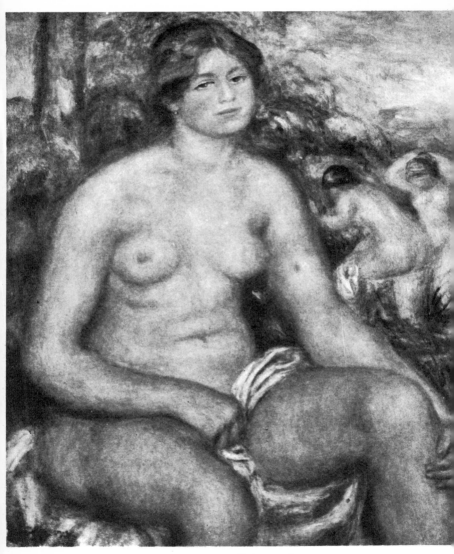

123. RENOIR.   Bather seated

and Ingres, different as they are from one another, would all have recognised him as their successor. Like him they would probably have spoken about their works as if they were simply the skilled representation of exceptionally beautiful individuals. That is the way that artists should speak. But in fact all of them were looking for something which had grown up in their minds from a confluence of memories, needs and beliefs : the memories of earlier works of art, the needs of their personal sensibilities and the belief that the female body was the token of a harmonious order. They looked with such eagerness at *Venus Naturalis* because they had caught a glimpse of her inaccessible twin sister.

CHAPTER V

Energy

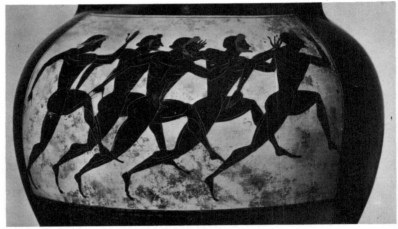

124. Pan-Athenaic amphora.   6th cent. B.C.

ENERGY is eternal delight ; and from the earliest times human beings have tried to imprison it in some durable hieroglyphic. It is perhaps the first of all the subjects of art. But the astonishing representations of energy in prehistoric painting are all concerned with animals. There are no men on the walls at Altamira, only a few wretched puppets at Lascaux ; and even on such evolved works as the Vaphio cups the men are insignificant compared to the stupendous bulls. These early artists considered the human body, that forked radish, that defenceless starfish, a poor vehicle for the expression of energy, compared to the muscle-rippling bull and the streamlined antelope. Once more it was the Greeks, by their idealisation of man, who turned the human body into an incarnation of energy, to us the most satisfying of all, for although it can never attain the uninhibited physical flow of the animal, its movements concern us more closely. Through art we can relive them in our own bodies, and achieve thereby that enhanced vitality which all thinkers on art, from Goethe to Berenson, have recognised as one of the chief sources of aesthetic pleasure.

The Greeks discovered in the nude two embodiments of energy, which lived on throughout European art almost until our own day. They are the athlete and the hero ; and from the beginning they were closely connected with one another. The divinities of other early religions were static, and everything that surrounded their worship was stiff and still ; but from Homeric times the gods and heroes of Greece proudly displayed their physical energy, and demanded such display from their devotees. Something of the sort had already appeared in the mysterious culture of Minoan Crete. We have hints of acrobatic dances, and famous representations of bull-vaulting. But how far this tradition of ritual athletics was carried on into the Hellenic world we cannot say. We only know that in the legendary beginnings of Greece Hercules is said to have founded the games at Olympia, and that in 776 B.C. the historical Olympiads were begun. Local festivals followed, and by the middle of the 6th century there was a four-yearly contest at Athens, which grew in fame as Athens became more evidently the political centre of Greece. At these games it was customary to present the winners with large jars, on which were painted representations of the branch of sport at which they had excelled : and from these vase paintings begins the long history of the nude in action [124], which stretches to the dancers of Degas. At first it is not graceful action. The early Greek convention for the active body, with its large arcs for hips, thigh and calf, does not promote what we have come to call physical beauty. Moreover, the athletes who raced and wrestled on the Athenian palestra were, in the 6th century, of ungainly build. The wrestlers were strong men, Homeric heroes hugging one another like bears. The runners had high shoulders, wasp-waists and swollen thighs. But they bound along with an elastic rhythm, more invigorating than the correct proportions of the next century, and we see for the first time what will recur at every turn in this chapter, that movement cannot be realised in art without some degree of distortion.

These prize pots, or, to give them their official title, pan-Athenaic amphorae, in spite of their vigorous directness have about them an element of mass-production ; but at the end of the 6th century we find the hand of an individual artist in the graceful reliefs of games players, formerly the base of a statue, in the National Museum of Athens [125]. The element of brute strength has diminished. These young men are still conspicuously muscular, but their bodies are neat and compact : how neat we can tell by comparing them to an engraving of nude men fighting by Antonio Pollajuolo [126]. For all their vigour, the Florentine nudes look gnarled and uncouth beside the stylish compactness of the Greek athletes. Pollajuolo comes first to mind as a term of comparison since he has used very much the same means to convey the sense of movement through the body. He was a student of Greek pottery, and his dancing figures in the Torre del Gallo are taken from Etruscan red-figure vases. But the resemblance goes deeper than mere imitation. There is the same rhythmic sense of interval between the figures, the same taut outlines and shallow internal modelling. Low relief, that beautiful frontier between drawing and sculpture, has always been well suited to the expression of movement precisely because it still operates through suggestion, and not through full statement. The moment a naked body in movement is put before us in its solid entirety problems arise which might seem almost insoluble by an intellectual approach.

The figures from the pediment of the Temple of Aegina illustrate this. Considering that they are almost the largest complex of sculpture to have survived from a period of Greek art—480 to 470 B.C.—to which we look with particular eagerness, how disappointing they are. They lack precisely that vitality which we should expect in the young conquerors of Salamis, and which their earlier admirers, dazzled by the literary sources, fancied that they could perceive in them. In part this is due to restoration, for in adding extremities the whole surface seems to have been rubbed down ; and probably they were always of provincial workmanship. But beyond this was the dilemma which faced Greek art throughout the 5th century ; how to achieve unity without sacrificing the geometrical clarity of the individual forms. It might have been possible, in decorative sculpture, to suggest movement by carrying on the lines of impetus from one figure to another. But this the

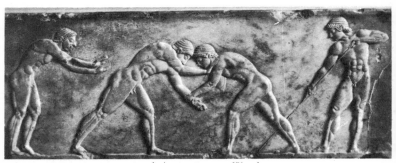

125. Attic. c. 480 B.C. Wrestlers

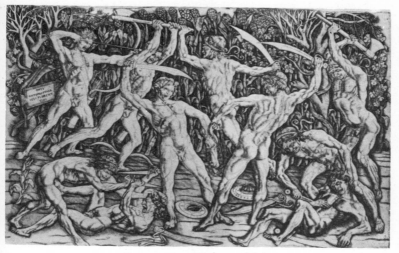

126. POLLAJUOLO. Nude men fighting

Greeks at first were reluctant to do. It is true that the figures at Aegina can be arranged in some credible relation to each other, but each remains enclosed within its outline. They seem to have been frozen, or suddenly forbidden to move, as in a children's game. Even when action is expressed in a single figure, and this was certainly achieved within a decade of its emergence in decorative groups, the same inhibition takes effect. The bearded god casting a thunderbolt, found in the sea off Histiaea, is almost the first single figure in action, and the only one to come down to us in its original bronze [127]. He is grand, commanding, authentic, and we may ask ourselves why, in the end, he is not completely satisfying. The answer is, surely, that the life-communicating power of movement is almost entirely absent. By his determination to preserve a geometrical point of balance in the centre of the figure, the Greek sculptor has made us more than ever conscious how plastically inconvenient is the human body. What can be done with those long attachments to the torso? Time usually answered that question; but there is another solution, which is to integrate them with the central mass by carrying their movement through the torso; and this is what the Zeus of Histiaea lacks. His torso is static, and if we had found it alone we should not have had the least indication of the attitude of the original. The sense of rhythmic life transforming the whole, which animates the drawings and reliefs of the 6th century, has been

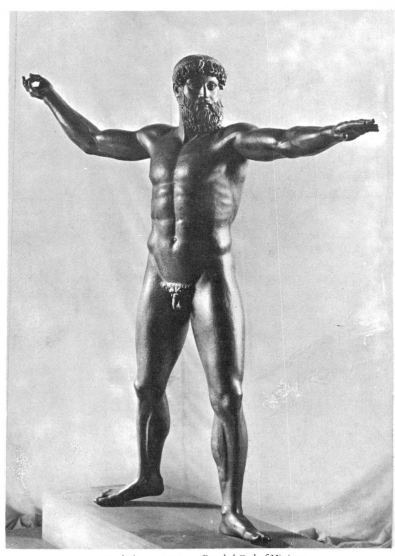

127. Attic. *c.* 470 B.C. Bearded God of Histiaea

sacrificed to a clear definition of individual parts. Sometimes, as in the metopes of the Parthenon, this mania for preserving each part of the body as a perfect entity has an almost comical effect. The Lapith who is being throttled by a centaur remains as stiff, erect and expressionless as a guardsman on parade [128]. This treatment of the body in (so to say) water-tight compartments is not due to a defect in skill or observation, but is part of that strange conformation of the Attic mind which demanded that all phenomena should be related to reasonable certainties.

Of all efforts to reconcile the body in action with geometrical perfection the most famous is the Discobolos of Myron [129], and even allowing for pre-cursors now lost, it remains one of those inexplicable leaps by which genius has advanced the range of human achievement. By sheer intelligence Myron has created the enduring pattern of athletic energy. He has taken a moment of action so transitory that students of athletics still debate if it is feasible and he has given it the completeness of a cameo. As with the Doryphoros of Poly-clitus this has involved a high degree of artificiality. The two problems were complementary. Polyclitus wished to represent a figure in repose which was poised for action ; Myron a figure in action which was balanced in equilibrium. As a sculptor he was attempting a more difficult task, for there is apt to be something painfully finite about a solid figure in arrested action. A body in lively repose is, as the French say, *disponible* : it may do anything. Whereas a moment of action must be absolutely fixed ; the next second the body will have escaped from the sculptural idea. Often to solve the problem at all is to solve it too completely, and to destroy that feeling of infinite possibility which the greatest works of art transmit. Rodin maintained that the only solution was to combine in one pose two different phases of the same con-tinuous movement, and the fact that students of athletics have found it so hard to interpret the action of the Discobolos suggests that this is what Myron has done.

This body, tense as a drawn bow, is in its totality like some Euclidean diagram of energy ; and within this main figure the disposition of the parts has a clarity and logic which only become apparent after comparison with all subsequent efforts of the same kind. To a modern eye it may seem that Myron's desire for perfection has made him suppress too rigorously the sense of strain in the individual muscles ; or, at least, has not given his interior modelling the rhythmic flexibility which would carry through the movement of the whole. But, in fact, the torso [130] is far from the rigid isolationism of the Parthenon metopes ; and if we object to his restraint and compression we are simply objecting to the classicism of classic art. A violent emphasis or a

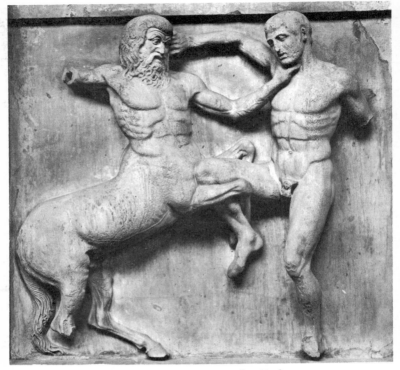

128. Attic. *c.* 440 B.C. Metope from Parthenon

sudden acceleration of rhythmic movement would have destroyed those qualities of balance and completeness through which it retained till the present century its position of authority in the restricted repertoire of visual images. What seems at first like deadness is, in fact, a means of conserving life. Compared to one of Michelangelo's athletes in the Sistine [131], and the comparison is not unfair, for Myron's sculpture is conceived so predominantly from one point of view as to be almost the equivalent of a drawing, the Greek figure looks almost too economical. Every form has been constrained to its bare essentials by the double pressure of Greek athletics and the Euclidean idealism.

Perfection closes the door. By their perfection Raphael's Madonnas deprived classic painting of a favourite subject ; perhaps Degas has done the same for ballet dancers. And this is particularly true of the representation of movement where, as I have said, any adequate solution seems to be exclusive, and becomes as fixed as a hieroglyphic. As a result, few single nude figures in violent action have come down to us from antiquity. Most of those which we know—the Youth of Subiaco, the so-called Iloneus, the bronze runner from Herculaneum—probably formed parts of groups : the idea of movement being more naturally communicable when it can be handed on from one figure to another. It must be admitted that these Hellenistic representations of athletes are surprisingly devoid of energy. Ideal beauty and high finish, two characteristics of later Greek sculpture, do not help to communicate aesthetic vitality. And beyond this stylistic impediment was a social one. By the end of the 4th century the religious earnestness of Greek athletics had given place to professional entertainment. The boy athlete had become a sentimental memory, and in sculpture his body assumed the curious smoothness characteristic of an art which aims at entertainment and self-preservation, the art of commercialised academies. Perhaps an exception should be made for a work once famous, and now unfairly neglected : The Wrestlers in the Uffizi [132]. If we can bring our eyes to rest on the unpleasant surface of a somewhat lifeless replica we discover that the original must have been a Lysippic bronze of masterly complexity and condensation.

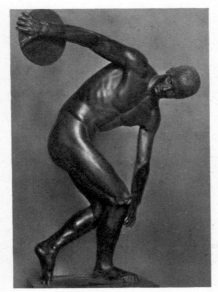

129. After Myron. *c.* 450 B.C. Discobolos (reconstruction)

In the rigorous nudity of the male athlete Myron and his successors had deprived themselves of the chief aid to the representation of movement which art has to offer : the rhythmic line of drapery. Clinging drapery, following a plane or a contour, emphasises the stretch or twist of the body ; floating drapery makes visible the line of movement through which it has just passed. Thus the aesthetic limitation of the nude body in action, that it is enclosed

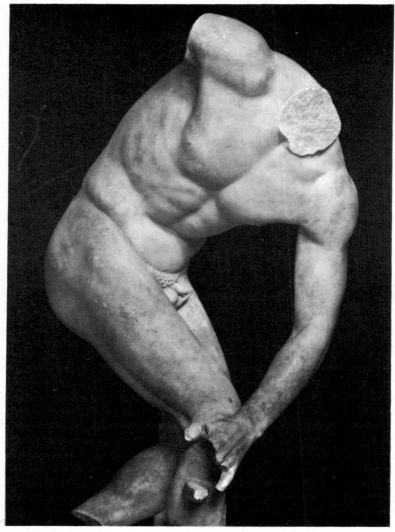

130. After Myron. *c.* 450 B.C. Discobolos of Castel Porziano

within an immediate present, is overcome. Drapery, by suggesting lines of force, indicates for each action a past and a possible future.

The Greeks at an early date used clinging drapery to enhance the female nude. When did they begin to recognise its power of suggesting movement? In sculpture the earliest example seems to be the small figure of a girl at Eleusis, running with head turned back, which dates from the beginning of the 5th century. The curves of her drapery cling to her body and seem to urge it on its way; but they follow the main lines of the movement without a break, and are as simple as the petals of a primitive acanthus. Not until fifty years later, in the

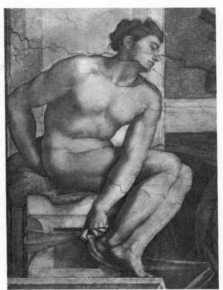

131. MICHELANGELO. Athlete

decoration of the Parthenon, is the line given a richer and more complex life. Of all the incredible developments of style which were achieved under the direction of Phidias none was carried further than the treatment of drapery. At Olympia, where many of the older Parthenon sculptors must have been employed, drapery is as formalised as that of the girl in Eleusis; in the later figures of the Parthenon it has attained a freedom and expressive power which has never been equalled except by Leonardo da Vinci. In the so-called Iris of the west pediment, the subtle and complex drapery both reveals the nude figure and accentuates its surging movement, like ripples on a wave [133]. Yet this noble embodiment of energy was one of the least prominent figures in the group. It was naturally in the figures of women that this convention of clinging and floating drapery was most fully developed; and perhaps the part it played in carrying movement through a composition may have been one of the reasons why a battle with Amazons so long remained a favourite subject with Greek sculptors, an iconographic motive surviving, as so often, simply because it was artistically manageable [134]. Male figures, their bodies totally undraped, were kept in motion by their flying cloaks. All through Greek art and in its post-renaissance derivatives this convention is used so shamelessly that we are hardly aware of it and have ceased to recognise how much the nude, as an expression of energy, depends on this artificial device. At every stage—the Temple of Bassai provides an early example—it tends to degenerate into mere space filling ; but it remains an instrument ready for the hands of an artist vigorous enough to use it. Such a one was the designer of the Mausoleum frieze, one of the finest works of the 4th century which have come down to us in the original. There are reasons for believing that this designer was Scopas himself, and although the execution is uneven, certain sections are worthy of a master. In these the figures race across the field like flames or swoop down on one another like eagles [135]. The frozen postures of the Aegina pediment and the impassive bodies of the Parthenon metopes are things of the past, and

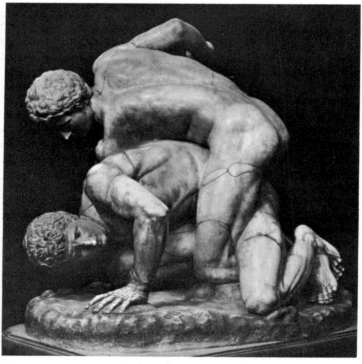

132. Greek. 3rd cent. B.C. Wrestlers

the charge brought against Greek art, that compared to the art of the Renaissance it was incapable of conveying movement, is refuted. On the contrary, comparison with the most vigorous works of the Renaissance can be sustained at every point. The horse with its Amazon rider firing a Parthian shot might be from the background of Leonardo's Adoration ; the Greek lunging forward and holding an Amazon by the hair [136] is equal, as an embodiment of energy, to the Hercules panels of Pollajuolo, and the tense triangle of assailants with a kneeling man crouching below two elliptical shields [135] recalls those drawings of Raphael in which he surpasses his Florentine models in the expression of movement.

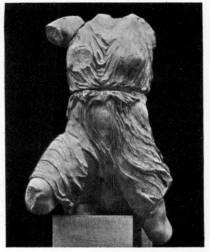

133. Attic. *c.* 440 B.C. Iris from west gable of Parthenon

But although the Greek sculptor shows a perfect understanding of human anatomy under the stress of action, his figures without the help of drapery would have looked stranded and self-contained, like dancers without a musical accompaniment ; and as we examine these reliefs more closely we begin to recognise the art with which their fluttering cloaks vary their rhythm according to the character of each action.

The Mausoleum also provides an admirable example of heroic energy, and in particular of the means through which it was so long expressed, that pose, or rhythmic accent, which I may call the heroic diagonal.

In every culture certain movements and gestures are recognised as speaking a clear symbolic language, and are thus employed in the arts, particularly the art of dancing. The dance, we know, had a profound influence on Greek sculpture, and accounts not only for rhythms of movement in frieze or relief, but also for the use of certain attitudes with the knowledge that they would be interpreted almost as precisely as the written word. At an early date it was accepted that a figure striding forward, one leg bent, the other forming a straight, continuous line with his back, should be the symbol of vigour and resolution. Thus were represented the tyrant-slayers, Harmodius and Aristo-giton, whose memorial by the sculptors Kritios and Mesiotes is the first

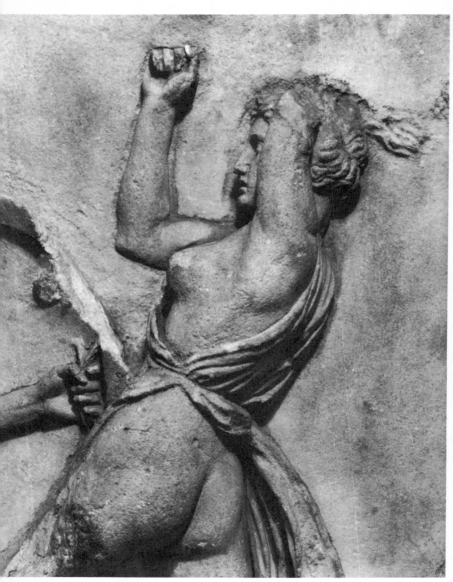

134. An Amazon. *c.* 350 B.C. From frieze of Mausoleum

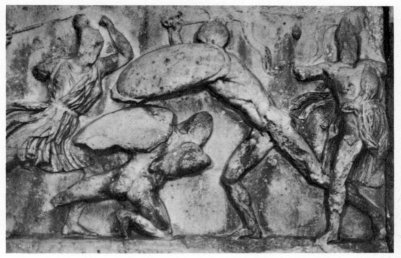

135. Greeks and Amazons. *c.* 350 B.C. From frieze of Mausoleum

piece of free standing sculpture of which both record and replica have come down to us. This is the pose which will reappear with the same meaning again and again throughout the centuries. It was much used by Phidias. The figure of Poseidon in the centre of the west pediment of the Parthenon was in this pose, and it is still to be found in a portion of the frieze in Athens. In scenes of violent action, for example the Amazon battles which decorated the shield of the Athene Parthenos and the base of her pedestal, the diagonals were more sharply accented. Of this we can judge only from fragmentary replicas and reminiscences; and from a few years later we have an original work, the frieze of the Temple of Bassai, which shows how, when the restraining influence of Phidias was removed, emphatic diagonals are repeated like oaths in popular speech. Not content with the line of leg and body, the sculptor has added shields and draperies repeating the same movement. What is done at Bassai with almost rustic crudity is refined upon with supreme art in the frieze of the Mausoleum. Nothing is heavily underlined, and the wilful insistence of diagonals is relieved by the curves of draperies and the arcs of shields or horses' necks. Euclidean intelligence, as this description indicates, controls the whole design. There are squares in which the diagonal of the figures runs from corner to corner, or groups in which two antagonists

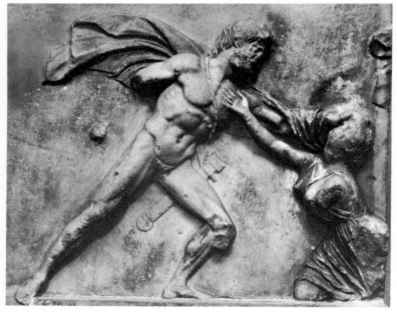

136. Greeks and Amazons. *c.* 350 B.C. From frieze of Mausoleum

form a regular equilateral triangle [137]. We must suppose that the Greek artist
began each composition with ruler and compass in hand, and the extraordinary
thing is that, in spite of the static and finite character of Euclidean geometry,
Scopas and his colleagues were able to fill their compositions with the feeling
of action.

The heroic diagonal survived into the less idealistic art of the Hellenistic
age, and was the basis of one of its most famous works, the Borghese Warrior
[138], signed by Agasias the Ephesian. The resolute stride of Harmodius and
Aristogeiton has been lengthened, accelerated and dramatised, but two hundred
years later the 'idea remains the same. Agasias (if, indeed, he invented the
pose and did not merely make a marble copy of an earlier bronze) shows
himself to be the last descendant of Lysippus and the sculptors of Pergamon.
All were official artists in the employment of victorious generals, and the heroic
diagonal itself has a quality of exhortation which has fitted it all too well for
impressive public monuments. Such are the two Dioscuri of the Quirinal,
once among the most famous antique statues in the world ; and if, as I believe,

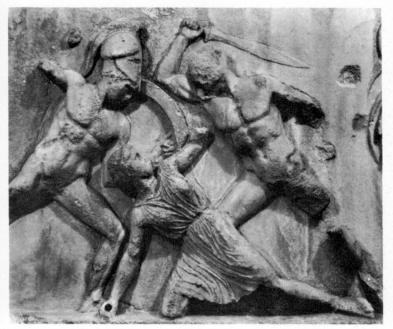

137. Greeks and Amazons. *c.* 350 B.C. From frieze of Mausoleum

they are really reminiscences, however crude, of a Phidian original, we can say that his image of heroic energy survived the middle ages unforgotten, linked even with his name, flourished in the Renaissance and was ready to hand in the revival of heroic ideals which dominated the classicism of the French revolution. Canova made it the motive of two famous groups, the Hercules and the Theseus ; it was a favourite with the sculptors employed to celebrate the glories of Napoleonic France, and when the English sculptor, Westmacott, wished to express through the nude the vigour which (in the opinion of his countrymen) had saved Europe from Napoleon, he chose the same pose.

Once more the nude has transferred its meaning from the physical to the moral sphere. And if we ask how that word can be applied to the pose of a figure in action, we need only compare the reliefs from the Mausoleum to those from, say, the Temple at Amaravati a few yards away in the British Museum. The soft, nerveless and extravagant shapes of Indian art emphasise by contrast the taut, resolute and economical forms of the Greek. We feel

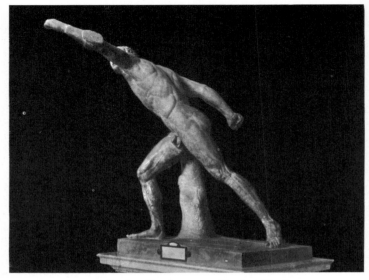

138. Greek. (?) 3rd cent. B.C. Borghese Warrior

in every line of these purposeful bodies a capacity for endurance and self-sacrifice for which the word moral is not inappropriate. Of this the Greeks themselves were, of course, perfectly conscious ; and it was an embodiment of moral energy, triumphing through physical means, that they created the myth of Hercules.

No doubt because he was a moral symbol, Hercules was one of the principal ambassadors between the antique and the mediaeval world. He was for the nude what Virgil was for poetry, and perhaps with less alteration of his original meaning. As always, survival as symbol is closely connected with existence as pattern. At a very early stage certain episodes in the legend of Hercules took the form they were to retain for over two thousand years. Most of these are based on the heroic diagonal. It is with this action that he assaults the Hydra, as we see on 6th-century vases in the Louvre and Vatican, which are the direct precursor of the most vivid depiction of energy in the early Renaissance, Pollajuolo's small picture in the Uffizi. The diagonal is also the basis of what must have been one of the grandest of all representations of Hercules, the metopes from Olympia. In one of them, the Cleansing of the Augean Stables, it is used in contrast to the calm, authoritative verticals of

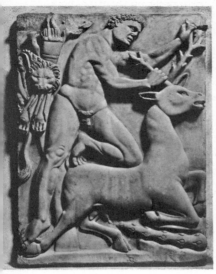

139. Late antique of 4th cent. Hercules and Stag

Athena ; in another, which must before its mutilation have been the noblest nude in action of pre-Phidian art, the diagonal of Hercules' body crosses the counter-diagonal of the Cretan bull, filling the square of the metope with a conflict of energies. Sometimes the diagonal is bent, like a bow, by the intensity of the labour and one knee is planted on the victim's back. This is the traditional pattern of Hercules and the Stag, and appears in the best preserved of the metopes from the Athenian Treasury at Delphi, almost the earliest great carvings of the Hercules cycle ; it is also the subject of the latest, a relief in the Museum at Ravenna of the 4th century A.D. [139], in which the antique style still resists the advancing tide of eastern pattern-making. Superficially, it seems that the long curve of classic art has almost returned to its starting-point. In the balance of line and modelling, and the decorative use of detail, the Ravenna relief seems to resemble the archaic style. But as expressions of energy the two carvings differ completely. In the first we feel that an inexhaustible vigour is compressed into the formalised body of Hercules ; in the second the nude has become a pattern, having little more relation to physical energy than the palmette has to organic growth. All the artistic vitality of the time has left the human body, and been transferred to ornament.

Although he was last to leave and first to return, Hercules did not escape the banishment of the Olympians. But whereas his fellow gods and heroes, when they appeared in the middle ages, did so in timid and pitiful disguises, so that their real significance is lost, Hercules, like many subsequent refugees, kept his status by changing his name. He took the name of Samson, some of whose exploits were similar to his own and may well have had the same origin : that is to say, the authors of the book of Judges and the creators of the Hercules myth may both have seen Mesopotamian gems or seals of a

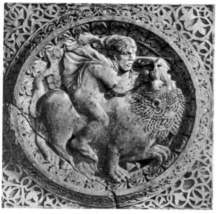

140. Tuscan. 12th cent. Samson and Lion

strong man struggling with a lion or stag, and have absorbed this memorable image into their own legend.

Mediaeval representations of Hercules and Samson show clearly how an idea may gain its value through its visible form rather than through a written description. As an example we may compare the picture of Hercules and the Lion in a French Gothic MS. of the mid-15th century with a 12th-century relief in the Museum at Lucca [140]. The late Gothic Hercules, confined by his dress and armour to some definite time and place, is a ludicrous figure. He does not grapple with the lion, but brandishes his club—sole survivor of iconographic tradition—above his head, and holds the querulous, but unresisting, animal at full length. With the loss of a compact, traditional design, based on the nude, all idea of resolute energy has vanished. The relief in Lucca is no more than a fragment of decoration, and the workman who carved it had a rudimentary knowledge of the nude. But because he was working in Italy, so little estranged from classical tradition, he has still retained the close-knit pattern of the Hercules idea (the relief, of course, is intended to represent Samson) and some of the concentration of the remote original. Even the flying cloak of antiquity has survived. A little more science and knowledge, and this idea becomes the classical Hercules of the antiquarian Renaissance, as we see it in the bronze reliefs of the Mantuan court sculptor who called himself Antico [141].

The Hercules-Samson figures of the middle ages, for example the Fortitudo of Nicola Pisano or the Samson of the Porta della Mandorla, are static, and it is not till after the middle of the century that the symbol of passive strength became, once more, the embodiment of active energy. The change seems to have occurred in the three great paintings of the labours of Hercules which Antonio Pollajuolo executed for the Medici Palace. According to Antonio (but no renaissance artist ever gave a correct date, even for his birth) they were painted in 1460, and he was assisted by his brother. These large canvases, twelve feet square, were amongst the most famous and influential works of

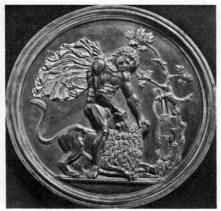

141. ANTICO. Hercules and Lion

their time, and remained so for over fifty years. Like nearly every canvas of the date, they have perished, but fortunately there remains a quantity of evidence by which two of them can be reconstructed—engravings by Robetta, made in about 1500, an original drawing for Hercules and the Hydra, and above all, two miniature replicas by Antonio himself, which until 1943 were in the Uffizi [142, 143]. These alone are enough to distinguish Pollajuolo as one of the two or three chief masters of the nude in action and as one of the originating forces in the history of European art, whose importance has been underrated partly owing to the accidents of time, and partly, perhaps, owing to a name which looks difficult to pronounce. Pollajuolo's true position was recognised in his own day and for the next half-century. Vasari says that his treatment of the nude is 'more modern than that of any of the masters who preceded him' and that 'he dissected many bodies to examine their anatomy, being the first to show how the muscles must be looked for if they are to take their proper place in representation of the figure'. As early as 1435 Leon Battista Alberti had recommended the scientific study of anatomy as if it were an established practice; and this is confirmed by the nude figures of both Donatello and Castagno. But not until Pollajuolo are we conscious of anatomical knowledge as a positive means of artistic expression; and this may therefore be a convenient point to ask how closely it is related to our subject.

If art is to be taught in academies and not by workshop practice, it must be reduced to rules. The fact that perspective and anatomy, two codifications of visual experience, are still taught in art schools, is a proof of how necessary to the teacher these rules became. But were they necessary to the artist? The Greeks, we know, did not study anatomy scientifically until the end of the 4th century, and, from 'Kritios' to Lysippus, produced some of the most perfect nudes in art. But it does not follow from this that the scientific enthusiasm of the Renaissance was an error. The Gothic approach to form, with its complex articulation, made it difficult for the classicists of the *quattrocento* to see the body with the unity and geometrical simplicity of the Greeks.

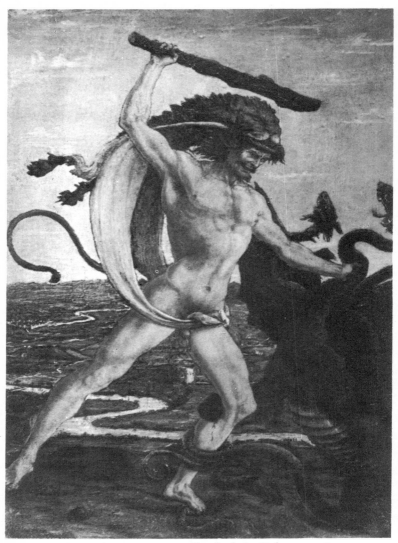

142. POLLAJUOLO. Hercules slaying Hydra

They needed some other means of animating each form, and this they achieved by adding knowledge to visual experience. The eye always knows more than it sees ; and this knowledge can heighten the artist's powers of perception to a point at which they can be more vividly communicated. Such is the sense of life which we derive from the muscles and sinews of Pollajuolo's Hercules, and, later, from Michelangelo's athletes. Each form is tense and full ; there are no slack or inflated sections. And each form confirms some knowledge which we have in ourselves without being aware of it. A dim and diffuse awareness of our own bodies suddenly becomes vivid and precise. Knowledge has become an aesthetic experience.

A restless search for the mechanism of the body and an emphasis on its components, therefore, gives to Pollajuolo's embodiments of

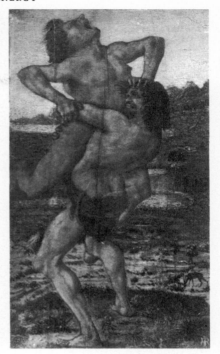

143. POLLAJUOLO. Hercules and Antaeus

energy a character very different from that of the Antique. His Hercules slaying the Hydra [142], going back, as we have seen, to a most ancient iconographical source, was derived from one of those numerous sarcophagi decorated with the labours of Hercules, which were sculpturally amongst the liveliest relics of antiquity ; for there had been a condensed vitality about the first patterns of Hercules which no amount of copying could destroy. These sarcophagi seem to have been based on Scopaic originals and we may therefore take as a term of comparison the striding figure of a Greek from the Mausoleum frieze which has already been compared to a Pollajuolo [136]. The similarity in the position of the legs is obvious ; but equally striking is the manner in which he has abandoned the antique diagonal. Just as the Greek passion for geometry led them to imagine a profile in which the nose continues the line of the forehead, so they constructed these figures, in which the body continues the

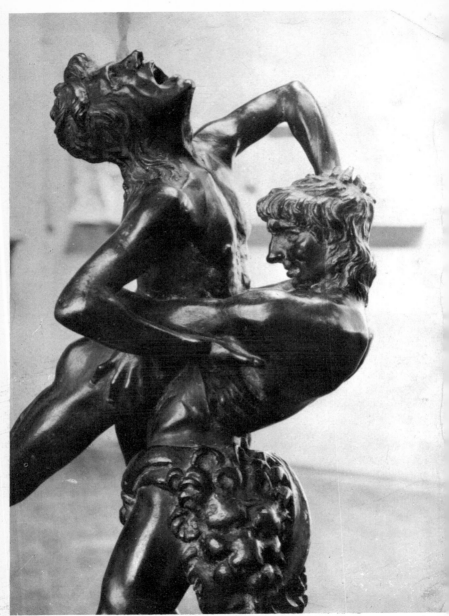

144. POLLAJUOLO. Hercules and Antaeus

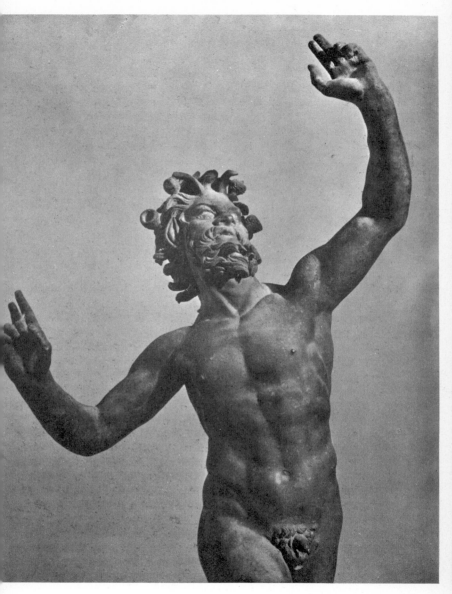

145. Graeco-Roman.   Dancing Faun

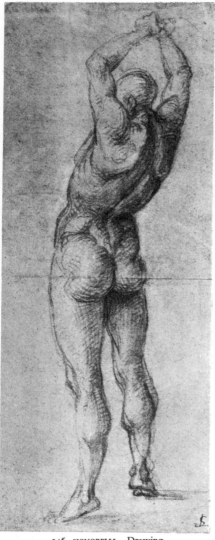

146. SIGNORELLI. Drawing

same diagonal as the extended leg. This Pollajuolo's more articulate style could not admit. The lower half of Hercules may be derivative ; the upper is unprecedented in the history of the nude. And even the legs show that nervous linear articulation peculiar to *quattrocento* art, which makes Greek form look, by comparison, simple and compact.

In Pollajuolo's other panel [143] Hercules lifts Antaeus from the ground and squeezes the breath out of his body, a subject which plays a great part in renaissance art, but was surprisingly rare in antiquity. Indeed the only widely diffused example seems to have been a coin of Antoninus Pius, in which Antaeus twists his body away from Hercules in an effort to escape. This was the source of inspiration used by the archaeologically minded artists of North Italy, as in an engraving which must derive from Mantegna and a bronze by Antico. But as far as I know nothing in Greek art anticipates the pose of both Pollajuolo's versions of the subject, where the antagonists are face to face, and Hercules has hollowed his back to hoist Antaeus onto his terrific chest. His miniature replica is one of the most marvellous realisations of muscular strength in all painting. 'A most beautiful picture,' says

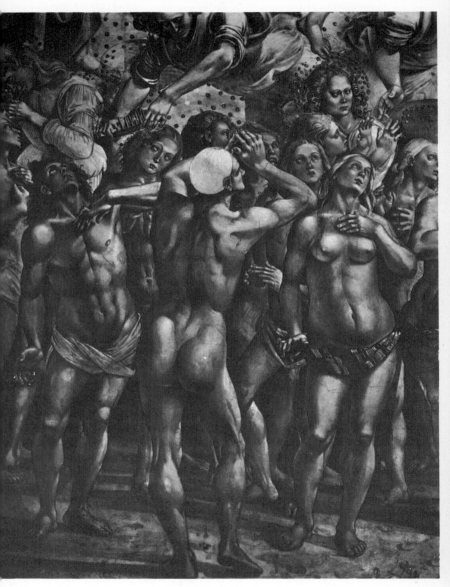

147. SIGNORELLI. The Blessed

Vasari, describing the lost original, 'in which one really sees the effort of Hercules in squeezing, for the muscles and tendons of his body are all concentrated on bursting Antaeus ; and as for his head, one sees him grinding his teeth in a way which corresponds to all the other parts of the body, right down to his toes, which swell with the effort.' Subsequent criticism has not greatly improved on this first appraisal, and Vasari is right in stressing how Pollajuolo's anatomical knowledge has allowed him to show the effect of muscular tension in every member. But of course his knowledge has been used with a power of vivid selection and emphasis, based on observation. It is one of the forms of intellectual discipline which must be applied to direct perception ; and just as we may imagine a Greek artist sitting down to his work with compass and ruler in hand, determined to unite the physical beauty he had observed on the palestra with geometrical perfection, so Pollajuolo must have watched the swelling muscles of some Florentine mason, as he hammered a pile or hoisted a basket of stones, and found his pleasure doubled because it confirmed long hours of anatomical investigation.

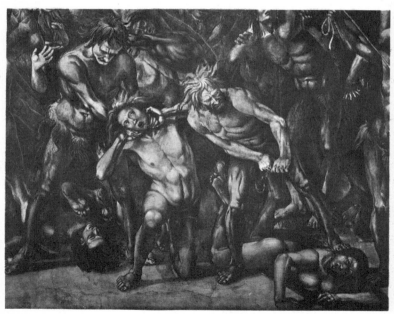

148. SIGNORELLI. The Damned

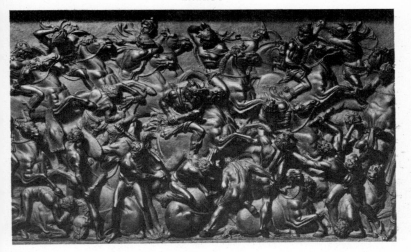

149. BERTOLDO. Battle piece

The bronze statuette of Hercules and Antaeus [144], now in the Bargello, shows even more clearly how Pollajuolo's means of conveying energy differed from that of antiquity. The silhouette, with its sharp excrescences, its flying buttresses of form, would have shocked a classic eye and the clear emphatic planes of the internal modelling would have seemed crude and abrupt. A fair term of comparison is the Dancing Faun at Naples [145] which is of higher quality than most of the furnishing bronzes found at Pompeii and Herculaneum. The pose is light and graceful, the modelling well understood, the general sense of movement admirably sustained. But to anyone trained in renaissance art the whole impression is artificial and dead, and as our eye glides on without the stimulus of sharply contrasted planes we begin to lose interest, and turn with delight to Pollajuolo's Hercules, his back and shoulders jutting out like some rocky escarpment.

In the planes of the shoulders the *quattrocento* discovered a symbol of energy almost comparable to the antique torso. There is a large, uncompromising angularity about this shape which seems to be inherently Florentine ; but in fact its greatest exponent came from the borders of Umbria : Luca Signorelli [146]. Whatever his origins, his early painting of the Flagellation in the Brera leaves us in no doubt that he discovered his true bent when he first came in contact with the art of Pollajuolo. In this picture the nude flagellators might be by a

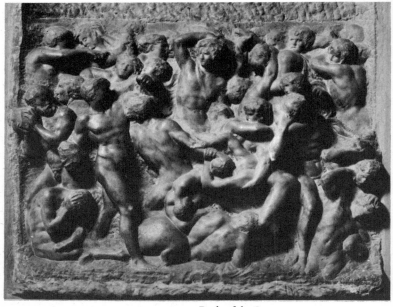

150. MICHELANGELO. Battle of the Centaurs

Florentine so closely do they follow his kind of articulation and emphasis ; but after about 1490 Signorelli developed a new architecture of the human body which departs even further than Pollajuolo from classical precedent. His simplification of certain contrasting masses—shoulders and buttocks, chest and stomach—gives his nudes [147] a disturbing plastic force, as if we had been suddenly endowed with a sort of stereoscopic vision. There are few things in painting to which the term tactile values has a more valid application ; and as we look at the vigorous rotundities of the figures crowded together in his frescoes at Orvieto, we begin to share the Florentine passion for the solidly comprehensible, that which can be grasped alike by mind and hand. In the scene of The Blessed his vigorous blend of sense and intellect is latent in the forms, but in the still more astonishing scene of The Damned it is released and rages with purposeful ferocity [148]. Signorelli does not attempt to make his nudes the vehicles of beauty. Muscles and sinews are given unflinching emphasis, so that some of his devils are like *écorchés*. They do not embody the victorious energy of athlete or hero, but a demonic energy, triumphant, too,

190

in its way, which was to reappear in the romantic movement of the early 19th century, in the slave-drivers and executioners of Géricault and in certain evil spirits in Blake.

The history of art could be written in terms of a sequence of compulsive subjects which seem to succeed each other for purely internal or artistic reasons. Such, for example, was the succession of apples, harlequins and guitars which occupied artists in the early years of the present century. And in Florence, from about 1480 to 1505, the compulsive subject was a battle of naked men. It had no social or iconographic justification ; it was simply art for art's sake. The subject seems to have appeared first in the work of Pollajuolo as a pretext for the combination of nude figures in action, and has come down to us in an engraving and several drawings. In these he no doubt had in mind an antique battle sarcophagus such as that in the Campo Santo, but he never approaches its evolved Scopaic style. About 1490 a battle-piece of truly classical character was produced by a much less gifted artist, Bertoldo [149]. He was keeper of Lorenzo de' Medici's collection of antiquities and it is understandable that his masterpiece, the bronze relief now in the Bargello, should have had a dogmatically antiquarian character. To us it gives all too clear an indication of the fate which was to overtake Italian art when the antique manner had been correctly understood. But to the young men of that date it seemed a model worthy of serious study. No doubt Michelangelo, who worked as a boy under Bertoldo's eye in the Medici gardens, believed that his marble relief of

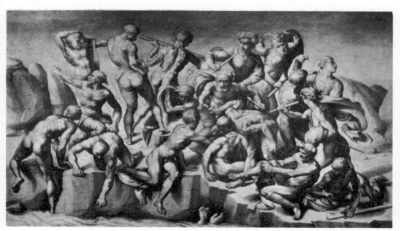

151. After Michelangelo.   Copy of Cascina cartoon

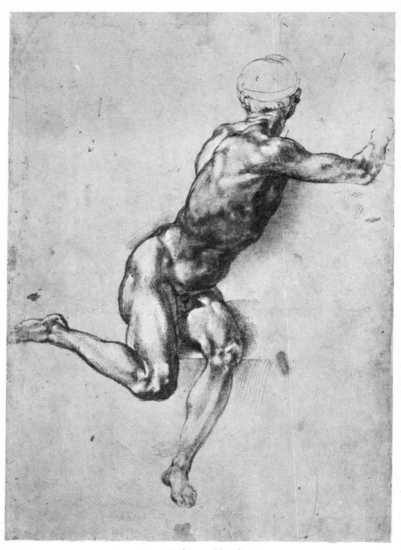

152. MICHELANGELO. Bathing Soldier for Cascina cartoon

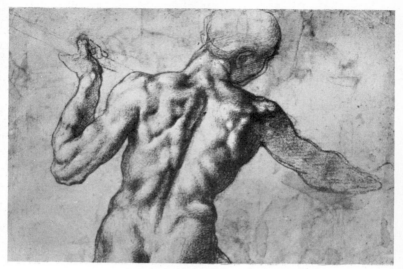

153. MICHELANGELO. Study for Cascina cartoon

the Battle of the Centaurs [150] was rough and clumsy compared to that of his master.

It may have been executed in the Medici garden shortly before Lorenzo died in 1492, and is thus only a few years later than the nude battles of Pollajuolo ; but what a gulf separates it from the light-limbed compositions of the *quattrocento*. As with Leonardo's Adoration, we seem to be looking into the boiling cauldron of his mind, and fancy that we can find there, forming and vanishing, the principal motives of his later work, figures from the Battle of Cascina, from the lunettes of the Sistine and the Medici tombs, above all from the Last Judgment. We know how this small nucleus of energy will expand, and how each pose will reappear, polished by art and weathered by experience, to create a new heroic style of painting. The young Michelangelo could not know that he had released a world of shapes which were to travel with him all his life, and prove, after his death, a Pandora's box of formal disturbance.

In the cartoon of soldiers surprised while bathing [151], which he executed for the Palazzo Vecchio in 1504, Michelangelo steps back into his own time. Iconographically it was not very suitable for public commemoration. The incident depicted was unimportant and slightly discreditable. It was chosen solely as a pretext for depicting the nude in action, and as such was accepted with enthusiasm; indeed, of all his works it was that which his contemporaries, and in particular his colleagues, were best able to appreciate. It revealed to them, and demonstrated to perfection, their belief that the highest subject of art was a group of nude male figures, physically perfect, and so arranged that their bodies could convey through movement a life-giving energy. This had been the aim of Myron and Scopas, but the men of the early 16th century could not remain satisfied by the limited range of poses employed in antiquity. Nor were they content to spread their figures out at regular intervals in one plane as on a frieze, or pile them flatly on top of one another as in a Roman sarcophagus. Michelangelo's Battle of Cascina demonstrated the value of twist and foreshortening, which not only increase the stock of admirable attitudes, but make it possible to compose in depth. These devices also increase the power of communicating energy. Twist accelerates movement; foreshortening is an urgent appeal to the eye, which must hasten to recognise in a small space what it is accustomed to visualise in extension. But

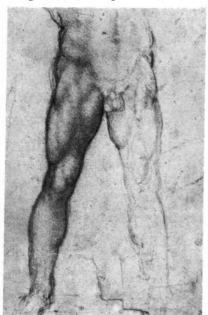

154. LEONARDO DA VINCI. Muscular legs

in the end these compositional devices are subordinate to one over-riding intention, to enhance, by movement, the beauty of the naked body. An example is the figure in the centre of the group seated on the bank and twisting back-wards, for which, fortunately, we have Michelangelo's original draw-ing [152]. This famous sheet, which, since the Renaissance, has been considered the summit of academic drawing, is one of a type which has lately been viewed with a certain suspicion. True, it lacks some of the graphic spontaneity through which great draughtsmen have communicated to us their first responses to life and movement; yet if we regard it as an independent and final creation, how splendidly it realises Michelangelo's desire to close on a complete form and follow it as it turns away, concentrating on every vital juncture, pressing round it with the passionate chisel strokes of his pen. The same is true of a study for the figure in the background thrusting with a lance, which shows his anatomical knowledge assimilated and subordinate to an ideal [153]. The musculature is no longer harsh and schematic, as in Signorelli's devils, but flowing and continuous ; and at every point it contributes to the movement of the figure. And what drawings must be lost ! As we pass from one figure to another in the Holkham copy, and picture each

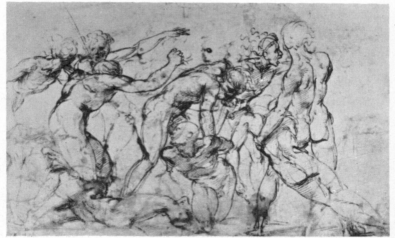

155. RAPHAEL. Men fighting

one in the light of our two or three surviving studies, we grow to share the Florentine passion for the *bel corpo ignudo* ; we recognise what a noble ideal was then intended by the sacred word *disegno*, and we understood why the cartoon continued to be, in Vasari's words, 'the school of all the world' even after it had been torn in pieces, like Dionysus, by its admirers.

Among the artists to be inspired by the Battle of Cascina were Leonardo da Vinci and Raphael. We think of Leonardo as the inventor of forms, the giver, rather than the receiver, of ideas. But where the nude is concerned he is derivative. The graceful, active figures of his early drawings are in the style of Pollajuolo, the drawings for the Battle of Anghiari are clearly influenced by Michelangelo. Between them come the first anatomical studies, for the most part factual, although seldom entirely without an underlying sense of

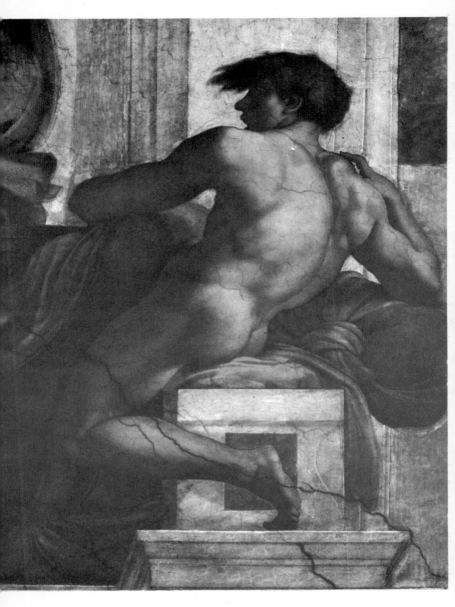

156. MICHELANGELO. Athlete

nobility. The finest nudes are those done in Florence during the years when his commission in the Palazzo della Signoria brought him into open rivalry with Michelangelo. They assume, with extraordinary skill, the heroic manner ; but even so the scientific interest predominates. In one of the most impressive the arm is cut off and the muscles numbered, as for some anatomical demonstration. Others are simply *écorchés* in warlike attitudes. Only in his magnificent studies of muscular legs has Leonardo used the body to convey an idea rather than a quantity of information [154]. These are his symbols of human energy, superbly powerful, and yet, because they are human, less important to him than the cascades and water-spouts which are his symbols of the energy of nature.

Raphael is at the opposite pole. His confidence in humanity was greater than that of any artist since the 4th century B.C., and his anthropocentric system of order was closer to antiquity than the restless researches of the Florentines. But during the later years of his stay in Florence he absorbed the heroic-classical style of Bertoldo and Michelangelo. Whether the three magnificent drawings at Oxford of naked men fighting [155] were done before or after the Battle of Cascina we do not know, and Raphael's almost telepathic gift of absorbing the artistic ideas of his time makes it unwise to guess. In any case they remain, with Michelangelo's drawings, the finest surviving testimony

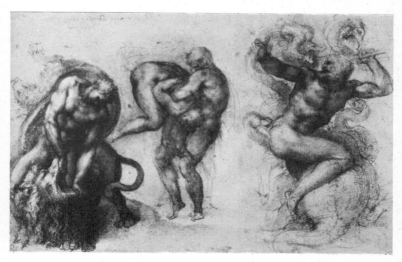

157. MICHELANGELO. Three Labours of Hercules

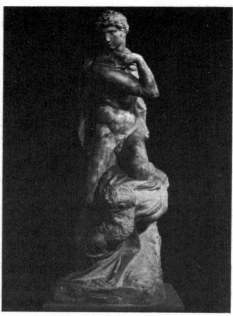

158. MICHELANGELO. Victory

of this noble ambition. Raphael equals the Florentines in the communication of energy, and surpasses them in clarity. The way in which outline, by the variation of its accent, is made to suggest both movement and weight is a model of classical draughtsmanship. Did Scopas, we wonder, make such drawings for the frieze of the Mausoleum ?

The nude figures in Michelangelo's drawings for the Battle of Cascina are graceful and perfectly poised, as well as being strong and resolute. Heroic and athletic energy are one. And it is under the title of athletes that we refer to the most famous nudes in all painting, the young men who represent, we are told, the *animae rationali* of the prophets on the Sistine ceiling. Whatever their precise intention, it is clear that Michelangelo intended them as mediators between the physical and the spiritual worlds. Their physical beauty is an image of divine perfection ; their alert and vigorous movements an expression of divine energy. The beautiful bodies of young men, controlled by the forms of Greek idealism, have been so charged with the spirit that they can enter the service of Christianity. Several of the athletes of the Sistine are derived from antique originals, notably the two earliest which are in poses which have come down to us in gems. In these there remains the same basic rhythm of movement which first appeared in the Discobolos of Myron ; but already there is a sense of urgency expressed in every inflection of the outline, in every transition of modelling, which the Greeks would have considered fretful or undignified. In spite of his movement, the Discobolos exists entirely in the physical present ; the Michelangelo athletes are struggling towards some bodiless future, which may perhaps be a past :

L' anima, della carne ancor vestita,
Con esso è già più volte aciesa a Dio.

This ceaseless tremor, this feeling that every form is, so to say, pawing the ground in its anxiety to be gone, can make its effect only because it is confined by knowledge of anatomy, without which the winds of expressionism would blow the figures out of shape.   Conversely, it is this knowledge which allows Michelangelo to take poses from antiquity and develop them to a point of expression far beyond the classic norm.   An example is the athlete beside the Persian Sybil [156].   Strangely, his pose seems to have been suggested by an Ariadne reclining in the lap of Bacchus on a Hellenistic relief.   But the muscles of his right shoulder are unlike those of any antique figure, let alone that of a woman.   If we compare his back with a classical athlete, for example the Iloneus at Munich, we see how far Michelangelo could depart, even in 1512,

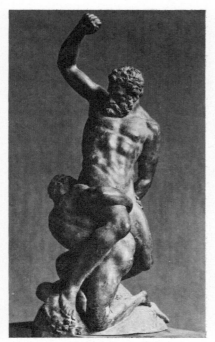

159. After Michelangelo.   Samson defeating Philistines

from orthodox classical proportion. These immense shoulders tapering abruptly into tiny buttocks are, by any standards, a distortion.   Yet we accept them because a compelling rhythmic force drives every inflection of the human body before it.   The outline of the back may seem almost as abstract as the profile of a moulding in one of Michelangelo's own magnificent architectural drawings ; and yet it would not convince us unless it was based on a profound knowledge of anatomy.   Nor, perhaps, would the moulding.

The athletes of the Sistine confirm a statement made at the beginning of the chapter : that some degree of exaggeration is necessary to a vivid representation of movement.   This accounts, in part, for the distortions in the athlete of the Persica, where the line of the thigh and back twists round with terrific emphasis, and shoots forward along the upper surface of the arm. But the curious physical structure of Michelangelo's nudes is not simply a pictorial device ; it is part of the inward-looking character of his whole art. If we imagine the figures of 4th-century sculpture suddenly come to life, they would be dazzlingly beautiful men and women ; but Michelangelo's athletes exist purely as vehicles of expression. In life they would be squat and disproportionate. The graceful youth to the left of Jeremiah is almost the only one whose beauty would survive realisation. His companion, based on the Torso Belvedere, would be a monster. Now, it is obviously foolish to criticise Michelangelo's nudes from the point of view of a supposed norm of human beauty. But it remains true that Michelangelo's intensely personal use of the

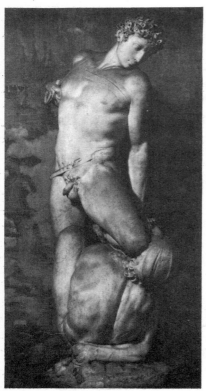

nude greatly altered its character. He changed it from a means of embodying ideas to a means of expressing emotions ; he transformed it from the world of living to the world of becoming. And he projected his world of the imagination with such unequalled artistic power that its shadow fell on every male nude in art for three hundred and fifty years. Painters either imitated his heroic poses and proportions, or they reacted against them self-consciously and sought a new repertoire of attitudes in the art of 5th-century Greece. In the 19th century the ghost of Michelangelo was still posing the models in art schools, and compelling would-be realists to see a system of forms invented to express his own troubled emotions. Géricault has used one of the athletes of the Sistine as the culminating figure in his Raft of the Medusa, and even the arch-realist Courbet, in his Wrestlers, was not able to shake off what Blake called that Outrageous Demon.

160. VINCENZO DANTI. Honour

Michelangelo's use of the nude as a means of expressing emotion will be treated more fully in the next chapter ; but there remains in his work another embodiment of energy which must be mentioned here, more particularly since it brings us back to the theme of Hercules. The ambassador of antiquity in the middle ages was equally suited to the heavier and more heroic mood of the high-Renaissance. Already in the 13th century he had appeared on the seal of the city of Florence as an emblem of good government, and by the 16th century he had become a favourite political symbol, claimed equally by both parties, like the word democratic. His appearance in the adornment of public buildings was thought to promise the cleansing of corruption and a resolute conduct of affairs. The power of a symbol is shown by the way in which this figure spread to the remotest part of Europe, so that in Sweden or Wales the public buildings of the late 16th century were decorated with the Labours of

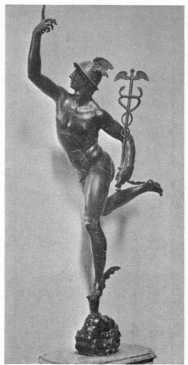

161. GIOVANNI DA BOLOGNA. Mercury

Hercules. As his was the first nude figure to penetrate the darkness of the middle ages, so he was the first to spread the image of naked energy among the Hyperboreans. It was inevitable that Michelangelo should turn his attention to Hercules. His youthful statue of the hero leaning on his club was sent to Fontainebleau, and is lost ; but in 1508 Pietro Soderini, head of the free Florentine republic, who had already commissioned the battle cartoon, invited Michelangelo to execute a gigantic Hercules as a companion to his other huge embodiment of heroism, the marble David. Largely for political reasons the Medici popes prevented him from executing it. The plan dragged on for twenty years, and in the end the commission was transferred to his enemy Bandinelli, who executed almost the largest and certainly the ugliest Hercules in existence. But several of Michelangelo's thoughts on the subject have survived in visible form, and are a turning-point in the subject.   Three of them, contained in a drawing at Windsor, are not studies for sculpture but independent graphic ideas, worked out for presentation to a friend [157]. In the Hercules and the Lion, a living texture of modelling is compressed within a simple outline ; in the Hercules and Antaeus, the forms are knotted so closely that we seem to feel the tension which pulled them together. Thus Michelangelo says the last word on two iconographical motives which had occupied the imagination of Mediterranean man for two thousand years.

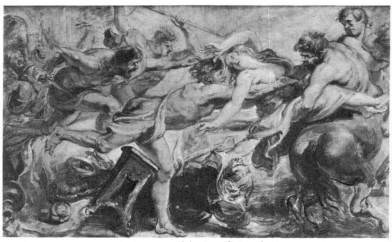

162. RUBENS.   Abduction of Hippodamia

In two pieces of sculpture the idea of Hercules creates a new motive in which the nude was to take some of the most vigorous forms in the next century.   The first of these is not ostensibly a Hercules.   It is the marble figure in the Palazzo Vecchio, in which a youthful embodiment of energy kneels in triumph over a bearded man who is not so much a defeated enemy as caryatid to the beautiful youth who bestrides him [158].   His head shows no anguish of defeat, but only a sad and troubled resignation.   Whatever this may mean as a symbol, as design it is of great importance, for it solves a major problem of the nude in action, a problem which had defeated sculptors ever since the bronze Zeus from Histiaea, how to avoid the spindly effect of striding legs and support the weight of the torso on a solid base.   Michelangelo's victor can turn his body with a violence which would have upset his sculptural stability had he not been securely planted on a living plinth ;   and by this spiral movement he can achieve an effect of energy which the two-dimensional geometry of the Discobolos could not give. This was the principle on which, as we know from several models, Michelangelo intended to execute his gigantic group of Hercules. It involved changing the episode from Hercules and Antaeus to Hercules and Cacus, since the point of the Antaeus legend was that he was lifted from the earth, and Michelangelo's design required the second figure to be at Hercules' feet ; and it is an indication of how little

strict iconographic considerations weighed with the great artists of the Renaissance, that just as he turned his Apollo into a David, so half-way through this commission he changes his Hercules into a Samson defeating the Philistines [159], simply because he required two figures instead of one at the base of his composition.

These models show a full development of the motive which was to dominate sculptural representations of energy during the baroque period. In contrast to the heroic diagonal, we may call it the heroic spiral. Its potentialities were barely understood by Michelangelo's immediate followers ; for example

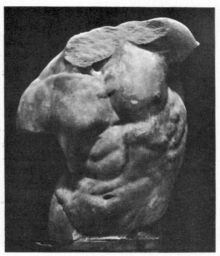

163. Greek. 2nd cent. B.C. Torso of Satyr

Vincenzo Danti's group of Honour pulling out the tongue of Falsehood in the Bargello [160], although one of the finest compressions of energy in sculpture, is still thought of in separate aspects, whereas Michelangelo's movement in space is continuous. Perhaps the first sculptor to recognise the possibilities of the heroic spiral was Giovanni da Bologna, who made it the basis of those impressive, heartless groups in the Loggia dei Lanzi and the Bargello. It was Giovanni da Bologna, incidentally, who, in the Mercury, created one of the few images of energy which have gained a place in the popular memory [161]. Just as the Venus of Milo has become a trademark for Beauty and the Discobolos of Myron is still given as a prize for athletics, so the Mercury has become an accepted symbol of victorious speed. Giambologna has set out to solve the same problem as Myron : to give balance and finality to an almost inapprehensible movement. But unlike the Discobolos, we do not believe that the Mercury's movement is possible. By his memorable clarity he stands out among the confused and redundant figures of the late 16th century, but he is a piece of rhetoric, intended to persuade rather than to convince, and the self-consciousness of his pose is very different from the seriousness with which the Discobolos concentrates on his task.

The twist into depth, the struggle to escape from the here and now of the picture plane, which had always distinguished Michelangelo from the Greeks, became the dominating rhythm of his later works. That colossal nightmare, the Last Judgment, is made up of such struggles. It is the most overpowering accumulation in all art of bodies in violent movement. But can we speak of energy before these tortured giants ? Certainly not in the sense that we can before the Mausoleum frieze or the Hercules of Pollajuolo. They do not enhance our vitality by their own but rather induce in us a feeling of insignificance, or mere terror. However, the Last Judgment had to be mentioned in this chapter, for the twisting movement it epitomises, and many of the actual poses it contains, were to be used as embodiments of energy by later painters from Tintoretto to Blake. Whether we admire or deplore that shattering of the classical scheme which is now described by the word mannerism, we must admit that it released a current of energy. Nude figures, derived from classical antiquity, suddenly took on the feverish violence of the north. Winds which had curled the draperies of Gothic saints, now blew round naked, elongated bodies, and swept them into the air or shot them headlong out of the clouds. Tibaldi may not have possessed, as Sir Joshua Reynolds believed, 'the true, genuine and noble mind of Michelangelo' ; but the use he made of motives from the Sistine Chapel is not devoid of energy, even when, as in the Palazzo Poggi, it takes the form of cynical caricature. In spite of repeated protests, the word mannerist must be applied to Tintoretto. Of course his strong conviction is far from the irresponsibility of Tibaldi ; yet what we may call his thematic material is often the same, and in the nude particularly he relied on the inventions of Michelangelo. He owned casts of the Medici tombs and drew them repeatedly from every angle. His Fall of the Damned is peopled with figures from the Last Judgment of the Sistine. In his later studies the Michelangelesque musculature is reduced to a few dots and dashes, which look at first like a formula ; but the long discipline of *disegno* has them under control, and these scribbles are as precise, in their life-communicating force, as a prehistoric drawing of a buffalo.

The other major transformation of Michelangelo's poses into abounding energy was achieved by Rubens. I have already referred to his laborious study of the past, and, of all his predecessors, it was Michelangelo whom he copied the most frequently and the most faithfully. We have careful drawings done after almost all his works, from the Centaur relief to the Last Judgment, and anyone so minded could discover a number of these reproduced with little change in Rubens' paintings. An example is the sketch in Brussels of the Abduction of Hippodamia [162], in which the chief figure is obviously taken from Michelangelo's drawing at Windsor of Archers Shooting at a Mark. This in turn has been derived from a decorative painting in the Golden House of Nero,

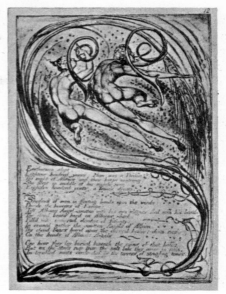

164. BLAKE. From *Europe*

now destroyed, but well known to the Renaissance, which certainly reproduced one of the great pictures of antiquity. So this vivid embodiment of speed and vitality, like so many others, reflects an image first minted in the great age of the figure arts. Its value as independent form can be gauged from the fact that although the figures were originally flying forwards, in the Rubens they are supposed to be pulling in the opposite direction : and yet we accept it without question. It is curious how seldom the male nude (except in the form of satyrs) appears in Rubens' finished paintings. His men are all draped or dressed in armour, often no doubt to provide a contrast with the shining nakedness of his women. It seems that he was reluctant to accept the convention by which male figures are nude when the subject does not warrant it. For this reason he treats his nude male figures like quotations, as in the Miracle of S. Benedict, where the figures climbing the wall and clinging to the column are obviously taken from Raphael's Stanze, one in the foreground from Michelangelo's Last Judgment. Like all great artists, Rubens was able to borrow so directly because he knew that he could give to his transcriptions his own abundant vitality and rhythmic buoyancy. The

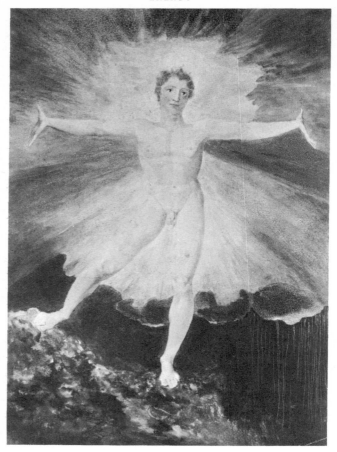

165. BLAKE. Glad Day. Colour print

rhythm is exactly the opposite of those early Greek artists whom I mentioned as being incapable of communicating the flow of movement through the body as a whole. That the Greeks themselves overcame this limitation we know from the art of Pergamon, and Rubens must have been greatly influenced by Pergamene sculpture, not only by the Laocoön, but also by the torso of a satyr, now in the Uffizi [163]. Thus he evolved a style very different from the nervous agitation of mannerism, fuller, weightier, more unified.

Behind it lies not only the vitality of Rubens as an individual, but the force of a living popular belief. His figures draw some of their energy from the same source as the façades of the great baroque churches in Rome, from the conviction that thus, and only thus, can all shapes work together to the glory of God.

In 18th-century painting, with its diminished force and seriousness, the embodiment of energy almost disappears ; but towards the end of the period there is an unforeseen explosion. Roman connoisseurs and artists took a

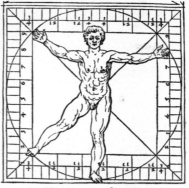

166. Vitruvian Man from Scamozzi

fresh interest in Michelangelo and Tibaldi ; and this mannerist revival was brought back to England by the numerous artists who had studied there, above all by Fuseli. This was the material which formed the style, and furnished the imagination of William Blake. He had an exceptional power of secreting retinal images, and it was, to some extent, the unconscious memory of these images which he identified with inspiration. He was justified in saying that 'All forms are perfected in the poet's mind', but it was seldom in his own mind that the forms in his work had originally been perfected. The long and painful interaction between ideal form remembered and natural appearances observed, which is the foundation of all great drawing from Michelangelo to Degas, was beyond his powers. But although the outlines of his nude figures were borrowed from 16th-century Rome and Bologna, he was able to give them a fresh energy which was his own. Sometimes it is as if the old Celtic spiral had been wound up tight and was ready to impel his figures through space [164] ; and sometimes his spiritual radiance shines through a dead form and transfigures it. Such is the splendid design known as Glad Day [165], which is derived from a woodcut of Vitruvian Man [166] in an old edition of Scamozzi's *Idea dell' architettura universale*. Blake must have seen it as a young man, for the figure occurs first in one of his earliest drawings, and have recognised the importance to him of its geometrical clarity. In the engraving of 1780 it has become a symbol of liberated vitality ; the arms are no longer stretched out for the convenience of measurement, but as a gesture of eager acceptance ; the right leg is no longer bent to fit into a circle, but to give the impression of movement. Geometrically perfect man is given back

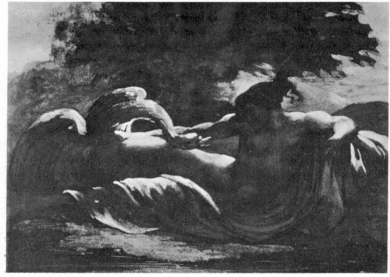

167. GÉRICAULT. Leda

some of Apollo's lost vitality. On one print of the engraving Blake wrote the words 'Albion arose from where he laboured at the mill with slaves'; which in his symbolic language meant precisely that the human imagination has freed itself from the doctrines of materialism. He might equally have written the words with which this chapter opens (and which in fact he wrote in that burning bush of wisdom, *The Marriage of Heaven and Hell*), 'Energy is eternal delight'.

I have observed how, in the 19th century, the nude came to mean, almost exclusively, the female nude. This applies even to the nude of energy. The superb drawing of Leda by Géricault provides a revealing example [167]. Formally it is an almost direct transcript of the so-called Ilissus of the Parthenon which Géricault had drawn from a cast when in Rome in 1817. But the Ilissus has undergone two transformations. It has changed its sex; and the slow movement of an Olympian has become a spasm of physical excitement. These changes have involved Géricault in certain difficulties of construction not perfectly solved; but in spite of them, how much more authentic is this female nude than are the male figures in, for example, the Fualdes drawings, which show that aspect of Géricault correctly described by Degas

as his *Côté Bandinelli*. The subjects in which nude women can be represented in violent action are limited, and it is curious that two of the most
intelligent painters of the 19th century, Delacroix and Degas, turned to the
passage in Euripides which describes how Spartan girls stripped naked and
competed with the boys on the palestra. Delacroix considered using the
motive in one of the pendentives of the *Chambre des Députés*, and his drawing
of girls wrestling [168], their bodies round and solid, like the nudes in Michelangelo's Deluge, is one of his most considered designs. But it remains
archaeological and, in the highest sense, academic. Delacroix's real conviction
of energy derived from his passion for wild animals, and the shoulders of a lion
grappling with a horse was to him what the back of a *bel corpo ignudo* had been
to Michelangelo. Degas was a natural humanist who needed no substitute
for the human body, and had the power of mind, hand and eye to reinterpret it.

If we allow to the word 'drawing' the meaning which a 16th-century
Florentine implied by the word *disegno*, Degas was the greatest draughtsman
since the Renaissance. His subject was the figure in action, his aim to

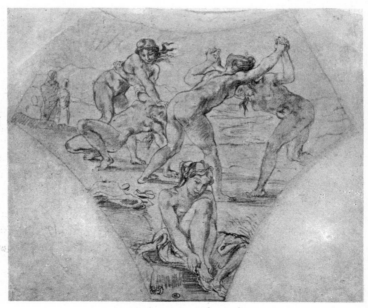

168. DELACROIX. Girls wrestling

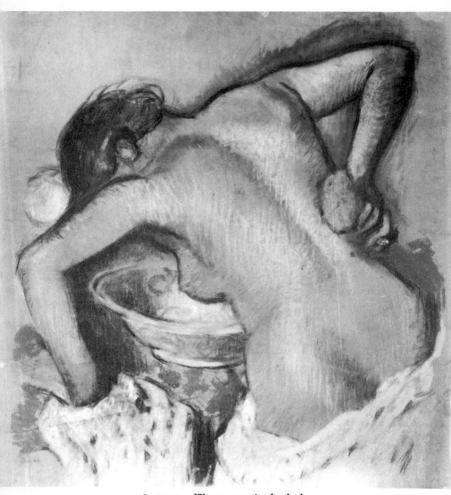

169. DEGAS. Woman sponging her back

communicate most vividly the idea of movement ; and he felt that vividness of movement must somehow be expressed through shapes which convince us that they are complete in themselves. This is the characteristic of *disegno* : that it enhances the vitality of a form by our recognition of its completeness. The great draughtsmen of this kind—Signorelli or Michelangelo—are not content to record a movement, as a Tiepolo might do, but press round it, till it approaches some ideal pattern which lies at the back of the imagination : hence the continual hammering at the same motive, the tracings, copies and replicas which so much astonish the profane.

One of Degas' earliest drawings is a copy—no doubt from Marcantonio's engraving—of those figures in the Battle of Cascina which I mentioned earlier as being the triple essence of Florentine design ; and looking through the drawings and pastels of his later years, when he was entirely himself, it is surprising to see how little his sense of form changed. The woman getting into her tub is still the soldier scrambling up the bank ; the woman sponging her back [169] is still the soldier fastening his armour. But before he could achieve this transformation Degas had to pass through an intermediate stage. Already in 1860 he recognised that his gifts for classic draughtsmanship might lead him into false academism ; so, having done the most beautiful life drawings of the 19th century, he renounced conventional 'beauty', and in his *Jeunes Filles Spartiates* [170] imagined two groups of defiant adolescents, whose awkward bodies seem to gather up and realise the points of resemblance between Pollajuolo's drawings and the vase paintings of 6th-century Greece. This feeling that immature forms have a vivid truthfulness which the developed body has lost guided his choice of the *rats de l'Opéra*. In his earlier drawings of the ballet, nudes are relatively rare, and we may deplore the accident by which the dancers in the Paris Opera rehearsed in *tutus* instead of the tights usual today. But gradually his dancers come to be conceived as nudes, till finally the pretext of the ballet school almost disappears. At the same time their bodies become more mature. Pollajuolo turns into Michelangelo. Having gone back to the sources of *disegno* in the severe style of the *quattrocento*, Degas feels free to repeat in himself the evolution which took place in Florence between 1480 and 1505, and is no longer afraid of false classicism because he knows that he has absorbed a new kind of truth.

But on the word truth a gulf seems to open between him and Michelangelo. Instead of almost worshipping beautiful young men, Degas said with satisfaction of his models, 'la femme en générale est laide'. Instead of conceiving the body as the repository of the soul, he said, 'J'ai peut-être trop considéré la femme comme un animal'. The gulf should be unbridgeable,

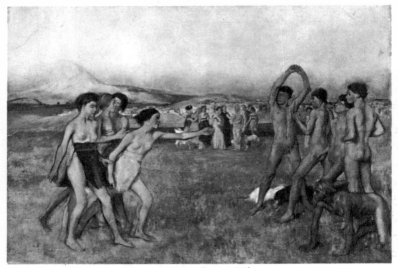

170. DEGAS.   Spartan Girls

but for some reason it is not.   For we are back to our first observation that in the nude of energy the body as such is easily forgotten in our pleasure at the life-enhancing completeness of art.

As I mentioned earlier, many of Michelangelo's figures, if they came to life, would be monsters, and would shock us more than Degas' women who, as he always maintained, are normally well-developed specimens.   It is true that they do not provide the same elaborate muscular scheme as the athletes of the Sistine.   They depend more on outline and the direction of the larger planes, and in this respect are closer to Signorelli.   We must also grant that Degas retained from his Impressionist period something which was contrary to the principles of classic art : the element of accident or surprise.   Photographs and Japanese prints are said to have revealed to him how this quality could be achieved ; we may also claim it as something Gothic, and we can catch a likeness to the angular movements of the Last Judgment at Bourges [253]. But this 'Gothic' movement is entirely without the self-conscious, protesting character of German nudes.   It remains classic in its concentration on formal values.   So by an unequalled combination of skill, intelligence and honesty, Degas won a place near the summit of that European tradition which had crushed so many of his contemporaries, or forced them into rebellion.

Already in 1911 the Futurist manifesto suggested as a contemporary symbol a racing motor-car, with great pipes like snakes with explosive breath, 'a roaring motor-car which seems to run on shrapnel'. This antediluvian monster of 1911 would look ridiculous to us, but it seemed a dragon to Marinetti, and since that date what new manifestations of mechanised energy have been evolved, whizzing, screeching, flashing, supersonic. The vast crowds which attend a motor race or an air rally are there to witness a display of power of a different order to anything they could see in an athletic stadium. The poor human body has been put back where it was in the stone age ; or lower, for it was at least on the same plane of activity as the sabre-toothed tiger and ruled by the same natural laws ; yet perhaps it will be a long time before we renounce our old symbol which, for almost three thousand years, has provided the invigorating joys of self-identification.

CHAPTER VI

Pathos

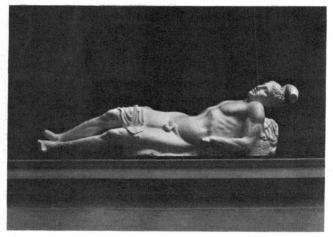

171. Greek.   (?) 5th cent. B.C.   Son of Niobe

I N the nudes of energy the body triumphed.   Hercules triumphed over the
tasks imposed upon him, the athlete triumphed over gravity and inertia.
But there is also a nude which expresses defeat.   The beautiful body,
which seemed secure and serene, is defeated by pain.   The strong man
who has overcome all obstacles by his strength is defeated by fate.   Hercules
triumphant becomes Samson Agonistes.   This nude embodiment, which I
have called pathos, is always the expression of the same idea, that man in his
pride has suffered the wrath of the gods.   And because this may be interpreted
as the triumph of the divine over the material, it admits of this development ;
that the body must be sacrificed to the spirit if man is to preserve his status
'a little lower than the angels'.

The early legends in which the gods assert their divinity are often, to our way of feeling, cruel and unjust. Because the Greek gods were so handsome we tend to forget that they were as jealous as Jehovah, and less merciful. Four of these legends above all touched the imagination of the Greek artists, and through the images they created were to affect the whole course of European art. They were the destruction of Niobe's children ; the death of a hero, Hector or Meleager ; the agony of presumptuous Marsyas ; and the fate of Laocoön, the disobedient priest.

Of these themes only the first belongs to the Classic period of the 5th century, and in pre-Phidian art the works in which the body by itself is expressive of pathos are few and doubtful.

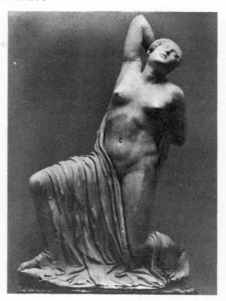

172. Greek. (?) 5th cent. B.C. Daughter of Niobe

In the Acropolis Museum, the gravestone of a crouching foot soldier, datable about 500 B.C., is a possible exception, for whether wounded or merely fatigued at the end of a race, his hands raised to his breast and the inclination of the head make a touching effect which is surely intentional. The fallen warriors from the Temple of Aegina, although they are cold and mechanical, like all the figures from that unlovable assembly, show that the twisted body was already recognised to be a vehicle of pathos. But it is not given emotional resonance till the earliest Niobids. Two of these have been dated in the second half of the 5th century, a recumbent son in Copenhagen [171] and a kneeling daughter in the Museo delle Terme, Rome [172]. In both, pain is expressed by the tension of the body, by the head thrown back and arm stretched above it, a gesture which we might connect with relaxation, but which was accepted by the Greeks as symbolising anguish ; and in the kneeling figure the rising, tapering line has the quality of a cry or of that sensation of pain which seems to shoot higher and higher till it reaches the summit of our nerves. To the Greeks, pain and beauty were almost contrary states, and these two figures are perhaps the first in which they have been united. In doing so, a little of the pure Greek sense of form has been sacrificed ; there is something uneasy, for example, about the relation of the daughter's neck to her shoulders, and the son's body shows a stress and contraction which might have seemed too painfully physical to Polycletus or even to Phidias. No doubt this is the reason why the Niobids had so strong an influence on the artists of the high-Renaissance.

The death of the hero is a sarcophagus motive, and like many such it probably goes back to great paintings of which no record remains ; and it is as a painting that the theme first appears, in those drawings on white Lekythoi showing Sleep and Death carrying a corpse to the tomb. From this group is evolved the design of the dead hero carried by his companions from the field of battle [173]. His right arm hangs limp, his left is raised by a friend who looks at him for some sign of life. The hero is sometimes Hector or Sarpedon, sometimes an unknown soldier ; and in addition to such generalised scenes of military death, there was also depicted the particular fate of

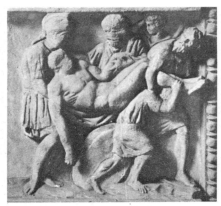

173. Graeco-Roman. Soldier's Gravestone

Meleager. We see him stretched out on his bier, dying before our eyes, as the wooden brand, his life token, is consumed by fire, and the group of women who surround him cry out in horror at the sight of his emaciated body. It is a strangely un-classic scene ; and indeed the whole legend, with its background of forest hunt and blind destiny, gives us a feeling of the cloudy north. Perhaps, after all, that is why Swinburne could make the subject into his masterpiece, and Donatello, with so little alteration, could adapt it to the Gothic motive of lamentation over the dead Christ.

The other embodiments of pathos in antique sculpture almost without exception originate in the art of Pergamon. For over fifty years this kingdom of Asia Minor defended Hellenism from the attacks of the Gauls. The struggle was desperate and unceasing, and when victories were commemorated it was with a sense of gravity and of the tragic character of all conflict ; so the sculptors who worked at Pergamon, and who came, no doubt, from all over the Greek world, had to give their efficient Lysippic style an added seriousness. The two famous figures of defeated Gauls which have come down to us, copies of the bronze figures dedicated about the year 230, express this mood of heroic tragedy with admirable restraint, and if we cannot quite claim the Dying Gaul in the Capitoline for this chapter, it is because the pathos is expressed through the head rather than the lean and leathery body. The first Pergamene school did, however, produce one work in which the body was a direct means of communicating emotion, the figure of Marsyas hanging with his hands and feet bound to a tree, waiting in terror for the knife [174]. In its origins this myth had expressed the cruel arrogance of the Apollonian idea ; but the men of Pergamon, with their romantic respect for barbarians, felt enough sympathy with Marsyas to make his figure into a tragic symbol. The stretched-out body is as defenceless as a dead animal in a butcher's shop, and the columnar form allows a concentration, a bare basic simplicity, which was to satisfy the final need of Michelangelo.

The high seriousness of

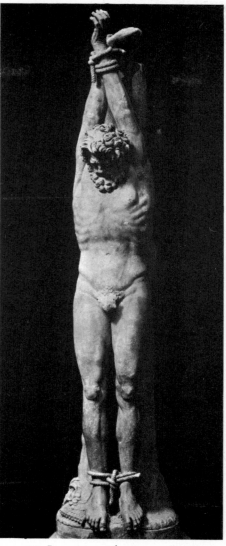

174. Pergamene. 3rd cent. B.C. Marsyas

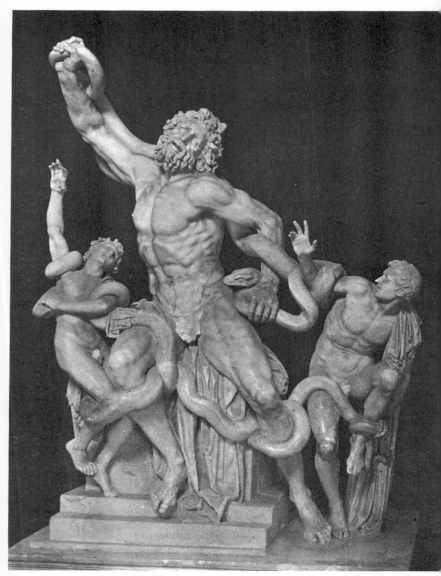

175. ? Pergamene.   2nd cent. B.C.   Laocoön

Pergamene art did not last for long. An enormous altar, dedicated in the beginning of the next century, is an example of that inflated official art with which the 19th century made us so familiar. It was, however, out of this milieu that there emerged the most influential of all embodiments of pathos, the Laocoön [175].

Of the once famous works of art which, in this study of the nude, I have tried to see with fresh eyes, the Laocoön is the most tarnished by familiarity. It is also the one whose fame can be least easily dismissed as an error of taste or the residue of earlier excitement ; and the artists, poets, critics and philosophers who have praised it have done more than read into it their own needs and poetic aspirations. In fact one of the greatest of critics, Lessing, used it as an example of those excellences which are peculiar to the visual arts. That this work, so highly recommended, should have failed in its effect during the last fifty years, is due to a quantity of causes, of which two may be mentioned now, its elaborate completeness and its rhetoric.

Antique art has come down to us in a fragmentary condition, and we have virtuously adapted our taste to this necessity. Almost all our favourite specimens of Greek sculpture, from the 6th century onwards, were originally parts of compositions, and if we were faced with the complete group in which the Charioteer of Delphi was once a subsidiary figure, we might well experience a moment of revulsion. We have come to think of the fragment as more vivid, more concentrated and more authentic. That revelation of personal sensibility, the quality of the sketch, to which Croce has given a philosophic justification, is overlaid and smothered by labour. We can test this by imagining, or seeing in a cast, a fragment of the Laocoön, for example the father's torso and thigh. How life-enhancing they are when allowed to make their effect by formal qualities alone, without encumbering detail. There is scarcely another nude in which emotion is communicated with such abolute mastery of means. The accessory snakes and sons seem to lessen the immediacy of this effect. Now, I think we should be wise to mistrust an aesthetic which habitually prefers the part to the whole ; and in this instance we know that the anguished strength of Laocoön's body is intended to gain in effect by contrast with the exhausted relaxation of his younger son. The criticisms of Winckelmann and Lessing are not mere literary exercises ; they indicate that a great masterpiece must fire off more than one gun. The first aesthetic shock is not enough. But to appreciate this demands time and a continuous state of alert receptivity, and in a philosophy of art based on the immediate sensation it is not easily achieved.

Then, as to rhetoric : the Laocoön is too rich for our frugal taste, and, in particular, we are apprehensive of this sauce by which our parents were

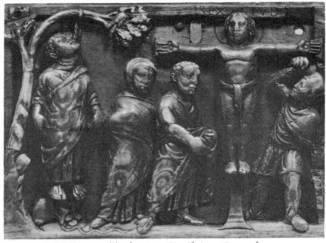

176. Rome. (?) 4th cent. Crucifixion. Ivory plaque

persuaded, as we believe, to swallow many impure substances. No one will deny that rhetoric, the mechanism of art used to persuade us through our emotions, has been generously employed in the Laocoön. But rhetoric is not necessarily a garnishing added to an idea to make it persuasive ; it may invest the idea so closely as to become a part of it, as in some famous speeches of Shakespeare ; and such, it seems to me, is the case with the Laocoön. It contains no movement which cannot be justified by necessity as well as art, except some which are due to its restoration in the 16th century. We know that the father's right hand was originally behind his head, the symbolic gesture of pain, and Montorsoli's eloquent reconstruction not only deprived the group of its classical enclosure, what I have called the cameo quality of antique art, but has also introduced a new kind of oratorical language. More-over, we must not confuse rhetoric with sentimental exaggeration. Winckel-mann stressed particularly the restraint of the Laocoön : 'He raises no terrible shriek. . . . The pains of body and grandeur of soul are, as it were, weighed out and distributed with equal strength throughout the whole frame of the figure.' Winckelmann was contrasting it, of course, with the works of the decadent baroque tradition, the current style of his youth, which his own writings were about to displace. For a hundred and fifty years artists had been trying to enhance the effectiveness of their works by gestures and expressions which went far outside the warrant of their subjects. The result was not precisely rhetoric, because in such a work as Guido Reni's Samson the nude figure is not trying to persuade us to feel any emotion, except satisfaction in the art itself : it is as much a piece of art for art's sake as a sculpture by Brancusi, and in certain moods we welcome it because it is at such a comfortable remove from reality. In the Laocoön, on the other hand, although the situation is improbable, the conduct of the fable is remarkably real and afflicting. To quote Winckelmann again : 'The pain discovers itself in every muscle and sinew of his body, and the beholder, while looking at the agonised contraction of the abdomen, without viewing the face and other parts, believes that he almost feels the pain himself'.

Such, then, were the four chief motives through which, in antique art, the nude communicated the pathos of defeat. Each of them was to be revived at the Renaissance. But during the long banishment of the body there arose one symbol of pathos more poignant, more inclusive, and more compelling than all others : Our Lord on the Cross. The Son of Man, the embodiment of

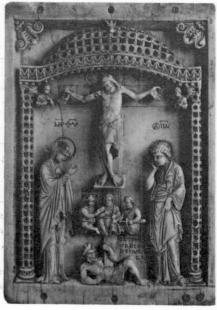

perfect goodness, has suffered the will of God ; but the spiritual power which has caused His death has come from within Himself. Nothing in our subject shows more decisively the ideal character of the antique nude than that, in spite of the Christian horror of nakedness, it was the undraped figure of Christ which was finally accepted as canonical in representations of the Cruci- fixion. Early images of the Crucifixion are of two types, that which shows the Crucified undraped, the so-called Antioch type, and that which shows Him draped in a long tunic, the so- called Jerusalem type. Both are extremely rare in early Christian iconography and do not date from earlier than the 5th century, partly, it is said, because the

177. Constantinople. 10th cent. Crucifixion

221

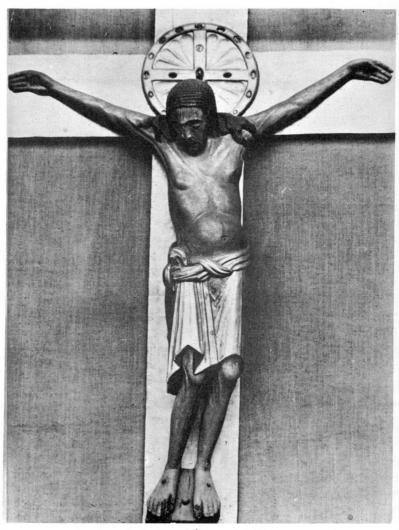

178. German. 10th cent. Gero Cross

memory of the Crucifixion was thought less likely to make converts than that of the Resurrection, or the miracles ; and partly because of the great theological difficulties which the subject involved. An ivory plaque in the British Museum [176] and a panel from the doors of Santa Sabina, which are, with the doubtful exception of some engraved gems, our earliest surviving representations of Christ on the Cross, show a classical figure, nude save for a loin-cloth, standing erect and frontal, with no indication of pain or death. Very shortly after come the draped figures, of which the Monza ampullae and a miniature in the Codex Rabulensis are the first datable examples. We might have supposed that this would have been more acceptable to the monastic west, but there is evidence that the nude version survived the dark ages. Towards the end of the 6th century Gregory of Tours tells how in the Cathedral of Narbonne there was a painting of a 'naked Christ upon the Cross, and that Christ appeared to the Bishop in a dream and commanded that His body be covered with drapery'. Under Charlemagne the self-conscious imitation of antique forms naturally involved a nude figure. Sometimes it is the Incarnate Word, upright and free from pain ; but in ivories of the later 9th century [177], and in such manuscripts as the prayer book of Charles the Bald, we see a nude figure with a drooping head and a compensating bend of the body. It has ceased to be a symbol of the Word and has become the pathetic image of the Son of Man. Once this element of pathos, expressed through movement, was established, the stiff conventional drapery of the Jerusalem type became impossible, and when some puritanically minded patron insisted that the pathetic body should be draped, as in an ivory plaque in Cluny, the figure appears to be dancing, and the spiritual quality is lost.

It is a curious fact that the origin of this image, which became of such supreme importance to western man, is totally obscure. We do not know whether, like much of Carolingian art, it was a revival, or a new invention of the time : and if the latter, whether it was invented in Constantinople or in the west. In any case, this was the image which was to satisfy mediaeval Christianity ; and in the Germanic north it soon takes on the intense poignancy which it retains, and develops to the limits of sanity, during the next five centuries. A strangely early example is the Cross in Cologne Cathedral [178], made for Archbishop Gero (d. 976), which anticipates the German Gothic spirit in every pitiful line of the body. We see the same rhythms in simplified, linear form in certain Anglo-Saxon drawings, or on the reverse of the Cross of Lothair in Aix-la-Chapelle. In evolved Gothic the head drops further, the emaciated body sags, the knees are bent and twisted : it is a hieroglyphic

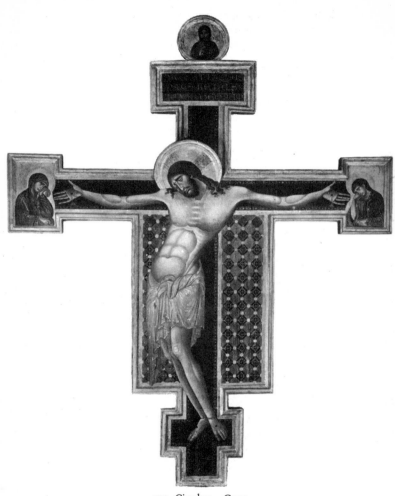

179. Cimabue. Cross

of pathos. In Italy this image of the Crucified appears at the same time as the rigid, hieratic figure ; but when the followers of St. Francis, in their eagerness for a human, emotional Christianity, preferred the more poignant image of the dead Christ, it seems to me probable that they looked for their iconography, as they did for their architecture, to the more fervent and vital rhythms of the north.

Once more the body has become a controlled and canonised vehicle of the Divine. But in the contrast between the Apollo of Phidias, smooth, solid and serene, and the painted Crosses of Cimabue [179] and Coppo di Marcavaldo, the human capacity for creating a God in man's image has been stretched to its fullest extent. Since suffering is precious in the domain of the spirit, and prosperity in the domain of the body, the image of suffering is no longer corporeal, but has become a sort of ideograph ; and of all the symbols used by man to stimulate his faith, to take him out of his natural, daily preoccupations and awaken the consciousness of a soul, these painted Crosses are perhaps the most powerful. The sweep of the torso, like the polyphonic wailing of a choir, the sustained rhythm with which every detail of head, hands and feet adds its cry of anguish to the whole, the thick dark outlines which stamp this terrible image on our minds, all express with irresistible force those impulses which turned mankind away from body-worshipping paganism. And yet, the basis of this ideograph is still the nude, which still obeys, as in the canon of Polyclitus, laws of compensation and balance. We can recognise this as soon as the figure of Christ on the Cross is accompanied by the two thieves. For centuries theologians had been troubled by the question : if Christ really died upon the Cross, how then did His body differ from those of the thieves ? But when the three Crosses appear in western art, the problem is solved by purely aesthetic means. Long before the epoch of realism, the cruci-fied thieves are realistic. Their coarse, ungainly bodies twist and writhe with pain. They are accidental, the Crucified Christ is essential : because, like the earliest nudes of Greece, His body conforms to a canon and satisfies an inner ideal.

It is true that certain of the greatest artists broke through this formula. They did so because it seemed to them that any convention, by holding the truth at arm's length, lessened the emotional impact of the tragedy ; and looking at the smooth, peaceful figures in certain Crucifixions by Perugino, we may share their feelings. It was, in fact, exceedingly difficult to take the formalised figure of iconographic tradition and make it into the body of a real man without loss of spirituality. Giotto has done so in his Cross in S. Maria Novella, and such is the grandeur of his imagination that we do not feel any lessening of divinity. But before the Crucifixions of Andrea del Castagno we instinctively ask ourselves if Christ could have been so muscular and so coarsely built ; and Donatello's crucifix in S. Croce, touching as it is, does not entirely satisfy us, not, as Brunellesco said, because the Christ is a peasant, but because in Italian art our feeling of divinity is so closely united with an ancient tradition of form.

The further we go from the main centres of classic art the less does this apply. The spiritual disease which, from the Black Death onwards, made trouble in all the arts, demanded that the body of the Crucified should display the utmost degree of anguish. The spectators must be roused to the same pitch of horror as they were by the ghastly recitations of Lenten sermons. This hysterical emotionalism occurs in provincial Italian art, but it is of course

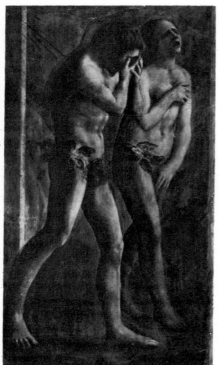

180. MASACCIO. The Expulsion

in the north that the body is subjected to the most painful indignities. The tragic intensity of the Gero Cross continues in wood carving and in such paintings as the Barbara Altar in Breslau, till it culminates in that horrifying masterpiece, Grünewald's Isenheim altarpiece, where the scars and blood-stains made familiar in popular woodcuts or *biblia pauperum* are overwhelmingly magnified. This is the most corporeal of all Crucifixions, in which every line contributes to the image of a living organism in torment. Never before or since have the sufferings of Christ been made so real to us. We may speculate on the feelings it would have aroused in those doctors of the early Church who first allowed a naked body to be shown on the Cross, provided that it symbolised the Incarnate word, incapable of pain or death.

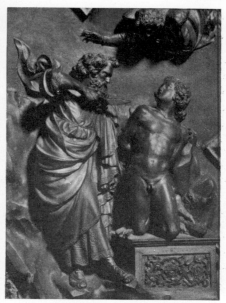

181. GHIBERTI. Sacrifice of Isaac

The subjects of Christian art in which nude figures are appropriate or permissible are, with one exception, subjects of pathos: the Expulsion, the Flagellation, the Crucifixion, the Entombment and the *Pietà*. And so we may imagine the artists of the early Renaissance, who recognised that the nude was the creation of classical art, searching eagerly among disorderly fragments of antique sculpture for motives which could be adapted to Christian needs, and discovering those four embodiments of pathos with which this chapter begins. There were, of course, subjects to which antiquity provided not even the most fanciful parallel, and renaissance artists had to invent for the body poses and gestures which were entirely new. Such was the Expulsion of Adam and Eve from Paradise, one of the first subjects of Christian art to inspire expressive nudes. Yet both Masaccio [180] and de Limbourg gave to Eve the pose of the Venus Pudica, and in general the artists of the Renaissance showed an astonishing clairvoyance in divining the original meaning of a classical fragment, and transposing that meaning into a Christian context. An example is the first classically beautiful nude of the *quattrocento*, the Isaac in Ghiberti's trial relief of Abraham's sacrifice [181], which was certainly inspired by one of Niobe's children. The young figure, kneeling in fear and silent supplication, aware that he must accept the fate prepared for him by a jealous God, has passed easily from one legend to the other.

The interpenetration of Christian and Classic imagery is well seen in two great subjects of pathos, the Entombment and the *Pietà*. The Entombment had been given satisfying shape in northern art, but the most memorable product of the Gothic imagination was that legendary incident known as the *Pietà* when the dead body of Christ was supported on His mother's knees. It is first represented in the 14th century, in German carved wooden figures of

227

great intensity, but its perfected expression belongs to the mid-15th century, and in painting may be found in that masterpiece of French art, the *Pietà* of Villeneuve-lès-Avignon [182]. It is a design composed of angles, rising and conflicting, like the buttresses and gables of Gothic architecture ; and from the first the key and centre of this construction is the harsh accent of Our Lord's emaciated ribs. Thus the moving quality of the design depends directly on

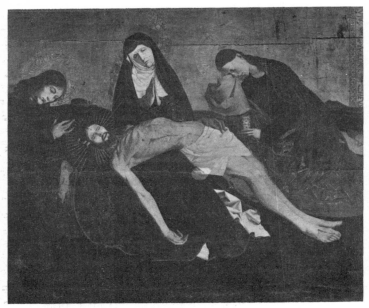

182. Provençale. 15th cent. *Pietà*

the distress of the body, on a condition which is exactly the reverse of physical beauty. Now, what could the Italians, with their thirst for bodily perfection, make of this ungraceful motive ? A few accepted it. Ercole Roberti, almost untouched by the forms of antique art, painted a *Pietà* which could, at first sight, be a Flemish picture of unusual economy. Botticelli, in his final rejection of paganism, made this moment of intimate pathos into the choric lamentation of the *Pietà* at Munich. But this Gothicism could not satisfy the creators of the classical Renaissance. They had somehow to reconcile the subject with their own ideals. Donatello took the first step by recognising that the death of a hero could be transformed, practically without alteration, into an Entombment. This did not at once result in bodily beauty, for, as we have seen, the body of Meleager is sometimes shown as wasting away, and even Donatello could not surpass the tragic horror of the Meleager sarcophagus in the Louvre. Yet, the antique motive once admitted, the classic sense of form would follow inevitably. Meanwhile Donatello took from Gothic art another image of the dead Christ, that which shows His body half-way out of the tomb supported

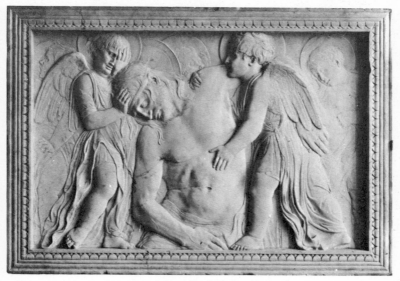

183. DONATELLO. Dead Christ with Angels

by child angels ; and in a marble relief now in London [183] gives it a drooping movement, one side crumpled, the other stretched to its extreme, a Niobid movement which was to inspire one of the most beautiful drawings of Michelangelo.

Different as is this heroic torso from the undeveloped bodies of the north, it is not so beautiful as to disturb us, and conveys through its modelling a sense of tragedy and pain. It was for Giovanni Bellini, Donatello's greatest disciple, to carry this development a stage further. He begins with northern stress and angularity and produces, in the Brera *Pietà*, one of the most soul-piercing pictures in the whole of art, where the stiff, wintry body, with no obvious signs of pain, yet seems to have a tragic structure, as have certain austere

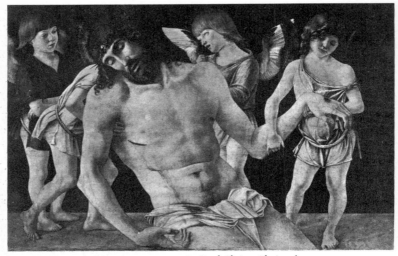

184. GIOVANNI BELLINI. Dead Christ with Angels

façades of mediaeval churches. A few years later, probably in about 1480, there is a decisive change. In the Dead Christ supported by Angels at Rimini it is for the first time the beauty rather than the anguish of Our Lord's body which enhances our pity [184]. Still later, in a picture of the same subject formerly in Berlin, the torso is almost Greek, as beautiful as a son of Niobe, but more peacefully resigned.

Thus Bellini asserts the victory of the spirit by exalting the body's beauty rather than by dwelling on its corruptibility. He himself was probably unconscious of the neo-Platonic doctrines implicit in these Olympian torsos, but towards the end of the century the same idea was developed with full consciousness of its meaning by an artist steeped in neo-Platonism, Michelangelo. His *Pietà* in St. Peter's is one of those sublime conjunctions of Classic and Christian philosophy to which, for a few years either side of 1500, Italian art could give visible expression [185]. He has accepted the touching northern iconography of the subject, the Christ stretched out on His mother's knees, and yet has given to Our Lord's body such an extreme refinement of physical beauty that it makes us hold our breath, as though to suspend the action of time. Michelangelo has adapted antique perfection to its northern setting by giving the body a rhythmic structure the reverse of that in the Gothic *Pietà*. Instead of rising in a series of angular gables, it sags like a garland ;

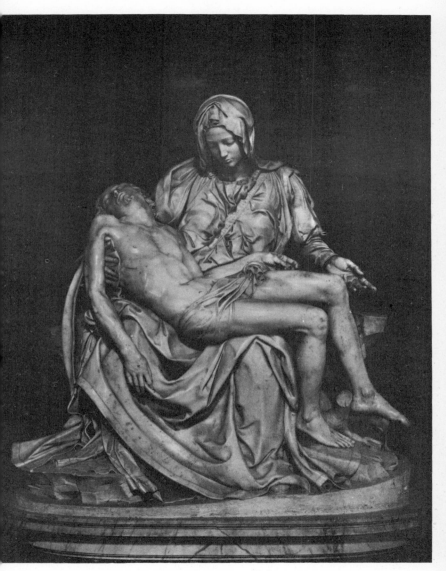

185. MICHELANGELO. *Pietà*

and in fact it is inspired by an antique relief, the death of a hero or *pietà militare*, in which the figure is being carried. Perhaps only Michelangelo, with his unequalled power of *disegno*, could have thus reversed the original function of a pose, and yet made us accept it as inevitable. The stages by which he did so are lost to us—not a single drawing for the St. Peter's *Pietà* survives—but

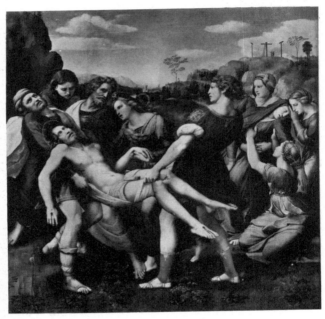

186. RAPHAEL. Entombment

it happens that we can trace the adaptation of the same motive in another famous work of art, Raphael's Entombment in the Borghese [186]. It was commissioned by Atalanta Baglioni, and was intended to commemorate the execution of her son. The events leading up to his death, as narrated by the chronicler Matarazzo, still seem to have the quality of antique tragedy, and in the drawings for Raphael's composition we see him giving his Christian subject a more antique character at every stage. First come drawings in a Peruginesque style, which show the holy women weeping over the stretched-out body of the dead Christ. This Lamentation becomes an Entombment; and in effecting this change there can be no doubt that he had been influenced by an antique

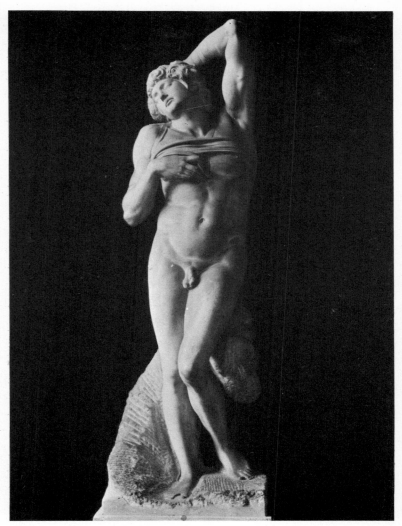

187. MICHELANGELO. Dying Captive

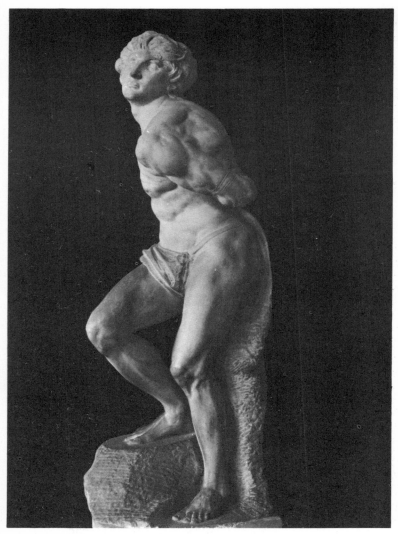

188. MICHELANGELO. Struggling Captive

grave relief or sarcophagus, perhaps the actual piece illustrated on Plate 173. The sag of the body, the limp right arm, the action of the lifters all make this clear. An intermediary drawing at Oxford is catalogued as the death of Adonis and may in fact have some pagan intention. It is revealing that after some uncertainty as to how to treat the limp left hand, he follows exactly the antique iconography by which the central figure raises it and gazes intently at the dead man's face : a motive which would be literally appropriate if, as in the case of Meleager, there were still doubt that the hero was dead. Through these drawings we can see how miraculously the spirit of some Greek artist whose name and work are forgotten, has been transmitted by crude derivatives and re-created by a genius equal to his own. In the end, however, Raphael returns to his own time : for it can hardly be doubted that the figure of Christ in the Borghese picture has been influenced by Michelangelo's *Pietà*. Even allowing that both artists were inspired by the same original, there is in Raphael's Christ a *morbidezza* which he could have found only in the work of his overwhelming contemporary.

After the Battle of Cascina almost all Michelangelo's nudes have this quality of pathos. The body can no longer triumph in its physical perfection, but feels itself vanquished by some divine power. And in the post-Christian world this power is no longer the external agency of a jealous God, but comes from within. The body is the victim of the soul. But, as Michelangelo's work develops, it is truer to put this position in reverse and say that the soul is the victim of the body, which drags it down and prevents its union with God.

The two Captives in the Louvre illustrate his attitude [187, 188]. The first, as I have said, is inspired by a Niobid : and it is hard to believe that Michelangelo did not know some figure with the emotive power of the young man stretched on the ground, now in Copenhagen; although it had not then been discovered and the most probable source of his inspiration is a mediocre figure in the Casa Maffei Collection, Rome, much admired by artists of the Renaissance. He had recognised the meaning of that ancient signature of pain, the head bent back, supported by the hand, and may even have had in mind some version of a wounded amazon. But no direct expression of physical pain remains ; it is more the gesture of a sleeper, half sunk in the luxury of sleep, half anxious to struggle free from some oppressive dream. This is the passive attitude to our mortal bondage. The second prisoner represents the active. Whereas the Dying Captive touches with languid finger the line of drapery on his chest, the heroic captive twists and struggles to be free from his bonds. The mood has changed, and with it the source of inspiration. The first is like a commentary on the ideal beauty of the 4th century ; the second derives from the charged and convulsive rhythms of Pergamon. This is one of the first of many references in Michelangelo's work to a decisive event in his career as an artist, the discovery of the Laocoön.

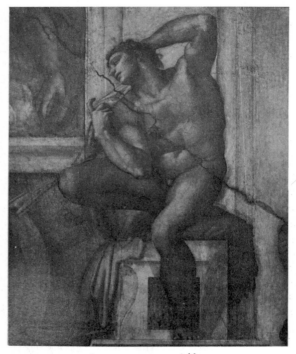

189. MICHELANGELO. Athlete

It happened on Wednesday, 14th January 1506, in a vineyard near S. Pietro in Vincoli ; and within a few hours Michelangelo was on the spot. Pliny's description of the Laocoön group had touched the imaginations of renaissance artists, and even before its excavation attempts had been made to draw what it could have been like. Michelangelo, and his friend Giuliano da Sangallo, identified the newly discovered group immediately. He also recognised that this was the sanction of his deepest need. From the Centaur relief onwards he had wished to make violent muscular movement expressive of something more than a physical struggle. But he had found little authority for this aim in classic art which was his only criterion where the nude was concerned. And then, from a subterranean chamber, marvellously intact, there appeared the authority he wanted, the statue which Pliny himself described as a 'work of art to be preferred above all else in painting and sculpture'. Even at this distance of time there is something miraculous about the whole event, because after centuries of excavation the Laocoön remains an exceptional piece of antique sculpture, and one of the few which does anticipate the needs of Michelangelo.

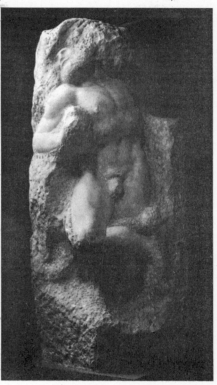

But although we may justifiably imagine the deep sense of confirmation which Michelangelo derived from the group on its first appearance, it had no immediate influence on his style. In the first period of work on the Sistine ceiling, 1508–9, the movements of the athletes grow more violent in each bay, but there is no reflection of the Laocoön. When, however, Michelangelo resumed work on the ceiling the athletes change their characters. A few are still in the mould of classic beauty ; others are highstrung to the point of hysteria ; others seem to be wrestling with intolerable burdens. Of these last, one who is probably the latest of the series is based on the other antique discovery which so greatly influenced Michelangelo,

190. MICHELANGELO. Captive

the Torso of the Belvedere, and is almost like an attempt to reconstruct its pose in reverse. But the muscular body of the athlete has, by its weight and a feeling of thundery oppression, become an embodiment of pathos rather than energy. Diagonally across the panel from him is a reminiscence of Laocoön's elder son [189], also in reverse, but with his broken arm put back behind his head in the position of the Dying Captive. Of all the athletes

237

this is the one who best shows the predicament of physical beauty when burdened with a soul.

But the strangest examples of spiritual struggle manifested through the body are the four Captives now in the Florentine Academy, in which each figure is only just emerging from the marble block [190]. This 'unfinished' element in Michelangelo's work may at first seem to have no bearing on our subject. Yet when we search for reasons why he left so many of his works in a condition far removed from the artistic ideals of the Renaissance, we find that one, at least, of the explanations is connected with his concept of the nude as a vehicle of pathos.

The influence of antique art on Michelangelo's style derives from works of two different kinds. On the one hand were the gems and cameos, which nourished his sense of physical beauty, that smooth perfection of limb realised in such a drawing as The Dream of Human Life. On the other were the battered fragments, the fallen giants half buried in the weeds and rubbish of the Campo Vaccino. In these the eye could comprehend the large lines of movement and then come to rest at those places sufficiently intact to provide it with a nucleus of form. May we not suppose that these noble ruins, which seemed to be struggling to give some message of eternal order through the

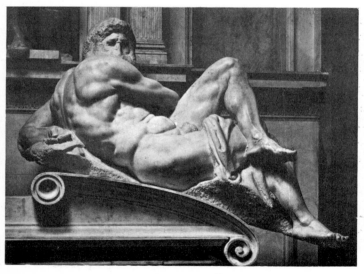

191. MICHELANGELO. Day

chaos of time and decay, became associated in his mind with the pathos of the human body, just as the figures from gems were associated with its sensual perfection? Such, at least, is the effect which these figures still have on us. Moreover, his contemplation of half-obliterated antiquities sanctioned a practice which he had followed in his earliest drawings: the concentration on certain passages of modelling, which were by themselves so expressive that the rest of the figure needed no more than an indication.

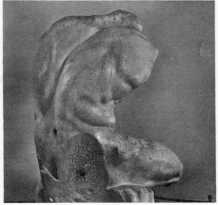

192. Graeco-Roman. The Torso Belvedere

I have already, more than once, spoken of the eagerness with which all great lovers of form grasp at certain closely knit sequences of the body, the muscle-landscape of the torso, or the knot of muscles round the shoulder and on the knee. At such points they find the elements of tension and relaxation, firm and soft, following a logical pattern. They are the most concrete examples of those formal relationships which artists are trying to discover everywhere in the natural world. Michelangelo, in his nudes of energy, fastened upon these nuclei and made them the focal points of his drawings; and when he came to use the body chiefly as an instrument of pathos, he developed an extraordinary power of communicating his feelings through knots of muscles, often presented to us almost without a context. How can a mere detail of anatomy move us so deeply? It is true that our instinctive familiarity with the body makes us sensitive to every inflection; but the answer must also lie in the nature of the classic scheme. Since the Greeks had turned the body into a kind of independent harmony, it was possible by almost imperceptible changes of emphasis to alter its whole effect. Just as in architecture where, with the same components, a classical façade may be serene or tragic, ominous or gay, so Michelangelo with a few elements, the muscles of the torso and thighs, above all the junction of the thorax and abdomen, can evoke an immense range of emotional effect.

The four Captives in the Accademia are the supreme illustration of this power. Their heads only just emerge from the stone, and in two cases are practically invisible; their hands and feet are equally buried in their parent

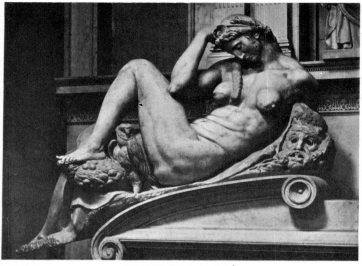

193. MICHELANGELO. Night

marble. They speak to us through their bodies alone. Their pathos, as was appropriate to figures intended to decorate the tomb of Julius II, is heroic. The body, in its struggle with the soul, still commands a Promethean energy. In the Medici tombs this heroic character is abandoned. The figures no longer attempt to free themselves, or to shoulder their burdens. They are languid and resigned, as if drowned in some deep sea of melancholy. 'Yet even here encumbered sleepers groaned.' From this great depth the *ascensio*, the upward flight of the spirit to God, has become almost beyond hope. The pose which Michelangelo has chosen to express his despair is one of great plastic and emotional power. From the pediment of Olympia onwards recumbent figures have been amongst the most satisfying forms of sculpture. Stretched on the ground, the body loses its look of instability and the sculptor needs no devices of tree-stump or drapery to make us believe in its equilibrium. The human race is no longer hoisted above the natural world on stilts, but seems to belong to the earth, like a rock or root. This closeness to the earth is associated in our minds with the loss of animation, with sleep or death, and the Evening is connected with an image of death of an obvious kind, a Roman tomb figure. Although Michelangelo has modelled the torso with an eloquence beyond the powers of late antique craftsmen, this remains the least expressive of the four great figures. On the opposite side of the chapel is the grandest example of Michelangelo's muscle-architecture, the Day [191], where the shoulders of the Torso Belvedere [192] have been 'developed', like a theme of Beethoven. Before this majestic landscape of hill and hollow, each undulation tense and purposeful, each related to the other by laws of natural growth, it seems that the transformation of human anatomy into an instrument of expression can go no further. That it was a transformation and not a mere imitation of a muscular back may be seen if we compare it with the antique bronze boxer in the Museo delle Terme, an able and obviously a truthful piece of work, but one so grossly material that we flinch from it, as from the carcass of a bull. These slabs of muscle weigh us down, whereas, in contemplating the back of Michelangelo's Day, we seem to leave the material world and ascend in our imaginations, as into a cloudy sky.

The Medici Chapel is peculiar in Michelangelo's sculpture in that two of the chief figures are women [193, 194]. We know, from a quantity of evidence, that Michelangelo considered the female body inferior to the male. Only one drawing of a woman done from life has come down to us, and his studies for female subjects, such as the Leda, are invariably drawn from men. It is true that in the Sistine ceiling he had been compelled by his theme to introduce the naked body of Eve, and in the history of the Fall had created two vivid and

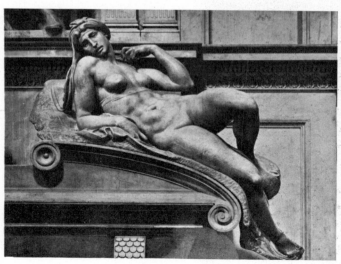

194. MICHELANGELO. Dawn

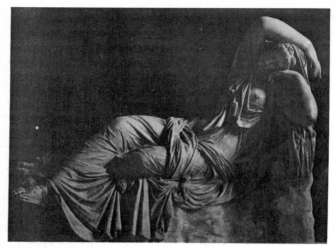

195. Greek. ? 2nd cent. Ariadne

valid images of woman, the temptress twisting her body with heroic sensuality
and the cowering animal fleeing from Eden. But the compulsion had been
dramatic rather than formal, and it is at first hard to know why, of his own
free will, he should have introduced the female body into a work so oppressively
personal as the Medici tombs. One answer may be that he felt the need of a
contrast to the emphatic muscularity of the other figures, and since this was
the period of his life when he was most troubled by his erotic feelings for
young men, he may not have trusted himself to include in the Chapel a male
embodiment of softness and grace. There was also, in the emotional atmo-
sphere of the Medici Chapel, a passive character which the female body could
express better than the male. This distinctively feminine pathos had been
recently revealed to renaissance artists by the discovery of a splendid and
moving work of antiquity, the so-called Ariadne of the Vatican [195] ; and
although neither of Michelangelo's figures imitates her pose, both sustain the
same flow of languid movement. But in spite of a feminine rhythm, they
are entirely without those basic sequences of form by which artists had given
a plastic order to physical passion. The breasts, for example, which from
the 5th century onwards had been intermediaries between geometry and the
senses, and in the profoundly sensual art of India are made to dominate
the whole body, are reduced, in the Night, to humiliating appendages ;

and the stomach, instead of being a soft modulation of the other spheres, is a shapeless trunk cut across by four horizontal furrows.

Several preliminary studies for the Night have survived. They are done, as usual, from male models and show how much more at ease he was with the rocky male thorax and abdomen, but they also show that in the sculpture Michelangelo has given the thigh a female character, and has gained a new plastic interest from its tapering form. The body of the Dawn [194] is a little less far from our normal conception of beauty, and represents a sort of agreed version of the female body which could be incorporated into the Michel-angelesque style without inconsistency. Although its feminine attributes have been so drastically stylised, it is not without a latent sensuality, as we can tell from the numerous variations which mannerist sculptors and painters were to play upon this form during the next hundred years, ranging from the elegance of Amanati to the feverish lubricity of Spranger and Cornelisz of Haarlem.

Strange as these figures are when judged by the criterion of the classic nude, as embodiments of pathos they are creations of genius. Every line of the Dawn's body is like a lamentation at the sovereignty of the senses; as for the Night, Michelangelo has allowed his statue itself to speak in the poem which he addressed to a friend who had said, wishing to flatter him, that it might wake and come to life:

> Caro m' è 'l sonno et più l' esser di sasso,
> Mentre che 'l danno et la vergogna dura.
> Non veder, non sentir m' è gran ventura;
> Però non me destar, deh! parla basso.

> (Welcome to me is sleep, and dearer still,
> While wrong and shame endure, my stony death.
> Neither to see nor hear is my good luck.
> Do not awake me: pass with bated breath.)

At two periods of his life, in his youth and old age, Michelangelo's mind was occupied by the subject of the Crucifixion. Soon after the death of Lorenzo de' Medici in 1492 he made for the prior of Santo Spirito a carved wooden crucifix, just below life size, which was placed over the high altar. It is lost, and was never, perhaps, one of his major works; but this commission is important in the formation of his spirit, because it was under the protection of the prior that he was first able to study anatomy; and at the same time he had his first vivid experience as a Christian, the preaching of

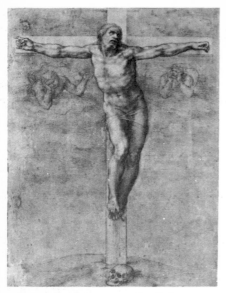

196. MICHELANGELO. Crucifixion

Savonarola. Although never a direct follower—his life's work is a refutation of the *frate's* puritanism—he studied Savonarola's works throughout his life, and, sixty years later, told Condivi that he could still hear the *frate's* voice ringing in his ears. These two great experiences, the study of anatomy and the teachings of Savonarola, came to him at the same impressionable moment, and whatever the immediate result in the Santo Spirito Cross, the final outcome seems to commemorate Savonarola's tragic denunciation of human vanity.

The later Crucifixions begin with a famous drawing done by Michelangelo for his friend Vittoria Colonna in about 1540 [196]. It was the result of special circumstances. The recipient was a pious lady of aristocratic birth who might equally have been found in the Rome of St. Jerome or the Paris of Bossuet, exercising an influence out of proportion to her intellectual powers. To Michelangelo she symbolised a release from the tyranny of the senses. His long struggle with physical passion was almost over, and as with many other great sensualists, its place had been taken by an obsession with death. So the drawings done for Vittoria Colonna represented with an eloquent poignancy the death of Christ, the Crucifixion and the *Pietà*. They were in the polished style of the sheets presented to his friends, and this was no doubt pleasing to their recipient, who wrote that she had examined them with a magnifying glass, and could find no mistakes in them. But since this high finish is combined with an emphatic sentiment anticipating that of the counter-Reformation, this Crucifixion was not to the taste of early 20th-century connoisseurs. The pose seemed artificial, the turn of the body too elegant, the modelling too smooth. It was, therefore, long dismissed as a copy. I think we may safely accept it as an authentic drawing, and surrender ourselves to his eloquence ; but it was not a communication of Michelangelo's deepest feelings. Fifteen years later he penetrated beyond these conventions of style and piety, and produced a series of drawings in which the idea of the Crucifixion, in all its tragic solemnity, is given its most concentrated form [197, 198]. Looking back at our antique prototypes of pathos, we can say that Michelangelo has turned from the second style of Pergamon to the first, from the Laocoön to Marsyas. He has felt how the body hanging stark and defenceless has a quality of truth far more moving than the elaborate *contra posto* of the Vittoria Colonna drawing. But the terrible strain which, as a means of touching our emotions, has taken the place of the *curva bizantina*, depends on the arms being raised high above the shoulders; and in order to achieve this Michelangelo has revived the Y-shaped Cross sometimes found in mediaeval

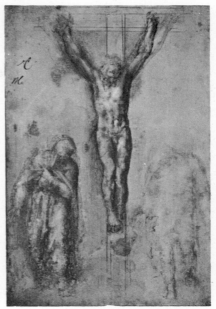

197. MICHELANGELO. Crucifixion

art. The two drawings which follow this pattern gain in tragic force from our feeling that this, in actual fact, is how a body would hang. Other drawings in which the body is straight, but the arms are extended, may belong to a stage before he had thought of the Y-shaped Cross ; or they may represent a sort of recoil from his own originality, a feeling that at all costs the ancient, sanctified image of the Crucifixion must be preserved. Plate 19 supports this second alternative, for the figures of the Virgin and St. John, which have been used to express a whole range of emotions—fear, horror, pity, repulsion and attraction—are brought close to the Cross in a mood of transcendent union ; and we feel that this must be the last of the series.

In these drawings, as in certain passages of Dante or St. John of the Cross, we reach a realm of the spirit where analysis is inappropriate and critical language inadequate. We can only be grateful that we have been permitted to catch a glimpse of the *nobilissima visione*. For a second those great mysteries of our faith, the Incarnation and the Redemption, are made clear to us by an

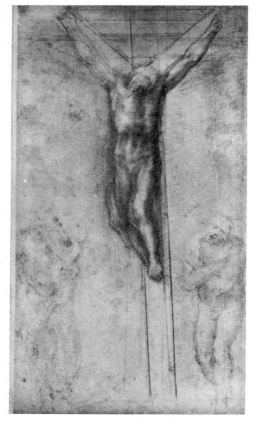

198. MICHELANGELO. Crucifixion

image of the naked human body. Has Michelangelo finally achieved the aim which had haunted him since the Sistine ceiling, and before : to grasp physical beauty so firmly that he may carry it with him to the realm of the spirit ? Not entirely, for he has been forced to awaken from that dream of antiquity, in all its strength and radiance, which had been the first inspiration of his art. His three last *Pietàs*, those carvings on which he worked in secrecy and self-imposed loneliness almost to the day of his death, show that in the end the ideal of physical beauty had to be abandoned. In the Palestrina *Pietà* [199] the

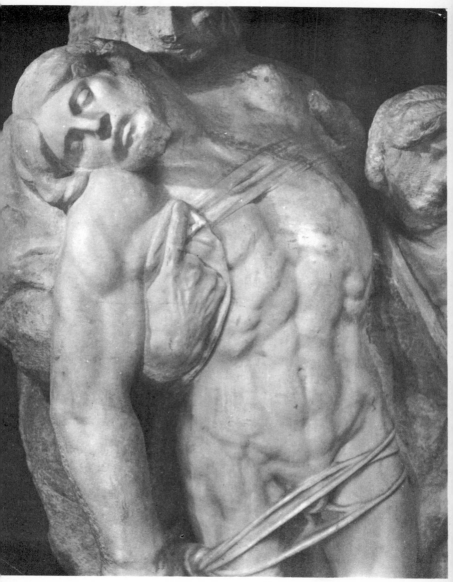

199. MICHELANGELO. *Pietà* (detail)

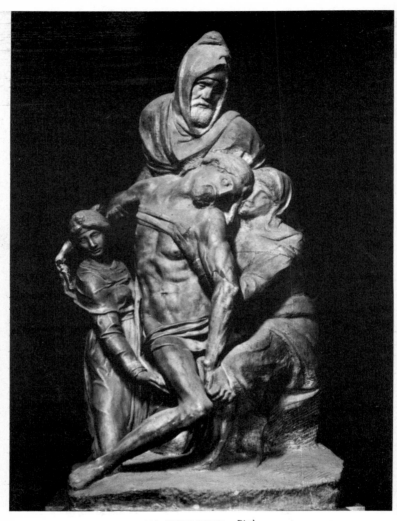

200. MICHELANGELO. *Pietà*

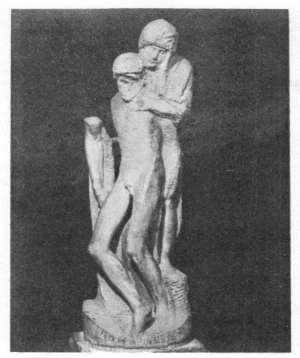

201. MICHELANGELO. *Pietà*

distortion is so great that certain critics have doubted its authenticity. The gigantic arm and torso weigh down the body of Our Lord, so that the legs seem crushed, and almost disappear, and even the torso itself has lost its firm physical structure and become like some ancient rock-face pitted by the weather. In the group in the Duomo [200] the nude figure follows an angular, criss-cross movement which is entirely unclassical. This is not the suave geometry of the godlike body, but the stressful geometry of the great cathedrals. Finally, the Rondanini *Pietà* [201] where, in the humility of his last years, Michelangelo has pared away everything which could suggest the pride of the body, till he has reached the huddled roots of a Gothic wood carving. He has even eliminated the torso, for we can deduce from a drawing that the right arm, which now stands in a strange isolation, was once attached to the body. And the sacrifice of this form, which for over sixty years had been the means of his most intimate communications, gives to this shattered trunk an incomparable pathos.

In the general collapse of humanism of the later 16th century, the nude survived as an instrument of pathos, for it could be made to satisfy the intense emotionalism which accompanied the religious upheavals of the time. The death of Our Lord and the sufferings of the saints were, for about a hundred years, almost the only way in which the naked human body could be represented without official disapproval. But the use of the nude was not limited by an external sanction alone : there was also a decline of confidence in the body. And with this decline it was no longer possible to lift the physical to the spiritual plane ; all that could be done was to abstract from the nude certain ideal elements, which had already been discovered by Michelangelo or in antiquity, and offer them in an almost disembodied state.

Such is the procedure of those two neurotics with whom the anti-classical movement of the 16th century begins, Rosso and Pontormo. Already in the 1520's in two pictures of the Descent from the Cross, which were to remain their finest works, each of them had produced figures of the dead Christ which are, once more, like hieroglyphs of pathos : only the hieroglyph is based on Michelangelo and not on the tradition of Byzantium. In the Rosso it is, in fact, the Christ from the St. Peter's *Pietà* in reverse, and the fact that a figure designed for a recumbent position is now used with the body vertical shows how little the solid reality of matter entered into Rosso's calculations. The most curious of these abstract nudes of pathos are to be found in that eccentric work, Moses and the Children of Jethro [202], painted by Rosso in about 1523. All that the humanist nude had aimed at, from the Greeks onwards—the rounded limbs, the smooth, full forms—has been abandoned. The bodies in the foreground are flat and angular, the transitions abrupt. There is an insistence on pattern rather than solid form, which looks back to the fallen knights in Uccello's San Romano and forward to the dead bodies in Douanier Rousseau's *La Guerre*. Yet this hysterically anti-classical work is based on an antique original. The nude figures in the foreground come from the lid of a Niobid sarcophagus, and the woman in the centre is actually a figure of Niobe, which Rosso clearly thought was too good to be omitted, although she has nothing whatsoever to do with the scene depicted.

This early revolt against the tyranny of the Antique, where the nude was concerned, may be illustrated by another example. Titian, who passed so easily from the humanism of Sacred and Profane Love to the counter-Reformation sentiment of the Frari Assumption, had borrowed freely from the Laocoön in his Brescia altar-piece. The risen Christ is one aspect of the famous group ; the St. Sebastian is another [203]. Yet the authority of Laocoön was so oppressive that he was impelled to produce a drawing in which the father and his two sons are represented as monkeys ; and, incidentally, he has studied the group with such care that his reconstruction of the missing parts is more accurate than that adopted in Montorsoli's restoration of the original. That the drawing was reproduced as a woodcut proves its popularity ; and,

in fact, it expressed two eternally popular opinions : that nature is superior to art, and the authority of famous masterpieces is a bore. The monkeys are not ridiculous but natural and are part of the rich vegetable landscape in which Titian has placed them. The nude body of the Laocoön was ideal and belongs to the arid intellectual world of museums, already in the 16th century peopled with theorists and pedagogues.

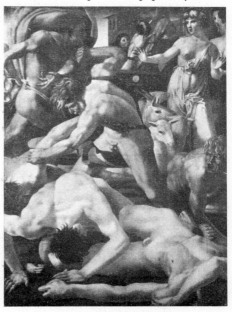

202. ROSSO. The Children of Jethro

Titian's protest against idealism and authority anticipated a general reaction. In the realistic painting of the early 17th century the suffering bodies of martyrs are so emphatically un-ideal as almost to persuade us that they should be treated in a later chapter. But, as with Rosso's Jethro, a closer consideration shows that they have not in fact departed very far from the themes of pathos in antiquity and the Renaissance. Marsyas, Meleager and the children of Niobe all reappear, but with unshaven faces and dirty finger-nails. We may turn for an example to the arch-realist himself, to Caravaggio's Entombment in the Vatican [204]. Fundamentally it is a renaissance composition, grandiose and compact, and less Baroque than Raphael's Transfiguration. The body of Christ has a genuine pathos rare in Caravaggio, and we recognise that this is due to his having retained the motive of the antique *pietà militare*.

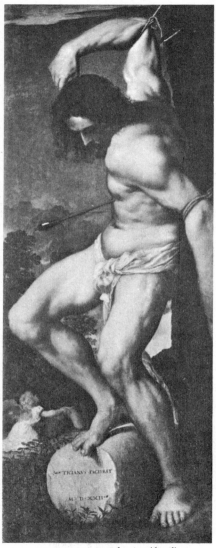

203. TITIAN. St. Sebastian (detail)

He has, in fact, followed it more closely than Raphael, but instead of making the body more graceful, he has added the coarse hands and feet which were his usual declaration of independence. A similar procedure may be found in the work of the chief Spanish realist, Ribera. In his picture of the Trinity in the Prado, the figure of Christ is claimed as an example of extreme realism. Yet it touches the imagination chiefly because it derives from the inventive genius of Michelangelo. True, the physical type is very far from heroic; but the pose is almost that of the Christ in the Duomo *Pietà*. Very rarely, as in his Martyrdom of St. Bartholomew, do we feel that the suffering body is primarily a record of something which Ribera has seen. This is realism at its best, in which facts achieve the dignity of art from the grave and simple manner in which they are presented. Complementary to it, academism at its best, is the *Pietà* of Annibale Carracci in Naples. The figure of Christ is a Michelangelesque invention, corrected and smoothed out, but with such art that we are not offended ; on the contrary, such high-minded eclecticism almost amounts to creation. Yet in neither Ribera nor Carracci does the body achieve that role of a

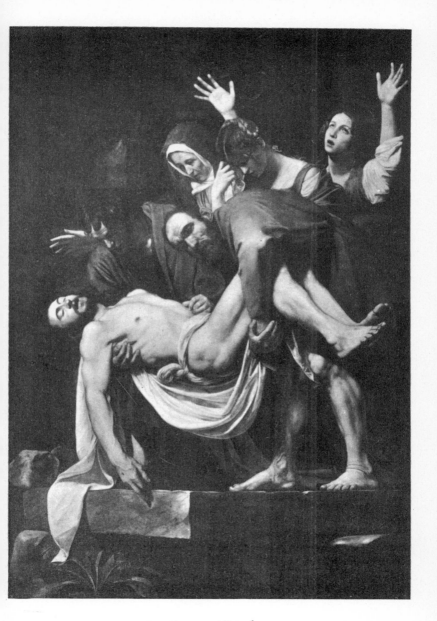

204. CARAVAGGIO. Entombment

complete and independent means of expression which it held in antiquity and the Renaissance. It is not part of a style, inseparable from the architecture of the time. This reintegration could be achieved only by an artist in whom the appetite for life and the mastery of style were equally powerful.

Peter Paul Rubens painted his two masterpieces of baroque pathos for the Cathedral of his native Antwerp soon after his triumphant return from Italy, the Raising of the Cross in 1611, the Descent from the Cross in 1613 [205]. They were decisive battles in the history of art, and like David's Oath of the Horatii were recognised as such from the beginning. They were also intended to supplement one another in style and sentiment, and the eloquent chapter of *Les maîtres d'autrefois* in which Fromentin describes the contrast between them, must be amongst the few passages of criticism which would certainly have pleased the artist. Between them they establish the range of pathos as it could be expressed through the nude body, for the next century. I have already described in the chapter on Energy how laboriously Rubens had studied Michelangelo ; and in the central figures of his two great triptychs there are certain reminiscences of the Medici tomb and the Last Judgment, for example the twist of Our Lord's right arm in the Descent. More generally, the vigorous cursive style in which everything is described is ultimately derived, through Tintoretto and Michelangelo, from the Laocoön. But when this is allowed, it is Rubens' own splendid powers which have drawn together all the stylistic and emotional currents of the time. He was not only a master of his profession, but he had an immense generosity of heart through which he could take the commonplaces of sentiment and make them moving. When he painted the dead body of Our Lord his feelings were as sincere and heartfelt as when he painted the nude body of Helena Fourment. Thus the artificiality of the baroque style, the element of make-believe which had been present from Correggio onwards, is swept away by Rubens' glorious confidence in the body.

Or should we say in the flesh ? An old antithesis between flesh and spirit makes it, at first, hard to accept the part played by the surface of the body in Rubens' paintings of the Deposition and Entombment. Yet the painter, communicating with us through pictorial means, must use whatever elements in the visible world affect him most strongly ; and the skin was to Rubens almost what the muscles had been to Michelangelo. It may be convenient to call one response sensuous, the other intellectual ; but if we judge the resulting work of art simply by its effect on our emotions, we must grant that Rubens' feeling for the changing colour and delicate texture of flesh has added a new element to the nude of pathos. Titian, in that splendid expansion of the *pietà militare*, the Louvre Entombment, had emphasised the contrast between the pale body of Our Lord and Joseph of Arimathea's brown arm, and Rubens, who was a profound student of Titian, must have recognised how this simple device added poignancy to the traditional design. In his own nudes of pathos the colour of the flesh is often the main theme of the picture, and ranges from the deathly pallor of the Deposition to the incorruptible pink of certain *Pietàs*, where, the subject being symbolic rather than realistic, he has simply made the body as beautiful as he could ; and we feel that any insult to that unblemished surface would be more than ever cruel.

In addition to these pictorial achievements of the kind usually associated with Rubens, there are certain paintings of the Crucifixion and Deposition which have the stark directness of the greatest classic art. Such is the Crucifixion in the Van Beunigen Collection [206] where all three figures hang like Marsyas, and yet are subtly differentiated by the character of their bodies and by the incidence of the stormy light. The long tradition of Christian iconography by which the figure of Christ is ideal while that of the unrepentant thief has a

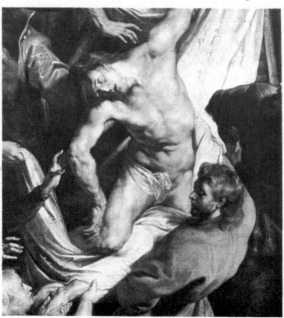

205. RUBENS. Deposition (detail)

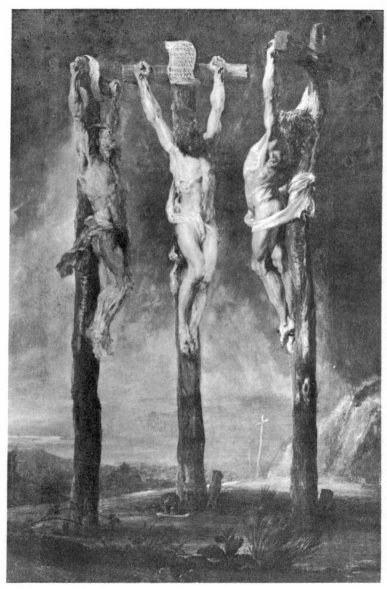

206. RUBENS. Three Crosses

brutal materiality, has seldom seemed more convincing, for, in spite of the divine beauty of Our Lord's body, Rubens has kept the three crucified men united by a sense of shared humanity. Equally concentrated is the small picture in Berlin of the two Marys mourning over the dead Christ [207]. It goes back to a classical relief both in the rigid figure, with arm hanging down, and in the severe frontal composition ; yet in painting it is as rich and dramatic as a Delacroix. It is one of the many inspired 'asides' in the great declamation of Rubens' religious painting, and seems almost to anticipate the so-called Classic Baroque which was to grow up under his shadow in the person of Nicolas Poussin.

For too long our responses to the powerful and moving quality of Poussin's imagination have been falsified by the stock epithets of criticism—'learned', 'judicious', even 'academic'. Such exclamations, foolish enough before his Bacchanals, must die on the lips when we contemplate his scenes of pathos. Of course he was familiar with the antique nudes of suffering, the Niobids or the dying Meleager ; but his transformation of his models was, in the end, almost as great as that of Rubens. An example is the death of Narcissus in the Louvre [208], where the figure seems to have been inspired by a relief in the Terme (No. 8074). Poussin has reconstructed such a figure in order to place at the centre of his composition the rectangular block of the chest and the contrapuntal movement of the arms ; and yet, as with all Poussin's most satisfying designs, these feats of pictorial architecture are subordinate to an intense imaginative participation in the drama. They are the means of forcing us to respond more vividly to the pathos of Narcissus' death. This is even truer of that tragic masterpiece, the Mourning over the Dead Christ, in Munich [209]. Here, instead of the rectangular torso of the Narcissus, there is the extruding thorax of a Gothic *pietà*, united with that of the dying Meleager. Apart from these correspondences in the pose, the body has evidently been studied from nature ; and this combination of realism with a full, frontal composition, extending no further into space than a relief, reminds us irresistibly of Donatello. That we should also think of him before the later drawings of Rembrandt, shows how the great spirits of the 17th century returned unconsciously to the serious, humane imaginative world of the first Renaissance.

In the 18th century this sense of tragic humanity was driven underground (where it was visited by Gluck's Orpheus and Mozart's Don Giovanni), and when it reappeared in the work of the great romantics it had grown more self-conscious, more assertive and more grandiloquent. In much of early 19th-century painting the nudes are as artificial in their pathos as in their pretensions to Apollonian beauty ; but from amongst the huge theatrical canvases of

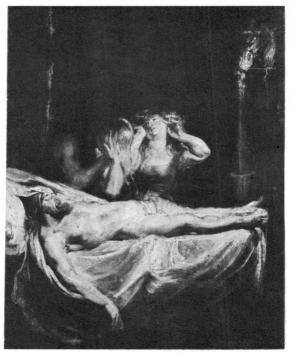

207. RUBENS. Mourning over the Dead Christ

Vernet, Girodet and Delaroche there emerges one even vaster which still convinces us, the Raft of the Medusa. It is a triumph for the Byronic, and gains its
authenticity from the fact that Géricault was a genuinely Byronic character—
impulsive, generous, unstable, pleased to be a child of the time, yet technically
traditional to the point of reaction. Just as Byron believed that there had been
no real poetry since Pope, so Géricault took his poses from antique reliefs and
his style from the mannered draughtsmen of the 16th century. When painting
the Medusa he fired his imagination by talking to the survivors, and had made
in his studio a model of the raft ; but he peopled it with figures from the
Sistine ceiling and from Raphael's Transfiguration. In spite of this reliance
on artifice, perhaps inseparable from the construction of so large a pictorial
unit, the Raft of the Medusa remains the chief example of romantic pathos
expressed through the nude ; and that obsession with death, which drove

Géricault to frequent mortuary chambers and places of public execution, gives truth to his figures of the dead and the dying. Their outlines may be taken from the classics, but they have been seen again with a craving for violent experience.

With Delacroix the romantic death wish was under the control of a lucid intelligence. No great poet ever had a clearer head ; yet he had visited the infernal regions and his first famous painting foreshadows the whole course of his imagination [210]. Somehow, with the help of Virgil, Dante will just succeed in crossing the Styx, as in later works Apollo will just succeed in conquering the Python and western thought just survive the ravages of Attila. And this survival of civilisation by so narrow a margin was symbolised for Delacroix by the formative genius of a few men, Gluck, Mozart, Shakespeare, Rubens, Michelangelo. Such is the spirit in which he approached the nude. The body is defeated, as the Gauls were defeated by the Romans, yet it survives because the great artists of the past had been able to give it perfection of form. The damned souls who cling to the barque of Dante, or float beside it, are such defeated Gauls, some with an antique form, others derived from Michelangelo, but transformed by Delacroix's imagination. After this magnificent beginning,

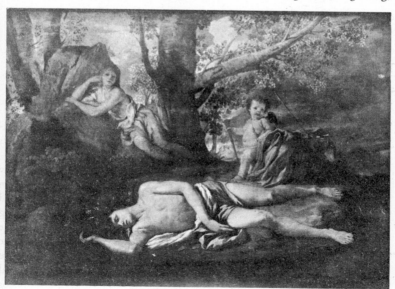

208. POUSSIN. Death of Narcissus

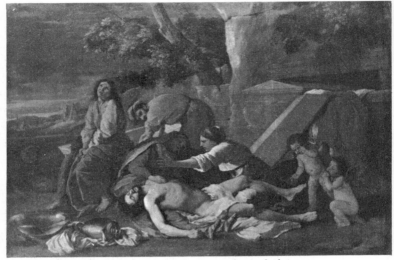

209. POUSSIN. Mourning over the Dead Christ

it is sad to find how seldom, in his later work, Delacroix attempted the nude. The chief exception is the half-naked woman, pale, delicate and defenceless, who in many of his pictures awaits the onslaught of brutality. She appears, with other admirable nudes, in the Massacre of Skios, she sprawls voluptuously on the funeral pyre of Sardanapalus, and kneels before the trampling hooves of the Crusaders as they enter Constantinople. She is that typically romantic image, the flower beneath the foot; but Delacroix treats her without a trace of sentimentality. His journey to the infernal regions had taught him that cruelty is a necessary part of creation. His contemporaries have recorded how closely he resembled the tigers which he painted with such loving admiration; and so in these 19th-century daughters of Niobe there is a new flavour of sadistic appetite, as if Delacroix, while pitying them, would willingly crunch them up.

The last heir of the great romantics was Rodin. This statement would not have pleased him, for he always claimed to be a disciple of the Greeks and of the Gothic sculptors. But no one can escape from his time, and seen in perspective we recognise him as extending into sculpture the pathos of Géricault and Delacroix, taking Michelangelo's inventions, making them more transient and more pictorial. His sense of form was remarkably close

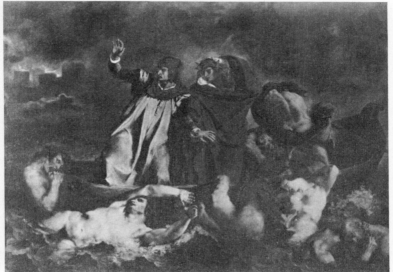

210. DELACROIX.   Barque of Dante

to that of Delacroix, and it is hard to believe that some figures from the Gate of Hell were not influenced by the lost souls who cling to the barque of Dante or the marble Danaid by the flower-like girl drooping before the Crusaders' horses. I make these comparisons to situate, not to belittle, him. In fact few sculptors have been less derivative, and many of his figures—the crouching woman, the prodigal son—add a new, convincing image to the restricted repertory of the nude.

No other artist of the 19th century had so profound a knowledge of the body. Like Degas he recognised that the deadness of the academic nude was partly due to the artificial and limited conditions under which the model was observed. That familiarity with the naked body, which the Greeks had acquired in the palestra and Degas had sought in the ballet school, Rodin achieved by having numerous models in his studio playing about and adopting their poses unconsciously. He moved amongst them, observing, noting in his incomparable shorthand, and acquiring an understanding of the body which none of his contemporaries could equal. But when, in a piece of considered sculpture, he coloured observation with thought, the result was almost always an embodiment of pathos. Rodin was so saturated with the

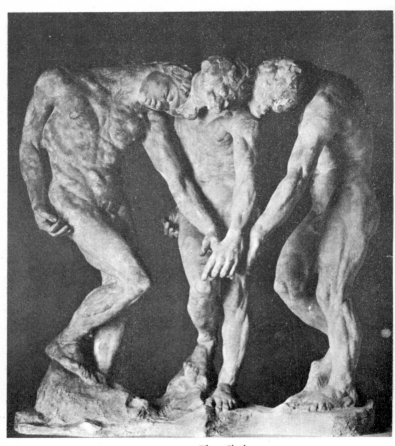
211. RODIN. Three Shades

feeling of man's tragic struggle with destiny that his figures could hardly move without expressing it. If they walk it is towards their doom, if they turn to look round it is for fear of some avenging angel. It was no accident that for thirty years his nude figures were thought of as parts of a grandiose, misconceived project, the Gates of Hell, and in fact 186 of them were fitted into the final scheme. Unfortunately Rodin was all too conscious of the soul-stricken character of his imagination, and occasionally exploited it, hollowing a cheek or accenting the tenseness of a muscle beyond conviction. But, like Wagner, the false and theatrical elements in his work are only an extension of the true, slightly vulgarised to suit modern conditions ; and his finest pieces, the Eve, the Three Shades [211] or the studies for the Burghers of Calais, are worthy of the tradition of sculpture which began with the Lapiths of Olympia, the daughters of Niobe and the Marsyas.

In spite of the vitality with which he maintained this tradition we feel that with Rodin an epoch and an episode have come to an end. The idea of pathos expressed through the body is in decay ; and the cause is fundamentally the same as that which led to the decline of belief in its divinity. In Greek mythology and the Christian religion, suffering was due to the direct inter-vention of a God. Michelangelo, it is true, made that suffering come from within, but he never doubted that God was there to superintend and ultimately to direct it. Pathos was focused. In the work of Rodin it is diffused. It is simply part of the *Götterdämmerung*, the death-wish that the poets of Romanti-cism had foreseen, and the technicians of the present century have so brilliantly accomplished.

CHAPTER VII

Ecstasy

'A LITTLE Olympus outside the greater' : with these words Walter Pater, in his *Study of Dionysus*, describes that population of satyrs, maenads, sylvans and nereids which represented, in the Greek imagination, the irrational elements of human nature, the remnants of animal impulse which the Olympian religion had attempted to sublimate or to subdue. And in art, too, beside the embodiments of measured harmony and justice, of celestial beauty and determination, were lesser embodiments of impulse, of abandonment to enthusiasm or panic, or to the mysterious influences of nature. The works of art in which these impulses are expressed are smaller and less impressive than the monuments dedicated to the Olympians ; yet just as the blood of Dionysus could flow into the cup of Christianity, so, in the history of art, Dionysian motives had a longer and more fruitful life, diffusing classical forms to the rim of the antique world, and reappearing as soon as the figure arts could receive them. At an early stage in Greek art painters, and perhaps sculptors, had discovered poses and movements which expressed something more than physical abandonment, which were, in fact, images of spiritual liberation or ascension, achieved through the Thiasos or processional dance ; and the Thiasos, whether of Bacchantes or nereids, became the favourite motive of sarcophagi ; for it showed death only as the passage of the soul through some less rigid element in which the body is remembered for its joy of sensuous participation rather than for its weight and dignity.

In the nude of energy the body was directed by the will. It lunged forward in a rigid diagonal, and even when it assumed the complicated poses of athletics it was under control. In the nude of ecstasy the will has been surrendered, and the body is possessed by some irrational power ; so it no longer makes its way from point to point by the shortest and most purposeful means, but twists and leaps, and flings itself backwards, as if trying to escape from the inexorable, ever-present laws of gravity [212]. The nudes of ecstasy are essentially unstable, and if they do not collapse it is not through conscious

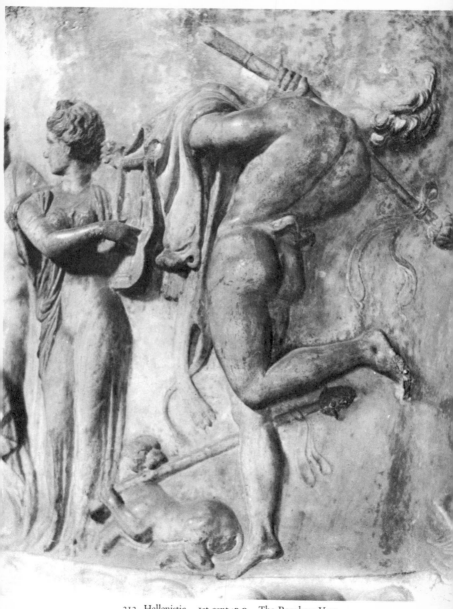

212. Hellenistic. 1st cent. B.C. The Borghese Vase

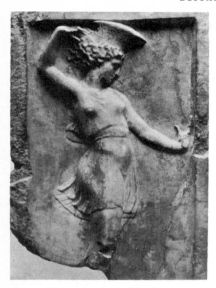

213. After Callimachus. (?) 4th cent. B.C.
Dancer

control, but through the precarious equilibrium of enthusiasm, the providence which is said, not always quite correctly, to look after drunken men.

The first Dionysiac scenes appear, appropriately, on drinking-cups, where, in the beginning of the 5th century, satyrs and maenads take the attitudes they retain for the next eight hundred years, the satyr leaping in the air, the maenad with head flung back and arm raised swaying forward in the processional dance. This was evidently a pictorial and not a plastic motive, and the sculptural form in which it has come down to us is, from its linear character, clearly inspired by painting. Two sets of reliefs show us something of what we have lost. One of them is of ritual dancers, perhaps priestesses of Apollo Karneios, wearing short kilts and the high straw hat called a calathiscos. They are almost certainly replicas of the 'Spartan girls dancing' mentioned by Pliny as the work of Callimachus. We know them from gems and Aretine ware, and from two marble carvings in Berlin so fresh and vivid that they might be the work of Desiderio da Settignano. Unlike the maenads their gestures are tense and controlled; but their flame-like movements give them an ecstatic quality and they are on tiptoe to leave the earth [213, 214].

The other series represents maenads or Bacchantes, their bodies abandoned to the ecstasy of the Thiasos, and probably derives from an altar of Dionysus [215]. These are known best from elaborate reliefs in New York and Madrid; later they provided motives with which to decorate urns, cisterns, pedestals and furniture of all kinds throughout Hellenistic and Roman times. Even in the earliest replicas they are highly artificial productions, and it is hard to believe that they were invented in the 5th century, although a quantity of evidence in vase-painting and on friezes confirms this early date. In contrast to the Spartan dancers, the maenads depend for their effect on clinging drapery, which not only accentuates their actions, but creates a pool of movement in which their bodies seem to swim. No doubt this swirling line, with its deep-rooted powers of visual excitement, helped to give them their long life as objects of art. We are half-hypnotised by its movement, as we are by swirling water, and, like the maenad herself, surrender our faculties of reason. But the predominance of drapery also led, as it so often does, to an ornamental unreality. The well-known maenad who holds in one hand the severed carcass of a kid and in the other brandishes a knife above her head is little more than a decorative hieroglyphic. Her bloodthirsty act is forgotten in the elegance of her pose, her body is subordinated to the convolution of her draperies. She anticipates the mere space-filling of Agostino di Duccio or Burne-Jones. Yet such is the

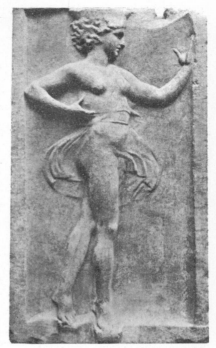

214. After Callimachus. (?) 4th cent. B.C.
Dancer

rhythmic completeness of these designs that few works of antiquity were to have a more liberating effect on the art of the *quattrocento*.

From its essential instability the ecstatic nude was unsuited to sculpture in the round and those pieces which attempt it, like the Hellenistic faun looking at his tail, are, for the most part, trivial. But in the 4th century both Praxiteles and Scopas took maenads as the subject of sculptured groups ; and, by rare good fortune, that of Scopas has come down to us in a small-scale replica which preserves some of the vitality of the original [216]. Scopas' figure was recognised in its own time as communicating, with unusual intensity, the sculptor's mastery of violence. 'Who carved this Bacchante ?' asks an epigram in the Anthology. 'Scopas. Who filled her with this wild delirium, Bacchius or Scopas ? Scopas.' This is just. The passionate energy which the Dresden maenad still radiates from her battered surface is the result of a highly developed skill. Her body has been given a double twist, to which her thrown-back head adds a third ; and her drapery is so artfully devised that one side being relatively austere enhances the sensuous shock of the other. Her naked flank combines the luxury of Hindu sculpture with the plastic vigour of a Donatello ; and yet the whole is kept within the bounds of classic form. Her ecstasy has the ferocious single-mindedness of the possessed, compared to which the Bacchantes of Titian are enjoying a romantic diversion. They are the highest product of decorative art ; she is still part of that antique religion of sensuality from which, in the end, the female nude derives its authority and momentum.

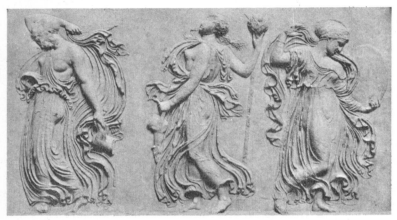

215. Graeco-Roman.   Three Maenads

The Dresden maenad, taken in conjunction with the frieze of the Mausoleum, leads us to believe that a number of Dionysiac motives which survive on reliefs and sarcophagi also originated in the workshop of Scopas. They are distinguishable from those of 5th-century derivation by a greater plasticity, and by a twisting movement. Instead of the stylised lines of transparent drapery, the maenad's cloak hangs from her shoulder and reveals her naked side. The figure striking a tambour, with head thrown back, hair and drapery streaming behind her, as she surges forward in the pursuit of the god, is worthy of the great sculptor of passionate movement ; and when we consider that it has come down to us only in the carvings of artisans done three or four hundred years later than the first source of inspiration, we can estimate the vitality of the original [217].

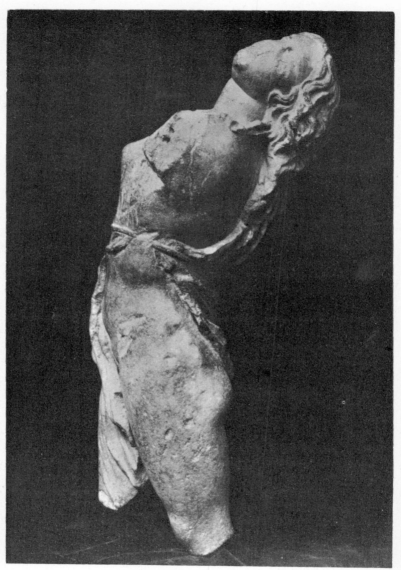

216. After Scopas. 4th cent. B.C. Maenad

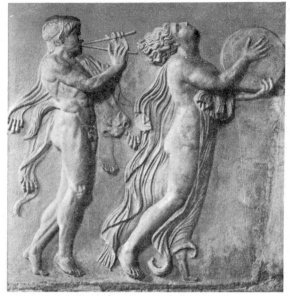

217. Graeco-Roman. Dionysiac procession

If the earlier maenads remind us of the *quattrocento*, of Agostino di Duccio and Botticelli, those deriving from Scopas recall the high-Renaissance, and the Bacchanals of Titian. A sarcophagus in the Terme, which preserves in stone the quality of a relief in bronze, has the bodily opulence and warmth of the great Venetians, and the Bacchante in the centre, standing with her arm bent across her chest which we rediscover in Giorgione's *Concert Champêtre*, has been referred to frequently in the chapter on *Venus Naturalis*. To the right we see the Scopaic twist at its most extreme [218]. The dancer with her back to us, standing on tiptoe, has turned her head right round to look at us over her shoulder. Evidently the sculptor was recording the dance of a Dionysiac votaress, for we find a similar pose in one of the finest surviving paintings of antiquity, the scene in the Villa Item, where a priestess purifies, by her orgiastic dance, a terrified initiate.

It seems that Scopas also provided vivid images of the other Dionysiac population, the nereids, tritons and *chorus phorci*, as Pliny calls them, describing his sculptured group after it had been brought to Rome by Domitius Aheno-barbus. Of this, too, there remain some fragmentary indications, less certain and less moving than the maenad, but retaining enough of the resonance of the original greatly to influence romantic art. One of them, the Grimani triton, looks unbelievably Giorgionesque, and must have been known to Venetian artists of the early 16th century. We might suppose it to be a renaissance forgery had not a small tritoness, apparently deriving from a group by the same artist, recently emerged from the excavations in Ostia. Her head is thrown back in ecstasy, her hair is thick and vital like that of the Dresden maenad, and her body is modelled with a sense of the flesh which gives her a strangely modern look [219].

But most of the nereids which have come down to us show no trace of a Scopaic origin. They are less charged with movement and more at ease in their surroundings than anything which we presume to be of his invention. These are the figures found on sarcophagi, and later on metalwork, which seem to have been made with the same pattern all over the antique world. Their origin is obscure, but they are (with one exception) consistent with one

another, and seem to derive from the design of a single artist. In general these nereids are un-Dionysiac. They sit comfortably on the backs of their fish-tailed companions, sea-centaurs or hippocamps [220], and turn to converse with them or look backwards with an air of pleasant detachment. The only one who resembles the maenads in enthusiasm is she who stretches out on her front and flings up her arms to embrace a goat or bull [221], with a gesture which leaves us little doubt of her significance. Her abandoned pose seems to derive from a source different to that of her more decorous sisters, and is perhaps of eastern origin. Amongst the seated figures are some which imply an advanced understanding of the nude ; but they are all resolved into plastic ideas so simple that a modest artisan could use them almost as easily as if he were carving an alphabet. We realise how rich and elaborate the original must have been only when we see them revived, almost unaltered, in the work of Nicolas Poussin.

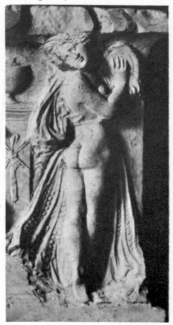

218. Graeco-Roman. Dionysiac sarcophagus (detail)

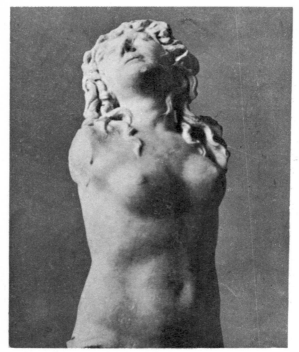

219. After Scopas (?). A Tritoness

The nereids, like the maenads, start as expressive sculpture, concerned with some important experience in human life ; and both end as decoration. It is worth digressing to discover, if possible, what this transformation of the Dionysiac nude implies.

Decoration exists to please the eye ; its images should not seriously engage the mind or strike deep into the imagination but should be accepted without question, like an ancient code of behaviour. In consequence, it must make free use of clichés, of figures which, whatever their origins, have already been reduced to a satisfactory hieroglyphic. From this point of view the nude provides a store of perfect decorative material. It pleases the eye, it is symmetrical and it has been reduced to a simple, memorable form almost as a condition of its survival. It can be used as a component part in building up a pictorial construction with only a faint flavour of its original intention being

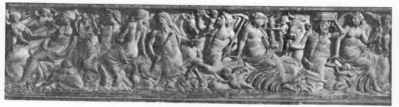

220. Graeco-Roman. Nereid sarcophagus

perceptible ; and yet there is always, in the human body, a latent warmth which can save such compositions from frigidity. But the nude figures which fulfil this function must be of a kind in which the rational faculties are superseded and the mind consents to be lulled out of its daily preoccupations ; and for this the subjects we have just described, the triumph of Bacchus and gambolling of sea-gods, are ideally suited. In both the reason is agreeably banished and its place taken by dreamy exultation and voluptuous instability. In the Bacchic scenes there is the grape, the wine-vat, the clashing of cymbals and the rhythmic dance to deprive us of our rational faculties ; in the other group the means are rather subtler and perhaps more profound, for the half-magical buoyancy of these tritons and nereids, the ease with which they ride on each other's backs or recline in the trough of a wave, appeals to our instinctive rebellion against the most inhibiting restraints of our body. In our dreams we fly or swim, and attain thereby a rapturous freedom which, in our waking lives, we know only in love. So the body, to be a perfect motive for decoration, must be in ecstasy, not only because it is then on a different plane of reality, but because, when no longer confined by stasis, it can be used with greater rhythmic freedom. It can flourish like the vine or float like the clouds, and thus achieves equality with the two chief sources of ornament in human history.

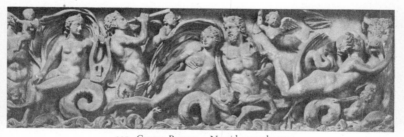

221. Graeco-Roman. Nereid sarcophagus

222. Late Antique.   *c.* A.D. 350.   The Mildenhall Dish

The history of the nereids shows how certain shapes will satisfy us and survive long after their iconographical meaning has been forgotten. Whatever may have been in the mind of the artist who first invented them, on sarcophagi they were accepted as symbolising the passage of the soul to another world ; but on Coptic needlework or the ivory caskets of Alexandria the nereid is purely ornamental. She is simply a form with agreeable associations, in which the stresses are resolved and enclosed, so that it can be included at any convenient point ; yet which has a cursive outline so that the eye is led on easily

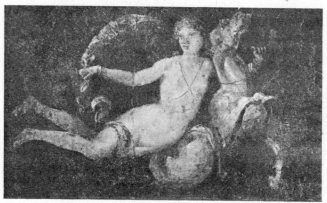

223. Graeco-Roman. 1st cent. A.D. Nereid

to the next unit of decoration. For this reason the nereid achieved, in the late Roman empire, a wider diffusion than has been the lot of any motive based on the nude. Pieces of silver, embossed or engraved with these compact, desirable shapes, were sent to the barbarian perimeter of the antique world, and nereids have been found in the most improbable places, in Northumberland and Baku, in Ireland and Arabia. A greco-buddhist carving in the Lahore Museum contains a nereid almost identical with one in Grottaferrata, which was a favourite in the Renaissance. The most elaborate of all Dionysiac dishes was recently turned up by the plough near the village of Mildenhall in Suffolk, and shows the two types of Thiasos combined : the Bacchic, complete with familiar maenads and satyrs on the rim, the Marine, with nereids, tritons and a gigantic head of Poseidon in the centre [222].

The proportions of these export-nereids are often exceedingly unclassical. Already in the 1st century a wall painting of a nereid from Stabia [223] shows the same long torso and short thighs as the Three Graces from Pompeii,

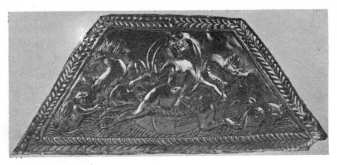

224. Late Antique. *c.* A.D. 380. The Casket of Projecta

and was presumably also of Alexandrian workmanship ; she is almost identical with the nereid on the lid of the silver casket of Projecta [224], which can be dated *c.* A.D. 370, and a century later the same figures, even further de-classicised, appear in the carvings and needlework of Coptic Egypt. The oriental luxury of their hips also reminds us how much the nereid must have contributed to art in India, where they appear in the 6th century, practically unchanged, as flying gandharvas [225]. And as we look at such figures, we realise that it was incorrect to imply that the nereid survived solely for formal reasons. Perhaps survival on those terms is impossible, and it is only when a form is valued as a symbol that it is also valued as a shape. For the nereid who was invented to symbolise the liberated soul continued to do so, in countries and times when

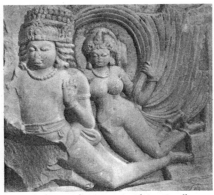

her first intention was unknown. In the middle ages she appears among the blessed in the Last Judgment, and even in such an emphatically Gothic work as the triptych of Hans Fries at Munich a sea maiden with wind-swept hair is being taken up to heaven. The painter could not resist that compact and eminently portable shape ; portable because, in the original, transported from cumbersome earth to the abodes of bliss [226].

225. Indian. 6th cent. A.D. Flying Gandharvas

It was this sense of floating

into new life which led to the nereid shape being transformed into the figure of Eve as she was evoked from the side of the sleeping Adam. The idea occurred first of all to that lonely exponent of bodily grace in the 14th century, the sculptor who designed the story of the Creation and Fall on the façade of Orvieto Cathedral. He seems, almost certainly, to have been the Sienese architect Lorenzo Maitani, and he would thus have been familiar with several sarcophagi, one of which was set over the doorway of the Cathedral workshop in his home town. His Eve [227], of

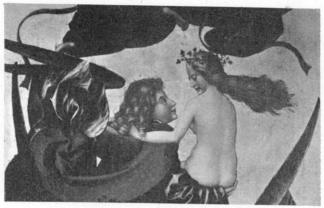

226. HANS FRIES. Last Judgment (detail)

course, is flatter and less voluptuous than a nereid, and instead of staring at her companion with level, amorous gaze she turns her long, serious face to God the Father with an air of submission. But her derivation is unquestionable, and she has retained, with her actual shape, some of the dream-like quality of the sea festival.

Over a hundred years later Ghiberti, who was familiar with the sculptures at Orvieto, uses the same idea in the second door of the Baptistery. He was a student and collector of antiques, and so was able to give his Eve a more classical sweep than was possible in the preceding century. She is not derived from a placid passenger nereid, but from one of her more active sisters ; and the source of her shape has determined her character. The Eve at Orvieto is modest and obedient ; Ghiberti's Eve is bold, the first, perhaps, of all the proud naked beauties of the Renaissance [228].

Ghiberti, by his artful mixture of Gothic and Classic rhythms, evolved a style which is often curiously outside its epoch. Many of his figures, if seen in isolation, could be dated a hundred years later. But when we find the same antique motives in the work of his contemporaries we realise how powerful the Gothic style remained right up to the middle of the 15th century. An example is the group of drawings by Pisanello and his pupils which are copies of Bacchic sarcophagi in the Campo Santo. No part of the body, chest,

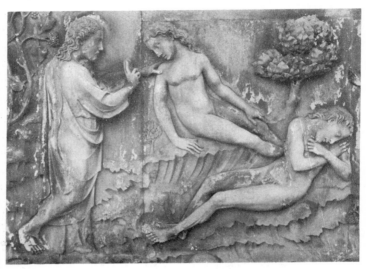

227. LORENZO MAITANI. The Creation of Eve

stomach or thighs is given its simple geometric shape, but each is accented and articulated with a restless eye for detail. Little is left of the antique except the iconographic motive. Yet Pisanello did not think of these pagan shapes purely as decoration. His figure of Luxury in the Albertina shows that he had recognised the character of the most enthusiastic nereid, and has added to her abandoned pose an evil thinness, a kind of Baudelairian corruption, which is quite unclassical [229].

As archaeological knowledge progressed this free, creative attitude to antiquity declined. I have mentioned more than once the sketch-books containing drawings of antique sculpture and architectural detail which were part of the stock-in-trade of certain *quattrocento* workshops. Turning the pages we see how much in demand were the subjects of Bacchic and nereid sarco-

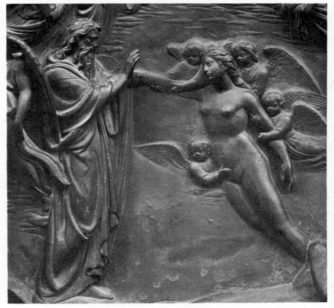

228. GHIBERTI. The Creation of Eve

phagi ; and the comparison of a drawing in the so-called Codex Escurialensis with the original sarcophagus from Santa Maria in Trastevere, now in the Louvre, shows how self-effacingly, and, on the whole, accurately, antique art was being recorded and diffused during the last decade of the 15th century. From this dead level of antiquarian knowledge there emerged those works of genius, Mantegna's engravings of tritons and hippocamps fighting, where pedantry is transformed by a severe and scrupulous technical skill. In fact Mantegna's use of depth is entirely un-antique, but it is improbable that he realised this, for his mind was fixed on giving to every detail a form which could be justified by reference to some vase, gem or relief.

The opposite approach to antique art, in which context and accuracy are ignored and only the rhythmic life is maintained, may be seen in two works of art in Florence, Donatello's Cantoria [230] and Pollajuolo's frescoes in the Torre del Gallo [231]. For many reasons I have excluded children from this study of the body ; but Donatello's *putti* must be an exception, for they are primarily symbols of Dionysiac abandon, and the childish character of their bodies is forgotten in our sense of liberated animal life. If in a photograph we cover their heads our first glance reveals a Bacchic sarcophagus more intricate and more vigorous than anything in antique art ; and only on looking more carefully are we aware of their fat tummies and chubby legs. The transference of Scopaic poses, invented to convey the climax of physical passion,

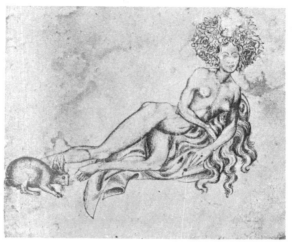

229. PISANELLO. Luxury

to the immature bodies of children, accounts for the feeling of uneasiness, of perversion almost, which this great masterpiece arouses in an unprejudiced mind. Pollajuolo's frescoes in the Torre del Gallo have suffered no such violent transposition. They are simply the figures from Etruscan pottery enlarged to the scale of mural decoration. We recognise familiar satyr poses, expanded and made more realistic by articulate Florentine outline. Under the influence of his antique model Pollajuolo has renounced the renaissance craving for depth. The light figures, stripped of all accessories, are silhouetted against a background of flat colour, and our whole attention is focused on their bodily movement. Our eyes, accustomed to the rigorous economies of cave men and of Henri Matisse, may be grateful that for once a renaissance painter has been willing to throw away some of the heavy baggage of his epoch.

Somewhere between the romantic archaeology of Mantegna and the rhythmic re-creation of Pollajuolo is the use made, throughout the *quattrocento*, of the maenad with clinging, wind-blown draperies. We find her first, I

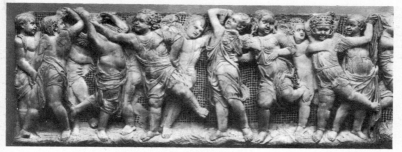

230. DONATELLO. Detail from Cantoria

believe, in the *predella* of Donatello's St. George, and she remains, to some extent, a pretext for introducing the free, cursive rhythm of antiquity into the rigid groups of *trecento* iconography. Often she is no more than a decorative adjunct, or visitant from another world, joining, in an unaccountable manner, the company of staid Florentine ladies, such as those who come to the bedside of St. Elizabeth in a fresco by that least Dionysiac of painters, Domenico Ghirlandajo. But, as with the nereid, her symbolic intention is not always forgotten, and it is in the person of Salome that she most often appears. On Donatello's marble relief at Lille she is in Herod's courtyard, dancing with arms raised above her head, one leg irresponsibly kicked up behind her ; a few years later we see her in Fra Filippo's fresco at Prato, where, however, she is decorously clothed, and retains something of Gothic stiffness. Botticelli also uses the same stock figure in his Sistine frescoes ; and not content to bring it in as a decorative adjunct, he makes the closest transcription of a Bacchic sarcophagus of the whole *quattrocento* in an engraving of Bacchus and Ariadne drawn in their chariot. It could almost have been copied direct from a relief, similar to one in Berlin ; but the weary droop of Dionysus' head and the half-trusting, half-diffident gesture of Ariadne retain some Gothic delicacy of human perception and seem to be his own invention.

Far beyond such a direct tribute to antiquity are the two flying zephyrs in the Birth of Venus, who are perhaps the most beautiful example of ecstatic movement in the whole of painting. Here for the first time (if Indian art be excepted) we see the defiance of gravity transferred from water to air. The dream of buoyancy, with all that it implies of liberation, becomes more rapturous and more invigorating. As with the first embodiments of ecstasy, the suspension of our reason is achieved by the intricate rhythms of the drapery which sweep and flow irresistibly around the nude figures. Their bodies, by an endless intricacy of embrace, sustain the current of movement, which finally flickers down their legs and is dispersed like an electric charge. Though we may find precedents for them in the flying Victories of antiquity, Botticelli's wind gods, like his Graces, are an individual inspiration, without sources or successors [232]. In the next century painters were to become much occupied with figures in the clouds, but only once again was the ecstasy of flight brought so near to us, in the Bacchus and Ariadne of Tintoretto. The nude is now an instrument in the hands of a virtuoso ; and the goddess Venus, who skims over the head of Bacchus without causing us a moment's anxiety, was, from the first, acclaimed as a *tour de force*. Yet this artifice is subordinate to a poetic purpose, and the flying figure is above all a projection of eager longing and imminent delight.

It was in Venice as Tintoretto's picture reminds us, that the nude of Dionysiac ecstasy regained its original warmth ; above all in the two great Bacchanals which Titian painted for Alfonso d' Este from 1518 to 1523. In these he imagines the protagonists of an antique relief, with added splendour of flesh and coloured silks, transported from their abstract setting into a landscape

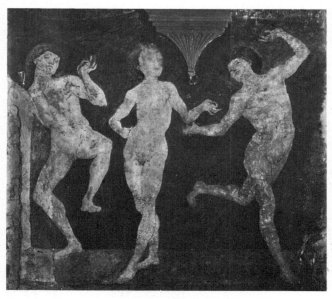

231. POLLAJUOLO. Dancing Nudes

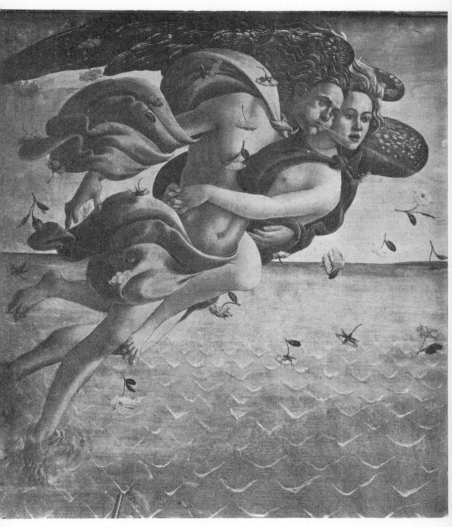

232. BOTTICELLI. The Winds (detail from Birth of Venus)

as sensuous as their bodies. In the Bacchus and Ariadne it is Bacchus himself [233] who expresses the idea of ecstasy, by the turn of his body, his fluttering drapery and his momentary pose. In the Madrid Bacchanal the reclining maenad [234], whom we often find in the corners of sarcophagi, overcome by the generosity of the grape, has been developed into one of the most splendid nudes of the high-Renaissance, an ecstatic counterpart to Giorgione's Venus. The utter relaxation of her head and stretched-back arm had been used already as a symbol of luxury by Perugino in the allegorical Victory of Chastity, which he painted for Isabella d' Este's study, and was to occur again in Poussin's Bacchus and Midas. Her firm, shameless torso must have been in Goya's mind when he painted the *Maja desnuda*.

At the end of his life, with undiminished appetite, Titian again drew his inspiration from a scene of Thiasos, this time from an amorous nereid whom he has transformed into a figure of Europa [235]. Although the motive is antique, the conception of the nude is profoundly unclassical. Titian has painted the open, full-blown body of his Europa entirely from nature, without any of those astringent simplifications which hitherto had refined away the accidents of the flesh. The folds and puckers of her right leg are as far from the basic severity of the Greek nude as anything in Rubens. Yet just as the Hellenistic Hermaphrodite is saved from mere eroticism by harmony of form, so this figure is raised to the highest realm of art by colour, and by the glowing consistency of Titian's imagination, through which he can both participate in and withdraw from the creative turmoil of the senses.

I have already contrasted the robust eagerness of Titian with Correggio's delicate tremor of the flesh. They are the sun and moon of sensuality. And it is this sense of nocturnal rapture which Correggio has realised in his picture of Io submitting to the cloudy embraces of Jove [236]. Her outline is like a pattern of ecstasy, combining the thrown-back head of a maenad, the naked flank of a nereid, and the outline of a figure of Psyche in a Hellenistic relief famous in the Renaissance as the *Letto di Policleto* ; and we can understand why this lineament of gratified desire could fill an ill-balanced nature with destructive envy. In the 18th century the picture passed into the possession of Louis d'Orléans, son of a famous lecher, the Regent of France. He at once ordered its destruction and is said himself to have struck the first blow with a knife. Can Dionysiac symbol ever have produced a more truly Dionysiac result ! Fragments of the canvas were surreptitiously collected by the Gallery director, Charles Coypel, and put together : all but the head, which had been completely destroyed. A merciful providence reincarnated Correggio in the person of Prud'hon, who painted the present head.

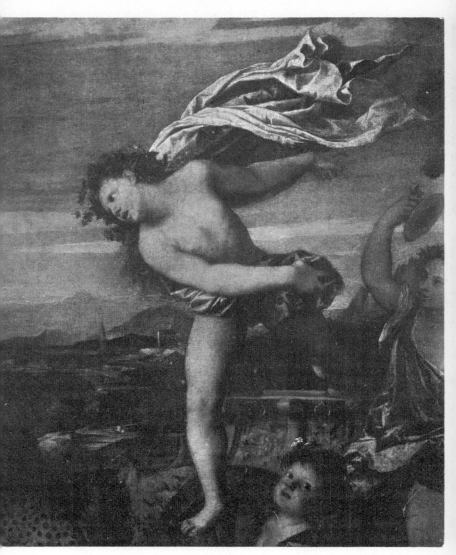

233. TITIAN. Bacchus (detail from Bacchus and Ariadne)

The line between sacred ecstasy and profane, fine-drawn at all periods of true religious fervour, was at its finest in the anxious years of the early 16th century. Correggio, the poet of pagan physical love, anticipated both in form and sentiment the art of the counter-Reformation. That other precursor of baroque imagery, Lorenzo Lotto, more closely concerned with Lutheran ideas, could not admit Correggio's easy, catholic acceptance of the flesh. He did not paint the nude, and avoided pagan subjects. There is, however, one revealing exception, the Triumph of Chastity in the Palazzo Rospigliosi [237]. In this the naked Venus, who is being driven away by an angry peasant Chastity, is taken direct from a nereid sarcophagus. Lotto has not attempted to disguise his source, and has hardly varied the outline of the torso, partly, no doubt, because nude figures of this sort were unfamiliar to him, but partly because he felt that this nereid was an accomplished symbol of desire. Just as the mediaeval sculptors had understood the transports of the sea-Thiasos in a spiritual sense, and used the nereids as souls on their

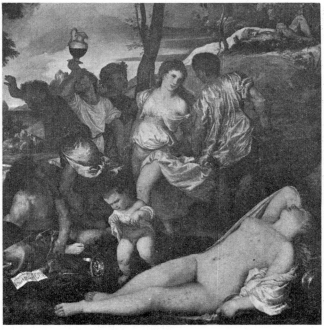

234. TITIAN. Reclining Maenad (detail from Bacchanal)

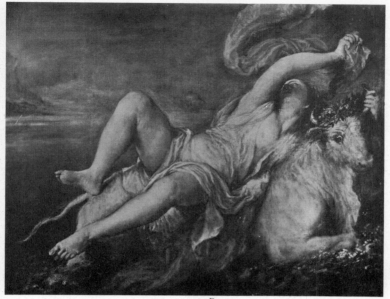

235. TITIAN. Europa

way to heaven, so Lotto has turned them the other way, the puritan way, as it was shortly to become, in which all that is expressed through the body is fundamentally evil.

Rubens is the noblest refutation of puritanism ; and in an earlier chapter I have tried to show how his religious and his pagan painting are the fruit of a single well-grown tree. But although he imagined so many scenes of Dionysiac enthusiasm, nude embodiments of ecstasy are rare in his work. The catalogues tell us that his nymphs have been surprised by satyrs but they show no sign of this emotion. They remain placidly seated and, only once, in the picture in the Prado, is there a widespread commotion. Nor do they give the feeling of freedom from gravity which characterises the nude of ecstasy as I have described it. They do not fly or float or seek to lose contact with the earth, of which they are such welcome offspring. On the other hand, Rubens' religious pictures often contain ecstatic gestures and expressions which show that such transports were not unknown to him. In this he showed himself a true son of the Catholic reformation, which although it encouraged a condition of spiritual self-surrender by no means devoid of sensuality, also

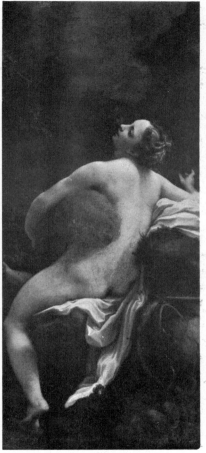

236. CORREGGIO. Io

frowned on the pagan nudity of the Renaissance. It is a proof of the sincerity with which Rubens' saints turned their eyes to heaven that (unlike Raphael) he did not give the same expression to Venus and Diana.

The Church's opposition to the nude was more effective in Italy than in the north, and the saints in ecstasy who play so prominent a part in the imagery of Bolognese and Roman Baroque are all enveloped in waves of billowing drapery. Out of the 17th century only one ecstatic nude comes to mind, the marble carving in which Bernini, taking as his points of departure the Apollo Belvedere and a nereid sarcophagus, has transformed them, through the unifying buoyancy of the baroque style, into the beautiful group of Apollo and Daphne [238]. This is the ecstasy of metamorphosis. All the figures described in this chapter have symbolised through the body some change or translation of the soul; and here Bernini has imagined how, when the body itself is changed, it must be like one of those great ecstatic moments, love, levitation or the sudden lift of a wave.

While, from Titian to Bernini, ecstatic motives were being used to enhance the sensuality of the nude, they were also being employed, as they always had been, in the interests of decoration. It may seem slighting to apply this word to Raphael's Galatea [239], and of course his great fresco is in a different category of art to the Mildenhall dish; yet, compared to Botticelli's Birth of Venus, decoration it remains, voluntarily renouncing just that sharpness of poetic reality which takes root in the imagination and grows there with an independent life. In the Galatea Raphael has taken the inhabitants of a nereid sarcophagus and, without greatly altering their occupations or their outlines, has given them a new character ; or perhaps we should say has given them back their old character, for I cannot resist the fancy that the Galatea must be miraculously like the great decorative painting of antiquity from which, in the first instance, the nereid sarcophagi derived. We must suppose, however, that Raphael's

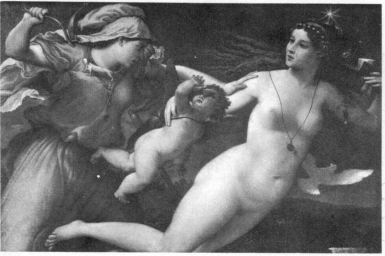

237. LOTTO. Triumph of Chastity

figures are more fully modelled than anything in early Greek painting and penetrate further into space ; and no doubt there is a difference in the whole intention of Raphael's design. Not only has he made the episodic oblong into an upright, but he has filled it according to the rules of renaissance geometry. Galatea's head is the apex of a triangle, the upper half of the space is related to the lower by the golden section, and the two are joined by intersecting circles. We know from a preparatory drawing that Raphael followed the same scheme in the Transfiguration. In these ways the Galatea leaves the realm of narrative and entertainment, to which decoration normally belongs, and enters that of philosophy ; and yet this is what makes its decorative qualities so deeply satisfying. A fresco in the Palazzo Vecchio by Vasari and Gherardi, in which all the elements united by Raphael into a logical system

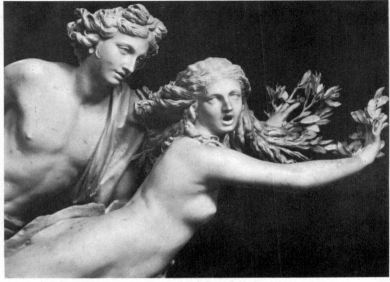

238. BERNINI. Apollo and Daphne

are once more spread out episodically over the surface, fails as decoration, for it has not recaptured the close, rhythmic structure of an antique relief, and we see how these nude figures, which seemed to be ornamental material of universal value, were in fact dependent on their close relationship with one another.

In the 17th century two triumphs of Galatea, by Agostino Carracci [240] and Nicolas Poussin [241], show alternative methods by which this can be done. Carracci reverts to the classical oblong and almost to the classical sense of space. His figures are not taken direct from antiquity, but he has given them that air at once sensuous and detached which fits them for classical decoration. His pictorial imagination is less fresh and vigorous than that of Raphael ; indeed the Galatea herself is more artificial than anything in antiquity. In antique sarcophagi the nereids who balance on the tails of tritons must have been studied from nature, for they are in exactly the pose adopted by their daughters in modern Italy who occupy an equally precarious seat on the pillions of motor scooters. But the attitude of Carracci's Galatea, like Guido Reni's Samson, is a piece of *coloratura*, in which the vocal line is accompanied by the orchestra of her floating drapery. The classical relief composition which Carracci has

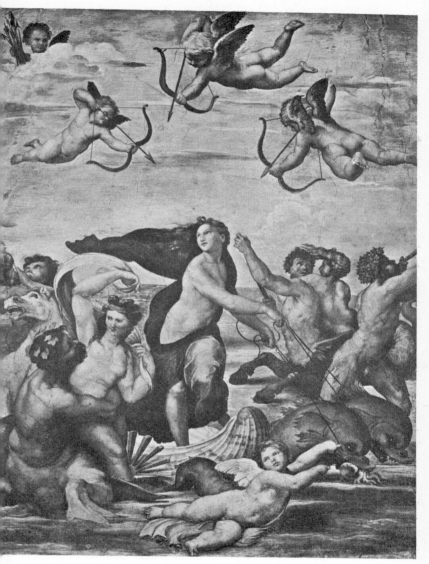

239. RAPHAEL. Triumph of Galatea

employed so skilfully cannot suppress the fact that he is a master of the Baroque. Poussin follows the opposite system, and proves the fundamental truthfulness of antique art. Almost every figure in his Triumph of Galatea is taken from an antique in pose and outline, but has been studied over again from nature. Most characteristic are the two nereids to the right. Although both are to be found on sarcophagi, he has accentuated their modelling and recombined them so that they achieve that quality of counterpoint, that logical interplay of contrary directions, which was his peculiar gift.

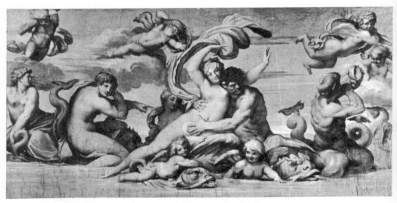

240. CARRACCI. Triumph of Galatea

As if to encourage the art historian in his analytic functions, Boucher's Triumph of Galatea in Stockholm illustrates a further stage of the same idea. Instead of Poussin's logic everything appears to be the result of fancy and happy coincidence. In fact, the picturesque façade of rococo conceals a solid science of composition, but the flickering outlines and wayward interruptions put us off our guard. Everything is in movement. The figures loll on the waves with a new abandon, and the customary loop of drapery breaks away and flies up into the air. Sweet, plump and desirable, the nereids have evidently been studied from nature, and then transferred, with no loss of substance, into a setting of enchanting unreality. If art, like cookery, existed solely to gratify the senses it could hardly go further.

The nude of ecstasy has continued to provide decorative material till the present day. In the 19th century, when decoration was not so much a matter of stylistic conviction as of *horror vacui*, the vacant spaces in theatres and restaurants were filled with a vulgarised Dionysiac imagery, unrelated to the real creative impulses of the time. Only one man, perhaps, gave this commercialised decoration any distinction, the sculptor Carpeaux ; and his group on the Paris Opera House, representing the Dance [242], provides a link between the false art of the post-industrial epoch and the true art which preceded it. Its relationship with Bernini's Apollo and Daphne is obvious,

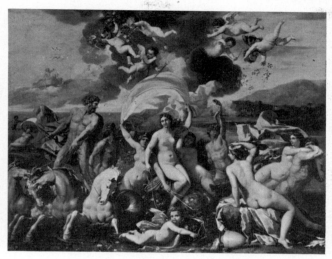

241. POUSSIN. Triumph of Galatea

and the female figures prolong the tradition of 18th-century French sculptors like Pajou and Clodion. They are, on comparison, lacking in style and substance, and their smiles betray some of the archness of the Second Empire ; but Carpeaux has given to the whole group the genuine movement of the dance, so that we discount the details and abandon ourselves to the ancient rhythms of ecstasy.

Ecstatic art began with the dance ; and heaven knows what splendid decorative paintings of Dionysiac dances are lost to us. We can only guess at them from Etruscan tomb paintings (no doubt executed by wandering Greek artists who carried with them memories of Attica and Ionia) and from the scenes of ritual dancing which from the mid-6th century onwards are to be found on some of the finest Greek vases. It is not by chance that two of the chief decorative paintings of our own day continue the same theme. These are the two great decorations by Henri Matisse, the first commissioned by

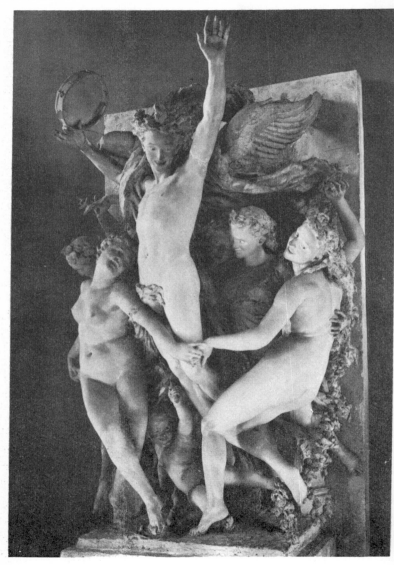

242. CARPEAUX. Dance

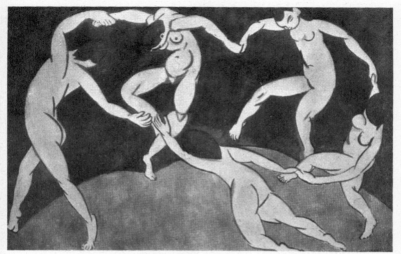

243. MATISSE. Dance

Shchukin in 1909, and still, I suppose, hanging in Moscow; the second commissioned by Dr. Barnes in 1931 and almost equally inaccessible in the suburbs
of Philadelphia. The ring of dancing figures of 1909 was one of the most
revolutionary works of its time [243]. It was painted with an inspired frenzy
which Matisse seldom regained, and communicates more vividly than any work
since the Renaissance the sense of Dionysiac rapture. Matisse maintained that he
had taken his theme from the rhythms and gestures of the *farandole*; perhaps
the sophisticated transports of Isadora Duncan also had some influence; but
artistically he has not disguised his indebtedness to early Greek painting, and
has revived not only the severe concentration of an expressive silhouette but
also the actual movements of 6th-century dancers. Whether or not he was
also aware of Pollajuolo's frescoes at the Torre del Gallo [231] I cannot say,
but in fact the enlargement of Greek motives has produced a similar result.

Over twenty years later, when Dr. Barnes commissioned the decorations
at Merrion, Matisse had come to mistrust the spontaneity of his earlier style.
Partly in order that his murals should not compete with the great pictures in
the gallery for which they were destined, and partly on account of a growing
preoccupation with essences, Matisse has eliminated all the life-giving accidents
inherent in the subject. Such Cartesian maenads may seem to involve an

internal contradiction ; and yet the drastic simplifications imposed, stage by
stage, on Matisse's design, have preserved—perhaps even intensified—the
fundamental rhythms of Dionysiac art. We recognise (in the first series) a
figure remarkably similar to the central dancer in the Carpeaux, we discover
the familiar satyr with head thrown back, who is ultimately changed into a
woman ; above all we are aware of that feeling of levitation and escape which
is the essence of the ecstatic nude. In the first series half the figures have actually

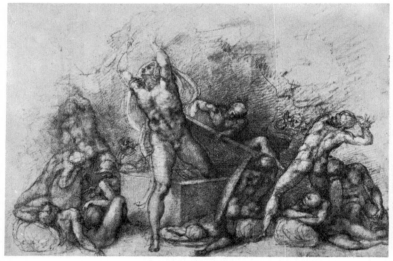

244. MICHELANGELO. Resurrection

shot up out of the lunettes so that only their legs remain visible—a movement
which, as photographic records show us, took place progressively as the work
proceeded. Like all Dionysiac art they celebrate the uprushing of vital forces
breaking through the earth's crust.

For the nude of ecstasy, even when it seems to be only a factor in decoration, is always a symbol of rebirth. Throughout its history it has been associated
with resurrection—on the sarcophagi of ancient religion where it shows the
solemnisations of fertility or the passage of the spirit to new abodes ; as the
Blessed Souls in the Last Judgment ; even in the early renaissance Eve who
rises out of the side of her sleeping spouse [228]. The 'lesser Olympus' of
Demeter and Dionysus had been peopled under pressure from the most ancient
of all religious instincts, those aroused by the rebirth of vegetable life after the

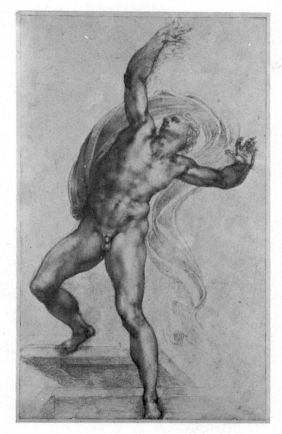

245. MICHELANGELO.   Risen Christ

death-like sleep of winter.   And, with this serious theme in mind, we may turn
back from water-frolics and decorative dances to the greatest embodiments
of ecstatic movement in art, Michelangelo's drawings of the Resurrection.

The subject began to occupy his mind in about the year 1532, at a period
of his life when the physical beauty of the antique world had laid its strongest
enchantment on him, and seemed to have been reborn in the person of
Tommaso Cavalieri.   Yet his Christian meditations continued, and of all the

themes which they suggested to him, none was more apt for pagan interpretation than that of the slain God emerging from the tomb. Iconographic
tradition had shown him only half awake from the trance of death ; but
Michelangelo imagined him as the embodiment of liberated vitality. A
carefully worked-out drawing at Windsor shows a Dionysiac scene beyond
the imagination of antiquity [244]. The sleeping soldiers to left and right are in
the poses of Bacchanalian stupor, the naked man starting back is like an
astonished satyr ; but the figure which bursts out of the tomb, gigantic and
irresistible as a force of nature, has a rhythmic singleness of purpose which
classic art never attempted. In antiquity the actual facts of the body were too
important for them to be so subordinated to expression. Not that, in treating
this theme, Michelangelo has wished us to forget the physical beauty of his

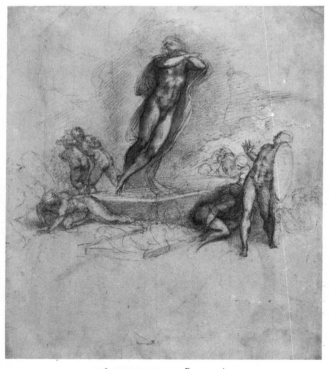

246. MICHELANGELO. Resurrection

reborn God. A finished study of the risen Christ, also at Windsor, is perhaps the most beautiful nude of ecstasy in the whole of art [245]. The thrown-back head, the raised arms, the momentary pose, the swirl of drapery, are all those of the old Dionysiac dancers. But how marvellously, even at this period of physical desire, Michelangelo has succeeded in spiritualising the body. Whether or not it is the latest of the series, Michelangelo's last word on the subject is a drawing in the British Museum in which the risen Christ does not burst from His sarcophagus like an explosion, but glides irresistibly into the air [246]. It is a movement more marvellous than any display of energy, and intensifies the visionary character of the scene. The guards, no longer like startled satyrs, gaze at Him with awe as if they were astonished as much by His divine beauty as by His emergence from the tomb. Perhaps no other nude by Michelangelo conforms more closely to our modern ideals of physical grace. If we compare this risen Christ with an image of earth-bound human beauty, as Michelangelo conceived it, that dreamer who is only just awakening to the claims of spiritual life in the drawing known as A Dream of Human Life, we realise how consciously he has refined away the encumbrances of flesh and muscle. It is the same process which led to the tragic mutilation of the Rondanini *Pietà* ; but as yet he has not lost faith in physical per-fection, and feels it almost as a recommendation to a higher world. *Ascender vivo fra gli spiriti eletti* : these words in one of Michelangelo's sonnets sum-marise his life's ambition, and nowhere more than in this drawing, where the human body, for all its sensuous beauty, has freed itself from the pull of the earth, do we feel that this prayer has been answered.

CHAPTER VIII

The Alternative Convention

Roots and bulbs, pulled up into the light, give us for a moment a feeling of shame. They are pale, defenceless, unself-supporting. They have the formless character of life which has been both protected and oppressed. In the darkness their slow biological gropings have been the contrary of the quick resolute movements of free creatures, bird, fish or dancer, flashing through a transparent medium, and have made them baggy, scraggy and indeterminate. Looking at a group of naked figures in a Gothic painting or miniature we experience the same sensation. The bulb-like women and root-like men seem to have been dragged out of the pro-

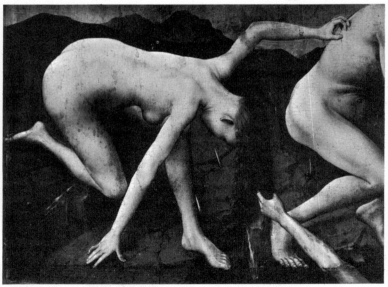

247. ROGIER VAN DER WEYDEN. Last Judgment (detail)

tective darkness in which the human body had lain muffled for a thousand years. Given my distinction between the nude and the naked, it may be asked by what criterion the Gothic body is included in this book at all. The answer is that since nakedness was required in certain subjects of Christian iconography, the body had to be given a memorable shape, and in the end the Gothic artists evolved a new ideal. We may call it the alternative convention.

In the first centuries of Christianity many causes had combined to bury the nude. The Jewish element in Christian thought condemned all human images as involving a breach of the second commandment, and pagan idols were particularly dangerous because, in the opinion of the early Church, they were not simply pieces of profane sculpture, but were the abode of devils who had cunningly assumed the shapes and names of beautiful human beings. The fact that these gods and goddesses were, for the most part, naked gave to nudity a diabolical association which it long retained. But iconoclasm and superstition were in the end less powerful factors than the new attitude to the body which accompanied the collapse of paganism. To some extent it was a survival of the old platonic contention that spiritual things were degraded by taking corporeal shape ; and this, like so much else in Hellenic philosophy, became amalgamated with Christian morals. We still say morals. Modern psychologists might maintain that the privations enjoined by the founders of monasticism, their denunciations of the pleasures of the senses, and their wholesale condemnation of women were not so much ethical judgments as symptoms of hysteria or of mental illness. Yet they were, and have remained, effective. Even today we cannot turn the pages of Petronius or Apuleius without being slightly shocked by the absolute matter-of-factness with which the antique world accepted the body, with all its animal needs ; and perhaps in the end the half-crazy austerities of the anchorites were necessary in order to establish a balance between spirit and senses.

But as a result the body changed its status. It ceased to be the mirror of divine perfection and became an object of humiliation and shame. The whole of mediaeval art is a proof of how completely Christian dogma had eradicated the image of bodily beauty. That human beings were still conscious of physical desire, we may assume ; but even in those subjects of iconography in which the nude could properly be represented the mediaeval artist seems to show no interest in those elements in the female body which we have come to think of as inevitably arousing desire. Did he deliberately repress his feelings ? Or is our own delight in a body, like our appreciation of landscape, partly the result of art ; dependent, that is to say, on an image created by a succession of peculiarly sensitive individuals ? At least there is

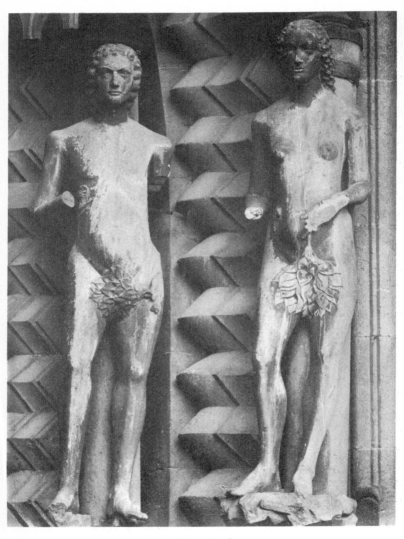

248. Adam and Eve. Bamberg. *c.* 1235

no doubt about the puritanism of the Christian tradition as we see it, for example, in the first full-size, independent nude figures of mediaeval art, the Adam and Eve at Bamberg. Their bodies are as little sensuous as the buttresses of a Gothic church. Eve's figure is distinguished from Adam's only by two small, hard protuberances far apart on her chest. Yet these statues have a gaunt nobility and an architectural completeness which makes them nudes and not naked people [248].

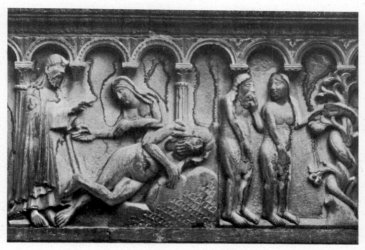

249. WILIGELMO. *c.* 1105. Adam and Eve

In general, the unclothed figures of the early middle ages are more shamefully naked, and are undergoing humiliations, martyrdoms or tortures. Above all it was in this condition that man suffered his cardinal misfortune, the Expulsion from Paradise ; and this was the moment in Christian story of his first consciousness of the body, 'They knew that they were naked'. While the Greek nude began with the heroic body proudly displaying itself on the palestra, the Christian nude began with the huddled body cowering in consciousness of sin.

The re-formulation of the naked body through Christian art took place in the west. Although nudes appear in Byzantine artifacts as late as the 9th century, occupying the labours of craftsmen when sacred subjects were prohibited, they are no more than freaks in a backwater of antiquarian dilettantism. In contrast to the naked imps of the Veroli casket, hopping and twirling with the irresponsibility of anachronisms, the Adams and Eves of early Romanesque art are heavy and crude. They follow a scheme of stylisation which is found in the most primitive representations of the figure. Eve's breasts hang down flat and formless, and there is no other attempt to suggest that the structure of her body differs from that of Adam. At the beginning of the 11th century there is a certain advance. Wiligelmo, who carved the reliefs on the façade of Modena Cathedral, was so intent on telling his story that he gave his Adam

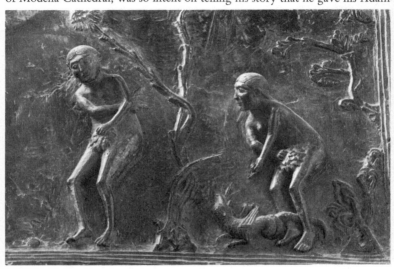

250. The Fall. Hildesheim. *c.* 1010

and Eve [249] a touching seriousness ; but almost fifty years later, on the façade of S. Zeno in Verona, the figures are still inexpressive blocks. The earliest works of mediaeval art in which the naked body becomes articulate are the five scenes of the Creation and Fall on the bronze doors of Hildesheim, executed for Abbot Bernward between 1008 and 1015 [250, 251]. They probably reproduce illustrations of a manuscript of the School of Tours and through it are remotely connected with classical antecedents ; but the sculptor's use of the figures is un-antique, not solely from lack of technical skill, but because he is aiming above all at dramatic expressiveness. In this he succeeds beyond every other sculptor of the early middle ages. Our first parents, accused of their sin, wince and double up with shame. Adam accuses Eve, and Eve accuses the serpent with a gesture of astonishing truth ; and when they are expelled from the garden Adam marches resignedly forward, while Eve turns back with a movement so revealing and so complex that anatomical crudities are forgotten.

For the next two centuries the sculptors of naked Eve in Romanesque and early Gothic style render the body with a kind of prehistoric brutality. Almost the only exception is the lintel of a door from Autun Cathedral, in which Eve

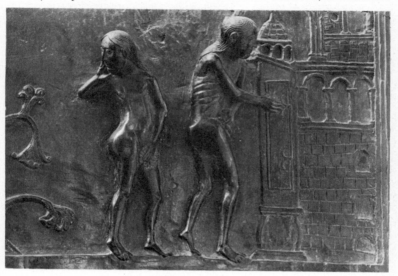

251. The Expulsion. Hildesheim. *c.* 1010

crawls or crouches on the ground. This beautiful relief makes an effect curiously like that of early Indian sculpture, but the similarity lies in the balance of form and decorative detail and the filling of the space, rather than in any likeness of physiology. Compared with the swelling thighs and abundant bosoms of Maurya sculpture the Eve at Autun is hard, flat and ribbed like a tree-trunk. Her body is still an unfortunate accident of her human condition, and instead of being presented as the summit of visual experience, it is made to go on all fours with ornamental leaves and fabulous animals [252].

In the middle of the 13th century, at almost the same date that the Gothic sculptors began to look attentively at leaves and flowers, and illuminators to look at birds, a new direction in iconography forced artists to study the naked human body. This was the decision that the encyclopaedic history of human

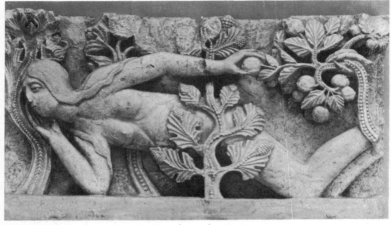

252. French. 12th cent. Eve

life portrayed on the great cathedrals should no longer end with the Apocalypse, but with the Last Judgment as described in the 24th and 25th chapters of St. Matthew. Human beings were to take the place of winged bulls and many-headed monsters. It was a visible victory for the humanism of the 12th century ; and in the instructions for artists usually followed, those contained in the *Speculum* of Vincent of Beauvais, the subject is given an interpretation directly derived from the humanist philosophy of Greece. It states that in the Resurrection the figures rising from the grave must not only be naked but that each one must be in a state of perfect beauty, following the laws of his being. What, we may imagine, were the feelings of a mediaeval craftsman confronted with this subject so greatly at variance with all those for which he had learnt a traditional stylistic equivalent ? Where did he look for his material ? In the 12th century, as at Autun, he took it from manuscripts, and his figures are mere puppets. But with the growing naturalism of the 13th century he sought other models. No doubt he looked at classical sarcophagi, as the sculptors at Chartres and Rheims had done, and found in defeated Gauls attitudes in which to represent the damned. But he must also have studied the figures from life, and probably have had recourse to those institutions so much condemned by mediaeval moralists, the public baths. When, in the 15th century, communal baths are represented in manuscripts, we recognise forms already made familiar in the Last Judgments of the preceding century.

Not all 13th-century patrons could bring themselves to accept the official iconography of the Resurrection. At Notre-Dame in Paris, for example, the figures were shown clothed, and at Rouen they are draped in their shrouds. But in the famous Last Judgment at Bourges [253] the sculptor has looked at the human body with an interest which had not been shown since antiquity. The man seen from behind pushing up the lid of his tomb has an action and a muscular back worthy of the *quattrocento*. In the middle of this group stands a

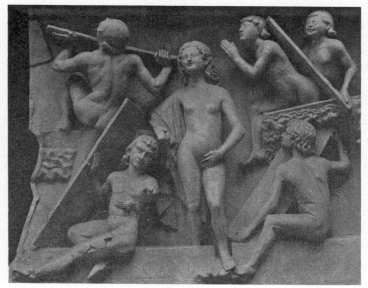

253. French. 13th cent. Last Judgment

maiden of confident virtue who shows, for the first time, the Gothic style applied to the female nude. Her body is exactly what we should expect the bodies of the Virgins on Gothic ivories to be like if, by some impious accident, they were divested of their exquisitely stylised draperies. Her form must owe something to the study of antique fragments ; she has, for example, a Polycletan stance, with the weight of her body borne on the right leg. But unlike those mediaeval sculptors, who incorporated the nereids of late antique industrial art as complete rhythmic entities, the Bourges master has reduced the classical model to the more rarefied Gothic style. The supporting hip is not a sensuous arc, but flattens out immediately after the hip-bone. The chest and stomach are also flattened into a single unit, in which the small breasts are placed far up and far apart. It was the perfect Gothic formula for the female nude, and if it was not immediately adopted, that is because few other sculptors could have been available at the time with the Bourges master's interest in the body and skill in depicting it.

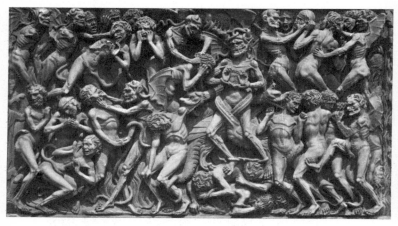

254. MAITANI. Last Judgment

The other great series of nudes in the high middle ages is to be found on the façade of the Cathedral of Orvieto, and dates from the early 14th century. The sculptor Lorenzo Maitani had a strong personal interest in the subject and deliberately chose to portray those scenes of sacred iconography, the Creation and Fall of Man and the Last Judgment, in which the nude must appear. I have pointed out in the preceding chapter how his Eve rising from Adam's side [227] was inspired by a nereid sarcophagus, then familiar to the sculptors of Siena. Her small breasts and large head follow the Gothic proportions, and in the scene which shows her standing beside the tree, listening to the admonitions of the Almighty, she scarcely differs from the mediaeval mould. But she is also delicately feminine, and we feel, almost for the first time, that a Christian artist has recognised the body as something which might contain and express the soul. The same is true of the sleeping Adam. His limbs flow into one another with a sweetness which only an artist who loved the human body could perceive ; and yet, as with Raphael, the body seems to reflect a state of spiritual grace.

In the Last Judgment Maitani returns to the tradition of the northern

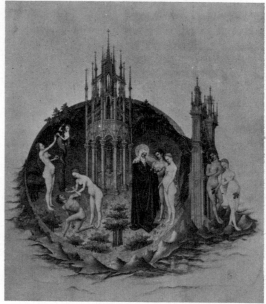

255. DE LIMBOURG. The Fall

cathedrals [254]. The melodious intervals of his Eden are abandoned in favour of the densely crowded, evenly accented composition which the Pisani had taken over from antique battle sarcophagi. Some of the figures are inspired by dying Gauls, others are completely Gothic, with tattered movements similar to those at Bourges. Right up to the time of Michelangelo the Last Judgment kept this character of an infernal rubbish-heap, as we see it in Memlinc's altar-piece in Danzig, where the broken and the uprooted have no cohesion, but only the haphazard angularity of haste. In Rogier van der Weyden's great polyptych at Beaune, the source no doubt of Memlinc's inspiration, the figures retain their identity [247] but still have the sharp scissor movements of the Gothic Judgment. They are amongst the most highly-wrought nudes of terror, an open, distracted cry, contrasting with the buried misery of Masaccio's Adam and Eve.

In its final form, which lasted for over a century, the alternative convention seems to have been evolved as part of the so-called international Gothic style. It first appeared in France, Burgundy and the Low Countries about the year

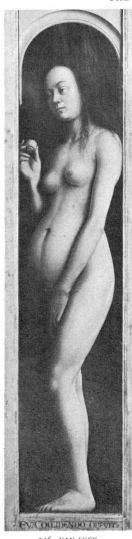

256. VAN EYCK.
Eve (detail of altar-piece)

1400, and the earliest datable example is in the manuscript known as the *Très Riches Heures* of the Duc de Berry executed in about 1410 by the brothers de Limbourg. One miniature shows the story of the Temptation and Fall of Man [255]. Within the Garden of Eden, circular like the known world, Eve is as naked as a shrimp, and seems at first entirely ignorant of her condition. But as she is reproved by the Almighty she grows conscious of shame, and when she is expelled through the traceried portico of Paradise she is in the attitude of the Venus Pudica, with a fig-leaf before her. De Limbourg was acquainted with classical models, for his kneeling Adam is taken from an antique statue of a conquered Persian or Gaul similar to those in the Attalos groups at Naples. Here, and elsewhere, he leaves us in no doubt that he appreciated the classical ideal of physical beauty and could reproduce it, if he chose to do so. But in the naked Eve he did not so choose, and has deliberately created, or adapted, a new feminine shape which was to satisfy northern taste for two hundred years. His Eve has the elongated torso which we first observed in the Three Graces of Pompeii. But the essential structure of her body is very different from that of Hellenistic art, however orientalised. Her pelvis is wider, her chest narrower, her waist higher; above all there is the prominence given to her stomach. This is what distinguishes the Gothic ideal of the female body: that whereas in the antique nude the dominating rhythm is the curve of the hip, in the alternative convention it is the curve of the stomach. This change argues a fundamental difference of attitude to the body. The curve of the hip is created by an upward thrust. Beneath it is bone and muscle, supporting the body's weight. However sensuous or geometric it may become, it remains in the end an

310

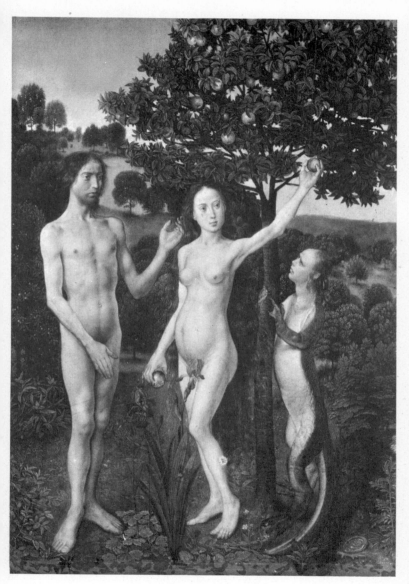

257. VAN DER GOES. Adam and Eve

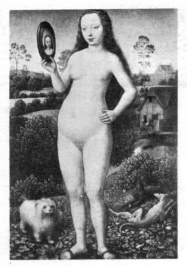

258. School of Memlinc. Vanitas

image of energy and control. The curve of the stomach is created by gravity and relaxation. It is a heavy, unstructural curve, soft and slow, yet with a kind of vegetable persistence. It does not take its shape from the will but from the unconscious biological process which gives shape to all hidden organisms.

Perhaps this is what historians have in mind when they say that the Gothic nude is realistic, for the words 'realistic' and 'organic' are often confused. If the former be taken to mean 'imitating a conjectural average', it is incorrect, for relatively few young women look like a Gothic Eve. But it is true that two painters of unflinching truth portrayed their Eves in this convention. The first

is Van Eyck, and his Eve in the Ghent altar-piece is a proof of how minutely 'realistic' a great artist may be in the rendering of details, and yet subordinate the whole to an ideal form. Hers is the supreme example of the bulb-like body. The weight-bearing leg is concealed, and the body is so contrived that on one side is the long curve of the stomach, on the other downward sweep of the thigh, uninterrupted by any articulation of bone or muscle. Above this relaxed oval the two spheres of the breasts also feel the pull of gravity, and the head itself weighs heavily on the neck [256].

The other unforgettable Eve of 15th-century Flemish painting is in the small painting of the Fall by Hugo Van der Goes, now in Vienna [257]. It was painted

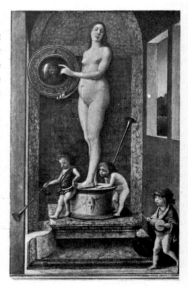

259. BELLINI. Vanitas

312

a generation later than the Van Eyck, but is in many respects less 'modern', and the pathetic little Eve, observed with loving accuracy, still illustrates the unfortunate condition to which the female body was reduced in the mediaeval mind. We may legitimately see her as the descendant of the Eve in the Hildesheim doors, with very similar proportions, although of course a more accurate command of such anatomical details as the placing of the breasts. The docile mother of our race, home-keeping, child-bearing, flat-footed with much serving, has seldom been depicted with so little attempt to modify the humble usefulness of her body. But can we be quite sure that these unathletic proportions, which are far from our own idea of grace and desirable beauty, aroused the same responses in a man of the 15th century? Several examples suggest that they did not.

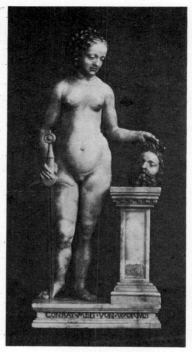

260. KONRAD MEIT. Judith

From the same circle of taste as Van der Goes' Eve, and painted only a decade or so later, is a picture at Strasbourg of the School of Memlinc, which symbolises female vanity, and was presumably intended to embody sensual charm, unabashed and irresistible [258]. The components of her body are identical with those of a Gothic Eve; the same large, sagging stomach, the same small breasts, the same short legs which can scarcely carry their owner to church or market. Even in Italy the nude Vanitas of Giovanni Bellini follows a similar pattern [259]. And if it be argued that in these examples the painter had some satiric intention, consider the alabaster figure of Judith by Konrad Meit, in the National Museum at Munich [260]. She follows the same bodily scheme as the Memlinc Vanitas but there can be no doubt that the sculptor has intended her to be physically desirable; and after the eye trained in classical proportions has allowed the first shock to subside, I think one must agree that he has succeeded.

At this point, a century after it was created, the alternative convention takes on a new character. From being an embodiment of humility and shame it becomes a means of erotic provocation. Given the nature of the Gothic nude, this was perhaps inevitable. In the popular imagery of the middle ages, a

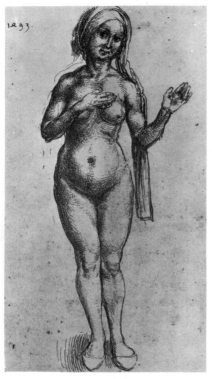

naked woman had exactly the same significance which she has retained in popular imagery ever since. And the very degradation which the body had suffered as a result of Christian morality served to sharpen its erotic impact. The formula of the classical ideal had been more protective than any drapery; whereas the shape of the Gothic body, which suggested that it was normally clothed, gave it the impropriety of a secret.

When, towards the end of the 15th century, northern artists became aware that a new liberation of the body had been taking place, for some thirty years, in Italian art, their feelings were those of schoolboys. They were shocked, curious and impressed. We may study the progress of their emotions in the work of the cleverest schoolboy of all, Albrecht Dürer. As an apprentice he must have learnt that naked women had become the subject of art, and in 1493 he made a drawing of a middle-

261. DÜRER. Naked Hausfrau

aged Nuremberg *hausfrau* in which horrified curiosity predominates [261]. A year later he began to study through prints and drawings the Italian masters of the nude, Pollajuolo and Mantegna; and by the time he reached Venice he was prepared to be impressed. He made his first attempt to conquer the Italian nude, which he was to use in various drawings and engravings during the next years, notably in the Dream, where the female who troubles the drowsy scholar is intended to suggest a pagan goddess.

Such classical fullness of form, however, was due to an effort of will. His other nudes of the same period show how much more his eye, with its appetite for accident, sought for the peculiarities of the body. In the drawing of the women's bath, dated 1496 [262], Gothic curiosity and horror are still uppermost, mixed with memories of Italy. The figure on the left is

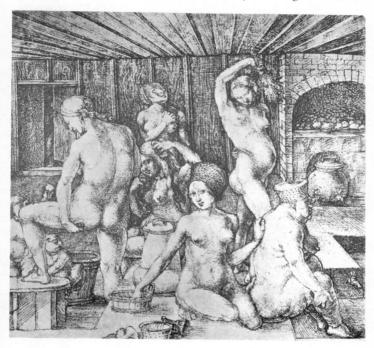

262. DÜRER. Women's Bath

almost Michelangelesque, the woman combing her hair in the centre is taken from a Venus Anadyomene, and the woman kneeling in the foreground is purely German. The fat monster on the right confirms his feeling of the obscenity of the whole situation and must have been observed from nature, although he might not have thought of introducing her without the example of Mantegna's Bacchanal engraving, where in fact the fat Bacchante is taken from an antique. The engraving of naked women known as the Four Witches, dated 1497 [263], shows clearly his unresolved mixture of curiosity and respect

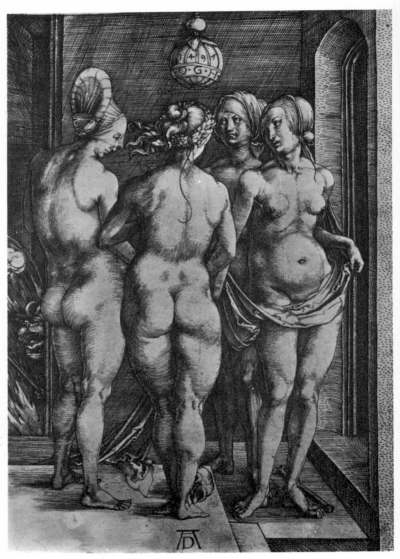

263. DÜRER. Four Witches

for classicism. He had seen and admired a relief of the Three Graces, and may have set out with the intention of producing his version of the subject. But already in the central figure his eye became engaged by the heavy irregularities of flesh, and the left-hand female, a formidable German matron divested of her clothes, but not of her local head-dress, upsets the classical scheme altogether. So the Three Graces become infernal gossips, with a skull at their feet and the devil peering round the corner.

The Four Witches has a further interest for us through its connection with an engraving of two naked women by the Venetian artist Jacopo de' Barbari. How far Dürer borrowed from Jacopo will always be a puzzle, because Jacopo's engravings cannot be dated with precision ; but he was probably twenty years older than Dürer, and had achieved the position of court artist to the Emperor Maximilian in the year 1500. Moreover, we have Dürer's own word for it that Jacopo had shown him two figures, a man and woman, constructed on geometrical principles, when he was 'still a young man and had never heard of such things' ; which can only mean when he was in Venice in 1494. Jacopo was a somewhat feeble though persistent draughtsman of the nude, whose elongated females look as if they were melting like fat tallow candles, and it is revealing that Dürer could not discover more genuinely classical models. But the examples of Rizzo and Bellini show that in Venice in the 1490's a Gothic conception of the female nude was still fashionable ; and perhaps the latent Gothicism in Jacopo's languorous figures made them easier for Dürer to assimilate than the relics of antiquity which ten years later were to inspire Giorgione. Dürer goes on to tell us that Jacopo had refused to explain how his figures were constructed ; thus setting up in Dürer's mind the conviction that the classical nude depended on a secret formula, a sort of masonic mystery guarded by Italian artists in order to surpass their German colleagues. In his determination to discover this secret Dürer began, and continued throughout his life, the elaborate geometrical analysis of the human figure which I have referred to in the first chapter. But somehow he felt that the mystery had escaped him, and as late as 1521, long after de' Barbari's death, he asked the Regent of Malines to present him with Master Jacopo's book. In common with all northern artists, he found it hard to believe that the harmony of the classical nude did not depend on a set of rules, but on a state of mind. In 1504, when he executed the engraving of Adam and Eve, he was in such a state and produced two figures at least as close to the classical ideal as anything in contemporary Italy. But the mood passed, and even after his most sustained analysis of proportion his painting of Eve, now in the Prado, remains essentially northern. Thenceforward his measured figures were not intended to demonstrate an ideal beauty but to analyse various laws of growth ; and since his aim was no longer aesthetic but scientific, what may be called his taste was free to revert to the bulbous proportions of the early drawings.

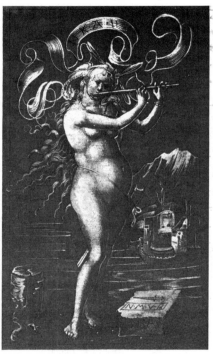

264. NIKLAUS MANUEL DEUTSCH. Masked flute player

The physical types evolved by Dürer in his attempt to reconcile the ideals of Nuremberg and Rome served as points of departure for a whole group of Swiss and German artists who, standing on his shoulders, could treat the nude without any of his struggles and anxieties. To Urs Graf and Niklaus Manuel Deutsch the fact that a painter was required to draw naked women was a rather comical piece of good fortune, to be accepted with hearty enthusiasm. Their drawings, which date from about 1520 to 1530, show the broad-hipped, full-bosomed, high - Renaissance Venus translated, with no loss of sensuality, into the alternative convention. An example is the masked flute player by Niklaus Manuel, whose stance is entirely classical, and may be derived from a Marcantonio engraving, but whose body has been turned round so that her right side is outlined by her generous stomach, which runs up to her breasts with an ogival sweep [264]. As a result, Dürer's condition that 'all things should rhyme alike' is better fulfilled than in many of his own nudes. With Urs Graf this Gothic swagger often degenerates into boisterous brutality. His *landsknechts* are the men who sacked Rome and cut short the revived authority of Apollo. His nudes are *Venus Vulgaris* undisguised, even when accompanied by the attributes of renaissance pedantry. But his vitality is irresistible. A drawing at Basle of a woman stabbing herself, hideous, horrifying and absurd, yet contrives to show the nude as a part of those organic forces which control the growth of roots and knotted trunks, and assimilate it to the swirl of late Gothic ornament [265].

There can be no doubt about the quantity or the kind of satisfaction which patrons of art in the Germanic countries derived from the nude during the first half of the 16th century. It became so much an accepted part of decoration that in 1519 naked women, with supreme impertinence, appear on the title-page of Erasmus' New Testament. Hundreds of popular prints and box-wood figures prove their popularity, and in the paintings of Lukas Cranach they delighted the most fastidious connoisseurs of the day.

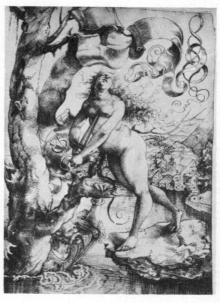

265. URS GRAF. Woman stabbing herself

Cranach achieved a version of the northern nude so personal and so perennially seductive that his work must be considered at greater length. Relatively early in his career, in 1509, he painted a life-size Venus and Cupid, now in the Hermitage [266], which clearly derives from a Mediterranean source. He is usually said to have been inspired by an antique, or a drawing of the antique ; but the way in which the figure is presented against a plain black background suggests that he had seen one of those paintings of Venus, deriving ultimately from Botticelli, which were fashionable in Italy during the last years of the *quattrocento*. Those by Lorenzo Costa [267] are the closest survivors, but he may have known an original Botticelli, and have made his own stiff translation. Evidently the patrons for whom Cranach worked in the provincial court of Saxony were too far off the trade routes of fashion to relish the nude : or perhaps his employer, Frederick the Wise, did not approve of it. For in spite of his natural gifts for the subject he seldom attempted it again till late in the 1520's, and the surprising series of naked beauties for which he is famous date from after 1530, when he was sixty years old. Taste and morals had changed. The post-Reformation appetite for provocative nudity, which I have already noted, had spread to all the Protestant states of Germany, and Cranach's third patron of the Saxon house, Johan Frederick, must have had a personal liking for these bibelots. The characteristic Cranach nude is, therefore, of a much later date than Dürer's experiments and bears no relation to earlier attempts of northern artists to master the Italian ideal. By this time, too, the Italian nude had been transformed, and we remember with a shock that Cranach's sinuous Lucretias are contemporary with the elongated figures of Pontormo. They are, indeed, most artful productions in which elements of

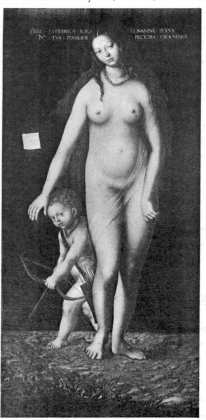

266. CRANACH. Venus and Cupid

mannerism and revived Gothicism are mingled and concealed.

How successfully Cranach gave new style to the Gothic body can be seen by comparing his paintings to those of his contemporary who took the greatest pains with the nude, Jan Gossart of Mabuse. Gossart was in Rome in 1508, and returned to Flanders full of ambition to excel in the Italian manner. In 1509 he seems to have entered into some sort of partnership with Jacopo de' Barbari, and it is from Jacopo that he derived the model for several highly polished paintings of the nude, such as the Neptune and Amphitrite at Berlin. In other works, such as the Adam and Eve in the same gallery, the Italian attitudes are rendered with a painstaking Flemish realism. This unresolved mixture of conventions has the result of making Gossart's nudes curiously indecent. They seem to push their way forward till they are embarrassingly near to us, and we recognise how necessary it is for the naked body to be clothed by a consistent style. This is what

Cranach achieves. Endowed with a sense of *chic* which should make him the patron saint of all fashion designers, he evolved a decorative convention for the nude equal to that of 10th-century India. It is, of course, a development of the sprightly Eves of 15th-century manuscripts—a conscious development, for Cranach was an ingenious archaiser who did actual copies of 15th-century pictures ; but his skill in combining sinuous line with shallow internal modelling is unprecedented in the north, and reminds us of Egyptian reliefs. With this sense of style went a highly developed appetite which allowed him to convince us that his personal taste in physical beauty is our own. He takes the Gothic body with its narrow shoulders and prominent stomach, and gives it long slender legs, a slender waist and gently undulating outline. As a result his naked charmers are as much to our taste today as they were to that of Johan Frederick the Magnanimous [268].

Cranach is one of those rare artists who have added to our imaginative repertoire of physical beauty. The necklaces and waistbands, enormous hats and filmy

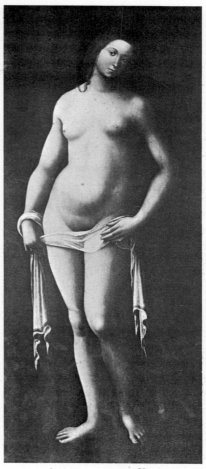

267. LORENZO COSTA. Venus

draperies worn by his goddesses leave us in no doubt that he did so with an erotic intention ; and it is curious how often Cranach has discovered devices used by purveyors of this kind of effect before and since. In some of his pictures of the Judgment of Paris [269] the rival ladies adopt exactly the same attitudes of seduction which we find in Indian painting of

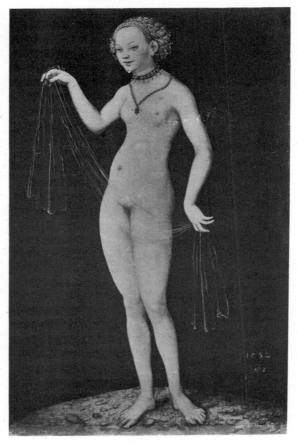

268. CRANACH. Venus

the 8th century [270] or in the illustrations of Ludwig Kirchener. In Europe aphrodisiac art is seldom successful. Cranach succeeds because he does not exploit the advantage of his universally attractive subject to the neglect of his precise and delicate style. In spite of their sidelong glances his sirens never cease to be *objets d'art*, to be enjoyed, by him who may, as dispassionately as crystals or enamels.

With Cranach the Gothic nude, in the narrow sense, fulfils itself and expires ; but anti-classical proportions are still perceptible in the nude figures of northern art up to the 19th century ; and this elongated elegance retains its physical impact, even when it is most strained and unnatural. The real successor to Cranach was the Antwerp painter Bartholomeus Spranger who as servant to Maximilian III supplied the court with presentable *erotica*, based on his training with the Zuccheri in Rome, but northern in their restless diabolism. The Mannerist formula, which I have already described, was itself influenced by Gothic urgency, and was more easily acceptable in the north than the Euclidean proportions of Raphael. Rosso and Primaticcio working at Fontainebleau felt free to make their nudes extravagantly unclassical, although at the same time importing from Italy bronze casts of classical sculpture which convey the spirit of antique art almost more persuasively than the originals. We must admit, however, that the most disturbing of all anti-classical elongations was made by a Florentine in Florence. It is to be found in a drawing by Pontormo where, as if in conscious defiance of antique measure, he has represented, or caricatured, the most harmonious of all classical subjects, the Three Graces. Their long, thin bodies are scarcely thicker than their legs ; their articulate arms twist in and out like branches. They remind us of some insatiable creeper, ivy or ancient vine, in which we often seem to discover obscene likenesses to the human body, here, in Pontormo's drawing, startlingly confirmed. To some extent this strange distortion is due to Pontormo's personal taste, to some extent it is the result of Michelangelo's cartoons for the Last Judgment, which dominated and obsessed the Roman and Florentine artists of the 1530's almost as the work of Picasso has obsessed international painting in our own day, and with a similar destruction of order. Cellini's Nymph of Fontainebleau, executed in the same decade as Pontormo's Graces, shows the same almost incredible deformations.

The Nymph of Fontainebleau makes an uncomfortable impression, less, perhaps, on account of her proportions than because Cellini, brought up on the tradition of *disegno*, could not quite abandon himself to mere modishness. In the Diana of Anet, traditionally ascribed to Goujon [271], unclassical proportion is acceptable because the unknown carver was content to produce a work of decoration, a super-fashion plate, in which peculiarities of drawing can be passed over. Instead of clearly defined and logically related areas of form, each part glides into the other, and the breasts, which gave the modulus to the antique geometry of the torso, have practically disappeared. All this is familiar in the Gothic nude, but the Diana is not Gothic. Hers is not a body which is normally clothed. She is as much at ease in her nudity as a Giorgione, and this sense of poise, which is also a balance between the northern and the

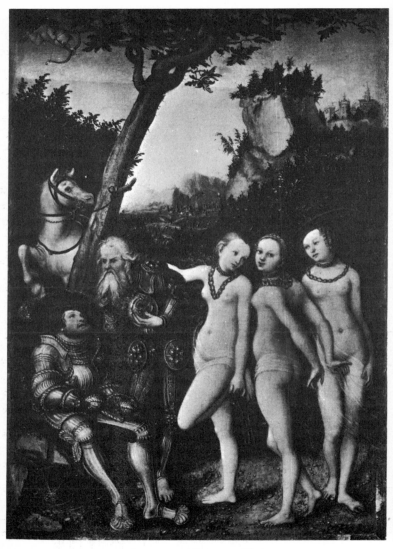

269. CRANACH. Judgment of Paris

Mediterranean spirit, has made her almost a symbol of the French Renaissance.
It is interesting to find that the two other
nude figures of women which seem to
fill, in French art, the same symbolic role
for their epochs, remain fundamentally
unclassical, the Diana of Houdon, whose
limbs and torso still aspire to the elongated ovals of Gothicism and the *Grande
Odalisque* of Ingres. Her long, sinuous
body and legs perversely crossed are
closer to Primaticcio's Fontainebleau
than to Raphael's Rome. In spite of his
obstinate professions of orthodoxy, some
instinct has inspired Ingres to follow the
alternative convention, with the result
that the *Grande Odalisque* is more authentic
and exciting than *La Source*.

After the erotic fantasies of Spranger
and Goltzius, and the splendid animal
exuberance of Rubens, it seemed as if the
humble body, from which the northern
nude had originated, could never again
be the subject of art. But in about the
year 1631 there appeared two etchings
of naked women in which the pitiful
inadequacy of the flesh is more unflinch-
ingly portrayed than in any representation before or since. They were the work
of a young Dutchman, then chiefly known
for his studies of beggars and expressive
heads, Rembrandt van Rhyn. What was

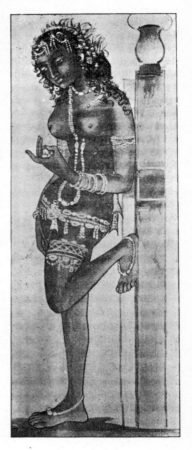

270. Indian. 8th cent.

in his mind when he felt impelled to set down these painful visions
of human nakedness? First of all, no doubt, a kind of defiant honesty.
Although Rembrandt was willing to adopt any device which would contribute to the technical development of his art, he was unable to accept a
formula which might compromise the truth of his vision; and such, pre-
eminently, was the artificial shape which his contemporaries, even among his

countrymen, had agreed to impose on the naked body. As a sort of protest Rembrandt has gone out of his way to find the most deplorable body imaginable and emphasise its least attractive features. Few young women in Amsterdam (and the face of the 'woman seated on a mound' suggests that she was still under thirty) can have had so huge and shapeless a stomach. We

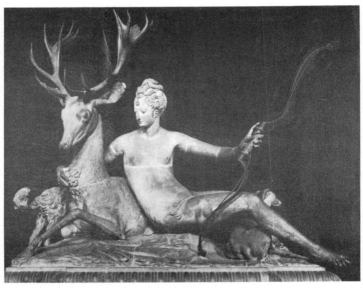

271. GERMAIN PILLON (?). Diana of Anet

can hardly bring our eyes to dwell on her : and that, I imagine, was exactly Rembrandt's intention. In the second etching the figure is less monstrous, but the defiance of classicism is more explicit, for the fat, flaccid creature has been given the attributes of Diana [272]. The drawings for the etching in the British Museum makes Rembrandt's intention apparent, for it shows a young Dutchwoman of average appearance and possible activity. In the etching his eye has dwelt on every baggy shape, every humiliating pucker, everything, in fact, which the convention of the nude obliterates, but which Rembrandt is determined that we shall see. The protest implied in these two etchings did not go unnoticed. The poet Andries Pels in his poem on the *Use and Misuse of the Theatre* describes these etchings in great detail and laments that Rembrandt should have misused his great gifts.

Flabby breasts,
Ill-shaped hands, nay the marks of the lacings
Of the corsets on the stomach and of the garters on the legs,
Must be visible if Nature was to get her due :
That is *his* Nature, which would stand no rules,
No principles of proportion in the human body.

Pels is not only recording contemporary opinion, but also, we may assume, Rembrandt's own justification, that appeal to Nature against rules which has been the repeated battle-cry of all great revolutionaries in art.

But what his critics naturally failed to see, for it only became plain in his later years, and what Rembrandt could not say for himself, is that another impulse beside defiant truthfulness had impelled him to do these etchings : Christian pity. Perhaps some element of curiosity led him to investigate these wrinkles of fat ; but the feelings they aroused in him were different from chilly repulsion which the women's bath aroused in Dürer. Still more did they differ from the many representations of the unfortunate body, fat men, cripples, drunken old women and the like, which have come down to us from antiquity. Sometimes, as in the Old Fisherman which so much distressed Winckelmann, this Hellenistic realism achieves an honourable stoicism. But it is without a breath of pity. The majority of such pieces were, I suppose, considered funny, and were popular because they flattered the spectator's sense of superiority. They are amongst the many elements in antique culture which make even the unbeliever grateful for Christianity. To Rembrandt, the supreme interpreter of biblical Christianity, ugliness, poverty and other misfortunes of our physical life were not absurd, but inevitable, perhaps he might have said 'natural', and capable of receiving some radiance of the spirit because emptied of all pride.

It is curious how this mediaeval view of our bodily estate led him to see the nude in the same shape as the artists of the middle ages. All his studies from life accept this Gothic convention, even when, as in the beautiful drawing on Plate 273, they represent a heroine of antiquity ; and his male nudes are as thin and flat as the Adams of Van der Goes or Van der Weyden. Just as he could have found plenty of girls in Amsterdam with firm young bodies, so there must have been boys with well-developed muscles. Yet, in general, Rembrandt's male models are as miserably thin as his women are embarrassingly fat. By a paradox, the academic search for perfection of form through a study of the nude has become a means of showing the humiliating *im*perfection to which our species is usually condemned.

This feeling of the inherent pitifulness of the body had another strange result : that the most considered nudes of Rembrandt's maturity, the three etchings dated 1658, are of old women [274]. Twenty-seven years have passed since the Diana which outraged Pels, and Rembrandt's truculence has subsided. He is no longer anxious to shock us ; and yet the idea of classical elegance still worries him so much that he prefers the Gothic hulk of an old body to the comely proportions of a young one. The etching of an old woman bathing

her feet in a brook is indeed a most noble piece of bodily architecture, the obstinate, un-defeated shape, as of an old boat, set down without a trace of sentimentality or extenuation. We try to think where else in art an aged body has been so grandly portrayed, and can re-member only Piero della Fran-cesca's Adam, one of Bellini's S. Jeromes and certain anchorites by Carpaccio. However, Rem-brandt's greatest painting of the nude is of a young woman, clearly intended to be physically attractive. This is the Bathsheba in the Louvre [275], one of those supreme works of art which can-

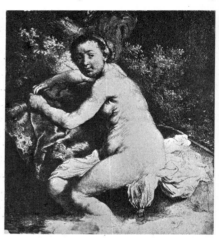

272. REMBRANDT. Diana

not be forced into any classification. The composition is derived from the combined memories of `two antique reliefs which Rembrandt had seen in engravings ; but his conception of the nude is entirely unclassical, and in fact must represent his beloved Hendrickje. Now, when the dogmatic insistence of his early etchings has been abandoned, we feel the value of Rembrandt's humble and scrupulous honesty. For this ample stomach, these heavy, practical hands and feet achieve a nobility far greater than the ideal form of, shall we say, Titian's Venus of Urbino. Moreover, this Christian acceptance of the un-fortunate body has permitted the Christian privilege of a soul. The conventional nudes based on classical originals could bear no burden of thought or inner life without losing their formal completeness. Rembrandt can give his Bathsheba an expression of reverie so complex that we follow her thoughts far beyond the moment depicted : and yet these thoughts are indissolubly part of her body, which speaks to us in its own language as truthfully as Chaucer or Burns.

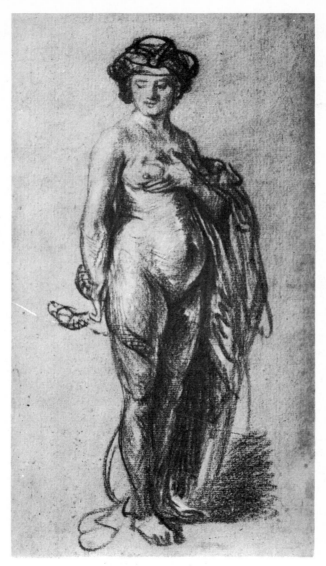

273. REMBRANDT. Cleopatra

The miracle of Rembrandt's Bathsheba, the naked body permeated with thought, was never repeated. But the late 19th century produced one or two memorable nudes of pity, of which the most pitiful is Van Gogh's Sorrow, an image so starkly terrible that we can hardly bring our eyes to dwell upon it ; and the most fully realised, as a work of art, is Rodin's *La Belle Heaulmière* [276]. This goes further than Rembrandt's etching. The body of Rembrandt's old woman, though lacking in grace, is still strong and serviceable. Rodin's old woman is a final image of decrepitude, a *memento mori*, reminding us of certain Gothic figures with exactly this intention. It has been compared with Donatello's St. Mary Magdalen in Florence, and there is a certain similarity in technique, both Rodin and Donatello modelling the furrowed flesh with the powerful nervous movement of their fingers, and creating thereby a living texture. But in sentiment the two figures are entirely different. Donatello's

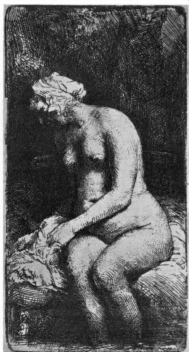

Magdalen is a female fakir whose small, sunken eyes, gazing across the desert, have beheld the vision of God. Her body is no longer of the least importance to her ; whereas Rodin's Heaulmière, although conceived in a graver spirit than the old courtesan of Villon's poem, is still bound to the body, and brooding on its deficiencies. Yet she is far from those pitiless figures of late Hellenistic art in which the worn-out body is represented as contemptible or derisory, for Rodin has seen in her shrunken members a Gothic grandeur of construction.

German painters of the last seventy years, both 'realists' and 'expressionists', have produced a number of nude figures which can be claimed for the alternative convention : that is to say, they still conform to proportions of the Gothic nude, with short legs and long body, and are still dominated by the sagging curve of the stomach. It is questionable, however, if we can apply the word convention to the

274. REMBRANDT. Old woman bathing her feet

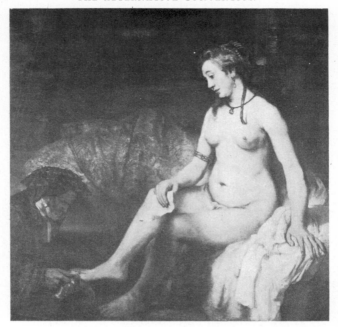

275. REMBRANDT. Bathsheba

welter of competing manners, each claiming to be based on truth, which at the beginning of this century had taken the place of a style. And perhaps the 'Gothic' character of the nude in recent German painting proves, simply, how true to observation were the original Gothic nudes. Any European artist who is unable imaginatively to accept the abstraction of the classic nude, seems to see the naked body in these terms. An example is Cézanne, the least Germanic of artists, whose only 'life study' of the nude [277] has a Gothic character simply because it aims at the truth. It is appallingly sincere, and proves that Courbet, for all his defiant trumpetings, continued to see the female body through memories of the Antique. But beyond mere realism there was another reason for depicting the naked body stripped of the garment of antique harmony ; and this, within the limits of language, I must now examine, for it represents the last violent twist in the history of the nude.

Few more horrifying images have ever been put before us than paint-

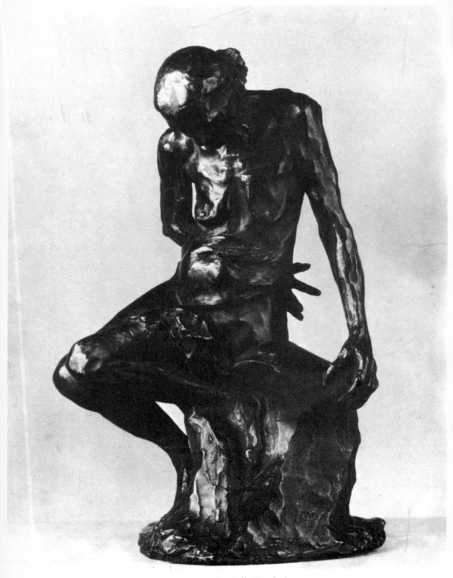

276. RODIN. *La Belle Heaulmière*

ings of naked prostitutes which Rouault executed in the years 1903-4 [278]. What had compelled the gentle pupil of Gustave Moreau to turn from biblical scenes and Rembrandtesque landscapes to these monsters of brutal depravity? Fundamentally, no doubt, the neo-Catholic doctrines of his friend Léon Bloy, by which in the lukewarm, materialistic society of 1900, absolute degradation came closer to redemption than worldly compromise. But the curious thing, for our present purpose, is that Rouault should have chosen to communicate this belief through the nude. He has done so precisely because it gives most pain. It has hurt him and he is savagely determined that it will hurt us. All those delicate feelings which flow together in our joy at the sight of an idealised human body, the Venus, shall we

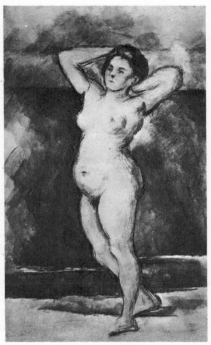

277. CÉZANNE. Nude

say, of Botticelli or of Giorgione, are shattered and profaned. The sublimation of desire is replaced by shame at its very existence ; our dream of a perfectible humanity is broken by this cruel reminder of what, in fact, man has contrived to make out of the raw material supplied to him in the cradle ; and, from the point of view of form, all that was realised in the nude on its first creation, the sense of healthy structure, the clear, geometric shapes and their harmonious disposition, has been rejected in favour of lumps of matter, swollen and inert.

And yet Rouault convinces us that this hideous image is necessary. It is the ultimate antithesis of the Cnidian Venus, appearing rather late, after more than two thousand years, but none the less inevitable. All ideals are corruptible, and by 1903 the Greek ideal of physical beauty had suffered a century of singular corruption. A convincing assertion of complementary truth began, perhaps, in the drawings done by Degas in brothels : thus suggesting how the formal falsity of the academic nude was also, to some extent, a moral falsity, for the amateurs who praised the nudes of Cabanel and Bouguereau had seen the real thing in the Maison Tellier. Degas' prostitutes are living beings, like obscene insects carved by an Egyptian sculptor, and Toulouse-Lautrec's pastels of the same subjects convey the character of an epoch and a society. Rouault's figure belongs to a different world. Like the Cnidian Venus, she is an *objet de culte*, though of a religion closer to that of Mexico than of Cnidos. She is a monstrous idol inspiring us with fear rather than pity. In this respect Rouault is also entirely unlike Rembrandt whom he so greatly admires, and who was his most fearless precursor in the exploitation of physical ugliness. Rembrandt's approach was moral, Rouault's is religious. This is what gives his menacing prostitute her importance for us. Her hideous body is ideal because conceived in a spirit of awe.

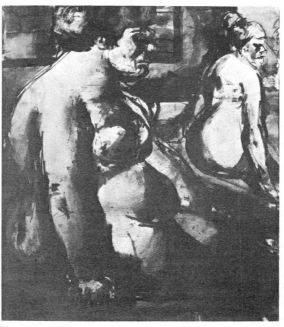

278. ROUAULT. A Prostitute

CHAPTER IX

The Nude as an End in Itself

IN this book I have tried to show how the naked body has been given memorable shapes by the wish to communicate certain ideas or states of feeling. I believe that this is the chief justification of the nude, but it is not the only justification. At all epochs when the body has been a subject of art, artists have felt that it could be given a shape which was good in itself. Many have gone further and have believed that they could find there the highest common factor of significant form. At the back of their minds is a notion similar to that which inspired the renaissance theorists with their mystic belief in Vitruvian Man or sent Goethe in his equally hopeless search for the *urpflanze*. They abandoned, of course, the Platonic fancy that Godlike man must conform to a mathematically perfect figure—the circle and the square ; but they continued to reverse the proposition and say that our admiration of an abstract form, a pot or an architectural moulding, has some analogy with satisfying human proportions. I myself have implied my acceptance of this belief many times in the foregoing pages—notably when I drew a parallel between the back of one of Michelangelo's athletes in the Sistine and his outline of a moulding for the Laurenziana. I must now examine rather more closely this notion of the nude as an end in itself and as a source of independent plastic construction.

The two reclining figures from the pediments of the Parthenon, the so-called Ilissus [279] and Dionysus, do not express particular ideas, and could not be classified under any of the headings of the preceding chapters. Yet they are indisputably two of the greatest pieces of sculpture in existence and they represent formal discoveries as valid as the formulations of a philosophic truth. During the Renaissance they were almost entirely inaccessible. They could not have been known to Raphael or Michelangelo. Yet both these artists discovered the same combinations of form and used them in some of their most memorable inventions. That relationship of the open legs to the twisted thorax, which we find so moving in the Ilissus, arouses a similar emotion when we encounter it in the dying Ananias of Raphael's cartoon or the stricken Paul of Michelangelo's sublime fresco. The Dionysus [45],

335

majestically accepting the earth from which the Ilissus struggles to be free, has an equally satisfying relationship of legs to torso, and this too was redis-covered by Michelangelo in his fragmentary river god [280] in the Florentine Academy. In both cases the interplay of axes, the balance of tensions and the rhythmic sequence of hump and hollow seem to convey an important truth,

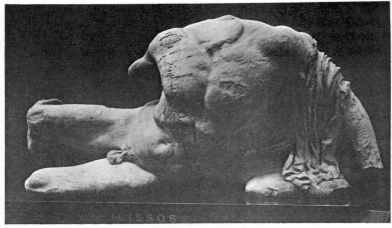

279. Greek. *c.* 438 B.C. Ilissus

although it is a truth which cannot be referred to the ordinary needs or actions of our lives. Or to take an example from the female nude : the Crouching Venus [281] which catalogues and textbooks attribute to Doidalsus but which certainly dates from the early 4th century. The plastic wholeness of her pear-shaped body has delighted all the ripening suns of art—Titian, Rubens, Renoir —till the present day, and in this case the reason is easily discovered, for this is the perfect symbol of fruitfulness, feeling earth's pull, like a hanging fruit, yet scarcely concealing in its structure a spring of sensual energy. But in other poses of the female nude our sense of completeness is almost inexplicable. Such, for example, is the outline which so enchanted the men of the Renais-sance, the figure of Psyche on a Hellenistic relief (now lost) known as the *Letto di Policleto*. Like a folk-song heard at a fair which, once discovered, serves as thematic material for generations of composers, we find this same outline in the masterpieces of Raphael, Michelangelo, Titian and Poussin, and feel that through it the nude has achieved an independent existence, just as the song has grown to be independent of the original words.

In addition to such poses which seem to achieve almost the status of ideograms, there are the thousands of nudes in European art which express no idea except the painter's striving for formal perfection. And this aspect of the nude has increased in importance during the last century as the importance of subject-matter, the story-telling part of painting, has declined. An Odalisque

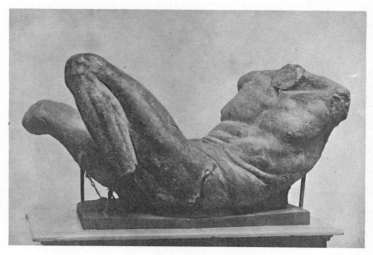

280. MICHELANGELO. River god

by Ingres, although from one point of view an exceptionally 'pure' pictorial construction, still embodies ideas attendant on the word Venus; the Blue Nude of Matisse [286] does not. To understand how this has occurred we must, I think, turn back to the point in the history of European art when the nude became the centre of academic discipline.

In the middle ages artists were resigned to being artisans, and the painter, sculptor or glazier was apprenticed to learn the rudiments of his craft like any other manual worker. When this old discipline of grinding colours, sizing panels and copying approved models was removed (and of course it was a gradual process), what new discipline took its place? Drawing from the nude, drawing from the Antique and perspective. This new approach has been strangely associated with the words scientific or naturalistic. In fact it is at the opposite pole. Instead of the late Gothic naturalism based on experience, it offers ideal form and ideal space, two intellectual abstractions. Art is

337

justified, as man is justified, by the faculty of forming ideas ; and the nude makes its first appearance in art theory at the very moment when painters begin to claim that their art is an intellectual, not a mechanical activity.

The doctrines of this new academism are clearly stated in the first treatise on the art of painting ever written, Leon Battista Alberti's *Della pittura*. It was

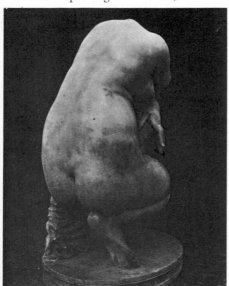

281. DOIDALSUS (?). Early 4th cent.
Crouching Venus

completed in August 1435 and dedicated to his friend Brunellesco, who may still be reckoned the inventor of mathematical perspective. In a dedicatory letter Alberti mentions as those who have restored the ancient glories of art their friends Donatello, Ghiberti, Masaccio and Luca della Robbia ; and we may therefore assume that throughout his treatise he is basing his theories on their practice. Now Alberti assumes that the basis of academic procedure is a study of the nude. He goes further, and recommends anatomical study of a kind which we associate with the next century. 'In painting the nude', he says, 'begin with the bones, then add the muscles and then cover the body with flesh in such a way as to leave the position of the muscles visible. It may be objected', he adds, 'that a painter should not represent what cannot be seen, but this procedure is analogous to drawing a nude and then covering it with draperies.' Here is a description of the academic practice which lasted till our own day. True, hardly any evidence of its employment in the early 15th century has come down to us, but that is due solely to the paucity of 15th-century drawings. Of the friends mentioned by Alberti, we have no drawings by Donatello, Masaccio or Luca della Robbia. We have, however, several scraps and copies from the workshops of Uccello and one or two superb originals by Pisanello to show that life studies existed in the early 15th century, and we have at least one drawing of nude figures used to form an academic composition. It shows a dozen naked youths posed round a polygonal structure, so that two disciplines of renaissance academism, perspective and the nude, are combined ; and, although it is in itself the work of an unskilled apprentice, is an indication of the sort of studies which preceded Ghiberti's relief of Joseph in Egypt or Donatello's reliefs of the miracles of Sant' Antonio.

In the second half of the 15th century we have plenty of evidence that

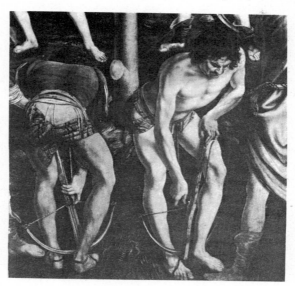

282. POLLAJUOLO. Bowmen (detail)

drawing from the naked model was a regular part of training. A score of silver point studies have survived from the workshops of Filippino Lippi and the Ghirlandajos ; and a large number of copies, no less than the testimony of Vasari, indicate that this was one of the chief occupations in the studio of the brothers Pollajuolo. It is, in fact, in a work of Antonio Pollajuolo that we find one of the first nudes to be included in a picture simply for our admiration, the man setting his crossbow in the foreground of the Martyrdom of St. Sebastian in the London National Gallery [282]. Admirable though he is, and admired by all good judges since Vasari, he is less expressive of energy than the clothed bowman beside him.

This is the aspect of academism which is concerned with anatomy. In an earlier chapter I have shown how the Florentine passion for anatomy was related to the idea of energy, by making our awareness of bodily movement more vivid and precise. But in addition to this quality of life-enhancement there is no doubt that the Florentines valued a demonstration of anatomical knowledge simply because it *was* knowledge and as such of a higher order than ordinary perception. Moreover, it involved the recognition of certain sequences of cause and effect, so that a 16th-century amateur must have followed the exact placing of every muscle and sinew with the same sort of enthusiasm as is aroused in the 20th-century mind by the contemplation of a Rolls-Royce engine. This explains the anatomical nudes which appear in so many compositions of the time without the smallest justification of subject-matter. They are like certificates of professional capacity. True these figures appear most frequently in the works of mannerists, whose display of anatomical skill is partly a mere compliance with fashion. The *écorché* statuette, which still survives as a neglected property in art schools, usually derives from a model by Cigoli and adds to its practical purpose some acquaintance with mannerist rhythm and gesture. But although a craving for details of musculature was partly a phase of style, the notion of the body as a complex of thrusts and tensions, whose reconciliation is one of the chief aims of the figure arts, remains eternally true. We are reminded once again of the *dipendenza* between the nude and architecture, and recall how, when we speak of architectural truth, we mean that in great buildings the interaction of shaft and vault or wall and buttress can be perceived intuitively as a harmonious balance of forces.

This feeling that a deeper truth is to be found in the knowledge of structure than in appearance also accounts for the practice recommended by Alberti by which, in composing a group, all the figures are first shown nude. One of the earliest and finest examples of the practice is a drawing by Raphael now in Frankfurt in which a group of nude athletic young men fill the places to be occupied by the church fathers and theologians to the left of the *Disputa* [283]. Visually such figures could have little connection with the finished painting, where the flow of ample draperies, colour and the contrast of light and shade would inevitably produce a different design ; but to Raphael the consciousness that nude figures had once stood where the draped ones came to stand was both a guarantee of their real existence and an assurance that the whole composition would 'work'.

Raphael's drawing reminds us that another element besides knowledge was needed to produce the academic nude : the quality known by the Italian connoisseurs as *gran gusto*. Pollajuolo's archer had the powerful body of a labourer, and the gawky youths who posed in Ghirlandajo's workshop were recognisably fellow apprentices. But at some point round about the year 1505 there was evolved a way of looking at the body which smoothed away abrupt transitions, gave a continuous flow to every movement and an air of nobility to every gesture. No doubt this thoroughgoing idealisation was based on the more perceptive study of antique sculpture which began when the young Michelangelo entered Bertoldo's academy in the Via Larga. But although the Battle of Cascina lies at the root of high-renaissance taste, Michelangelo always preferred strenuous Florentine movement to classical ease, and

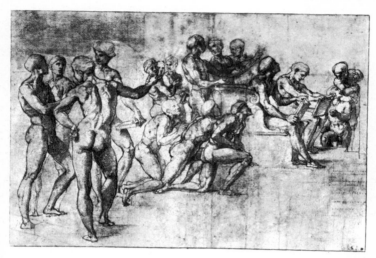

283. RAPHAEL. Drawing for *Disputa*

it is in the work of Raphael that the academic version of antique art takes its lasting form. We can, in fact, take two of Marcantonio's prints after his designs, the Massacre of the Innocents [284] and the Judgment of Paris [285], as containing almost all the characteristics and many of the actual properties which were to be approved and used in art schools till this century. The design for the Massacre of the Innocents dates from the first years of Raphael's residence in Rome, and the memory of Michelangelo's battle cartoon is still fresh in his mind. But there are two significant differences. First, many of Michelangelo's soldiers are replaced by women; and second, the male figures are shown as nude with no factual justification whatsoever. Michelangelo had taken pains to choose for his battle cartoon an incident when the soldiers really were naked, but no one could have supposed that Herod's executioners had laid aside their clothes. They were accepted, as the naked Greek soldiers in an Amazon battle were accepted, simply because their bodies could display grace of movement and knowledge of anatomy ; and their beautiful poses bear no more relation to their brutal intentions than if they were ballet dancers. This arbitrary use of the nude in 'historical painting' was, in fact, too Greek for the painters of the *seicento*. It was never attempted by Poussin, and even

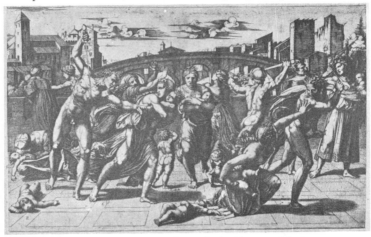

284. MARCANTONIO. Engraving after Raphael. Massacre of the Innocents

at the meridian of classicism the nude warriors in David's Intervention of the Sabine Women were included as an afterthought on the instigation of that most implacable prophet of the ideal, Quatremère de Quincy.

In Raphael's Massacre of the Innocents the women, following antique precedent, remain draped. We know from preparatory drawings how gladly he would have depicted their bodies, but he felt, and subsequent classicists agreed with him, that this was possible only in subjects drawn from Greek mythology. Of this he provided a model in his design for the Judgment of Paris. It is the crystallisation of the academic idea. We need think only of the mythological paintings of Poussin, the Realm of Flora of Dresden or the Venus and Aeneas at Rouen, to recognise how completely Raphael's design anticipates the use of the nude in learned picture-making. His naked divinities are there with no other purpose but to display themselves as perfect units of form, and in fact we recognise in the river god to the right and the naiad sitting at his feet two of these perennially satisfying poses referred to at the beginning of the chapter. That Manet used them in his *Déjeuner sur l'herbe* has been claimed as a sort of joke against academism ; in fact it was an intelligent acceptance of its value. The *un*intelligent acceptance is to be found in such a prize-winning composition as Poynter's Visit to Aesculapius, but even there a distant memory of Marcantonio's print has saved him from the more efficient banalities of the Salon.

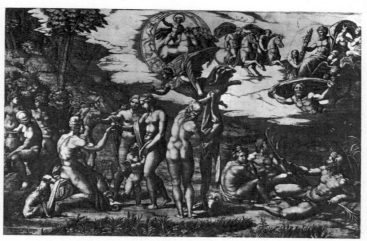

285. MARCANTONIO. Engraving after Raphael. Judgment of Paris

The predominance of the female nude over the male, of which Raphael's Judgment of Paris is the first example, was to increase during the next 200 years, till by the 19th century it was absolute. The male nude kept its place in the curriculum of art schools out of piety to the classical ideal, but it was drawn and painted with diminishing enthusiasm, and when we speak of a nude study or *académie* of that period we tend to assume that the subject will be a woman. No doubt this is connected with a declining interest in anatomy (for the *écorché* figure is always male) and so is part of that prolonged episode in the history of art in which the intellectual analysis of parts dissolves before a sensuous perception of totalities. In this, as in much else, Giorgione's *Concert Champêtre* is like a first spring of feeling and it is notable that there the classical practice is reversed : the men are clothed, the women nude. Giorgione's pastoral has already been quoted as one of the earliest triumphs of *Venus*

Naturalis, and no doubt in the eventual establishment of the female model the tug of normal sensuality must have a place. But it is also arguable that the female body is plastically more rewarding on what, at their first submission, seem to be purely abstract grounds. Since Michelangelo few artists have shared a Florentine passion for shoulders, knees and other small knobs of form. They have found it easier to compose harmoniously the larger units of a woman's torso ; they have been grateful for its smoother transitions, and above all they have discovered analogies with satisfying geometrical forms, the oval, the ellipsoid and the sphere. But may not this argument reverse the order of cause and effect ? Is there, after all, any reason why certain quasi-geometrical shapes should be satisfying except that they are simplified statements of the forms which please us in a woman's body ? The recurrent search by writers on the theory of art—Lomazzo, Hogarth, Winckelmann—for a 'line of beauty' ends, not inappropriately, in a question-mark ; and he who pursues it further is soon caught in the sterile fallacy of one cause. A shape, like a word, has innumerable associations which vibrate in the memory, and any attempt to explain it by a single analogy is as futile as the translation of a lyric poem. But the fact that we can base our argument either way on this unexpected union of sex and geometry is a proof of how deeply the concept of the nude is linked with our most elementary notions of order and design.

We have come to accept this almost as a law of nature, but mediaeval and Far Eastern art proves that we are mistaken. It is to a large extent an artificial creation due to the system of training which came into being at the moment of transition from mediaeval to modern art. From the antique room to the life class : this progression, inaugurated in the workshops of renaissance Rome and Florence, has lasted till the present day and western artists have unconsciously derived from it their sense of scale, their system of proportion and their basic repertoire of forms. A return to the fundamentals of design has always meant to them a return to the nude ; and yet to a creative artist the nude was deeply compromised by its subjection to the formulae of academic training. From this point of view let me examine the revolutionary painting of the present century.

Two pictures painted in the year 1907 can conveniently be taken as the starting-point of 20th-century art. They are Matisse's *Le Nu bleu* [286] and Picasso's *Demoiselles d'Avignon* [289] ; and both these cardinal, anti-academic pictures represent the nude. The reason is that the revolt of 20th-century painters was not against academism : that had been achieved by the Impressionists. It was a revolt against the doctrine, with which the Impressionists implicitly agreed, that the painter should be no more than a sensitive and well-informed camera. And the very elements of symbolism and abstraction which made the nude an unsuitable subject for the Impressionists, commended it to their successors. When art was once more concerned with concepts rather than sensations, the nude was the first concept which came to mind. But in 1907 it was a concept with many odious associations. It is difficult for us to realise how complacently the official and cultured world of 1900 accepted the standards of degraded Hellenism, especially in France. England had felt the influence of Ruskin and the pre-Raphaelites, America had already recognised Impressionism as the painting of democracy. But in France the great official edifice of the Beaux-Arts seemed impregnable, and the concept of *le beau* on which it rested was still not very far from that which had governed Louis XIV in his admission of antique statuary into the Galerie des Glaces. We may look back with nostalgia to such security of taste, but an artist sensitive to his time was bound to reject it ; and inevitably the two painters, who may, without apology, be taken as representative of their epoch, have treated the nude with considerable violence.

Matisse and Picasso, although posterity will be struck by the technical similarities in their work, are almost antithetical characters, and their reactions to the nude have been very different from one another. Matisse was a traditionalist picture-maker whose life drawings could almost be mistaken for those of Degas, and like Degas or Ingres he deduced from the female

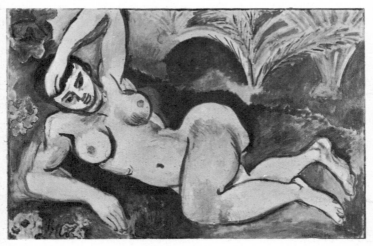

286. MATISSE. Blue Nude

nude certain pictorial constructions which satisfied his sense of form and which were to obsess him for a great part of his life. The Blue Nude represents such a construction. It was an important part of himself, and he not only carried out the same pose in sculpture, but brought it into numerous other compositions. This is the standard use of the nude as an end in itself or, in the convenient language of recent criticism, as a means of creating significant form. The revolutionary character of Matisse's picture resides not in the end but the means. That enjoyment of continuous surfaces, easy transitions and delicate modelling, which had seemed such an essential factor in painting the nude, is sacrificed to violent transitions and emphatic simplifications. This problem of simplifying the body was to obsess Matisse and all the most intelligent painters of his time. The classical system had been the hard-won solution of the problem, and when it was no longer acceptable some other form of simplification had to be found. Matisse sought for it in an earlier phase of the Greek tradition, and produced *La Danse* and *La Musique*, the two decorations painted for Shchukin. He sought for it in Japanese prints and in the Islamic Exhibition of 1910. Above all he sought to achieve it by the same sort of logical processes by which Paul Valéry tells us he was composing poetry. Sometimes his search is successful, particularly in his etched illustrations to *Mallarmé*, where the graphic medium preserves an illusion of spontaneity [287]. But sometimes he seems to grow exhausted in pursuit of a quarry which, like the unicorn, can be subdued only by love. Such is the impression we receive from a series of eighteen photographs taken of the stages in the completion of a painting known as the Pink Nude. Almost thirty years have passed since the Blue Nude, but the first stage is remarkably similar in pose. He is still clasping the same obsession. But the handling is less vigorous, and we can understand why the simplifications had to be achieved by argument and not by instinct. Perhaps only the countrymen of Descartes can believe that works of art come into existence in this way, and although the last stage of the Pink Nude achieves a monumentality absent from the preceding eighteen, it has, to my eye, the same august flatness as a copy of the Doryphoros.

But this is not because Matisse had lost interest in the body. On the contrary, at the same epoch that he was using the female nude as the basis for a 'pure' pictorial construction, he was doing a series of drawings of naked women which reveal a kind of frenzy almost without precedent in art. There are Rodin drawings in which the model rolls and stretches with an inhuman lack of modesty ; but even in these Rodin is further from his models and from us. Matisse breathes down our necks and brings us so close to the

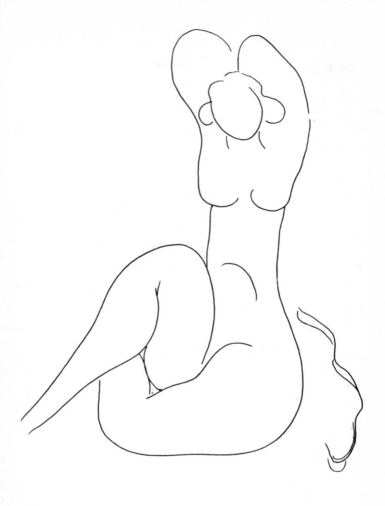

287. MATISSE. Nude. From *Poésies de Mallarmé*

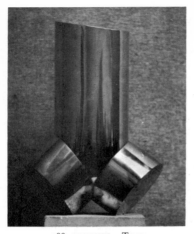

288. BRANCUSI. Torso

sprawling naked body that I, at least, retreat in embarrassment.

This contrast between the calculated formalism of Matisse's painting and the animality of his drawings supports one of our chief conclusions about the nude : that the antique scheme had involved so complete a fusion of the sensual and the geometric as to provide a kind of armour ; and the words *cuirasse esthétique*, used by French critics to describe the formalised male torso, could have been extended to the female torso as well. Once this armour had grown unwearable, the nude either became a dead abstraction or the sexual element became unduly insistent. In fact if this element is allowed to make itself felt at all, abstraction and distortion will tend to increase its impact. A more simplified version of the female torso than that by Brancusi [288] can hardly be conceived, and yet it is more disturbingly physical and, may we say, less decent than the Cnidian. This is partly because the eye instinctively looks for analogies and amplifies them, so that a face imagined in the pattern of a wallpaper may become more vivid than a photograph ; and partly because the discipline of art schools has given all skilful draughtsmen such innate sense of the construction of the female body that this can make its proportions felt through almost any disguise. The fullest illustration is to be found in the work of Picasso.

Unlike Matisse's steady, traditional pursuit of a few motives, Picasso's relation to the nude has been a scarcely resolved struggle between love and hatred. The *Demoiselles d'Avignon* [289] is the triumph of hate. Starting from a brothel theme, which seems to have owed something to Cézanne's groups of bathers, it developed into an enraged protest at everything involved in the conventional notion of beauty. This meant not simply representing ugly women, as Toulouse-Lautrec had done, but finding some formula for the treatment of the body which should owe nothing whatsoever to the classical tradition. As I have tried to show, this is extremely difficult. Even the Eve of Hildesheim and the dancers at Amaravati have some remote connection

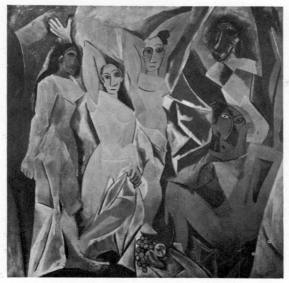

289. PICASSO. *Les Demoiselles d'Avignon*

with Greece. It happened, however, that the painting of the *Demoiselles d'Avignon* coincided with the first appreciative study of negro sculpture ; and there, at last, was a totally un-Hellenised stylisation of the body which, from its intuitive geometry, can be classified a nude. The date and degree of Picasso's indebtedness to the Congo is a matter of dispute, and perhaps only the heads of the two right-hand *Demoiselles* show a direct derivation ; but the general sense of form, with its sharp contours and shallow concave planes, indicates a moment when consciousness of African carving had begun and cubism was on the way.

With cubism come the first of Picasso's dismemberments of the nude. Compared to what was to follow it was relatively mild. The members are not monstrously displaced, but are simply subjected to a general law of refraction ; and the fact that he was voluntarily subject to a law gave to Picasso's cubist pictures a tranquillity very unlike the rest of his work. His love-hate relationship to the nude was temporarily suspended, because the classical style was at such a safe distance. But in 1917 Jean Cocteau persuaded him to join Diaghilev in Rome, and together they visited Naples and Pompeii. Here for the first time he realised that classical art had once been alive. In Paris he had

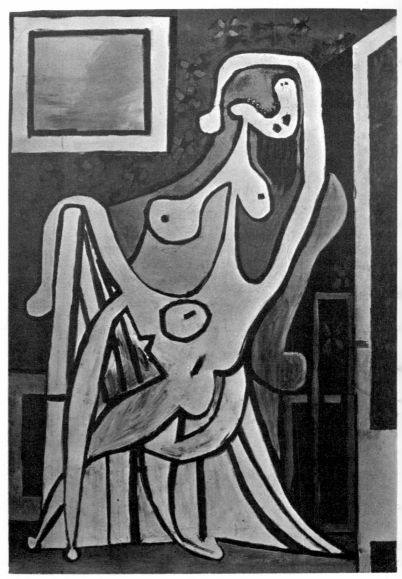

290. PICASSO. Woman in an Armchair

thought of it as a hollow machine used by the enemy in their battle with the rebellious young. But no man of imagination can tread the soil of Campania without feeling the nearness of paganism and the eternal freshness of its art ; and within a year Picasso had done the drawing on Plate 3 which I have compared to a Greek mirror-back, but which equally recalls a white Lekythos. Actually this experience of antiquity was to remain in absorption for another two years, and when it emerged it was as part of a reassertion of classical values which affected all the arts in the early 1920's. A slight element of modishness in this movement gives an air of expediency to some of Picasso's classical nudes. They furnish agreeably his illustrations to Ovid or Aristophanes, but when worked up into large drawings or paintings their wilful renunciation of vitality is rather oppressive. Picasso is above all things an animator, but this gift, which was so fascinating when manifested through the stubbornly inanimate materials of cubism, was not allowed to disturb the ponderous objectivity of his classical nudes. When vitality reasserted itself it was through new and more cruel distortions. No doubt there was an element of provocation, halfway between that of a naughty child and an angry god, in the indignities to which the body was subjected. In his rage Picasso no longer attacked the classic nude with its exhausted *beaux-arts* associations, but the accepted nude of contemporary painting. In the picture of a woman in an armchair of 1929 [290] the relation of the figure to the chair and of the chair to the wallpaper and picture-frame, all recall one of Matisse's Odalisques of three or four years earlier. To pretend that these savage distortions have been contrived solely in the interests of pictorial construction is to look at the picture with the mind half closed. On the contrary, the arm bent over the head, a motive frequently used by Matisse as a means of achieving a satisfactory shape, is here given some of its antique force as a symbol of pain, and the displacements of the members all contribute to the same expression of agony. The extraordinary thing is that we recognise them at all. Some of the 'bathers' done in the next five or six years show an even greater desire to displace and deform, although in these we often feel that hatred is accompanied by a certain pleasure in the metaphysical ingenuity and once more we are reminded of the naughty child. 'Look what I've made, Mummy ; it's a man. Yes, it *is* a man.'

Yet in the end the controlling impulse is godlike—to create in his own image something that shall have an independent existence as design. Parallel with the eighteen stages of Matisse's Pink Nude are the eighteen proofs of a lithograph of two nude women done in the winter of 1945–6 [291]. The subject is one of the few to which Picasso has frequently returned, and which

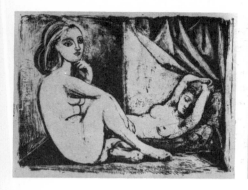

4th stage. 22 November 1945

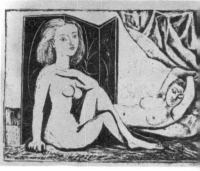

9th stage. 10 January 1946

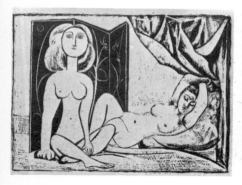

10th stage. 17 January 1946

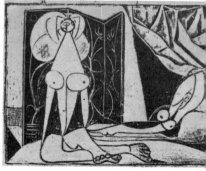

18th stage. 12 February 1946

291. PICASSO. Four of the eighteen stages of *Les Deux Femmes nues*

must be to him what the *Grande Baigneuse* and the Odalisque were to Ingres, one figure lying asleep, while the other sits and watches. Essentially it is the Cupid and Psyche motive, and in the years immediately preceding this lithograph he had executed a series of large drawings of the subject which seemed to me, when I saw them in his studio in 1944, to be amongst his finest works. In these the sleeper is a boy, the watcher a girl ; but in the lithograph both are women, and from the first we feel that the subject has lost some of its symbolic importance to him and become an exclusively pictorial problem. It is also evident that the watcher is so much more stylised than the sleeper (who is curiously reminiscent of a 19th-century art-school) that ultimately she will take command. She does so definitely in the tenth state, turning round to face us, and bequeathing her legs to the sleeper. Clearly this will not do, and in the next state the sleeper is transformed, becoming, in turn, more abstract than the watcher. A sort of competition then sets in between them, in which the watcher's body expands and contracts and the sleeper remains unchanged, until finally both achieve a high degree of independence. But, like an independence, it involves a further frustration. Aesthetic essences are never pure enough ; and if accidents must persist, the familiar accident of our bodily shape is perhaps preferable to a pattern so arbitrary and inconclusive.

The exhaustion of antique formalities which had led Matisse to approach the nude in two different ways, produced a similar duality in the mind of Picasso. But his response to the situation was less narrowly aesthetic. For one thing, he retained, and even exploited, erotic images in his abstract work. For another, he saw as clearly as any church elder that the flaw in the whole respectable edifice of the academic nude was the relationship between the painter and his model. No doubt an artist can achieve a greater degree of detachment than the profane might suppose. But does this not involve a certain callosity or dimness of response ? To scrutinise a naked girl as if she was a loaf of bread or a piece of rustic pottery is surely to exclude one of the human emotions of which a work of art is composed ; and, as a matter of history, the Victorian moralists who alleged that painting the nude usually ended in fornication were not far from the mark.

Picasso's drawings of the painter and his model go back to the illustrations he did in 1927 for an edition of Balzac's *Le Chef-d'œuvre inconnu*. In these the model is impassive and ideal ; in the struggle between art and nature, they represent a victory for art. As Balzac's story demands, her influence is not perceptible on the painter's canvases, but her classical outlines inform us that at the height of his surrealist period Picasso has by no means lost faith in physical beauty. A few years later he is still brooding on the relationship between art and nature in a series of etchings dated 1933. They show the artist and his model, both nude, contemplating various pieces of sculpture, amongst them one which Picasso himself was to execute in bronze. A puzzled Pygmalion, the sculptor seems uncertain whether the independent form of his own creation really excels the living girl who crouches beside him.

Finally, during the winter of 1953-4, in a series of 180 drawings, he set down his feelings on the painter-model relationship with ironical simplicity. The series has been compared to Baudelaire's *Mon Cœur mis à nu*, and some of the painter's admirers have made heavy weather of these sparkling pages. But whatever its bearing on Picasso's life, it is also a serious commentary on the whole practice of painting the nude as an accepted part of the academic system. This time the model comes off best and the painter, with few exceptions, cuts a poor figure. She is a satisfied animal, a work of nature more graceful and alive than anything he is likely to produce by art. He peers at her anxiously, myopically, hoping to calculate the exact curve of her behind. No wonder she prefers the company of a black kitten, or even a baboon. The most ravishing model of all poses for a resolute lady, who subsequently shows her canvas, huge and incomprehensible, to a group of complacent toadies. None of them think of looking at the model, who, in a pose of sensual relaxation, is a sight for the gods.

In later pages of his 'diary' Picasso shows the same short-sighted artists who had peered so painstakingly at a delightful body gazing with equal earnestness at the deplorable body of a middle-aged female. We are left in no doubt about his impatience at the occupational blindness of his colleagues, and indeed with the whole concept of drawing from the life as it had developed in the 19th century. The first inventors of the nude would have agreed with him. The Greeks wished to perpetuate the naked human body because it was beautiful. Their athletes were beautiful in life first, and in art afterwards. The physical perfection of Phryne was considered as important as the artistic endowment of Praxiteles. To draw from a misshapen model would have seemed to them incomprehensible and revolting, and when, in Hellenistic art, these subjects are represented, it is with the same cold-hearted contempt as in Picasso's drawings. For the same reason Greek artists did not think of the nude merely as a repertoire of forms. Even when they achieved independent plastic constructions as severe as the athletes of Polyclitus, they did so on the basis of a fervent admiration for physical beauty. To abstract from the model a number of plastic components without having regard to the totality of sensuous

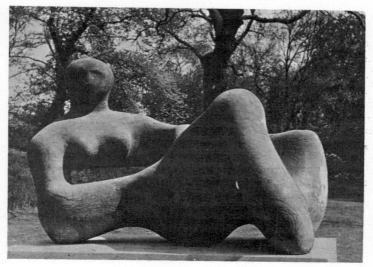

292. HENRY MOORE. Recumbent Figure

impression, as was the practice in neo-classic discipline no less than in the drastic simplification and rearrangements of the last thirty years, is fundamentally un-Greek.

This does not mean that the attempt to create an independent form on the basis of the human body is a lost cause ; only that the old approach by which art-school nudes are scrambled into a new pictorial language involves too great a sacrifice of fundamental responses. Such a metamorphosis, in so far as it seems to be necessary to our own peculiar needs, must take place deep in the unconscious, and not be achieved by trial or elimination. I may take as an example the work of Henry Moore.

Almost alone of the generation succeeding Picasso, he has not felt himself swamped or frustrated by that ruthless torrent of invention. It is true, of course, that he has found some of these inventions liberating and directive. Anyone familiar with Picasso's drawing of 1933 known as An Anatomy will find that it forestalls not only some of Moore's experiments of the succeeding years, but also his way of presenting them in rows or groups of three. But there the resemblance ends. Where Picasso is volatile, Moore is tenacious ; Picasso swoops, Moore burrows. A see-saw between love and hate, elegant

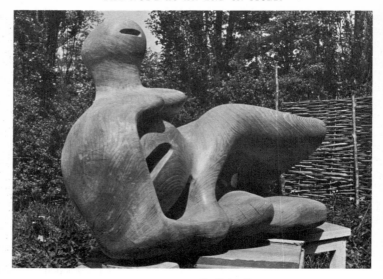

293. HENRY MOORE. Reclining Figure

classicism and enraged distortion is entirely foreign to his single-minded character. Moore is an impressive draughtsman of the nude, but practically none of his life drawings is directly related to his sculpture; none, for example, represents the figure in that reclining pose which was for long his favourite motive. His great sculptural ideas appear first in his notebooks almost exactly as they will be when executed in wood or stone. They are, so to say, abstract from the first; the metamorphosis has been intuitive, the result of some deep internal pressure. Yet they are clearly the work of a man in whom the body has aroused powerful emotions.

Two of Henry Moore's most satisfying works are the stone recumbent figure of 1938 [292] and the wooden reclining figure of 1946 [293]. Many different associations converge in these carvings: in the former there is the feeling of the menhir and the memory of rocks worn through by the sea; in the latter there is the pulsation of the wooden heart, like a crusader's head, burrowing in the hollow breast. But in both, these conflicting memories are resolved by their subordination to the human body, and in fact they develop two basic ideas of the nude which was first embodied in the Dionysus and the Ilissus of the Parthenon, the stone figure with bent knee rising from the earth like a hill, the wooden figure with averted thorax and open legs, struggling out of the earth like a tree, not without a powerful suggestion of sexual readiness.

Thus modern art shows even more explicitly than the art of the past that the nude does not simply represent the body, but relates it, by analogy, to all structures that have become part of our imaginative experience. The Greeks related it to their geometry. Twentieth-century man, with his vastly extended experience of physical life, and his more elaborate patterns of mathematical symbols, must have at the back of his mind analogies of far greater complexity. But he has not abandoned the effort to express them visibly as part of himself. The Greeks perfected the nude in order that man might feel like a god, and in a sense this is still its function, for although we no longer suppose that God is like a beautiful man, we still feel close to divinity in those flashes of self-identification when, through our own bodies, we seem to be aware of a universal order.

List of Books referred to
in Abbreviated Form

B.   Bartsch. *Le Peintre-Graveur.* Leipzig, 1854–1870. Volume given except in case of Marcantonio which is volume XIV.

B.B.   Bernard Berenson. *The Drawings of the Florentine Painters,* amplified edition. Chicago, 1938.

Escurialensis. Hermann Egger. *Codex Escurialensis.* Wien, 1906.

Lasinio. Lasinio, P. *Raccolta di sarcofagi, urne e altri monumenti di scultura del Campo Santo di Pisa.* Pisa, 1814.

Pausanias. *Pausanias's Description of Greece.* Translated J. G. Frazer. London, 1898.

Picard, Manuel. Charles Picard. *Manuel d'archéologie grecque. La Sculpture.* Paris, 1935–1954.

Pliny. *The Elder Pliny's Chapters in the History of Art.* Translated K. Jex-Blake. London, 1896.

Popham and Wilde. A. E. Popham and Johannes Wilde. *The Italian Drawings of the XV and XVI Centuries in the Collection of His Majesty the King at Windsor Castle.* London, 1949.

Reinach, Répertoire. Reinach, S. *Répertoire de la statuaire grecque et romaine.* Paris.

Reinach, Répertoire des reliefs. Reinach, S. *Répertoire des reliefs grecs et romains.* Paris, 1909–1912.

Tolnay. Charles de Tolnay. *Michelangelo.* Princeton, 1943–1954.

Vasari. *Le vite de' più eccellenti pittori, scultori ed architetti da Giorgio Vasari.* Ed. Gaetano Milanesi. Firenze, 1878–1885.

Venturi. *Storia dell' arte italiana.* Milan, 1908–1939.

Wiener Jahrbuch. *Jahrbuch der kunsthistorischen Sammlungen des allerhöchsten Kaiserhauses.* Wien.

Wilde, British Museum. Johannes Wilde. *Italian Drawings in the Department of Prints and Drawings in the British Museum. Michelangelo and his Studio.* London, 1953.

Wildenstein. Georges Wildenstein. *Ingres.* London, 1954.

Winkler. Friedrich Winkler. *Die Zeichnungen Albrecht Dürer's.* Berlin, 1936–1939.

Notes

Numbers in square brackets refer to illustrations in this book.

I. THE NAKED AND THE NUDE

p. 2. VELASQUEZ AND THE NUDE. We have records of at least five paintings of the nude by Velasquez. In addition to the National Gallery picture, which belonged to Don Gaspar de Haro y Guzman in 1651, there were a Cupid and Psyche and a Venus and Adonis in the possession of Philip IV, a nude woman in the estate of Domingo Guerra Coronel in 1651, and a recumbent Venus in the painter's own possession at the time of his death in 1660. There is some reason to suppose that the National Gallery painting was done in Italy, for Velasquez did not return to Spain till the summer of 1651 ; and it can hardly be earlier than his departure to Italy in 1649. Cf. Neil Maclaren, *The Spanish School*, National Gallery Catalogue, London, 1952, p. 76. It is commonly said that Velasquez took the pose of the Rokeby Venus from Rembrandt's etching of a negress lying down (Munz, 142), but as this is dated 1658 the connection between the two poses must be accidental. Ultimately it derives from the Borghese Hermaphrodite, now in the Louvre, which had attained great celebrity at the time Velasquez was in Rome, and had been restored by Bernini. Velasquez ordered a cast of it for the Spanish Royal Collection. See note on p. 377.

p. 6. *Beauty and Other Forms of Value*, Alexander, p. 127. In fairness to Professor Alexander it must be said that this has been for many years a commonplace of aesthetic philosophy, and is a branch of the accepted doctrine that our responses to subjects and situations represented in art are fundamentally different from our responses to the same subjects and situations in life. Experience suggests that they differ in some important ways, but not fundamentally.

p. 7. For the NAKED FIGURE IN JAPANESE PRINTS, cf. Stratz, *Die Körperformen der Japaner*, 1902, who demonstrates, by means of photographs, their naturalism. There are some beautiful naked figures by Utamaro, *e.g.* a print in the Musée Guimet of a woman stepping into a bath, reproduced in André Lhote, *Figure Painting*, London, 1953, pl. 92, which was apparently known to Matisse. But it is notable that in the so-called pillow books of Utamaro, which are illustrated guides to sexual intercourse, the whole naked body is never shown. That western man, even at his crudest, has rejected specialisation in this particular activity is to some extent a legacy of that Greek belief in wholeness which created the nude.

p. 8. ETRUSCAN TOMB FIGURES WITH BIG STOMACHS are known to archaeologists as *obesi*, perhaps in reference to the stock epithets applied to them by the Roman poets of the Augustan era, *pingues et obesi Etrusci*. It has been suggested that these prominent stomachs had a symbolic meaning and referred to the prosperity or status of the deceased. But in fact they are probably only one more example of the inherent naturalism of Etruscan art. The majority of men over middle age reclining in this position would show a similar proportion.

p. 8. PROFESSIONAL ATHLETES. The ugliest are to be found in the series of mosaics from the baths of Caracalla, now in the Museum of the Lateran. They represent the debased gladiatorial spirit which we associate with Imperial Rome. But professionalism and specialisation had begun to affect athletics already in 5th-century Greece. Socrates, in Xenophon's *Symposium* (II, 17), is made to lament that the bodies are not developed evenly, but that the runner has over-developed legs, the boxer enormous chest and shoulders, etc. Cf. Norman Gardiner, *Athletics of the Ancient World*, 1930, ch. vii *passim.*

p. 8. THE VEROLI CASKET in the Victoria and Albert Museum is one of a group of ivory caskets of which forty-three have come down to us complete and as many in separate panels. All are decorated with pseudo-antique motives derived from silver plate or manuscripts, put together with little understanding of the original significance. They are usually thought to have been made in Constantinople during the Icono-clastic period, *i.e.* 8th and 9th centuries ; see Victoria and Albert Museum, *Catalogue of Carvings in Ivory*, by Margaret L. Longhurst, 1927, p. 34.

p. 8. THE IVORY PANEL OF APOLLO AND DAPHNE in the Museum at Ravenna is usually dated in the late 5th century, and is related to a large number of Coptic ivories. Of the *objets de luxe* referred to, the most characteristic are the silver dishes which seem to have been made all over the eastern Mediterranean in the 6th century and are frequently decorated with pagan divinities, *e.g.* the dish with Venus and Adonis in the Cabinet des Médailles, Paris (illustrated in Peirce and Tyler, *L'Art byzantin*, vol. II, 1934, pl. 74). For silverware decorated with nereids cf. p. 275.

p. 8. The fate of the CNIDIAN VENUS IN THE MIDDLE AGES is considered in Blinken-berg, *Cnidia*, 1933, pp. 32-3. Picard, *Manuel*, III, 1948, pp. 562-3, implies that she was still in Constantinople in 1203, basing his statement on the chronicle of Robert de Clari. But the statue Robert describes was of 'copper' (bronze). According to him it was 'a good twenty feet in height', and although, in an otherwise accurate account, he tends to exaggerate sizes, it must have been over life-size. His description does, however, make it clear that the figure was a Venus *pudica*, so it was probably a copy or derivative of the Cnidian. Cf. Robert de Clari, *The Conquest of Constantin-ople*, edited by E. H. McNeal, Columbia University, New York, 1936.

p. 9. VILLARD DE HONNECOURT'S NOTEBOOK, containing drawings of the works of sculpture and architecture which had particularly impressed him, was compiled in the second half of the 13th century. It is now in the Bibliothèque Nationale, Fonds français 19093. The two antique figures on f. 22 are taken from representations of Dionysus and Hermes, probably in Gallo-Roman bronzes. For a list of similar figures, see Hahnloser, *Villard de Honnecourt*, Wien, 1935, p. 131. Another nude figure, also extremely ugly, is on f. 11 verso. It appears to be copied from a late antique mosaic, painting, or book illustration.

p. 13. VITRUVIAN MAN in the narrow sense of a human figure illustrating Vitruvius' doctrine of proportion appears first in Francesco di Giorgio's book on Architecture in the Laurenziana, Florence (Ashburnham, 361), which was owned and annotated by Leonardo. But the image of man as a microcosm of the universe is present in the background of mediaeval thought and goes back to Plotinus ; cf. R. Wittkower, *Architectural Principles in the Age of Humanism*, 1949, p. 15, note. There are many examples of mediaeval drawings showing man as a microcosm with arms and legs spread out filling a circle, remarkably similar to the Vitruvian Man of Cesarino [10], *e.g.* a representation of the Harmony of the Spheres in a Reims MS. of 1170, illustrated in Swarzenski, *Monuments of Romanesque Art*, London, 1955, p. 210.

p. 16. DÜRER NEVER WENT TO ROME, so that the clear reminiscences of the Apollo Belvedere in the studies which culminate in the Adam must derive from drawings of the recently discovered figure which he had borrowed or acquired. We know that Dürer armed himself with material of this kind when in Italy ; cf. his copies of drawings by Leonardo da Vinci and Pollajuolo. If his drawing in the British Museum inscribed *Apolo* [40] is really datable *c.* 1501, he must have acquired a record of the Apollo during his first visit to Italy, 1494–5. But this date seems to me doubtful (cf. note on p. 367) and I think his acquaintance with the Apollo must date from just before his second visit to Venice, *c.* 1504, and have led directly to the engraving of the Fall of Man. The schematised drawing on pl. 12 is traced, though, and made into a study for the Adam.

p. 16. DÜRER'S admission that either a stout or a thin figure may be beautiful occurs also in Leon Battista Alberti's *Della architettura*, Book IX, ch. v (in the original Latin edition of 1485, f. 164^{b}). It has long been assumed that Dürer was familiar with Alberti's *Della pittura* ; it seems probable that he knew the *de Re Aedificatoria* as well.

p. 23. NUDITY AND THE INQUISITION. The Inquisitor who made this reply to Paul Veronese was a cleric of exceptional enlightenment. In general after the decrees of the Council of Trent (1563), nudity was objected to in sacred subjects, and some of the more zealous Popes contemplated destroying or painting over Michelangelo's Last Judgment. In fact Paul IV instructed Daniele de Volterra to paint draperies over those parts which (in Alberti's words) *porgono poco gratia* ; which he did with such tact that they do not affect the composition. Clement VIII was prevented from destroying the painting completely by the appeals of the Academy of St. Luke. Nevertheless, it was largely owing to the unassailable prestige of Michelangelo that the nude survived the counter-Reformation. Even such an earnest interpreter of Tridentine doctrines as Gilio da Fabriano expressed his admiration for the Last Judgment. Cf. Anthony Blunt, *Artistic Theory in Italy*, 1940, pp. 118-24.

II. APOLLO

p. 26. APOLLO. Throughout this chapter I am concerned with the idea of male beauty based on harmony, clarity and tranquil authority. This idea is most shortly conveyed by the word *Apollo* ; but it will be seen that by no means all the figures referred to were intended to represent Apollo. The male beauty of an Olympian was subject to slight variations of proportion even in antiquity, although this was due far more to the taste of the epoch or the idiosyncrasy of the artist than to any set typological requirements. In the late Renaissance, however, the proportions and characteristics of the gods were schematised, *e.g.* the Apollo type was nine faces high, the Jupiter type ten faces, and so forth. Cf. Lomazzo, *Trattato*, ed. 1844, II, p. 77. Such artificial classifications in no way affect the argument of this book.

p. 26. KOUROI. Cf. Richter, *Kouroi*, Oxford University Press, 1942, where, however, the author's bias in favour of a narrowly naturalistic aesthetic is sometimes misleading.

p. 29. THE EPHEBE OF KRITIOS owes its name to a supposed resemblance of both head and body to the Harmodius and Aristogiton attributed to Kritios and Nesiotes by Pausanias, I, 8-5. The fragility of this evidence is apparent when we consider (1) that the head of the Naples Harmodius is a characterless copy ; (2) there is strong reason to doubt that the head of the Acropolis youth originally belonged to it, although it is of about the same date ; cf. Payne and Young, *Archaic Marble Sculpture from the Acropolis*, London, N.D., p. 44 ; (3) that comparison between a static body and a body in action is, at this date, bound to be incomplete, and even if a similarity can be maintained, it is agreed that the Tyrant Slayers would have been a later work. Nevertheless the name may be retained for convenience.

p. 30. UCCELLO SCHOOL DRAWING, BB. 2779C. Also from the circle of Uccello is a drawing in Stockholm (BB. 2779K) which shows a group of male nudes standing on a polygon, thus combining on one sheet the two roots of renaissance academism.

The earliest nude drawn from the life which has survived seems to be the sheet by Pisanello in the Boyman's Museum, Rotterdam (Degenhart, *Pisanello*, 3rd edn., Wien, pl. 26). Life studies from the Florentine workshops of *c.* 1450 are quite common ; cf. Berenson (BB. 545a), a youth leaning on a stick attributed to Benozzo Gozzoli, who is already posed to look like an antique, and so has some of the artificiality which 'academies' have retained.

p. 32. BRONZE AND MARBLE. The extent to which Greek sculpture has been traduced by the reproduction of bronzes in marble can be seen from one example in which an original bronze and a marble copy have both survived, the bronze athlete of Ephesus in the Kunsthistorisches Museum, Vienna, and the marble athlete of Ephesus in the Uffizi. In spite of the fact that the bronze had been broken into 234 fragments and the marble is a copy of high quality, the former remains a vivid, life-communicating work of art, the latter is dead.

p. 35. THE CUIRASSE ESTHÉTIQUE. At an early date the symbolic importance of this schematisation led to a form of armour known as the *cuirasse musclée*. It has been found in tombs of the 5th century B.C., but did not become usual till the 4th. It was Greek in origin, and seems to have been made of metal or leather covered with metal plates. In the 3rd and 2nd centuries it was usually made of hardened leather, and moulded even more closely to the torso (cf. Reinach, *Répertoire des reliefs*, III, 442 ii, 446 ii). During all this time it was reserved for higher ranks, and the more elaborate metal examples were worn by generals. In the first centuries of the Christian era its use was extended to centurions, and finally to ordinary soldiers (Reinach, *Répertoire des reliefs*, I, 264-7). From its frequent appearance in Roman relief, *e.g.* Trajan's Column, it was known in the Renaissance as armour *alla romana* and became *de rigueur* for all academic or mannerist compositions of the 16th century.

p. 35. IDOLINO : discovered in Pesaro in 1530, and long considered the only surviving bronze of the type and period of Polyclitus. Although archaeologists are temporarily united in classing it as an archaising work of the Roman epoch, it is of an altogether different quality from those furnishing bronzes from Herculaneum which attempt a 5th-century style, and could be an eclectic work of the early 4th century B.C. There is much evidence (*e.g.* bronzes in Cabinet des Médailles, Paris, and Metropolitan Museum, New York) that Polyclitan works were still being produced then.

p. 36. APOLLO OF CASSEL may not reproduce a figure of which we have a literary record, but certainly goes back to a Phidian original. A superior head of the same figure is in the Palazzo Vecchio, Florence. Cf. Picard, *Manuel*, 1939, II, p. 314 and fig. 133.

p. 39. HERMES OF PRAXITELES. It was discovered in 1877, and immediately identified as the figure mentioned by Pausanias, V, 17, 3. Two recent theories are worth noting. First, that it is of Roman date. The arguments are set out by W. L. Cuttle in *Antiquity*, June 1934, vol. viii, no. 30, and may be summarised as, first, that the back is carved by a flat chisel not used by the Greeks for body work ; second, that the hair is worked by a running drill ; third, that the drapery appears to be of a later date. These theories were first put forward by Carl Blümel whose latest work, *Hermes eines Praxiteles*, Baden-Baden, 1948, dismisses it also on stylistic grounds and suggests that Pausanias was referring to another Praxiteles of the Hellenistic epoch. The other theory is put forward by Oscar Antonsson, *Praxiteles Marble Group in Olympia*, Stockholm, 1937, who maintains that the figure was originally a Pan (signs of horns in the hair, only possible copy represents a satyr) and was altered in Roman times to a Hermes, thus accounting for the Roman tool marks. Neither theory has gained wide acceptance.

p. 41. LYSIPPUS. Of the works claimed as his on the basis of resemblance to the athlete scraping himself (Apoxyomenos), the most convincing are the Hermes tying his sandal (Copenhagen) and the Eros with a bow (the Capitoline). There is also a scrap of evidence that the Farnese Hercules and others of this type derive from Lysippus. Other attributions are purely hypothetical, and as he is said to have executed 1500 pieces of sculpture there is plenty of room for speculation.

p. 44. ANTINOUS. The chief surviving examples are two reliefs, in the Villa Albani and the Terme ; and two statues, known as the Mandragone and the Braschi, in the Louvre and the Vatican respectively. This new ideal of beauty must have been created between 130 (death of Antinous) and 138 (death of Hadrian), but given Hadrian's taste for early Greek art it is not impossible that the type was influenced by a Phidian Athena. Cf. Picard, *La Sculpture antique*, Paris, 1926, pp. 427-9.

p. 44. APOLLO BELVEDERE. The date of its discovery is unknown, but it appears in a *quattrocento* pattern-book of antiques, known as *Codex Escurialensis*, ff. 53 and 64, so must have been above ground in the 1480's. It was found in the garden of S. Pietro in Vincoli of which Giuliano della Rovere was Cardinal, and when he became Pope Julius II he took it to the Vatican, where it still stands. The *Escurialensis* drawings and Marcantonio's engraving, B. 331, show it as better preserved than it is today. (Incidentally the drawing on f. 53 is done from precisely the same viewpoint as the Marcantonio which, although about thirty years later, might have been taken from a common original.) Of the right hand only the fingers were broken. Before restoration the arm was chopped off at the elbow and the present arm, with its rhetorical gesture, was added by Montorsoli in 1532 (Vasari, VI, 633). The effect of opening out a closed composition is similar to that of his restoration of the Laocoön. The Apollo was drawn and engraved many times in the Renaissance, starting with Nicoletto da Modena's fanciful reconstruction of about 1500 (Hind, *Early Italian Engraving*, vol. v, p. 121, no. 34), and an early Marcantonio (B. 5) in which it is represented as David. Recent writers on Greek art think so poorly of the Apollo ('as a work of art little short of abominable', Dickins, *Hellenistic Sculpture*, p. 70 ; 'Present-day comparison with many statues of greater merit makes the encomiums of older critics appear ridiculous', Lawrence, *Classical Sculpture*, p. 337) that they have made no serious attempt to study it. Clearly it is a copy, made for the Roman market, of a Hellenistic bronze, but the date and provenance of the original are disputable. The old connection with the name of Leochares is purely hypothetical. It was certainly made after the period of Alexander, perhaps in Syria, as the head and hair are fundamentally un-Greek. The Diana of Versailles appears to me to reproduce a work by the same sculptor, and is so similar in both style and feeling that the original bronzes might have been a pair. The height of the Apollo is 224 cm. ; that of the Diana 211 cm.

p. 49. THE SPINARIO was one of the few antique bronzes which remained unmelted above ground throughout the middle ages. Its pose first appears (clothed) on Brunellesco's bronze trial piece for the Baptistery doors. At that time it was probably in the Lateran cloisters, and was accessible to Donatello during his visit to Rome. The quasi-archaic simplification of forms in relation to the technique of bronze casting is exactly that used by Donatello in the David. In a decree of 1471 Sixtus IV presented it to the newly constructed Palazzo dei Conservatori, where it has remained ever since. Towards the end of the *quattrocento* it became one of the most popular antiques, and was much reproduced in small bronze replicas, *e.g.* three in the Louvre, four in Vienna. Cf. Bode, *Die italienischen Bronze-Statuetten der Renaissance*, small edn., pl. 81. Archaeologists now tend to consider the Spinario an archaising work of the Roman period ; but the technical arguments are inconclusive, and in comparison with analogous bronzes in the Naples Museum (*e.g.* The Muses) it has a warmth and freshness which persuades us to believe that it is an original of the 5th century.

p. 53. DÜRER'S APOLLO DRAWING raises a number of problems. That it was originally inspired by Jacopo de' Barbari's engraving of Apollo and Diana (B. VII, 523, 16) is proved by the seated female figure on the right. Perhaps it was the unresolved pose of this figure which led Dürer to abandon his project (evident from the reversed inscription) of engraving direct from the drawing. He did not abandon the idea of contrasting the male and female nude, but having no model for the latter as canonical as the Apollo Belvedere, he undertook a series of systematised drawings from life (Winkler, vol. ii, nos. 411–18). He also executed another Apollo study (Winkler, 44) in which the pose of the Belvedere figure is varied by the head being turned in the direction of the weight-bearing leg. This is the pose used in the final engraving, *The Fall of Man* (B. VII, 30, 1), although for the head he has reverted to the original

Apollo drawing. The engraving is dated 1504, as is a drawing of the subject in the Morgan Library (Winkler, 333). It is usually assumed that the Apollo drawing was done some years earlier, but for this there is no evidence, and the resemblance to Michelangelo's drawings of *c.* 1501 makes an earlier date improbable. The legs are an almost exact copy of the Dionysus in Mantegna's engraving of the Bacchanal with a Wine Press (Bartsch, XIII, 240, 19), but the upper part of the figure is very close to the Apollo Belvedere, the right arm being shown exactly as it was before Montorsoli's restoration.

p. 54. MICHELANGELO AND CAVALIERI. A selection from Michelangelo's letters to Cavalieri is to be found in Tolnay, *Michelangelo*, III, 24. The same passionate admiration is given more complete expression in the poems. In Cavalieri's perfect body

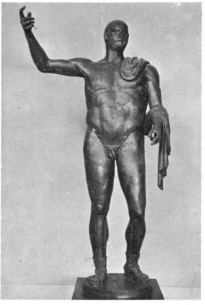

294. Roman. The Emperor Trebonius Gallus

he sees an image of universal beauty. He is the *forma universale* (Frey, *Dichtungen*, LXXIX). He is the incarnation of the divine idea, and contemplating his beautiful features Michelangelo feels himself ascending to God (Frey, *Dichtungen*, LXIV and LXXIX).

p. 55. MICHELANGELO'S DRAWINGS OF APOLLONIAN YOUTHS. The most important are : (1) The standing youth in the Louvre (R.F. 1086 *recto* ; BB. 1590) inspired by an antique, and perhaps drawn from nature ; usually dated *c.* 1501, but possibly earlier, as it was a drawing of this type which influenced Dürer's Apollo, cf. note above. (2) The figure, also in the Louvre (688 *recto*, BB. 1588), with Mercury's cap and Apollo's viol added later, apparently a memory of a Mercury in the Horti Farnesiani which was also used by Raphael for the Mercury in his fresco of the Council of the Gods in the Farnesina ; datable *c.* 1501. (3) The youth running with left arm extended in the British Museum (Wilde, *British Museum*, 4 *recto*, BB. 1481) ; a memory of the Apollo Belvedere, but turned into a figure in action, and used in relation to the Bathers cartoon ; so datable *c.* 1504. (4) A drawing known only from a copy in the Louvre (694, BB. 1730) which shows two views of an antique with a broken left arm, apparently a Hermes, but made by Michelangelo to look entirely 16th century.

p. 57. THICKENING OF THE TORSO may have been felt to give the figure super-human authority, for the same proportion is to be found in statues of the deified rulers of late antiquity, *e.g.* the colossal bronze statue of the Emperor Trebonius Gallus, 251-3, in the Metropolitan Museum, New York [294].

III. VENUS 1

p. 65. NAKED VENUS AND ORIENTAL CULTS. The nakedness of the Mesopotamian goddess Lilith was aggressive and symbolic, not merely convenient as in early Egyptian statuettes of slaves; cf. Frankfurt, *The Art and Architecture of the Ancient Orient*, 1955, pl. 56. To her naked body were added the wings of an owl and the feet of a lion. This witch and harpy was dreadful to both Greek and Hebrew thought. In the Authorised Version her name is rendered 'screech owl' or 'night monster' ; in the Bishops' Bible of 1568 the same word is translated as Lamia (Isaiah xxxiv, 14).

p. 67. SPARTAN GIRLS. The information that they stripped and wrestled with each other is in Xenophon, *Government of Lacedaemon*, I, 4. The tradition that they wrestled with the boys seems to derive from Euripides' *Andromache*, 596 ff. The girl runner of the Vatican is a late marble replica of a 5th-century votive bronze. Her authentic character can be recognised only when the restored arms are removed.

p. 67. ESQUILINE VENUS. Archaeologists have long been in doubt as to whether she is a fairly close copy of a 5th-century figure or a 'Pasitelean' (*i.e.* archaising) imitation ; and many have gone so far as to suggest that the upper half of the figure reproduces a 5th-century original while the legs are in a later style. However, the organic unity of the whole figure argues strongly against this theory, and the discovery of the Louvre torso, which is almost identical, suggests that both are copying some well-known original. It would probably have been in bronze and possibly of the school of Rhegium. As the support and other attributes have been added in the copy they cannot be used as evidence of the figure's original purpose, but it is unlikely that she represented a Venus. Amelung, *The Museums and Ruins of Rome*, English edn., 1906, vol. i, p. 207, was probably right in identifying the Esquiline copy as a Votary of Isis, but that cannot have been the subject of the original.

p. 69. THE NEREID MONUMENT is the name commonly given to the monumental tomb or *heroon* discovered in Xanthos, Lycia, in 1838 and now in the British Museum. The floating figures of women show an extreme use of clinging drapery, but this is no real evidence that the device originated in Asia Minor, for the nereids are slightly feeble in construction and are probably imitations of some more central style. The date usually accepted is *c.* 430, but on grounds of style a later date would be more convincing.

p. 70. VENUS GENETRIX. The beautiful figure which has come down to us in several replicas (Louvre, Boston ; and, in reverse, Terme, Rome, and Este Collection, Vienna) is now generally believed to have been the work of Callimachus. It has also been claimed for Alcamanes on the basis of its resemblance to the Nike tying her Sandal of the Acropolis ; but the attribution of the Nike is by no means certain. The inappropriate title by which this figure is commonly known is due to the accident by which it was represented, with the inscription VENERI GENETRICI, on a coin of the Empress Sabina. The Louvre replica was discovered at Fréjus in 1650. The replica known in the Renaissance was in the Casa Sassi. It was drawn by both Amico Aspertini and Martin van Heemskerck, and engraved by Marcello Fogolino (with a ridiculous head). Cf. Hind, *Early Italian Engraving*, vol. viii, p. 803.

p. 71. MUNICH BRONZE GIRL. Cf. Sieveking in *Münchener Jahrbuch der bildenden Kunst*, V, 1910, p. 1. The date usually assigned to her, *c.* 450 B.C., based on the hair and features, has sometimes been questioned. As with the Idolino, we may ask whether in the years of uncertainty at the end of the 5th century work was not sometimes produced with a slightly archaic flavour.

p. 71. CNIDIAN VENUS. All available information, including passage from the false Lucian, in *Knidia* by C. S. Blinkenberg, Copenhagen, 1933. The chief facts not mentioned in my text are : (1) We can identify the pose of the Cnidian Venus from the Roman coinage of Cnidos. (2) The colouring, which contributed greatly to its success, was by the famous painter Nikias. (3) A free copy of the original was evidently cast in bronze, and of this the second replica in the Vatican, the Venus of the Belvedere, is a rendering in marble. This was re-translated back into bronze in the 16th century by Pierre Bontemps, and the resulting cast in the Louvre is perhaps the most satisfactory surviving reminiscence of the Cnidian.

p. 76. MEDICI VENUS is a replica of a post-Praxitelean original, probably a bronze, usually dated about 200 B.C. From the type of the dolphin support it is thought to have been executed in the Augustan epoch, see Muthmann, *Statuenstützen und dekoratives Beiwerk*, 1951, pp. 28, 91 ff. The affected gesture of the right arm is a restoration, and the head has been broken and re-set at the wrong angle. The original position of the head can be seen from a replica in the Metropolitan Museum of New York, which is in other respects a very close copy. It is, however, slightly more fully modelled, and may be earlier. The correct position of the head gives it a more authentically Greek appearance. Cf. Christine Alexander in *Metropolitan Museum Bulletin*, 1953, vol. xi, no. 9.

p. 79. BYRON, *Childe Harold*, canto iv, xlix. But in a letter to John Murray, April 26th, 1817, he says that 'the Venus is more for admiration than for love'; and in *Don Juan*, when he felt free to tell the truth, he writes (of sculptors) :

> A race of mere impostors, when all's done—
> I've seen much finer women, ripe and real,
> Than all the nonsense of their stone ideal.
> (Canto iii, stanza 118)

p. 80. VENUS OF ARLES. Its history throws some light on the concept of ideal art in the 17th century. It was discovered in Arles in 1651 on the site of the ancient theatre, complete except for the arms. Under the direction of an artist named Jean Sautereau it was restored and placed in a cupboard in the Hôtel de Ville. Unfortunately the people of Arles boasted about this treasure and in 1684 decided to win royal favour by presenting it to the King. In spite of protests it was taken to Paris by water and placed in the Galerie des Glaces at Versailles in April 1685. The King found her torso too accented, and ordered Girardon to make it smoother ; also to provide her with arms and hands, one of which was to hold an apple, the other a mirror—thereby settling the controversy whether she represented Venus or Diana. Before the figure left Arles a number of casts were made, one by Jean Peru and at least seven others by Italian workmen. Only one of these survived the Revolution, and even this seems to have been damaged by a *sans-culotte*, and the breasts have been restored. It was rediscovered in 1911 and is now in the museum of Arles. Comparison with the original in the Louvre shows how much of the character of an antique had to be polished away before it could qualify for admission to the Galerie des Glaces.

p. 83. VENUS OF MILO. In his famous re-dating, Furtwängler, *Meister der griechischen Plastik*, 1893, p. 601, had suggested a date between 150 B.C. and 50 B.C. Of many attempts to situate her more exactly, the most convincing is that of Charbonneaux, *La Revue des Arts*, i, 1951, p. 8, who points out her similarity to a figure in the Louvre known as the Inopos, which is in fact an idealised portrait of Mithridates the Great. This gives a date between 110 B.C. and 88 B.C.

p. 84. HELLENISTIC VENUSES. Examples of the chief motives are as follows :

> Venus Anadyomene, with drapery held to her legs, marble ; Museo Nazionale, Syracuse.
> Venus Anadyomene, wringing the water from her hair, marble ; Vatican ; Palazzo Colonna, Rome.
> Venus putting on a necklace, bronze ; British Museum.
> Venus unfastening her sandal, bronze ; British Museum ; terra-cotta ; Metropolitan, New York.
> Venus putting on Mars' sword, marble ; Uffizi (but this may be a renaissance invention when restoring an antique).

In addition there are several fine original torsos of which the motive is uncertain, *e.g.* Bibliothèque Nationale, Paris ; Vatican ; Brussels. Their richer forms suggest Alexandrian workmanship.

p. 85. THREE GRACES. In addition to the group in Siena, renaissance artists were familiar with a replica in the Vatican, engraved, with a fanciful background of palm trees, by Marcantonio Raimondi, B. 340. The earliest reference to this is on a drawing in the Albertina of the Siena group, perhaps by Francesco di Giorgio or, as Salis suggests (*Antike und Renaissance*, p. 153), by Federighi, on which is written *in Roma anche*. There was also a rough but charming fragment in the Campo Santo which, although Roberto Papini, *Bollettino d'Arte*, 1951, claimed it as a 14th-century Pisan imitation, is certainly late Antique. In spite of the chaste character imposed upon them in the Renaissance there is reason to believe that Three Graces were frequently used as a sign for a brothel. Such is evidently the intention of a relief in Berlin inscribed *Ad Sorores IIII*. Cf. von Salis, *ibid.* p. 161.

p. 90. THE POPULAR CONCEPT OF VENUS NATURALIS. An example is the painted tray in the Louvre [75]. Among engravings cf. *Virgil the Sorcerer*, Hind, A1. 46.

p. 92. BOTTICELLI'S GRACES. For the literary inspiration cf. the admirable article by E. Gombrich in *Courtauld Warburg Journal*, 1945. Among other antique examples of transparent drapery Botticelli may well have known a replica of the Venus Genetrix type ; cf. note above. Already in the *Della pittura* (1435) Leon Battista Alberti had recommended painters to make their draperies seem as if blown by the wind, so that on one side the nude body is revealed, while on the other the draperies flutter in the air with a graceful movement (ed. Jantischek, p. 131). Clearly he was thinking of antique maenad figures, which are usually considered the chief source of Botticelli's Graces. For the elongated proportions he had many examples in Roman *stucchi*, of which those from the site of the Farnesina survive in the Terme.

p. 97. RUSKIN AND BOTTICELLI'S VENUS. In the appendix to *Ariadne Fiorentina*, 1873, Cook edn., XXII, p. 483, he prints as the 'probable truth' a note by Mr. Tyrwhitt in which he says that the Venus must represent Simonetta, and adds, 'Now I think she must have been induced to let Sandro draw her from her whole person un-draped, more or less ; and that he must have done so . . . in strict honour as to deed, word and *definite* thought, but under occasional accesses of passion of which he said nothing and which in all probability and by the grace of God refined down to nil, or nearly so, as he got accustomed to look in honour at so beautiful a thing. First her figure is absolutely fine Gothic ; I don't think any antique is so slender. Secondly she has the sad, passionate and exquisite Lombard mouth. Thirdly her limbs shrink together, and she seems not quite to have "liked it", and been an accustomed model.'

p. 99. TRUTH IN BOTTICELLI'S CALUMNY. Her extreme purity is in accordance with the various descriptions of the subject which Botticelli seems to have used, *e.g.* in L. B. Alberti's *Della pittura* when she is called *pudica et verecunda*, or in the poem of Bernardo Ruccellai who says

> *la tarda Penitenza in negro ammanto*
> *sguardò la Verità, ch' è nuda e pura.*

p. 102. SIGNORELLI'S ONE EXCEPTION, a straight borrowing from antiquity in the Ghirlandajo manner, is the nude young man seated in the foreground of the fresco of the Testament of Moses in the Sistine Chapel. That it is taken from a relief or gem is suggested by the wisp of drapery following the line of the arm. The same relief must have influenced the *ignudi* of Michelangelo, and more particularly the pose of the Erythrean Sibyl, who in fact is to be found above the Signorelli youth in the chapel. I should perhaps add that a figure of a youth in the background of Signorelli's *tondo* of the Virgin and Child in Berlin is in the pose of the Spinario.

p. 106. ANTONIO FEDERIGHI. The Sienese architect and sculptor born about 1420, died 1490. The scanty documents concerning him give no indication why his work has this strangely classicistic character. The Adam and Eve must in fact be one of his latest works, *c.* 1482. The symbolic contrast of male and female bodies does not seem to occur in antiquity, although it is common in Indian art : *e.g.* the 1st-century relief at Karle, Bombay, in Kramrisch, *The Art of India*, 1954, pl. 26. The first famous example in European art is Dürer's engraving of the Fall of Man, dated 1504 (cf. note on p. 367), which may well have induced Raphael to prepare his design for the engraving of Marcantonio.

p. 106. CARDINAL BIBIENA'S BATHROOM. Bembo in a letter to Cardinal Bibiena of April 19th, 1516, describes Raphael as at work on the bathroom and anxious for details of the subjects. These are in fact the History of Venus and Cupid and the Triumphs of Love. The room is, with the Villa Madama, the most complete reproduction of antiquity achieved by the Renaissance. Few of the scenes appear to have been touched by Raphael's own hand. Photographs of the bathroom are not available and access to it is discouraged, but the subjects have long been known through copies in the Hermitage (formerly in the Villa Mills on the Palatine) and in certain engravings of Marcantonio, B. 321, B. 325.

p. 109. MARCANTONIO'S ENGRAVINGS OF ANTIQUES. Cf. Thode, *Die Antiken in den Stichen Marcantons*, 1881. Of the famous nude figures given currency through engravings I may note : The Apollo Belvedere, twice, B. 328 and B. 331 ; The Crouching Venus, B. 313 ; The Three Graces, B. 340 ; The Ariadne of the Vatican, B. 199 ;· Fauns carrying a Child, B. 230—all generally attributed to Marcantonio. By Marco Dente da Ravenna : The Laocoön, B. 353. By Giovanni Antonio da

Brescia : The Venus of the Belvedere, Hind, Plate 536 (inscribed ROME NOVITER REPERTUM) ; The Torso of Hercules, Hind, Plate 539 (inscribed IN MONTE CAVALLO).

p. 110. For RIZZO'S EVE and the influence of van Eyck's nudes see p. 394.

p. 110. MANTEGNA'S REPRESENTATIONS OF THE FEMALE NUDE are all from the last decades of his life and his period of work for Isabella d' Este. In general they are taken from antiquity, *e.g.* the Venus in the so-called *Parnassus* of the Louvre. But a curious problem is presented by the beautiful drawing in the British Museum representing Mars between Diana and (?) Venus in which the figure of Venus is closely related to the right-hand Grace in Botticelli's *Primavera*. The disposition of the legs is identical, and the slender proportions are unlike Mantegna's usual classicising figures. The drawing is thought to be a late work (Tietze-Conrat, *Mantegna*, 1955, p. 206), so that there can be no question of Botticelli having been influenced by Mantegna. On the other hand, Mantegna was in Florence in 1466, and the *Primavera* was not painted till about 1477. The resemblance could be due to a common source in antiquity (*e.g.* on Aretine ware or the end of a sarcophagus in the Campo Santo, Lasinio, IC) or Mantegna could have seen a Botticelli drawing for the Graces ; or it is just possible that he visited Florence again.

p. 110. GIORGIONE AND THE CLASSIC VENETIAN NUDE. To the influences mentioned in the text must be added that of Jacopo de' Barbari who, although a second-rate artist, was undoubtedly a precursor where the nude was concerned ; cf. Dürer's interest in his studies of the human figure, p. 395, and note on Apollo, p. 367. Some of his engravings and drawings of the nude must date from before his huge woodcut of Venice (1500), and may account for such a classically Venetian nude as we see in Dürer's drawing, Winkler, 85, dated 1495 (this date and signature may, however, be apocryphal). Jacopo's engraving of *Victory and Fame* (B. VII, 524, 18) is usually thought to have influenced Dürer's engraving of *Four Naked Women* (B. VII, 89, 75) dated 1497 [263]. Jacopo was closely connected with the Fondaco de' Tedeschi, and it was here, in 1507–8, that Giorgione executed a series of nude figures as the main part of the decoration. These are known to us only from the etchings by Zanetti, *Varie pitture*, Venice, 1760, and they show that Giorgione had conceived his nudes in isolation, like antiques in niches. Taken in conjunction with the Hermitage Judith they make it probable that Marcantonio's engraving of a woman watering a plant (B. 383) is from a design by Giorgione. Michiel mentions in the collection of Pietro Bembo a copy by Giulio Campagnola after Giorgione of a nude woman lying with her back turned to us and another of a nude woman watering a tree (*The Anonimo*, ed. G. C. Williamson, London, 1903, p. 24). The former may well be represented in an engraving by Giulio (Hind, *Early Italian Engraving*, pl. 781). I am inclined to accept Wilde's suggestion that a picture by Girolamo da Treviso in the Kunsthistorisches Museum, Vienna, of a nude woman standing beside an Antique torso, is a copy of a

Giorgione. Her pose is repeated in the figure of Christ in the *Noli me tangere* in the National Gallery, London, which is perhaps a Giorgione finished by Titian, and is reproduced in Marcantonio's engraving of Venus and Cupid (B. 311).

IV. VENUS 2

p. 113. LEONARDO'S LEDA. He made at least two cartoons with a standing figure, and one with the figure kneeling. The earliest must have been done before 1505 since it was known to Raphael, who copied it in a drawing in Windsor Castle Library (12759). It could have been done earlier still, *i.e.* in Milan, though hardly before 1497. The second cartoon could be considerably later and we may deduce from the position of the babies that it was this which was carried out as a painting. The general idea of the standing figure must, of course, be taken from an Antique, but it differs from that of the ordinary Venus Anadyomene pose in that the arms are turned away from the weight-bearing leg. The kneeling figure could also have been influenced by a Venus Anadyomene kneeling in a shell, as on the sarcophagus (Robert and Roden-waldt, *Die antiken Sarcophagreliefs*, vol. v, 1939, p. 69).

p. 115. PATER'S ESSAY ON THE SCHOOL OF GIORGIONE was written in 1877 and so appeared for the first time in the second edition of *The Renaissance* (1st edn. 1873). It was in a sense a commentary on Crowe and Cavalcaselle's *History of Painting in North Italy* (1871) in which the traditional concept of Giorgione had been drastically and, as we now realise, quite incorrectly revised.

p. 115. RAPHAEL'S JUDGMENT OF PARIS was inspired by a sarcophagus in the Villa Medici ; cf. Cagiano di Azevedo, *Le antichità di Villa Medici*, p. 68, pl. xxviii. This belongs to a well-known type thought to represent the design of a lost painting ; certainly it is quite unsculptural and gains by re-translation into a graphic medium. Raphael has followed the subject closely, but used only a few of the actual outlines. It is commonly said that he was also influenced by a relief in the Villa Pamphili, but I cannot find one which bears any resemblance to the engraving.

p. 117. SEBASTIANO DEL PIOMBO AND THE FEMALE NUDE. It first appears in that extraordinary composition, *The Death of Adonis*, *c.*. 1511 (Uffizi, 916), which anticipates at almost every point the classical academism of the 17th century. If a series of pen drawings in the Uffizi representing Antiques, and generally attributed to him, *e.g.* Pallucchini, *Sebastian Viniziano*, pls. 86-9, are really from his hand, then we must assume that several engravings of nude women follow his design. The life drawing referred to, published by Philip Pouncey, *Burlington Magazine*, vol. xciv, 1952, p. 161, is for the Martyrdom of St. Agatha dated 1520.

p. 119.   TITIAN'S SACRED AND PROFANE LOVE.   For the classical exposition of the subject see Panofsky, *Studies in Iconology*, p. 150 *et seq.*, which establishes that in Titian's picture of the twin Venuses *Venus naturalis* is clothed.   Such may have been the raw material of iconography, but as transmitted to us by Titian the effect is almost the reverse.

p. 119.   ELLESMERE VENUS.   The date can hardly be established owing to Titian's own repainting, and other changes which can be seen in an X-ray.   Cf. Kennedy North in *Burlington Magazine*, vol. lx, 1932, p. 158.   The idea of isolating the figure derives from Giorgione's frescoes in the Fondaco de' Tedeschi.   Evidently there was an antique of Venus wringing the water from her hair in a Venetian or Paduan collection in the early 16th century, as the pose appears several times in Venetian art.   Probably it is represented in the early Marcantonio engraving (B. 312).

p. 123.   TITIAN'S DANAE was inspired by Michelangelo's *Notte* and not, as might have been expected, by his Leda ; *i.e.* the body is turned towards us to show the front of the torso and not away from us as if to enclose the Swan.   The position of the right arm, however, is that of the Leda, and may have been inspired directly, by the same antique relief of Leda which was known to Michelangelo.   See next note.

p. 128.   MICHELANGELO'S TRANSFORMATION OF THE NOTTE INTO A LEDA must be related to the fact that the *Notte* was itself taken from an antique relief of Leda.   The drawings for *Notte*, *e.g.* Frey, 217, at Oxford, date from *c.* 1525.   The drawings for the Leda, done from a male model, Casa Buonarroti, Tolnay, no. 98, and British Museum, 48 *verso*, are datable in 1530.   They prove that Michelangelo thought the figure out afresh, with many significant variations.   The body was more turned in and the right leg was bent under the left so that the legs enfolded the swan.   The whole subject will be treated in an essay by J. Wilde.   Michelangelo's painting of Leda is lost.   The fascinating and pathetic history of how Michelangelo gave the painting and drawing to his *garzone* Antonio Mini to take to France as a dowry and how Mini was swindled out of them by a tax collector in Lyons is told by Léon Dorez, *Bibl. de l'École des Chartes*, vols. lxxvii and lxxviii.

p. 129.   THE FLORENTINE SCULPTORS OF LATER 16TH CENTURY who produced the ideal of tapering elegance which is chiefly associated with Giambologna have not yet been studied with enough chronological detail for us to say to whom this ideal was chiefly due ;   also attributions remain uncertain, *e.g.* there is no real evidence that the bronze illustrated on pl. 102 is by Ammanati.   We can at least say that the fountain in the Piazza della Signoria, Florence (*c.* 1570), was executed under his direction, and that the elegant abstractions of the female body which surround it are his development of Michelangelo's Evening, although some of them, as Venturi suggests (*Storia*, X, 2, p. 416), may be the work of Andrea Calamecca.   Cellini may also have contributed to the ideal, although his Venus on the base of the Perseus (*c.* 1550) is less elongated and more naturalistic. Perhaps the most complete example is the latest—the marble Venus by Giambologna in the grotto of the Boboli gardens, which, from its setting, seems to have been consciously designed as a 16th-century equivalent to the Cnidian Venus (1583).

p. 139. SLAVES OF ACADEMISM. This sentence cannot pass without a reference to the greatest *master* of academism, Nicolas Poussin. The female nude is common in his early work and shows a profound study of Raphael (via Marcantonio), Titian and the Antique. But, as always, his learning is warmed by a noble sensuality, and some-times, *e.g.* his Sleeping Venus at Dresden, he permits himself an approach to the body more direct than anything in 16th-century Italian art. How well he under-stood the real purpose of the nude is evident from his letter to Chantelou quoted on p. 19. Nevertheless it is hard to say that Poussin adds anything to the history of the nude.

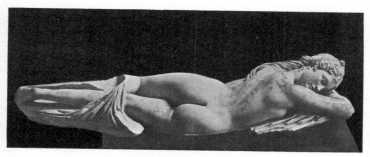

295. Graeco-Roman. Hermaphrodite

p. 140. SHE SHOWS US HER BACK. The more frequent appearance of the motive in the late 17th and 18th centuries is probably due to the prestige of the antique figure of Hermaphrodite of which the most famous example in the Borghese Col-lection had been restored by Bernini. This version [295], discovered in the early 17th century near the Baths of Diocletian, is now in the Louvre. Of many other replicas the best is that now in the Terme. Whether or not these figures reproduce the famous bronze Hermaphrodite mentioned by Pliny as the work of Polycles (*Nat. Hist.*, XXXIV, 80) seems to be an insoluble problem. In renaissance art the earliest example of a nude woman lying with her back to the spectator is the Giulio Cam-pagnola engraving (Galichon, *Gazette des Beaux-Arts*, Series I, vol. xiii, p. 344, 13) which probably represents a design by Giorgione, of which a miniature copy by Giulio Campagnola is mentioned by Michiel (see note to p. 110).

p. 143. UN CHINOIS ÉGARÉ. This justly famous *mot* concludes the malicious essay on Ingres by Théophile Silvestre in his *Histoire des artistes vivants*, 1855–6, p. 33. He can have seen very little Chinese painting, but deduced its qualities of prehensile line from porcelain, wallpapers, etc.

p. 143. INGRES' IDEAS OF THE NUDE. To the four mentioned in the text must be added a fifth, the beautiful figure of Angelica (Andromeda) which follows the main lines of the Bacchante figure on a sarcophagus in the Terme, but with head thrown back in languorous, Raphaelesque despair. The first dated example is the picture in the Louvre, 1819, for which there is (also in the Louvre) a study in oils (Wildenstein, 127), copied by Seurat. Ingres showed his satisfaction with the figure by repeating it several times, *e.g.* National Gallery, London, no. 3292 (*ex* Degas) ; Montauban, dated 1841 ; and Wildenstein, no. 287, dated 1859, but said to have been painted earlier. There is no evidence that Ingres thought of this figure much earlier than 1819, and it is therefore the last nude to come from his inner core. Following the *Grande Odalisque*, it shows a move away from classic fullness towards a more slender and youthful proportion.

p. 144. INGRES' VENUS ANADYOMENE AND LA SOURCE. They have a long and complex history. The earliest records (1807) are the two outline drawings at Montauban for the Venus, one showing her in the pose of the Pudica, the other with both hands placed below her breasts. In the second the disposition of the *amorini* at the feet is almost that followed in the final version. He must have carried the design much further in the next year, as the picture at Chantilly is inscribed *J. Ingres faciebat 1808 et 1848*, but we have no evidence as to whether he had adopted the all-important motive of the right arm bent over the head, as the drawings showing this motive, *Ingres, Dessins des maîtres français*, Paris, 1926, pls. 44 and 45, clearly belong to a later period. I believe that Ingres derived it from the famous relief of a nymph on Goujon's *Fontaine des Innocents*, of which a drawing by Ingres is in the Guy Knowles Collection, London. This derivation accounts for the fact that as early as 1820 Ingres had begun work on a second version of the figure in which the motive of wringing her hair was replaced by that of pouring from a pitcher, the origin of *La Source*. It is said that in 1821 and again in 1823 Ingres promised to complete the Venus Anadyomene for various patrons. He does not seem to have worked on *La Source* again till 1856, when he is said to have been helped in its execution by two pupils, Paul Balze and Alexandre Desgoffe. The story that he was fired by the sight of his concierge's daughter occurs frequently in Ingres literature, but I have not been able to trace it to a reliable source.

p. 145. THE TWO VERSIONS OF THE ODALISQUE ET L'ESCLAVE are in the Fogg Museum, Cambridge, Mass. (1839), and Walters Gallery, Baltimore (1842). The assumption that this Odalisque is the same as in the lost picture bought by Murat,

King of Naples, in 1809 rests not only on the early drawing referred to (Maruccia), but also on a number of small replicas (Wildenstein, 55, 56, 57), one of which, in the Victoria and Albert (Ionides Coll.), appears to be an original. The idea of re-using the figure in a scene of the Harem appears (with three attendants) in a sketch at Montauban (Longa, *Ingres inconnu*, 1942, fig. 84), on which Ingres notes the name of a French model, thus suggesting that the figure was re-studied from nature after his return to Paris.

p. 147. THE NOTE FOR L'ÂGE D'OR, reproduced in Longa, *op. cit.* 106, reads as follows : *Les adolescents à bord du tableau pour mettre de la beauté à droite ; cette beauté qui charme et transporte. Il faut bien passer les détails du corps humain, que les membres soient, pour ainsi dire, comme les fûts de colonnes—tels les maîtres des maîtres.* It is interesting to compare this with a letter from Poussin to Chantelou, printed on p. 19, which Ingres cannot have known.

p. 149. MANET'S DÉJEUNER SUR L'HERBE. In fact the derivation from Marcantonio's engraving was recognised almost immediately by Earnest Chesneau, in *L'Art et les artistes en France et l'Angleterre*, 1864, p. 190 ; but his discovery passed unnoticed till 1908, when it was made afresh in Gustav Pauli, *Raffael und Manet*, in *Monatshefte f. Kunstwissenschaft*, I, 1908, p. 53.

p. 149. HIRAM POWER'S CAPTIVE SLAVE, now in the Corcoran Gallery, Washington, D.C., does not seem to have been much criticised during the Great Exhibition, but when the Crystal Palace was moved to the purer air of Sydenham a number of protests were published. What troubled contemporary moralists was the use of nude models in art schools ; cf. as typical, a pamphlet entitled *The Statue Question. A Letter to the Chairman of the Crystal Palace Company, dated 8th July, 1854 : and An Appeal against the Practice of Studying from Nude Human Beings by British Artists, and in Public Schools of Design*, by William Peters. In such pamphlets anti-nudery is usually combined with anti-popery, chauvinism and bourgeois democracy : they are easily ridiculed. But the fact remains that a number of people staring intensely at a naked woman is, in ordinary human terms, a disturbing concept.

p. 151. COURBET'S BAIGNEUSE OF 1853 outraged judges of art more enlightened than Napoleon III ; Mérimée, for example, said she would be best appreciated in New Zealand where figures were valued on account of the flesh they would provide for a cannibal feast. But her enormous buttocks did not conceal from Delacroix her fundamental academism : *La vulgarité des formes ne ferait rien ; c'est la vulgarité et l'inutilité de la pensée qui sont abominables. . . . Elle fait une geste qui n'exprime rien* (*Journal*, April 15, 1853).

p. 159. RENOIR'S LATER NUDES POINT TO THE FUTURE (*i.e.* Picasso, Laurens), whereas the nudes of Maillol look to the past. Nevertheless it would be unfair to omit

Maillol altogether, as few men have rendered so well the completeness of the female torso. His small statuettes look Greek not because they are imitations of antique art—in fact they are far more realistic—but because he has the same plastic conviction nourished by the same uncomplicated sensuality. He is a pagan in the earliest sense of the word, the inhabitant of a country cut off from time ; and his work, like his personality, has nourished our belief in a Golden Age.

V. ENERGY

p. 162. LASCAUX CAVES. There is, in fact, one pinman with a bird-like head at Lascaux. The so-called human figure at Altamira is doubtful. See F. Windels, *Lascaux Cave Paintings*, p. 134, fig. 57.

p. 164. POLLAJUOLO DANCING FIGURES. The likeness to the dancers on Etruscan pottery was first pointed out by J. Shapley, *Art Bulletin*, II, 1919, p. 78, who does not, however, seem to appreciate how much all Pollajuolo's silhouetted figures in action must derive from the same source.

p. 164. TEMPLE OF AEGINA. Cf. Fürtwangler, *Aegina*. The pediment carvings, discovered in what would now be considered fairly good condition, were brought to Rome and restored under the direction of Thorwaldsen, then at the height of his fame. He felt no compunction in improving them : in fact, considering that they were spoken of as 'hyper-archaic', his restorations were remarkably self-effacing. Bought by King Louis of Bavaria for the Glyptothek at Munich.

p. 165. TIME AND THE TORSO. Probably our whole concept of a satisfying plastic unit has been influenced by the accident that antique sculpture has come down to us chiefly in the form of torsos. The modern sculptor's practice of offering a torso as a complete work of art might never have gained currency if antique art had survived in bronze rather than in broken marble.

p. 167. DISCOBOLOS OF MYRON. The three best-known versions are (1) the marble of the Palazzo Lancelotti, discovered 1781, complete with head ; (2) the marble from Castel Porziano, now in the Terme, lacking head, right arm and lower legs, not known till 1906 ; (3) a small bronze in Munich with a Hellenistic head. There are also representations on several gems, and presumably it was these which were known in the Renaissance, as figures in the round would have been too famous to have passed unrecorded. Illustrations are usually from a cast made up of the Castel Porziano body and the Lancelotti head coloured to look like bronze. Naturally all consistency of style and medium is lost.

p. 169. FEW SINGLE NUDE FIGURES IN VIOLENT ACTION. Here once more our whole concept of antique art may have been falsified by the fact that all the available bronzes were melted down, and we know it from the medium of marble. Other evidence (*e.g.* the reverses of coins) suggests that figures in action were not uncommon.

p. 169. FLYING DRAPERY. It is fair to assume that the flying draperies which appear in such an evolved form in Greek sculpture after about 450 B.C. derive from painting. For example, the draperies indicated in the background of the frieze of the Temple of Bassai (*c.* 420 B.C.) are plastically unrelated to the figures, and reveal a degree of artifice quite outside the range of the vigorous but rather rustic carvers who executed it. I should also predicate a graphic source for the relief in the heroon of Trysa (Gulbashi), *c.* 420 B.C. It must have been a rotula remarkably similar to the Joshua roll of the Vatican—showing how little antique art changed in 700 years.

p. 173. HARMODIUS AND ARISTOGITON recorded by Pausanias, I, 8, 5. The best copy is in Naples, to which has been added a cast of a head of Aristogiton in the Vatican, apparently a close copy of the original.

p. 175. SHIELD OF ATHENE. The various copies are important as this was probably where many of the most famous poses expressive of heroic action first made their appearance. The chief source is the so-called Strangford shield in the British Museum, round which may be grouped several fragments in Rome, the Piraeus and the Glyptotek, Copenhagen.

p. 176. HORSE TAMERS. Furtwängler, *Masterpieces*, ed. Sellers, 1895, p. 95, had the insight to recognise in these clumsy monsters a crude reflection of Phidian grandeur. It was through them that one of the great ideas of the nude of energy was transmitted through the middle ages to the Renaissance, and they recur repeatedly, *e.g.* on the pulpits in San Lorenzo begun by Donatello and finished by Bertoldo. They furnished the motive for two of the most popular pieces of sculpture in the Great Exhibition of 1851, the Arabian Horses of the King of Württemberg, from whence are descended the bronze ornaments still to be found in almost every English pawnshop.

p. 179. HERCULES AND MESOPOTAMIAN SEALS. It is now generally accepted that the Greek Hercules was an adaptation of an Asian deity. Whatever his prehistoric origin (for which see Levy, *Journal of Hellenic Studies*, vol. liv, 1934), his exploits are similar beyond coincidence with those of the deities Akkad and Sumer. The Greeks themselves seem to have accepted this oriental origin. Cylinder seals showing a standing hero overcoming a rampant lion date from the early dynastic period of Ur (3000–2340 B.C.). During the Akkadian and neo-Sumerian periods (2340–2025 B.C.) the motive evolves into a form not dissimilar from that taken over by the Greeks in vases of the 6th century or in the carvings at Delphi. The hero is sometimes shown struggling with a bull as well as a lion. Cf. Frankfort, *Cylinder Seals*, 1939, and the plates at the end of Zervos, *L'Art de la Mésopotamie*, Cahiers d'art, 1935.

p. 181. POLLAJUOLO'S SMALL HERCULES PICTURES. It has always been the practice of artists to make small replicas of their famous works at a later date, *e.g.* El Greco's *Espolio*, Ingres' *Grande Baigneuse* ; and the two miniature versions of the Hercules legend may have been painted considerably later than 1460 but have preserved the main line of the originals. They disappeared from the Uffizi when the gallery was evacuated during the 1940–45 war, and have not been seen since.

p. 186. HERCULES AND ANTAEUS. It is usually said that the numerous representations of this subject in the Renaissance go back to an antique marble group in the courtyard of the Palazzo Pitti, engraved in Rossi-Maffei, *Raccolta di statue antiche*, Rome, 1704, pl. 43 ; Reinach, *Répertoire*, I, 1920, p. 472. Of this piece, however, only the head, the torso and part of the left arm of Hercules are original. His legs, and the head, arms and legs of Antaeus are a restoration, perhaps by Vincenzo de' Rossi. There must have been some evidence of how his body joined that of Hercules, enough to suggest that Hercules was lifting a man and not some other victim, but not enough to justify any particular reconstruction. Antaeus was being raised on Hercules' right side. The fragment can therefore have had no influence on Pollajuolo. The drawing in the Windsor Castle Library, 12802, Wilde, no. 17, shows a pose accidentally similar to the present restoration, but in reverse. The Marcantonio engraving (B. 246), which looks like the copy of a Giulio Romano, probably derived from this fragment, although the reconstruction of the Antaeus is different. The numerous engravings by Giovanni Antonio da Brescia and other followers of Mantegna, Hind, *Early Italian Engraving*, vol. vi, pls. 515, 516, 517, 525, 527, 528, have a different origin. Another group is included in Reinach, *Répertoire*, II, 1908, p. 233, as at Wilton, no. 223. It is possible that a better preserved antique group of the subject existed in the Renaissance and is now lost ; but, given the rarity of the subject and the fact that it is not mentioned in any contemporary sources, this is improbable ; and Hercules and Antaeus emerges an almost complete creation of the Renaissance based on descriptions in literature, a few small reliefs and one fragment mutilated almost beyond recognition.

p. 191. BATTLE OF NAKED MEN. Ultimately the source of this motive was the series of antique sarcophagi of which those in the Campo Santo, no. II, Lasinio, CXXXVI, and no. XXX, Lasinio, CXII and one in the Duomo of Cortona seem to have been the most influential. But the fashion for the subject in late 15th-century Florence was probably due to a piece of sculpture by Pollajuolo of which Vasari, III, p. 296, says that he 'made a very beautiful battle of nude figures in low relief and of metal, which went to Spain ; and of this every craftsman in Florence has a plaster cast'. The bronze relief is lost and not one of the casts has survived, but we may trace the influence of the relief in both sculpture and drawings, viz. in Francesco di Giorgio's relief of Discord in the Victoria and Albert Museum, and probably in Raphael's drawings in the Ashmolean. I believe that some indication of the original may be provided by the Venetian sculptor Gambello in two bronze reliefs made for his tomb and now in the Museo Archeologico, Venice ; cf. Planischig's *Venezianischer Bildhauer*, p. 309, fig. 325. Bertoldo's bronze relief in the Bargello is a compound of the two Campo Santo sarcophagi, and was probably intended to correct the *quattrocento* style of Pollajuolo by insisting more dogmatically on antique taste.

p. 195. HOLKHAM GRISAILLE. This is the copy from which our knowledge of Michelangelo's cartoon for the Battle of Cascina is derived. It was made by Aristotile da Sangallo in 1542 from a (lost) drawing made in his youth before the cartoon was destroyed. It was already recognised by Vasari, VI (p. 433 f.), as being the only complete record of the cartoon, and comparison with Michelangelo's own drawings proves it to be remarkably reliable.

p. 198. THE ATHLETES OF THE SISTINE. Michelangelo had already employed the nude figures of young men as the background of a sacred subject in the Doni Tondo in the Uffizi, which was clearly inspired by the Signorelli Tondo in the same gallery. In the Signorelli, however, the young men are represented as herdsmen and have some factual justification. In the Michelangelo they are, so to say, a philosophic decoration. The scale and attitudes of the Sistine athletes were certainly influenced by Donatello school reliefs in the courtyard of the Palazzo Riccardi, Florence. These in turn were little more than enlarged copies of antique gems. The most famous of these gems, depicting Diana, belonged to Paul II and the Medici family. It was lost in 1494, but copies of it had already been made. For a list of possible sources for the athletes, see Tolnay, *Michelangelo*, II, 65-6. Some of the gems originally related to these figures may be renaissance copies, but antique originals undoubtedly existed. The Hellenistic relief of Bacchus and Ariadne which influenced the Persica is in the Vatican ; cf. Tolnay, *Michelangelo*, II, fig. 391.

p. 202. MICHELANGELO'S VICTORY. Obviously datable during the 1520's and related to the figures in the Medici tombs, but its exact date and intention are unknown. It was in Michelangelo's possession at his death and is first mentioned in a letter from Vasari to his nephew. Wilde, *Michelangelo : The Group of Victory*, Oxford, 1954, argues that it was one of the figures intended for the third version of the Julius Monument, on which Michelangelo was at work in Florence between 1516 and 1527. He believes that it was to be balanced by a Hercules and Cacus, of which the terra-cotta in the Casa Buonarroti is a sketch. He places it at the end of this period, 1526. One may doubt whether, by this time, Michelangelo undertook such a work with a precise intention in mind, but the date is convincing.

p. 205. ARCHERS SHOOTING AT A MARK. For a full discussion of problems connected with the date and authorship of this drawing see Popham and Wilde, *Windsor*, p. 248. The doubts as to its authorship expressed by such eminent students of Michelangelo as

Popp, Panofsky and Tolnay may come to be considered among the curiosities of modern connoisseurship. This, like some other of the so-called 'presentation' drawings, seems to have been a conscious effort to re-create a lost masterpiece of antiquity. The subject was known to renaissance artists through a decorated panel on a ceiling in the Golden House of Nero, now destroyed but recorded in a watercolour by Francisco de Hollanda ; cf. *Codex Escurialenis*, text, pl. III. A pupil of Raphael used the same motive in a decorative fresco in Raphael's Villa, now in the Villa Borghese.

VI. PATHOS

p. 215. FOUR LEGENDS. I originally included a fifth antique embodiment of pathos—the captive barbarians, either standing with hands bound before them or seated with hands bound behind, who once more embody the idea of defeated rebellion against a superior or quasi-divine power. But on examination few of these standing figures on sarcophagi and other reliefs are nude. The fact that they were represented naturalistically as dressed in their barbarian trousers was intended to distinguish them from the ideal nudity of Romans or Hellenes. The seated prisoners with arms bound behind them are more often nude. Cf. Bienkowski, *Die Darstellungen der Gallier in der hellenistischen Kunst*, Wien, 1908, pls. IV, Va, IXa, etc. Although nude standing captives were exceptional in antique art, their 'pathetic' poses appealed so strongly to the Renaissance that they are often shown nude in renaissance art, *e.g.* Bertoldo's battle relief in the Bargello. Seated prisoners are common, *e.g.* the relief of the Flagellation by Francesco di Giorgio in Perugia, influenced by the sarcophagus in Cortona which he had seen when at work on the church of the *Calcinaio* outside that city.

p. 215. THE EARLIEST NIOBIDS. The figures discovered in the garden of Sallust, Rome, now in the Terme and at Copenhagen, are usually considered 5th-century work, but archaeologists have always felt uneasy about their date and origin. The workmanship, especially in the Copenhagen figures, is lacking in vitality, and I believe them to be free copies of a pediment group of the same date as the east pediment of Olympia and perhaps by the same carver. Comparison of the dying son at Copenhagen with the river god Alpheus at Olympia [296] shows not only a similar sense of form, but also an identical treatment of details, *e.g.* the drapery. But the Olympia figure, where invention and execution were one, makes its appeal to our feelings directly through its plastic vigour and expressiveness, whereas the Niobid can only do so at second hand through identification of the subject. In fact we have no reason to believe that the river god Alpheus was intended to be in pain or sorrow ; otherwise this early masterpiece of contraposto could be cited as the first great embodiment of Pathos. The origin of these Niobid groups is wholly a matter of

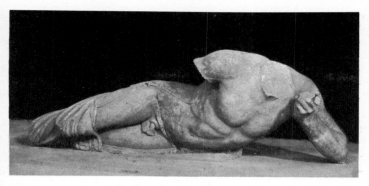

296. Greek. 5th cent. The River Alpheus

speculation. Archaeologists, on grounds of certain early representations on vases,
e.g. a *crater* at Orvieto, are inclined to trace them back to a painting by Polygnotos.
As usual in antique art, the main lines of the composition, some of the motives and
the general sentiment survived for 500 years. The most complete group, discovered
near the Lateran in 1588, is now in the Uffizi. By the time this group was made
(1st century A.D.?) its original purpose as part of a pediment had been forgotten.
Other magnificent Niobid poses, deriving from lost masterpieces of painting and
sculpture, are known only on sarcophagi, e.g. Vatican 1445 ; Lateran, Museo Profano,
etc.

p. 216. DEATH OF MELEAGER. See A. von Salis, *Antike und Renaissance*, 1947,
pp. 61 *et seq.*

p. 217. MARSYAS. The group of the flaying of Marsyas was one of the most popular
works of sculpture of the Hellenistic period. It was probably in bronze and consisted
of three figures : Apollo, a slave sharpening his knife and Marsyas hanging by his
hands. Their general disposition can be seen on the sarcophagus of Harmogenes
in the Ny-Carlsberg Glyptotek, Copenhagen. Of these figures the Apollo has come
down only in a fragmentary copy (Berlin), the slave in a famous marble in the
Uffizi known as the Arrotino, and the Marsyas in a large number of marble copies
(Rome, Florence, Berlin, the Louvre, Constantinople, etc.). They are of two types,
one invariably in red marble, the other in white. Of these the red are more expressive
and probably represent the bronze more closely ; the white go back to a prototype
copy in marble in which the emotion was softened. The restrained and classical
character of the body, no less than the treatment of the hair, resemble the dying Gauls
(Campidoglio, Terme), which are copies of the bronze groups dedicated by Attalos
soon after 240 B.C. ; and the Marsyas clearly belongs to this epoch rather than to the

more 'baroque' style of the Pergamon altar in Berlin, which was about fifty years later. Many replicas of the Marsyas were known in the Renaissance. In the Medici Collection alone there were both a red and a white version. The former was restored by Verrocchio, and is mentioned both in Tommaso's inventory (Crutwell, *Verrocchio* p. 243) and in Vasari, III, 367 ; it has now disappeared. The latter was said by Vasari, II, 407, to have been restored by Donatello. If this is true, it must also be lost, as the two figures of Marsyas now in the Uffizi are restored by a poor artist at a later date.

p. 219. LAOCOÖN. The date and authorship have been much disputed. Pliny, XXXVI, 37, says 'out of one block of marble did the illustrious artists Hagesander, Polydorus and Athanadorus of Rhodes, after taking counsel together, carve Laocoön his children and the wondrous coil of snakes'. There are several signatures on bases of Athanadorus, the son of Hagesandros, and the coincidence of these two names has naturally led archaeologists to assume that these were identical with the carvers of the Laocoön. The inscriptions are datable in the 1st century, and two men of this name (actually brothers) are recorded as receiving honours in 22 and 21 B.C. Against this i has been argued by Gisella Richter, *Three Critical Periods in Greek Sculpture*, Appendix p. 69, that these names were common in Rhodes throughout the Hellenistic period. She concludes that the Laocoön is by other sculptors of the same name who lived in the second Pergamon period, *i.e.* early in the 2nd century. The stylistic affinity of the Laocoön with the Pergamon altar formerly in Berlin (destroyed by bombing, 1944) is unquestionable. I do not, however, agree that it is an original marble of that period, and that the 1st-century dating of the names of two of the sculptors is a mere coincidence. The whole sculptural character of the Laocoön suggests that it was originally conceived and executed in bronze. It is well known that practically all the signatures on marbles of the Roman period are of the craftsmen who executed the copy. Names of the original artists are hardly ever preserved; cf. Richter, *op. cit.* pp. 45-7. It therefore seems probable that the names recorded by Pliny were those of the copyists, whose virtuosity in rendering an elaborate bronze group in marble was much admired. (Incidentally, Pliny is mistaken in saying that it is carved from single block.) The fact that Pliny is our chief source of written information about antique art must not lead us to place much reliance on his judgment in artistic matters. As with the Apollo Belvedere, we have only to look at the bronze cast of the Laocoön by Bontemps in the Louvre to see how much more satisfying it is in that medium. Pliny's contention that the marble is the work of three craftsmen is borne out by the fact that it exhibits three different degrees of skill. It would be hard to believe that the admirable carver of the father's torso should also have executed the lifeless surfaces of the elder son's body. The Laocoön was restored in 1532 by the Florentine sculptor Fra Giovanni Montorsoli (Vasari, VI, 633). The greater part of the original father's arm is in the Vatican and could be put back in its correct position behind his head, had not the present restoration become itself a historical document.

p. 221. THE ORIGIN OF THE 'PATHETIC' CRUCIFIXION ; see Johannes Reil, *Christus am Kreuz in der Bildkunst der Karolingerzeit*, Leipzig, 1930, which reproduces the earliest example of the *Curva bizantina* from the later 9th century, the prayer-book of Charles the Bald (pl. IX) and the Drogo-Sakramentar (pl. X). For the diffusion of the pathetic crucifixion through the spread of Rhineland crucifixes, see an admirable article by Gezo Francovich, *L' origine e la diffusione del crocefisso gotico doloroso* in the *Jahrbuch der Bibliotheca.Hertziana*, vol. ii, 1938.

p. 223. GREGORY OF TOURS: The passage is quoted by Schlosser, *Schriftquellen des frühen Mittelalters*, 1891, p. 9.

p. 223. THE DRAPED CRUCIFIXION fell out of use from Carolingian times onwards, partly, no doubt, because it could not be accommodated to the 'pathetic' body. An example of a Crucified Christ who, because of His drapery, seems to be dancing is an ivory plaque in the Musée de Cluny, Paris. By the 15th century the Jerusalem type of Crucifixion had been so completely forgotten that when it survived, *e.g.* at Lucca, it was thought to represent a bearded woman and became identified with the legend of a saint, variously known as Liberata, Wilgefortis, Kumernus and Uncomber, who grew a beard in order to preserve her virginity.

p. 225. THE TWO THIEVES. In the earliest representation of Christ crucified between two thieves, a panel on the doors of S. Sabina, Rome, 4th century, the thieves are miniature replicas of the Christ, and stand in the same pose. But at some point it was felt necessary to distinguish between their human agonies and the sublime sufferings of Christ. Early in the middle ages they were taken from their straight crosses, which involved the same schematic image as the Christ, and put on rough-hewn trees, *e.g.* an ivory plaque of the Metz school *c.* 850 in the Bibliothèque Nationale, MS. lat. 9388 [297]. When the figure of Christ was shown hanging in pain, the attitudes of the thieves had to be more contorted, *e.g.* in Germany, a picture of a Bavarian artist at Schleissheim, *c.* 1441 (Glaser, *Zwei Jahrhunderte deutscher Malerei*, 1916, p. 48) ; or, in Italy, Antonello da Messina's picture in Antwerp, 1475. In the *Grandes Heures de Rohan* (mid-15th century) the profane character of the thieves is emphasised by their being depicted in their underclothes. They were thereby given a status as natural man, whereas Our Lord was associated with an ideal form of geometry.

p. 227. MASACCIO'S EVE, as has frequently been observed, *e.g.* Mesnil in *Burlington Magazine*, 1926, pp. 91-8, is in the pose of a *Venus pudica*. That at least one antique of this type was known to artists of the 13th century is proved by the Temperance of Giovanni Pisano (see p. 89), and Masaccio, who had spent the preceding year in Pisa, may have derived the pose direct from Giovanni's figure. The earliest description of a *Venus pudica* is in Benvenuto Rambaldi da Imola's commentary on Dante's

Divina commedia which must date from about 1340. Cf. the edition of 1855 (Imola) translated by Tamburini, vol. ii, p. 207. He says that he saw it in a private house in Florence, and adds that it is said to be a work of Polycletus, but he does not believe it. The Venus described by Ghiberti in his *Memoriale* (ed. Schlosser, I, 62) cannot be the same, as she had draperies half-way up her thighs, *i.e.* the type of the Venus of Syracuse.

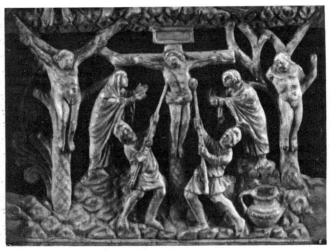

297. Metz. *c.* 850. The Crucifixion

p. 227. GHIBERTI'S ISAAC AND THE ANTIQUE. There can be little doubt that it was inspired by a Niobid, but no figure in precisely this attitude has survived. It has been thought to derive from the Iloneus in Munich, which was at one time believed to have been in Ghiberti's own collection. Cf. Grünwald in *Wiener Jahrbuch*, XXVII, 1907–9, p. 155.

p. 227. PIETÀ was one of the last great motives to be added to Christian imagery. It originated in Germany in the early 14th century out of a fusion of the Lamentation over the dead Christ and the Madonna and Child (in the earliest *Pietàs* the Christ is as small as a child). No detailed study of the subject is known to me, but cf. a booklet by W. Pinder, *Die Pietà*, Leipzig, 1922.

p. 232. RAPHAEL'S ENTOMBMENT. In addition to the antique *Pietà Militare* and Michelangelo's *Pietà*, we must note the influence of Mantegna's engraving of the

Entombment (B. XIII, 229, 3), of which a copy exists in the so-called Raphael sketch-book. From this Raphael took the man carrying Our Lord's body on the left, the disposition of the fainting Virgin on the right, and many other compositional ideas.

p. 238. FALLEN GIANTS. Of those who inspired Michelangelo's 'unfinished' style, the most influential was the fragment of a group (probably Menelaus with the body of Patroclus) known as the *Mastro Pasquino* which stood, and still stands, at the side of the Palazzo Braschi, Rome. As was first pointed out by Grünwald, *Wiener Jahrbuch*, XXVII, 1907–9, p. 130, Michelangelo certainly had this figure in mind when he executed his earliest 'unfinished' figure, the St. Matthew.

p. 242. THE ARIADNE OF THE VATICAN was discovered in the early 16th century and identified as a Cleopatra. It was part of a group of Dionysus and Ariadne, and the magnificent bronze cast by Bontemps in the Louvre suggests that the original may itself have been a bronze. This group must have been similar to the originals of the Uffizi Niobids, and both may ultimately derive from Scopas, although their enhanced pathos suggests a later date. The Ariadne was drawn by Raphael at the time when he was at work on the Parnassus. A photograph of a copy of this drawing was shown to me by Fischel but I can no longer trace it. The droop of her head, and still more the turn of Niobe's head as we know it in several replicas, *e.g.* Brocklesby Park, provided the model of feminine pathos from Raphael onwards. Niobe is the origin of all the eye-rolling, heaven-supplicating martyrs of counter-Reformation art, and was the subject of a drawing by Ingres inscribed *mon 1ᵉʳ dessin 1789* (Lapauze, *Ingres : sa vie et son œuvre*, p. 19).

p. 244. THREE DRAWINGS DONE FOR VITTORIA COLONNA. Of these only one has survived, the Crucifixion in the British Museum ; and even this was considered a copy by every critic except Thode until its recent vindication by Johannes Wilde, *British Museum : Michelangelo*, 1953, no. 67. He dates it between 1538 and 1541. Provenance (it was in the collection of the King of Naples) and comparison with numerous copies (Oxford, Louvre, British Museum) persuade me to accept it as the original.

p. 245. THE Y-SHAPED CROSS is almost certainly an invention of the Rhineland. It appears first in an ivory of the Metz school of *c.* 850 in the Bibliothèque Nationale (see above and [297]), but is there assigned appropriately to one of the thieves. It seems to have been transferred to the Cross of Our Lord in the 11th century and must have been widely diffused in Italy. Rhenish crosses of this type are to be found in many Italian churches (Pisa, Orvieto, Spalato, etc.), but most of these are late 13th century, and the first datable instance of the motive is Nicola Pisano's pulpit in the cathedral of Siena, 1265. It may be fairly assumed that this was derived from a cross of the Rhineland school, now lost. Either this, or Giovanni Pisano's somewhat similar Crucifixion in Sant' Andrea, Pistoja, was probably what lay at the back of Michelangelo's mind when he adopted the Y-shaped cross ; but we know from the St. Peter's *Pietà* that he appreciated the pathos of Gothic carving, so he may also have been thinking of a Rhineland crucifix. The Y-shaped cross is rare in painting, the only examples known to me being in a diptych in the Florence Academy in the style of Berlinghieri and a picture by Ugolino in the Siena gallery, no. 34.

p. 251. MONKEY LAOCOÖN. This woodcut [298], which is neither signed nor dated, is first mentioned by Carlo Ridolfi, and his attribution to Titian has never been questioned. It is in a style similar to that of the woodcuts after Titian executed by

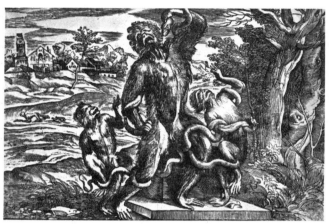

298. BOLDRINI. After Titian. The Monkey Laocoön (woodcut)

Boldrini, who was working for Titian in 1566, but there is no reason to assume that Titian's design was so late. The correct position of the Monkey Laocoön's left arm suggests a date earlier than Montorsoli's restoration of the original (1532). Many theories have been put forward to explain this group. The earliest, that it was intended to satirise Bandinelli's copy of the Laocoön, is improbable on many counts. The latest, Janson in *Art Bulletin*, 1946, p. 49, is that it was connected with a famous controversy on the nature of human anatomy in which Vesalius had accused Galen of describing the structure of an ape, not a man. There is not sufficient evidence for this ingenious theory, and the simplest explanation is the best : that Titian was satirising the excessive admiration bestowed on the group and on classical art in general. To ridicule the solemnities of human life by depicting them as being enacted by animals is a universal artistic practice, *e.g.* the so-called Toba Soja role (early 12th-century Japanese), and the many thousands of carvings and manuscript borders of the middle ages. The fact that Titian admired the group and owned a cast of it would no more prevent him ridiculing it than a priest of the mediaeval church was prevented from carving a monkey mass on a miserere seat.

VII. ECSTASY

p. 264. NEREID SARCOPHAGI. The only systematic study is in *Die antiken Sarcophagreliefs* (Robert and Rodenwalt), vol. v, *Die Meerwesen* by Andreas Rumpf, Berlin, 1939. An almost complete corpus, classified iconographically, but throws little light on the subject from the point of view of form or pictorial invention.

p. 266. SPARTAN GIRLS DANCING. The Saltantes Lacanae of Callimachus, mentioned in Pliny, were evidently celebrated, for in addition to the reliefs in Berlin they have come down in certain coins of Abdera, on a number of pieces of Aretine ware and on fragments of Roman glass. They also appear together with the maenads mentioned in the next note, on a marble base from the Grimani Collection in the Museo Archeologico, Venice. Cf. Rizzo, *Thiasos*, figs. 29-30. The identification of these figures with the passage in Pliny is confirmed (*a*) by their short Spartan kilts ; (*b*) the crownlike hat, presumably of Egyptian origin, known as the calathiscos, was worn by Spartan priestesses of Apollo at Delphi.

p. 266. MAENADS. Cf. Rizzo, *Thiasos*, for a full treatment of the linear type and their relation to Callimachus. The Scopaic type has not, as far as I know, been examined. No doubt both types incorporate much iconographic material of an earlier date of which we find evidence in vase paintings throughout the 5th century from the famous cup by Makron in Berlin (*c*. 490) onwards.

p. 267. ECSTASY IN THE ROUND. The satyr looking at his tail was evidently popular and exists in several replicas, *e.g.* in the Terme (499) and the Uffizi. The so-called Dancer of Tivoli (Terme, 108596) is the best example of a type which also exists in Berlin and Vienna, and which, through Canova's free variations, became popular in the 19th century.

p. 268. THE DRESDEN MAENAD was discovered at Marino, not far from Lake Albano. Up to 1944 it was in the Albertinum, Dresden (no. 133). From its likeness to plaque 1014 of the Mausoleum (cf. pl. 134) and from other characteristics, it has always been accepted as a copy of the Maenad of Scopas, but one of an unusual kind. Instead of the lifeless 'pointed' copy generally supplied to the Roman market, it is much reduced in scale (the height of the fragment is 60 cm.), and is executed with exceptional freedom, amounting in places to roughness. One is led to suppose that this is the work of an individual artist making, so to say, a sketch of the original, rather than of a professional copyist. The numerous Bacchic figures on reliefs and vases in a style related to the Mausoleum and the Dresden Maenad are all decorative derivations by more or less competent craftsmen. The most famous is the Borghese Vase, now in the Louvre [212], found (like the Niobids) in the gardens of Sallust. It probably dates from the 1st century B.C., and the Scopaic motives have been considerably altered for decorative purposes.

p. 271. THE ORIGIN OF THE NEREIDS seems to be an insoluble problem, since the sarcophagi in which they appear are all later than the 1st century B.C., whereas the motives can be traced back to the 4th century. They were obviously taken from 'pattern books' which probably reproduced famous paintings. We can say that these patterns were of two types, the decorous and the abandoned, representing classicising and orientalising tendencies in Hellenistic art ; but this is only art historians' patter. The abandoned nereid, in the same outlines which were to last till the 5th century A.D., is to be found painted on duck-shaped *askos* in the Louvre, discovered in South Italy, datable 4th century B.C. ; only there she is represented as a winged genius.

p. 275. THE DIFFUSION OF NEREIDS in the 4th century is a subject that would resolve itself into a study of trade routes in the late Roman empire. L. Matzuluvitsch, *Byzantinische Antike*, Berlin, 1929, pl. 6, reproduces one found in Baku. Foucher, *L'Art buddhique*, fig. 130, reproduces a nereid relief in the Lahore Museum.

p. 282. TITIAN'S BACCHANALS were intended to be re-creations of antique painting, and the subjects were drawn directly from antique literature. The Bacchus and Ariadne, as pointed out by E. Wind, *Giovanni Bellini's Feast of the Gods*, 1948, p. 56, illustrates a passage in Ovid, *Fasti*, III, 505-8, although certain details are taken from Catullus, *Carmina*, LXIV, as was originally observed by Lomazzo. Since Wickhoff, *Jahrbuch der Preussischen Kunstsammlungen*, XXIII, 1902, p. 118, the Madrid Bacchanal is always said to have been derived from a passage in Philostratus, *Imagines*, I, 25, describing how, on the island of Andros, Bacchus caused a river of wine to flow. Philostratus says quite definitely that this river shall be the subject of the picture, but Titian depicted only the resulting Bacchanal and may well have had some other source in mind.

p. 284. LETTO DI POLICLETO was the name given to a marble relief of Cupid and Psyche at one time in the possession of Lorenzo Ghiberti, which had an extraordinary influence on renaissance art. From the figure of Psyche Raphael derived the nude woman (? Hebe) in the foreground of his fresco of the Wedding of Cupid and Psyche in the Farnesina, Correggio derived the Io (*c.* 1530), Titian derived the Venus in his Prado Venus and Adonis (1553) and Poussin derived (in reverse) the nereid to the right of his Triumph of Galatea. Of the recumbent male figure

(Cupid) we have a copy by Michelangelo at Windsor, Wilde, 422, *recto*. The relief passed into the hands of Ghiberti's grandson Vittorio, himself a sculptor and friend of Michelangelo ; it was later sold to Cardinal Bembo. Its subsequent history is hard to follow, as there was at least one other relief of the same subject (? a forgery) and also a bronze. We may deduce that the motive was common in antiquity, as it appeared on Aretine ware, for which an original mould stamp is in the Metropolitan Museum, New York ; cf. *Museum Bulletin*, vol. xxxii, 1937, pp. 96-7. All three have disappeared and our only replica of the original is a rough 17th-century copy in the Palazzo Maffei, Rome (illustrated in Goldscheider, *Michelangelo Drawings*, London, 1951, fig. 143). Cf. Popham and Wilde, *Windsor*, p. 246 ; Schlosser, *Ghiberti's Denkwürdigkeiten*, II, p. 172.

p. 284. THE MUTILATION OF CORREGGIO'S IO. The story quoted in the text, although it appears in standard works, *e.g.* Corrado Ricci's *Correggio*, does not withstand an examination of the picture's history, as the Io was definitely in the Imperial Collection in Vienna by 1702. The Correggios in the Regent's Collection were the Leda and the Danae, and it was the former which was destroyed by Louis d'Orléans. It seems to be true that Coypel collected the pieces and that the head was missing, but the present head cannot have been painted by Prud'hon (as is often said), as in 1755 the Leda passed into the possession of Frederick the Great. It is equally impossible that Prud'hon should have painted, or restored, the head of the Io in Vienna. Perhaps the confusion arose from the fact that the Regent owned a *copy* of the Io which was also destroyed by Louis d'Orléans. In view of this fact I have let the passage in the text stand as I gave it in the lecture.

VIII. THE ALTERNATIVE CONVENTION

p. 301. PAGAN IDOLS. The most accessible summary of post-classical attitude towards representation of the Olympian gods is Edwin Bevan, *Holy Images*, 1940 ; but he does not allow sufficiently for variations in different parts of the Empire or for sporadic revivals of paganism. Cf. A. Arföldi, *Die Kontorniaten, ein verkanntes Propagandamittel der stadtrömischen heidnischen Aristokratie in ihrem Kampf gegen das christliche Kaisertum*, Budapest, 1943.

p. 304. BRONZE DOORS. See Goldschmidt, *Die deutschen Bronzetüren*, 1926, p. 23, and von Einem, *Zur Hildesheimer Bronzetür: Jahrbuch der Preussischen Kunstsammlungen*, 1930. The doors can be dated precisely between 1008 and 1015. Several artists were employed, of which far the most gifted and individual was the portrayer of the Creation and Fall. The sense of spacing suggests a 9th-century Tours manuscript, *e.g.* the Bamberg Bible, but the animation is far superior, and the author may have seen antique prototypes, now lost, on which the Tours Bibles were also based.

p. 306.   The idea of basing a LAST JUDGMENT ON AN ANTIQUE SARCOPHAGUS, representing the victory of Romans over Barbarians, first appears on Nicola Pisano's pulpit in the Baptistery at Pisa, 1260.   Not only are individual figures imitated, but the whole compositional idea is the same, the defeated grovelling below, the victorious in dignity above.   This explains why the Last Judgment at Pisa differs so strikingly from the other sides of the pulpit.   At Orvieto, Maitani does not follow the classical composition, but many of his sufferers are clearly inspired by defeated Gauls.   In the Last Judgments of Roger van der Weyden and Memlinc at Beaune and Danzig the figures are more naked and defenceless, and are in fact an instance of the un-flinching truth of late Gothic art ; as we realise when we see photographs of Belsen or of the struggle for the sacred baton at the Kwannon Temple, Saidaiji (cf. *Illustrated London News*, Jan. 1, 1955, p. 18).

p. 310.   DE LIMBOURG AND ANTIQUE SCULPTURE.   His patron, the Duc de Berry, although a great collector, does not seem to have owned any antiques : at least none is mentioned in his inventories.   So de Limbourg probably saw the kneeling figure from which his Adam is derived during his visit to Italy.   It was a figure in the round, not a coin or gem, as it appears again drawn from a different angle on f. 34, v (Durrieu, *Les Tres Riches Heures du duc de Berry*, Paris, 1904, pl. XXV).   It was evidently a type similar to the Youth of Subiaco in the Terme, and so could be either a Niobid or, more probably, a vanquished Persian from a group such as the Attalus figures in Naples.

p. 314.   GOTHIC NUDES IN ITALY.   One famous painting of nudes, presumably in what I have called the alternative convention, reached Italy early.   This was Jan van Eyck's picture of women in a bathroom, which was the property of Cardinal Octavian, who was created Cardinal in 1408.   It is described at length in Bartolomeo Facio's *de Viris Illustribus*, written *c.* 1455 (ed. Florence, 1745, p. 46).   It contained several figures, some lightly veiled, and of one it was possible, by means of a mirror, to see her back as well as her breast.   This remarkable work is usually identified with the painting by Jan van Eyck referred to by Vasari '*al duca d' Urbino Federico II, la stufa sua*' (ed. Milanesi, I, p. 184, who points out that Vasari must mean Federico I).   Another picture by van Eyck of a nude woman and her maid, recorded in van Haecht's copy of C. van der Geest's gallery, is sometimes confused with the picture mentioned by Facio, but does not tally with his description.   Pisanello, who had probably visited France and Burgundy, gave a Gothic character to his nudes, even when they were free copies of the Antique.   A similar character is to be found in two *cassone* panels, a Judgment of Paris in the Burrell Collection and a Diana and Actaeon in the Fuld Collection, now attributed to the workshop of Domenico Veneziano, and datable *c.* 1460. There are numerous Gothic nudes in popular engravings evidently derived from German cuts. In sculpture, a curious example is one of the figures supporting the holy-water stoup at the main door of Siena Cathedral by Antonio Federighi (*c.* 1460–70). The most famous 'Gothic' nude in Italian art is the Eve of Antonio Rizzo on the Arco Foscari of the Doge's palace in Venice. It has frequently been compared to Jan van Eyck's Eve on the Ghent altar-piece, but no direct influence is probable or necessary. It is, however, somewhat earlier (*c.* 1483) than the German bronze and boxwood figures which it so closely resembles.

p. 315. THE FAT BACCHANTE IN MANTEGNA'S ENGRAVING (B. XIII, 240, 20) was based on an antique relief, presumably a Bacchic sarcophagus, recorded in a pattern-book of the Renaissance of which a few sheets are in the Ambrosiana, don Beltrami. Cf. *Rassegna d'Arte*, X, 1910, p. 6. It was probably in Rome as were the other antiquities recorded in this pattern-book, *e.g.* the Triton and Nereid now at Grotta-ferrata (see p. 275).

p. 317. DÜRER AND JACOPO DE' BARBARI. The whole story of their relationship is full of puzzles on which we must hope that scholars of Dürer will shed more light: *e.g.* if the masterly drawing of a nude woman seen from behind in the Louvre (Winkler, 85) is really 1495, why did Dürer do a timid imitation of Jacopo on his second visit to Venice in 1505 (ex-Lubomirski, Winkler, 410)? And why, after all his researches of 1505, did he still wish to possess Jacopo's book? By 1521 he must have seen prints and drawings of antiques and of Raphael's work far more evolved and systematic than anything by Jacopo. Incidentally, the Regent of Malines refused to let him have the book, saying that she had promised it to her court painter, Bernard van Orley ; cf. Veth and Müller, *Albrecht Dürer's niederländische Reise*, 1918, I, 84.

p. 319. TITLE-PAGE OF ERASMUS' NEW TESTAMENT OF 1519. For this Froben used a woodcut known as *Imago Vitae Aulicae* by Ambrosius Holbein, which seems to have been published in the preceding year. Apparently no one commented on its inappropriateness ; which gives some justification to the later strictures of the Council of Trent.

p. 323. THE DIANA OF ANET. Maurice Roy, *Artistes et monuments de la renaissance française*, Paris, 1929, I, p. 320, shows that the attribution to Goujon is of recent origin and cannot be upheld. Nevertheless it is hard to believe that such a perfect and individual work is by an unknown carver, and on grounds of style one would gladly accept the suggestion put forward by Anthony Blunt, *Art and Architecture in France, 1500–1700*, London, 1953, p. 76, that it is the work of Germain Pillon, were it not that the Diana was in place in 1554, and Pillon himself gave the date of his birth as 1536 'or thereabouts'. Even allowing that he was precocious (he undertook the sculpture for the tomb of Francis I in 1558), the Diana is an incredibly assured work for a young man of about twenty.

p. 326. ANDRIES PELS, *Gebruik en misbruik des tooneels*, Amsterdam, 1681, p. 36. This passage from the poem is quoted with approval by Arnold Houbraken in his Life of Rembrandt (*Groote Schonburgh der Nederlantsche Konstschilders*, vol. i, Amsterdam, 1718, translated in *Rembrandt Selected Paintings*, Phaidon Press, 1942, p. 26). Houbraken himself says, 'His nude women, however, the most wonderful subject of the brush to which all celebrated masters from time immemorial have given the best of their industry, are too pitiful (as the saying goes) for one to make a song about'. This represents the conventional attitude to the nude in which both classic and baroque schools of thought concurred. That there was in fact a certain demand for 'nudes' of a grossly plebeian kind had been proved by the success of Jordaens.

IX. THE NUDE AS AN END IN ITSELF

p. 335. THE PARTHENON was not entirely unknown in the Renaissance as Cyriac of Ancona had visited it in 1435 and 1437 and made a drawing of the West Front, published by Mommsen, *Jahrbuch der Preussischen Kunstsammlungen*, 1883, p. 78. This drawing may have been used by Giuliano da Sangallo in his representation of the Parthenon in his book of studies in the Vatican Library, although this contains evidence of knowledge of the metopes, which was not included by Cyriac ; cf. Huelsen, *Il libro di Giuliano Sangallo*, 1910, pp. 41-2. Cyriac had turned the sculpture in the pediment into Gothic figures (the Neptune is a woman in a fashionable Burgundian dress) and the indication of sculpture in Giuliano's drawing was certainly not clear enough to have had any influence on artists. In so far as similarities between Michelangelo's reclining figures and those on the pediments of the Parthenon are not due solely to a similar feeling for the architecture of the body, they arise from reminiscences of Phidian motives still to be found in Graeco-Roman sarcophagi.

p. 336. THE ASSOCIATION OF THE CROUCHING VENUS with the name of Doidalsus of Bithynia derives from a corrupt passage in Pliny, *Naturalis Historia*, XXXVI, 35, ed. Jex-Blake, pp. 208-9. It reads *Venerem lavantem se sedaedalsus stantem Polycharmos*. As the word *sedaedalsus* is meaningless, scholars have supposed that it is a corruption of Doidalsus who is said by Eustathios to have been a Bithynian sculptor working in the 2nd century The representation of a crouching Venus appears on various coins, cf. Pliny (*ibid.* p. 239), and on vases such as the Attic Hydra of Thetis in the British Museum and it was certainly current early in the 4th century. The appearance of this pose on coins of Bithynia of the 2nd century need, therefore, be related to

Doidalsus, even supposing that the emendation which produced his name out of the incomprehensible passage of Pliny is correct.

p. 338. THE NUDES OF PISANELLO are of two kinds. The more numerous are studies from the Antique to which Pisanello has given the accent of late Gothic realism. These are to be found in the Ambrosiana, cf. Degenhart, *Antonio Pisanello*, 3rd edn. N.D. Wien, figs. 30 and 31 ; in Rotterdam, Degenhart, *op. cit.* fig. 33 ; and in the Louvre, *fonds Vallardi*. There are also a few studies from the life, amongst which we must class *Luxuria* in the Albertina [229]. Of these the most remarkable is a sheet in the Boymans Museum, Rotterdam (formerly Koenig's Collection), Degenhart, *op. cit.* fig. 26, which bears four studies of a naked woman done direct from the model, with practically no reference to antiquity either in pose or proportion (the right-hand figure in the pose of the Venus Anadyomene is clearly drawn from life). Almost equally surprising is a drawing from Pisanello's workshop (not from his hand) in the Print Room, Berlin, no. 487, reproduced Meder, *Die Handzeichnung*, 1919, fig. 155. It shows a naked woman lying, seated and bending over a wash-basin in totally unclassical poses. These two sheets remind us how little our scanty evidence permits us to know of the background of *quattrocento* art.

p. 338. THE DRAWING OF NUDE FIGURES USED TO FORM AN ACADEMIC COMPOSITION is in the National Museum, Stockholm, Inv. 11 ; cf. Berenson, *Drawings of the Florentine Painters*, Chicago, 1938, no. 2779K. It is reproduced in Meder, *Die Handzeichnung*, 1919, fig. 304. Although Berenson classifies it as 'school of Uccello', I believe that such studies were also common in more conservative workshops. Similar drawings are attributed to Benozzo Gozzoli, *e.g.* Berenson, *op. cit.* 445a ; and the nude figures in the background of the Adoration in the National Gallery, Washington, now considered a joint work of Fra Angelico and Filippo Lippi, may derive from similar academic studies.

Berenson, *op. cit.* 176[e], also classes with 'following (in the widest sense of the word) of Fra Angelico' one of the earliest nude drawings of a woman, British Museum, *Catalogue*, 1950, no. 273, plate CCXXXVI. The foreshortened hand and tall head-dress show us that this was inspired by a calathiscos dancer similar to one on the Grimani altar, and probably known to the draughtsman from a piece of Aretine ware. A similar use of the antique is to be found in a drawing, also in the British Museum, *Catalogue*, 1950, 152, inspired by the Horse Tamers of the Quirinal which seems to come from the same Benozzo-Filippo Lippi circle, although Berenson, *op. cit.* 986, attributes it to Granacci.

p. 340. THE ORIGIN AND DEVELOPMENT OF THE ÉCORCHÉ figure deserves to be studied. The earliest surviving examples are in drawings by Leonardo da Vinci, *e.g.* Windsor, 12625, 19003 R. and V., 19013 V., 19014 R. and V. ; but several drawings from the following of Antonio Pollajuolo suggest that *écorchés* from his hand once existed. There is a long-standing tradition that Michelangelo made an *écorché* figure, known as *La Notomia di Michelangelo* ; cf. Bottari in his edition of Vasari's *Vita di Michelangelo*, Roma, 1760, p. 172. Dr. Wilde tells me that three drawings at Windsor (nos. 439–441), which he now ascribes to Michelangelo, and two at Haarlem, Teyler Museum (Frey and Knapp, *Die Handzeichnungen Michelangelos Buonarroti*, Berlin, 1925, nos. 333, 334), imply that the tradition is correct. Michelangelo probably made small anatomical models of parts of the body similar to those in the Victoria and Albert Museum, 1854, 4109 to 4113, and these seem to be referred to in a letter from Sebastiano del Piombo, *Les Correspondants di Michelange*, ed. Milanesi, Paris, 1890, p. 100. But if he had made an *écorché* figure of any size such an important event in the artistic life of 16th-century Italy would surely have been recorded. The tradition that Marco d' Agrate's figure of St. Bartholomew of 1562 in Milan Cathedral, admired by generations of tourists including Mark Twain in *Innocents Abroad*, was based on a model by Michelangelo is first recorded by F. Le Comte, *Cabinet des singularitez*, Paris, 1699/1700. This figure, which scarcely deserves its notoriety, has no obviously Michelangelesque characteristics. On the other hand Cigoli's bronze *écorché* in the Bargello does recall, both in pose and physiological type, some of the Leonardo drawings in Anatomical MS. A. Windsor, 19003 V., and suggests that an *écorché* model from his hand may once have existed.

p. 340. RAPHAEL'S COMPOSITIONS OF NUDE FIGURES. An interesting point is raised by a famous drawing in the Albertina, Inv. no. 17544, which shows all the figures in the Transfiguration nude. This is certainly not by Raphael, and the question arises whether it is a copy of an original drawing or whether some 16th-century artist has translated the transfiguration into nude figures. Meder, *Die Handzeichnung*, 1919, p. 318, note 2, holds the second view, and uses it to prove the academic mannerist craze for nudity. In view of the authentic drawings by Raphael in which he has made up compositions of undraped figures, including two for the Transfiguration itself, *e.g.* Fischel, *Raphael's Zeichnungen*, Strassburg, 1898, nos. 339 (Louvre) and 340 (Ambrosiana), I am inclined to think that the Albertina drawing follows a Raphael original.

Index

Plate numbers are indicated by italic figures

Academism, 337-41, 377

Adam and Eve, in art, 47, 276-7, 301-12 *passim Representations.* 5th-century ivory, *36.* 47 ; of Michelangelo, *44.* 59 ; of Raphael, *83. 86.* 104 ; of Federighi, *85.* 106 ; on Bamberg Cathedral, *248.* 303 ; of Wiligelmo, *249.* 304 ; of Maitani, *227.* 277 ; of Ghiberti, *228.* 277 ; at Autun, 12th century, *252.* 305 ; of Van Eyck, *256.* 312 ; of Memlinc, *14. 18. See also* Fall

Aegina, Temple of, sculpture from, 164, 215, 380

Aelian, 31

Agasias the Ephesian. Borghese Warrior, *138.* 176

Agostino di Duccio, 267, 270

Agrate, Marco d', 398

Ajanta, *see* Indian art

Alberti, Leon Battista. *Della pittura,* 10, 181, 338, 340, 372 ; *Della architettura,* 363

Alcamenes. Garden of Aphrodite, 70-1 ; Nike, 370

Alexander, Professor, 6, 361

Alexandria, nereids on work from, 275-6

Alpheus, river god, *296.* 384

Altamira, 162

Amaravati, sculptures from, 71, 177, 348

Amazons, battle with, as a subject in Greek art, *134. 135. 136. 137.* 172-5

Ambrogio Lorenzetti, 88

Amelung, 369

Ammanati, 243

    Works. Fountain in Piazza della Signoria, *1-3,* 376 ; Venus, *102.* 129, 376

Andrea del Castagno, 57, 181 ; Crucifixion of, 226

Antaeus, *see* Hercules

Antico, 186

    Works. Copy of Apollo Belvedere, 53 ; Hercules and the Lion, *141.* 180

Antinous, head of, used on statues of the gods, 44, 366

Antique gems, 383

Antonello da Messina, 387

Antoninus Pius, coins of, 186

Apollo, Ch II, *364* ; Belvedere, *35.* 19, 38, 44-5, 366 ; influence in Renaissance, 53-4, 288 ; of Cassel, 36, 38, 365 ; at Olympia, *29.* 36-7 ; of Piombino, *23.* 29, 30 ; of Tenea, *21.* 27, 30 ; of the Tiber, *30.* 38 ; and Daphne (ivory panel), 8, *362. See also* David in art, Dürer, Michelangelo, Perugino, Poussin, Praxiteles, Sansovino

Apollo Belvedere, *see* Apollo

Apuleius, 301

Architecture and the nude, 17-19, 335

Aretine ware, 266, 374

Ariadne of the Vatican, *195.* 106, 242, 373

Aristotle, 9, 10

Aspertini, Amico, 370

Athene Parthenos, shield of, 175, 381

Athletics, Athletes, Greek conception of, 29 ; on Greek vases and pan-Athenaic amphorae, *124.* 19, 20, 163 ; professional athletes, 8, 362 ; of Polyclitus, 33, 35 ; participation of women in, 67 ; as embodiment of energy in Greek art, *125. 163. See also* Olympic Games, Wrestlers

Autun Cathedral, 12th-century Eve in, *252.* 305

Bacchantes, Ch. VII *passim. See also* Maenads

Bacchus, *233.* 267, 282, 284, 392

Bacon, Francis, 16

Baldassare Peruzzi, 106

Balzac, Honoré. *Le Chef-d'œuvre inconnu,* 353-4

Barnes, Dr., 295

Bassai, frieze from Temple of, 172, 175, 381
Battle scenes, nudes in, *126. 149. 150. 151. 155.* 191-8, 382. *See also* Amazons
Baudelaire, 130, 143
Bellini, Giovanni, 110, 119, 229-30, 317
  Works. Woman at her toilet, *88.* 110; Dead Christ with Angels, *184.* 230 ; Pietà (Brera), 229; St. Jerome, 328; Vanitas, *259.* 110, 313
Bembo, Pietro, 374, 393
Benvenuto Rambaldi da Imola, 387
Berenson, Bernard, 125, 163, 397
Bernini, 361. Apollo and Daphne, *238.* 53, 288, 293
Bernward, Abbot, 304
Berry, Duc de, *see* de Limbourg
Bertoldo, 191-3, 341
  Work. Battle piece, *149.* 191
Bibiena, Cardinal, bathroom of, 106, 373
Blake, William, 11, 21-2, 119, 191, 200, 204, 207-8
  Works. Illustration from ' Europe ', *164.* 207 ; Glad Day, *165.* 207
Blanc, Charles, 144
Bloy, Léon, 333
Boddhisatvas in Khmer sculpture, 47
Boilly, 143
Boldrini, *298.* 390
Bontemps, Pierre, 370, 386, 389
Borghese Vase, 392
Bossuet, 244
Botticelli, 50, 65, 92-102, 125, 144, 281-2, 333, 372
  Works. Birth of Venus, 77. *232.* 15, 97-8, 281 ; Calumny of Apelles, *78.* 99-100, 373 ; Pietà (Munich), 228 ; *Primavera, 76.* 92-7
Boucher, 127, 139-42 *passim,* 158, 159
  Works. Diana, *110.* 140, 151 ; Miss O'Murphy, *109.* 140 ; Triumph of Galatea, 292
Bouguereau, 152, 334
Bourges, 13th-century Last Judgment at, *253.* 307
Brancusi. Torso, *288.* 348
Bronze doors, *see* Hildesheim
Bronze girl (Munich), *62. 63.* 71, 370
Bronzino. Allegory of Passion, *101.* 128
Brunellesco, 50, 226, 338, 367
Burne-Jones, 267

Burns, Robert, 328
Byron, Lord, on the Medici Venus, 79-80, 371

Cabanel, 152, 334
Calamecca, 129, 376
Calathiscos, the, 266, 391
Caligula, 44
Callimachus. 'Spartan girls dancing', *213. 214.* 266, 391
Campo Santo (Pisa), collection of antiques in, 191, 278, 372, 374, 382
Campo Vaccino, 238
Canova, 149, 391
  Works. Perseus, *50.* 62 ; Hercules, 177 ; Theseus, 177
Caravaggio, 150, 152
  Work. Entombment, *204.* 251-2
Carpaccio, 328
Carpeaux. The Dance (Paris Opera House), *242.* 293, 296
Carracci, Agostino. Galatea, *240.* 290-292
Carracci, Annibale, 252
  Work. Pietà (Naples), 252
Castagno, *see* Andrea del Castagno
Cavalieri, Tommaso, 54, 297, 368
Cellini, 129
  Works. Perseus, *34.* 41, 130 ; Nymph of Fontainebleau, 130, 323
Cennini, Cennino, 9
Cesarino, his edition of *Vitruvius,* Vitruvian Man, *10.* 15, 363
Cézanne, 124, 348
  Work. Life study, *277.* 331
Chantelou, 19, 377, 379
Charbonneaux, 371
Charioteer, The (from Delphi), 219
Chasseriau, 127
Chaucer, 328
Chesneau, Ernest, 379
Chigi, Agostino, 106, 107
Christianity, and the nude :
  In Northern art : Ch. VIII *passim.* Rejection of, in early middle ages, 23, 301 ; Romanesque and early Gothic representations of, 301-5 ; development in, 13, 305-8 ; influence of Antique on, 306-7, 310

Christianity, and the nude—*contd.*
  In Renaissance : Ch. VI *passim.* First interpretation of classical nude in Italy, 48, 89
  See also Adam and Eve, Crucifixion, The Entombment, The Fall, Last Judgment, *Pietà*, Resurrection
Cigoli, 340, 398
Cimabue. Painted cross, *179.* 225
Claudel, Paul, *Partage de midi,* 19
Claudius, 44
Clodion, 127, 159, 293
  Work. Nymph and Satyr, *112.* 142
Cnidian Venus, *see* Praxiteles
Cocteau, Jean, 349
Codex Escurialensis, 53, 279, 366, 384
Codex Rabulensis, *see* Crucifixion in art
Coleridge, Samuel Taylor, 22
Cologne Cathedral, Gero Cross in, *178.* 223, 226
Colonna, Vittoria, 244, 389
Congreve, 130
Coppo di Marcavaldo, painted crosses, 225
Coptic needlework, nereids on, 275-6
Correggio, 39, 125-7, 254, 284-6
  Works. Antiope, *99.* 125 ; Danaë, *100.* 127 ; Leda, 127, 139, 393 ; Io, *236.* 284, 392, 393
Cos, 71
Costa, Lorenzo. Venus, *267.* 319
Courbet, 116, 124, 150-6 *passim,* 200, 331
  Works. La Source, *4.* 4 ; *Femme au perroquet,* 150 ; *Baigneuse* (1853), 151, 379 ; *L'Atelier du peintre,* *118.* 151
Cranach, 102, 319-23
  Works. Venus and Cupid, *266.* 319 ; Venus, *268.* 321 ; Judgment of Paris, *269.* 321
Critobalus, 20, 21
Crucifixion in art, Ch. VI *passim,* 387, 389 ; draped, 221-3, 387
  Representations. Ivory plaque (British Museum), *176.* 223 ; Monza ampullae, 223 ; miniature in Codex Rabulensis, 223 ; 9th-century ivory, *177.* 223 ; in prayer book of Charles the Bald, 223, 387 ; Gero Cross, *178.* 223 ; Cross of Lothair, 223 ; Painted crosses, *179.* 225 ; Barbara Altar (Breslau), 226 ; at Metz, *297.* 389. *See also* Andrea del Castagno, Giotto, Grünewald, Michel-

Crucifixion in art (*Representations*)—*contd.*
  angelo, Rubens, Thieves in Crucifixion, Y-shaped Cross
cuirasse esthétique, 35, 49, 348, 365
Cyclades, marble dolls of, *52.* 64

Dance, the, Dancers in art, and Greek art, 163, 173, 293 ; Dancing Faun, *145.* 189 ; of Matisse, *243.* 293-6 ; of Pollajuolo, *231.* 164, 279-80, 295. *See also* Callimachus, Degas
Danti, Vincenzo. Honour, *160.* 203
David. Intervention of the Sabine Women, 342
David in art, transformation of, by Donatello, *38.* 48-9, 367 ; of Michelangelo, *43. 46.* 58-9
de Berry, Duc, *see* de Limbourg
de Chirico, 94
de Clari, Robert, 8, 362
Decoration, the nude as, 212-13, 288, 292-5, 374
Defeated Gauls, 306, 309, 394
Degas, 153-4, 261, 333-4, 345 ; and nudes of energy, 209-12 ; dancers, 163, 168-9, 211
  Works. Jeunes Filles Spartiates, *170.* 211 ; Woman sponging her back, *169.* 211
déhanchement, 71, 106, 149
de Honnecourt, Villard, 9, 363
  Work. Nude figures from notebook, *8.* 9
Delacroix, 257, 259-61
  Works. Girls wrestling, *168.* 209 ; Barque of Dante, *210.* 259 ; Massacre of Skios, 260
Delaroche, 258
de Limbourg and antique sculpture, 394
  Work. Très Riches Heures du Duc de Berry, *255.* 96, 310
Desiderio da Settignano, 266
Deutsch, *see* Niklaus Manuel Deutsch
Diaghilev, 349
Diderot, 137
Diogenes, 4, 9
Dionysus, 47, 63, 368 ; from the Parthenon, *45. 59,* 335 ; Dionysiac scenes in Greek art, Ch. VII *passim*
Dioscuri of the Quirinal, 176-7, 381
Dipendenza, 17, 19, 340
Doidalsus. Crouching Venus, *281.* 84-5, 134, 336, 396-7

Domenico Veneziano, 394

Domitius Ahenobarbus, 270

Donatello, 181, 216, 226, 228-9, 257, 281, 338, 339, 381
  Works. David, *38.* 48-9 ; Crucifix in S. Croce, 226 ; Dead Christ with Angels, *183.* 229 ; Cantoria, *230.* 279-80 ; St. Mary Magdalen (Florence), 330 ; Reliefs in Palazzo Riccardi, 383

Drapery, in Romanesque art, 4 ; *draperie mouillée*, 68-9, 94, 106, 169-71, 266-7, 369 ; flying, 171-2, 266-7, 381

Du Fresnoy, 10

Duncan, Isadora, 295

Dürer, Albrecht, 7, 53, 314-18, 327, 363, 367 ; his search for ideal beauty, 10, 16, 363 ; and proportion of the human body, 15-17, 317
  Works. Nemesis, *11.* 15 ; Apollo, *40.* 53, 367 ; Naked Hausfrau, *261.* 314 ; Women's Bath, *262.* 315, 327 ; Four Witches, *263.* 315-317 ; Measured nude, *12.* 15 ; Fall of Man (engraving), 16, 363, 367

Eastern art, 47, 65, 86, 369, 373. *See* Indian art, Japanese art

Écorché, 190, 340, 397-8

Egyptian art, nude figures in, 26, 71, 86

Eleusis, running girl from, 171

Entombment, The, in art, 227-32 *passim,* 251-5 *passim*
  Representations : of Caravaggio, *204.* 251 ; of Raphael, *186.* 232 ; of Titian, 254-5

Ephebe of 'Kritios', *see* 'Kritios'

Erasmus, New Testament of (1519), 319, 395

Etruscan tomb figures, 7. 8, 362

Etty, 116, 150

Euclid, 167, 175, 176

Euripides, 209

Fabriano, Gilio da, 364

Facio, Bartolomeo, *de Viris Illustribus,* 394

Falconet, 142

Fall, The (and The Expulsion), 227, 304-5, 308-12 *passim*
  Representations. Masaccio, *180.* 227 ; the Hildesheim doors, *250. 251.* 304 ; de Limbourg, *255.* 310 ; Van der Goes, *257.* 312-13

Federighi, 106, 372, 373
  Work. Font at Siena, *85.* 106

Filarete, 90

Fragonard, 142

Francesca, Piero della, *see* Piero della Francesca

Francesco I, bronzes in Studiolo of, 129

Franciabigio, *cassone* panels of, 139

Fromentin, 254

Furtwängler, 83, 371, 381

Gambello, 383

Geometry, importance in Greek art, 11, 27, 183 ; in nude drawings of de Honnecourt, 9. *See also* Dürer, Euclid

Géricault, 145, 191, 258-60
  Works. Leda, *167.* 208-9 ; Raft of the Medusa, 200, 258-9

Gero, Archbishop, cross in Cologne Cathedral, *178.* 223

Gerolamo Campagna, 129

Gherardi, 289

Ghiberti, 88, 277-8, 338, 339, 393
  Works. Golden doors, 8 ; Sacrifice of Isaac, *181.* 227, 388 ; Creation of Eve, *228.* 277, 296

Ghirlandajo, Domenico, 281, 339, 340, 373

Giambologna, *see* Giovanni da Bologna

Giorgione, 106, 110, 112, 115-17, 159, 270, 333, 374, 376, 377
  Works. Concert Champêtre, *92.* 110, 115-117, 343-4 ; Dresden Venus, *89.* 110, 112 ; Frescoes of Fondaco de' Tedeschi, 110, 117, 376

Giotto, 39
  Work. Cross in S. Maria Novella, 225-226

Giovanni Antonio da Brescia, 109, 373-4

Giovanni da Bologna, 129, 203-4, 376
  Works. Astronomy, *103.* 129 ; Mercury, *161.* 203-4

Girardon, 139, 158

Girodet, 143, 258

Giulio Campagnola, 374, 377

Glück, 257, 259

Goethe, 163, 335

Goltzius, 325

Gossart, Jan, 320

Goujon, 122, 158, 395
  Work. Diana of Anet, *271.* 323-5, 395
Grandes Heures de Rohan, 387
Great Exhibition of 1851, 379
Gregory of Tours, 223, 387
Grünewald. Isenheim altar-piece, 226

Hadrian, Emperor, 44
Handel, *Messiah,* 84
Hans Fries. Last Judgment, *226. 276*
Harmodius and Aristogiton, 173, 364, 381
Hazlitt, 80
Hector, 215, 216
Henner, 152, 154
Herculaneum, 189 ; antique paintings from, 94 ; bronze runner from, 169
Hercules, in art, 22, 41, 48, 163, 178-89 ; origin of, 178, 381 ; Labours of, 201-3 ; and Antaeus, *143. 144.* 186-9, 382 ; and the Cleansing of Augean Stables, 178 ; and the Hydra, *142.* 183-6 ; and the Lion, *141.* 180 ; and the Stag, *139.* 179. *See also* Samson
Hermaphrodite, 141, 284, 295. 377
Hermes, 44, 45-6, 366 ; from Antikythera, 41. *See also* Lysippus, Praxiteles
Hero, the, in Greek art, as embodiment of energy, 163 ; death of, *173.* 215-16, 232, 235. *See also* Hector, Meleager
Hildesheim, bronze doors of, *250. 251.* 304-5, 348, 393
Histiaea, bearded God of, *127.* 165, 202
Hogarth, 344
Holbein, Ambrosius, 395
Holkham Grisaille, *see* Michelangelo, cartoon
Horse tamers, *see* Dioscuri
Houdon. Diana, 325

Ideal beauty, theory of, 9-11
Idolino, the, *27.* 35, 365
Ilissus, the, from the Parthenon, *279.* 208, 335
Iloneus, 169, 199, 380-1
Indian art, 145, 147, 275, 305, 373, 392 ; flying Gandharvas (Gwalior), *225.* 276 ; 8th-century painting (Ajanta), *270.* 321-2. *See also* Amaravati

Ingres, 4, 143-9, 158, 161, 337, 378
  Works. Baigneuse de Valpinçon, *113.* 144 ; the *Bain Turc,* 117. 114, 149 ; Drawing of Maruccia, 147 ; the *Grande Odalisque, 115.* 145, 325, 353, 378 ; Jupiter and Thetis, 143 ; *La Source,* 145, 325, 378 ; Study for *L'Âge d'or, 116.* 147, 379 ; Venus Anadyomene, *114.* 114-5, 378
Inquisition, the, and nudity, 23, 363

Jacopo de' Barbari, 317, 320, 367. 374, 395
Japanese art, *6.* 7, 67
Jordaens, Jacob, 131

Keats, 116
Kirchener, Ludwig, 322
Kouroi, *20.* 26-7, 30, 47, 364. *See also* Apollo, of Tenea
'Kritios', Ephebe of, *22.* 29-31, 33, 67, 364 ; Harmodius and Aristogiton, 173, 364, 381

Laocoön, the, *175.* 127, 206, 219-21, 251, 254, 386 ; discovery of, and influence on Michelangelo, 236-7 ; the Monkey, *298.* 251, 390
Lascaux cave paintings, 162, 380
Last Judgment, in Gothic art, 226, 247. *253. 254.* 276, 306-9, 394 ; of Hans Fries, *226.* 276 ; of Van der Weyden, *247.* 309 ; French 13th century, *253.* 307 ; of Maitani, *254.* 308-9, of Memlinc, 309
Lawrence, D. H., 63, 151
Leighton, Lord, 152
Lekythoi, drawings on, 216
Leonardo da Vinci, 113-15, 125, 195-7, 397
  Works. Vitruvian Man, *9.* 15 ; Leda, *91.* 113-15, 375 ; Last Supper, 84 ; Adoration, 173, 193 ; Drawing of muscular legs, *154.* 197 ; Drawings for Battle of Anghiari, 195
Lessing, 219
Letto di Policleto, 284, 336, 392
Limbourg, *see* de Limbourg
Lippi, Filippino, 339
Lippi, Filippo, 281, 339, 397
Lomazzo, 344, 364
Lorenzetti, *see* Ambrogio Lorenzetti

Lorenzo de' Medici, 191, 193, 243
Lorenzo di Credi. Venus, 79. 102
Lorenzo di Pierfrancesco de' Medici, 92, 97
Lotto, Lorenzo. Triumph of Chastity, 237.
    286-7
Louis XIV, 81
Louis d'Orléans, 284
Ludovisi throne, 59. 60. 69
Lysippus, 42-3, 176, 181, 366 ; attribution of
    Hermes to, 42 ; a statue of Venus dis-
    covered in Siena, 88-9

Maenads (and Bacchantes), Ch. VII, 94 passim,
    391 ; of Scopas, 216. 267-71, 391
Maillol, 67, 379
Maitani, Lorenzo, 277
    Works. Creation and Fall (Orvieto), 227.
    277, 308 ; Last Judgment, 254. 308-9, 394
Malherbe, 31
Mallarmé, 159, 346
Manet. Déjeuner sur l'herbe, 116, 149, 343,
    379 ; Olympia, 119. 152-3
Mannerism and Venus, 127-31
Mantegna, 53, 110, 314, 374
    Engravings. Tritons and Hippocamps
    fighting, 279 ; Bacchanal, 315, 395 ; En-
    tombment, 388
Marathon, Praxitelean boy from, 33. 41
Maratta, 106
Marcantonio, 53, 318 ; engravings of
    antiques, 109-10, 121, 373, 382
    Engravings : of Raphael's Temptation, 84.
    104 ; of Raphael's Judgment of Paris, 285.
    115, 341 ; of Raphael's Massacre of the
    Innocents, 284. 341
Marcello Fogolino, 370
Marsyas, flaying of, in Pergamene art, 174.
    26, 215-17, 245, 251, 385 ; with Apollo,
    by Perugino, 39. 50-1
Masaccio, 338
    Works. Expulsion, 180. 227, 309 ; Eve, 387
Mastro Pasquino, 389
Mathematics, Greek passion for, 11. See also
    Geometry, Proportion
Matisse, Henri, 280, 293-6, 344-8, 351
    Works. Dance, 243. 295, 346 ; Blue Nude,
    286. 337, 344, 346 ; Pink Nude, 346 ; Illus-
    tration to Mallarmé, 287. 346

Mausoleum, frieze of, 134. 135. 136. 137. 172-5,
    183, 204
Medici Chapel, see Michelangelo
Meit, Konrad, 110
    Work. Judith, 260. 313
Meleager, 215, 216, 235, 251, 257, 385
Memlinc. Eve, 14. 18 ; Last Judgment, 309 ;
    School of, Vanitas, 258. 313
Mengs, 106
    Work. Parnassus, 49. 62
Mérimée, 379
Mesiotes. Harmodius and Aristogiton, 173
Mesopotamia, gems and seals from, 179-80,
    381
Michelangelo, Buonarroti, 17, 23, 54-61, 127-
    128, Ch. V passim, 230-62 passim, 335,
    336, 389, 398
    Works. Paintings—In Sistine Chapel :
    Creation of Adam, 44. 59 ; Last Judgment,
    47. 23, 61, 193, 204, 323 ; Athletes, 131.
    156. 189. 168, 183, 198-200, 212, 237-8, 335,
    383 ; Leda, 376. Sculpture—'Davids', 43.
    46. 41, 58-9 ; Battle of Centaurs, 150. 191-
    193 ; Victory, 158. 202, 383 ; Samson
    defeating Philistines, 159. 203 ; Dying
    Captive, 187. 235-7 ; Struggling Captive,
    188. 235-6 ; Captive, 190. 238. For
    Medici Chapel : Day, 191. 240-3 ; Night,
    193. 123, 128, 240-3 ; Dawn, 194. 128,
    240-3 ; Pietà, 185. 199. 200. 201. 230-2, 246-
    250, 252, 299 ; River god, 280. 336. Car-
    toon—Copy of Cascina cartoon (Holkham),
    151. 193-4, 341-2. Drawings—Apollonian
    Youths, 41. 42. 54-7, 368 ; Bathing Soldier
    for Cascina cartoon, 152. 194-5, 368 ; Study
    for Cascina cartoon, 153. 194 ; Three
    Labours of Hercules, 157. 201-2 ; Archers
    Shooting at a Mark, 205, 383 ; Crucifixions,
    19. 196. 197. 198. 25, 243-5 ; Resurrections,
    244. 245. 246. 297-9
Mildenhall Dish, the, 222. 275
Milton, 31
Montorsoli, 220, 251, 366, 368, 386
Moore, Henry, 3, 355-7
    Works. Recumbent Figure, 292. 356 ; Re-
    clining Figure, 293. 356
Moreau, Gustave, 333
Movement, Ch. V passim ; and Polyclitus,
    32-3 ; Florentine love of, 50

Mozart, 257, 259
Muscles, stylised development of, in early Greek sculpture, 30-1
Myron, 31, 50
  Work. Discobolos, *129. 130.* 167-9, 198, 203-4, 380

Neo-classicism, 22
Neo-Platonists, 23, 230 ; and Botticelli, 92
Nereids, Ch. VII *passim*, 392 ; monument, 69, 369 ; on sarcophagi, *220. 221.* 271, 275, 391 ; on metalwork, *222. 224.* 271, 275-6 ; wide diffusion of, 275-6, 392
Nero, Golden House of, 205, 384
Nicolo del Abate, 129
Nikias, 370
Niklaus Manuel Deutsch. Masked flute player, *264.* 318
Niobe, Niobids, *171. 172.* 215-16, 227, 235, 250-1, *296.* 384-5, 389

Olympia, sculptures, character of, 37, 171 ; metopes from, 178-9 ; River Alpheus at, *296.* 384. *See also* Apollo
Olympic Games, 20, 163

Paganism, 107, 393
Paionios, Nike of, 69-71
Pan-Athenaic amphorae, *124.* 163. *See also* Athletics
Panofsky, 15
Parmigiano, 127
Parthenon, the, knowledge of, in Renaissance, 396 ; frieze of, 33 ; metopes from, *128.* 167 ; Iris from W. pediment, *133.* 171 ; Poseidon from W. pediment, 175 ; Dionysus, *45.* 59, 335-6, 356 ; Ilissus, *279.* 335-6, 356. *See also* Phidias
Pater, Walter, 53, 115, 264, 375
Pattern books, antiquarian, use of, in Renaissance, 50, 278, 392 ; Codex Escurialensis, 53, 279, 362
Pels, Andries, *Use and Misuse of the Theatre*, 326-7, 396
Pergamon, art of, 206 ; pathos in, 216-21, 236, 245. *See also* Laocoön, Marsyas
Peru, Jean, 371

Perugino, 103, 225
  Work. Apollo and Marsyas, *39. 50*
Petronius, 301
Phidias, 36-9, 175, 365 ; and art of Parthenon, see Parthenon. *See also* Apollo, of Tiber, of Cassel
Philostratus, 119 ; and Titian's Bacchanals, 392
Photography, Photographers, and the nude, 4
Phryne, 74
Picasso, 323, 348-55 ; link with Greek art, *3.* 2-3
  Works. Les Demoiselles d'Avignon, *289.* 344, 348-9 ; Woman in an Armchair, *290.* 351 ; Les Deux Femmes nues, *291.* 351-2
Pico della Mirandola, 92
Piero della Francesca, 50, 328
Pietà, 227-63 *passim*, 388 ; of Villeneuve-lès-Avignon, *182.* 228. *See also* Bellini, Botticelli, Carracci, Michelangelo, Roberti
Pillon, 139
  Work. Diana of Anet (?), *271.* 395
Pisanello, 338 ; drawings from the Antique, 278, 365, 397
  Work. Luxury, *229.* 278
Pisano, Giovanni, 89, 109, 387, 389
  Work. Venus Pudica on pulpit, Pisa, *74.* 89
Pisano, Nicola, 89, 389, 394
  Work. Fortitudo on pulpit, Pisa, *37.* 48, 180
Plato, 64
Pliny, the elder, 10, 42, 71, 97, 236-7, 266, 367-9 ; rules of proportion, 11
Poliziano, 15, 53, 97
Pollajuolo, 50, 211, 340, 363 ; and nude figures of energy, 164, 178, 180-9, 191, 204 ; and the Antique, 279-80
  Works. Nude men fighting, *126.* 164, 191 ; Hercules slaying Hydra, *142.* 183, 382 ; Hercules and Antaeus, *143.* 186, 382 ; Hercules and Antaeus (bronze statuette), *144.* 189 ; Frescoes in Torre del Gallo, *231.* 164, 279-80, 295, 380
Polyclitus, 31-6, 50 ; canon of, 11, 33, 225
  Works after : Diadumenos, *25.* 32, 36 ; Doryphoros, *24.* 32, 35, 167, 346 ; Discophoros, *28.* 35 ; Torso from Miletus, 33
Polygnotos, 385

Pompadour, Madame de, 140
Pompeii, 189 ; wall paintings at, 86
Pontormo, 250, 320, 323
  Work. Descent from the Cross, 250
Portrait heads used on ideal body, 43-4
Poussin, 19, 31, 61-2, 257, 271, 336, 342, 377
  Works. Apollo crowning Virgil, *48.* 61 ;
  Death of Narcissus, *208.* 257 ; Mourning
  over Dead Christ, *209.* 257 ; Galatea, *241.*
  290-2
Power, Hiram. Captive Slave, 149, 379
Poynter. Visit to Aesculapius, 343
Praxiteles, 39-41, 71, 103, 159
  Works. Cnidian Venus, *64. 65.* 8, 71-6,
  85, 156, 333, 362, 370, 377 ; Hermes (at
  Olympia), *31.* 19, 39, 366 ; Apollo Sauroc-
  tonos, *32.* 39 ; Faun, 39 ; Apollino, 39. *See
  also* Venus, of Arles
Primaticcio, 129, 323, 325
Projecta, Casket of, *224.* 276
Proportion, and the nude, 9-19 *passim*, 23,
  25 ; in Greek art, 11-13, 16-17, 33, 41,
  86 ; Vitruvian theory of, 13-15 ; of female
  body, 17-19 ; of Esquiline Venus, 67-8
Prud'hon, 127, 143, 284, 393
Public baths, 306
Pythagoras, 13, 26
Pythagoras of Rhegium, 29

Raphael, 103-9, 159, 168, 173, 335, 336, 340-3 ;
  and antique art, 53-4, 103-6, 398
  Works. Galatea, *239.* 15, 107, 156, 288-9 ;
  Apollos in *Stanze della Segnatura,* 54 ;
  School of Athens, 54 ; Parnassus, 53, 54, 106 ;
  Three Graces, *81.* 103-4 ; Leda, *82.* 104 ;
  Temptation, *83. 84.* 104 ; Venus, *86.* 106 ;
  Kneeling Girl, *87.* 107 ; Judgment of Paris,
  285. 115, 341-3, 375 ; Naked men fighting,
  155. 197 ; Entombment, *186.* 232-4, 388 ;
  Drawing for *Disputa, 283.* 340 ; Massacre
  of Innocents, *284.* 341-3 ; Wedding of
  Cupid and Psyche, 392
Ravenna, Apollo and Daphne ivory at, 8, 362
Rejlander, photograph of nude by, *5.* 4
Rembrandt, 124, 325-30, 334
  Works. Danaë, 122 ; Diana, *272.* 326 ;
  Cleopatra, *273.* 327 ; Old woman bathing
  her feet, *274.* 328 ; Bathsheba, *275.* 328-30

Reni, Guido. Samson, 221, 290
Renoir, 6, 116, 121, 137, 154-61, 336
  Works. Baigneuse au griffon, 120. 154 ;
  Anna, 156 ; Torso (Barnes Collection),
  156 ; *Baigneuse blonde, 121.* 156-8 ; Three
  Bathers, *122.* 158 ; *Grandes Baigneuses,*
  158-9 ; Bather seated, *123.* 159
Renoir, Madame, 156, 159
Resurrection, The, Michelangelo drawings of,
  244. 245. 246. 297-9
Reynolds, Sir Joshua, 204 ; *Discourses,* 11
  Work. Cymon and Iphigenia, 2
Ribera, 252
Rizzo, 317
  Work. Eve, 110, 395
Robbia, Luca della, 338
Roberti, Ercole. *Pietà,* 228
Robetta, 181
Rodin, 167, 260-3, 330, 346
  Works. Eve, 263 ; Three Shades, *211.*
  263 ; Burghers of Calais, 263 ; *La Belle
  Heaulmière, 276.* 330
Rolls-Royce, 340
Rosso, 129, 250-1, 323
  Works. Descent from the Cross, 250 ;
  Moses and the Children of Jethro, *202.*
  250-1
Rouault, 333-4
  Work. A Prostitute, *278.* 333
Rousseau, Douanier. *La Guerre,* 250
Rubens, 6, 65, 84, 124, 129, 131-9, 159, 254-7,
  259, 287-8 ; influence of predecessors,
  133-4, 205-7, 254
  Works. Three Graces, *104.* 131, 141 ;
  Venus and Area, *105.* 133-4 ; Rape of
  Daughters of Leucippus, *106.* 134 ; Diana
  and Callisto, 134 ; Helena Fourment, 135,
  254 ; Perseus and Andromeda, *107.* 137 ;
  Life drawing, *111.* 141 ; Abduction of
  Hippodamia, *162.* 205 ; Miracle of S.
  Benedict, 205 ; Raising of the Cross, 254 ;
  Descent from the Cross, *205.* 254 ; Three
  Crosses, *206.* 255 ; Mourning over Dead
  Christ, *207.* 257
Ruskin, 97, 345, 372

St. Thomas Aquinas, 137
St. Wilgefortis (or Uncomber), 387

Samson, in art, as embodiment of energy in mediaeval art, 179-80 ; and the Lion, in relief, *140*. 180 ; of the Porta della Mandorla, 180 ; defeating the Philistines, after Michelangelo, *159*. 203 ; of Guido Reni, 221, 290

Sangallo Aristotile da, 383

Sangallo, Giuliano da, 236

Sannazaro, 115

Sansovino, 119
    Work. Apollo, *15*. 19

Santa Sabina, doors of, 223

Sarcophagi, as source of antique motives in Renaissance : Battles and Hercules, Ch. V *passim* ; in Campo Santo, 191, 383. Dionysiac and Nereids, Ch. VII *passim*, 391, 392 ; in Terme, *218*. 113, 270

Sautereau, Jean, 371

Savonarola, 100, 244

Scamozzi, *see* Vitruvian Man

Scheffer, 152

Schiller, *Piccolomini*, 22

Scopas, and Mausoleum frieze, 172, 198 ; maenads of, 267-70 ; nereid devised from, 270-1
    Works. Dresden maenad, *216*. 267, 391 ; Tritoness, *219*. 271

Sebastiano del Piombo, 106, 375
    Works. Life drawing, *93*. 117-19 ; Death of Adonis, 375

Seurat, 31

Shakespeare, 259

Shchukin, 295, 346

Signorelli, 102, 373 ; and nudes of energy, 189-91, 211, 212
    Works. School of Pan, *80*. 102-3 ; Drawing, *146*. 189 ; The Blessed, *147*. 190 ; The Damned, *148*. 190 ; Tondo (Uffizi), 373

Silvestre, Théophile, 378

Sistine Chapel, 204. *See* Michelangelo

Spartan girls, 67, 369. *See* Degas, Delacroix

Spenser, 23

Spinario, the, 49, 109, 367

Spranger, 323, 325

Stabia, wall painting from, *223*. 275

Stoldo di Lorenzo, 129

Subiaco, youth of, 169, 380-1

Swift, 137

Swinburne, 216

Tebaldeo, 115

Thiasos, 264-75 *passim*

Thieves in Crucifixion, 225, 387

Three Graces, The, in art, Romanesque, *18*. 22 ; Graeco-Roman, *71*. *73*. 85-6 ; knowledge of, in Renaissance, 372 ; of Botticelli, *76*. 92-6, 372 ; of Raphael, *81*. 103-4 ; of Pontormo, 323

Thucydides, 20

Tibaldi, 204, 207

Tintoretto, 204, 254
    Works. Fall of the Damned, 204 ; Bacchus and Ariadne, 282

Titian, 119-24, 125, 137, 250-4, 282-4, 336
    Works. Venus of Urbino, *90*. 110, 112, 119, 127, 328 ; Venus del Pardo, 110, 121, 376 ; Sacred and Profane Love, *94*. 119, 376 ; Venus Anadyomene (Ellesmere Coll.), *95*. 119-21, 156, 376 ; Venus and the Organ Player, *96*. 122 ; Danaë, *97*. 123, 376 ; Diana and Actaeon, *98*. 123-4, 156 ; Callisto, 123-4 ; St. Sebastian (from Brescia altar-piece), *203*. 251 ; Monkey Laocoön, *298*. 251, 390 ; Entombment (Louvre), 255 ; Bacchanals, *233*. *234*. 282-4, 392 ; Europa, *235*. 284

Tiziano Aspetti, 129

Torso, 239, 369 ; treatment in early Greek sculpture, 30 ; perfection and schematisation of, by Polyclitus, *26*. 35 ; and Michelangelo, 57-8, 369 ; from Miletus, 33 ; Esquiline Venus, *57*. 67 ; of Discobolos of Myron, 167 ; of a satyr, 206 ; of Brancusi, *288*. 348

Toulouse-Lautrec, 154, 334, 348

Trebonius Gallus, Emperor, bronze, *294*. 369

Très Riches Heures, see de Limbourg

Uccello. Rout of San Romano, 250 ; School of, 30, 338, 397

Urs Graf, 318-19
    Work. Woman stabbing herself, *265*. 318

Utamaro, 361

Van der Goes, 327
    Work. Adam and Eve, *257*. 312-13

Van der Weyden, 327
Work. Last Judgment, *247.* 309
Van Eyck, 394
Work. Eve, *256.* 312
Van Gogh, 330
Van Heemskerck, 370
Vasari, 181, 186-8, 195, 289, 339
Velasquez, 124 ; and the nude, 361
Work. Rokeby Venus, *1. 2,* 141
Venus, Chs. III, IV ; Greek and Hellenistic,
64-87, 371 ; on mirror handle, *53.* 65 ;
Esquiline, *57. 58.* 67-8, 71, 369 ; on
Ludovisi throne, *60.* 69 ; Genetrix, *61.*
70, 106, 370 ; of the Capitol, *66.* 76-9,
106 ; Medici, *67.* 76, 83, 370 ; of
Arles, 80-3, 84, 371 ; of Capua, 83; of Milo,
68. 83-4, 371 ; of Cyrenaica, *70.* 85 ;
Crouching, *281.* 84-5, 109, 336, 396.
See also Ammanati, Botticelli, Cranach,
Giorgione, Ingres, Lorenzo Costa, Lorenzo
di Credi, Lysippus, Praxiteles, Raphael,
Renoir, Rubens
Vernet, 258
Veroli Casket, 8, 303-4, 362
Veronese, Paul, 23, 363
Vignola, 119
Villa Item, antique paintings in, 270
Villa Medici, 375
Villa Pamphili, 375

Villard de Honnecourt, *see* de Honnecourt
Vincent of Beauvais, the *Speculum,* 306
Virgil, *48.* 61, 178
Vitruvian Man, 363 ; influence on Renaissance, 13, 15 ; Como *Vitruvius, 10.* 15,
363 ; in Scamozzi's *Idea dell' architettura
universale, 166.* 207, 335

Walpole, Horace, 39
Watteau, 124
Work. Judgment of Paris, *108.* 139
Westmacott, 177
Whistler, 4
Wiligelmo. Relief on Modena Cathedral,
249. 304
Winckelmann, 38, 44-5, 62, 80, 147, 219-21,
327, 344
Wölfflin, 135
Wordsworth, 80
Wrestlers, Greek, *125. 132.* 163, 169

Xenophon, 20, 21, 362, 369

Y-shaped Cross, 245, *297.* 389

Zeuxis and five beautiful maidens, 10
Zuccheri, the, 323